The Renaissance
Philosophy of Man

PETRARCA · VALLA · FICINO · PICO · POMPONAZZI · VIVES

The Renaissance
Philosophy of Man

Selections in translation, edited by
ERNST CASSIRER · PAUL OSKAR KRISTELLER
JOHN HERMAN RANDALL, JR.

THE UNIVERSITY OF CHICAGO PRESS
CHICAGO & LONDON

The University of Chicago Press, Chicago 60637
The University of Chicago Press, Ltd., London

16 15 14 13 12 11 10 09 08 07   22 23 24 25 26

ISBN-13: 978-0-226-09604-9 (paper)
ISBN-10: 0-226-09604-1 (paper)
LCN: 48-9358

♾ The paper used in this publication meets the minimum
requirements of the American National Standard for Information
Sciences—Permanence of Paper for Printed Library Materials,
ANSI Z39.48-1992.

PREFACE

THE purpose of this volume is to acquaint the student of philosophy with certain major thinkers of the early Italian Renaissance through English translations of some of their more important works. To understand any author, the best way is to read his writings in the original, the second best is to read them in a faithful translation, the worst is to rely upon short summaries found in reference works or in textbooks. Most of the treatises included in this volume have never before been published in an English version. The only exceptions are certain letters of Petrarca; Pico's *Oration*, of which another translation appeared last year in *View* magazine, long after the present one had been ready for publication; and Pomponazzi's treatise on immortality, the present translation of which, now out of print, was published privately in 1938 at Haverford, Pennsylvania, and is now republished with the translator's permission and in a revised version approved by him. It is hoped that these translations will prove useful even to those able to read the original texts, especially since some of the latter are not easily accessible.

While this volume was being prepared for publication, one of the editors who had taken an active part in its planning suddenly passed away. The death of Ernst Cassirer will be a serious loss for the readers of this volume, since he had promised to contribute a general introduction from his pen. Conscious that they are not able to supply what he left undone, the remaining editors have tried to fill the gap as well as they could.

PAUL OSKAR KRISTELLER
JOHN HERMAN RANDALL, JR.

COLUMBIA UNIVERSITY
NEW YORK CITY

CONTENTS

[vii]

CONTENTS

V. PIETRO POMPONAZZI

*Translated by William Henry Hay II, revised by
John Herman Randall, Jr., and annotated
by Paul Oskar Kristeller*

VI. JUAN LUIS VIVES

Translated by Nancy Lenkeith

SELECTIVE BIBLIOGRAPHY

INDEX

GENERAL INTRODUCTION

By PAUL OSKAR KRISTELLER and
JOHN HERMAN RANDALL, JR.

THE period of the Renaissance, which we take to extend from about the middle of the fourteenth century to the end of the sixteenth, has been widely admired and studied for the great changes it witnessed in society and the church and for its achievements in the arts and in literature, in the sciences and in classical learning. But it has not attracted much interest, especially its earlier phases, from students of philosophy. The studies that have been devoted to the thinkers of the early Renaissance are hardly known outside a small circle of specialists.

The reasons for this neglect are not hard to understand. The Renaissance produced no philosopher of the very first importance; and, once a thinker acquires the reputation of not being "great," his chances of being read and studied are slight indeed, in a day when influential writers and educators are reiterating that we need read nothing but their own books and the hundred greatest works of world literature. Moreover, many students of philosophy are convinced that the progress of science and thought since the seventeenth century has superseded everything that came before, with the possible exception of Plato and Aristotle. For their part, the admirers and followers of medieval philosophy are often inclined to think that the impressive development which culminated in the thirteenth century with Thomas Aquinas was followed by a period of complete decay and disintegration.

We are convinced, however, that a reader whose curiosity extends beyond the limits of a strictly rationed intellectual diet is likely to be rewarded and that the works of many so-called minor thinkers, including those of the early Renaissance, deserve attention and study for the intrinsic interest of their ideas. Moreover, such lesser thinkers fill in the historical vacuum left between the greater minds, and thus they help us to understand them and to see their relations to one another. A mountain climber cannot jump directly from one peak to the next. On the way he must traverse many valleys and ascend lower foothills, which also command interesting vistas and are still high enough in comparison with the plains far behind.

The philosophical literature of the Renaissance is in fact rich and diversified, and its extent appears still greater if we include the writings of theologians, scientists, artists, historians, and classical scholars that are of related interest to the student of intellectual history. To give a complete picture of this whole literature would be impossible within the limits of a single book. The present volume aims to illustrate merely one part of the entire period—the earlier Italian Renaissance. The opening phase was first selected because its contribution to philosophical thought is comparatively unknown. It was then determined to emphasize Italian thinkers, since during that period Italy held a dominating place in many fields of culture, and since several intellectual impulses then originated in that country were later transmitted to the rest of Europe. Our selection does not presume to minimize the contributions made during the later Renaissance, or in other lands, or in other fields of thought and literature. On the contrary, it is hoped that some of these other aspects of Renaissance thought will be treated in further volumes of the present series.

The philosophical thought of the early Italian Renaissance may be grouped into three major currents or traditions: Humanism, Platonism, and Aristotelianism.

To understand the Humanistic movement, it would be well to remember that during the Italian Renaissance the term "Humanism" denoted primarily a specific intellectual program and only incidentally suggested the more general set of values which have in recent times come to be called "humanistic." Humanism appeared in Italy toward the end of the thirteenth century. It was in part an outgrowth of the earlier traditions of professional teaching in rhetoric and grammar in the medieval Italian schools. However, the emphasis on classical studies, which was to remain the distinctive characteristic of the Humanism of the Renaissance, was a new development that may have been encouraged by influences from France and from Byzantium. The earlier beginnings of the movement were very modest. Petrarca, who was not so much its initiator as its first major representative, may still be called the "father of Humanism," since his authority and influence gave the whole movement a strong impulse. He was followed by a great number of other Humanists who, during the fifteenth century and later, exercised an extremely important influence on the cultural life of Italy. After the middle of the fifteenth century, Humanism spread to the other European countries, where it reached its climax during the sixteenth.

The major concern of the Humanists was an educational and cultural program based on the study of the classical Greek and Latin authors. In dealing with these texts, they elaborated methods of historical and philological criticism which contributed greatly to the later developments of these disciplines. Yet the interest of the Humanists in the classics was not merely scholarly but also served a practical purpose. They emphasized the ideal of literary elegance and considered the imitation of the Roman authors the best way of learning to speak and to write well in prose and in verse. Moreover, admiration for the classical models extended from their form to their content, and it became increasingly fashionable to quote their words and to restate their ideas. At the same time the demands of the present were by no means neglected for a search after the distant past. The Humanists tried and managed to express the concrete circumstances of their own life and their personal thoughts and feelings in a language and a style largely borrowed from classical models.

The interests of the Humanists ranged from rhetoric and poetry to history and moral philosophy. Work in each of these fields comprised both the study of the appropriate classical authors and the composition of original writings patterned on their model. For this group of disciplines the scholars of the time, following certain ancient precedents, coined the comprehensive term, *Studia Humanitatis*, or "the Humanities," and hence called themselves "Humanists." It is from this designation that nineteenth-century historians derived the term "Humanism." Although "the Humanities" is merely another name for these particular studies, the choice of the term implies a claim very characteristic of the cultural and educational ideal of the Humanists: the cultivation of the classics or "the Humanities" is justified because it serves to educate and to develop a desirable type of human being. For the classics represent the highest level of human achievement and should hence be of primary concern for every man.

It is for this reason, as Petrarca's words clearly show, that the Humanists profess to despise the study of logic and of natural philosophy, so much cultivated during the preceding centuries. Yet the polemic of the Humanists against the teaching of the schools was largely a struggle between one field of learning and others and not, as it often appears, between a new philosophy and an old. On the other hand, the opposition to medieval logic and natural philosophy found in many of the Humanists was far from being an opposition to the Church or to the Christian religion. The teaching of the medieval Italian universities was scientific and often anticlerical in its interests, and to such interests the Humanists were opposing their own religious and moral aims. Petrarca, in posing as the defender of religion against the atheism of his Averroist opponents, or Valla, in appealing from philosophical reason to blind faith, is obviously trying to detach theology from its dangerous link with Aristotelian natural philosophy and metaphysics and to join it instead with his own different type of learning, with eloquence or with Humanistic studies. This religious tendency was strong among many of the Humanists and found its culmination in the Christian Humanism of Erasmus.

The literary production of the Humanists makes clear that their interest in philosophy was but secondary and was limited primarily to the field of ethics. Compared with the enormous number of translations, commentaries, poems, speeches, letters, and historical, grammatical, and rhetorical works they composed, their treatises and dialogues on moral subjects are of slight extent or importance. Their direct contribution to philosophy must hence be called rather modest. But their indirect contribution is much greater. They influenced the style and form of philosophical literature; they vaguely formulated new problems that furnished material to the thought of more serious thinkers; they made available a considerable number of ancient philosophical texts not known to the Middle Ages; and, with the help of these new sources, they encouraged a great deal of philosophical eclecticism or paved the way for the revival of several ancient philosophies besides Aristotle's. The Humanistic movement, with the classicism it brought about, is the most pervasive element of Renaissance culture. Its influence may be traced in every country and in almost every field of intellectual endeavor. Its cultural and educational ideal survived long after the Renaissance, at least until the end of the eighteenth century; and certain faint traces of it are still discernible in the midst of our own "progressive" age.

For those who demanded a more intellectual philosophy, there was Plato, the natural refuge of those fleeing Aristotle and his fundamentally scientific interests. Most of the Humanists had rejected this scientific interest for other concerns, practical, artistic, and at bottom religious. What they objected to in the organized Aristotelian learning of the universities was not its synthesis with religious values, and certainly not any otherworldliness and asceticism. It was rather in behalf of a purer and deeper religious life that Humanists on both sides of the Alps opposed Aristotle. The Neo-Platonism of the Florentine Academy or the "philosophy of Christ" of an Erasmus or a Lefèvre d'Étaples is a turning-away from scientific questions to the problems of the moral life and the religious imagination.

Platonism was the most imposing alternative to the Aristotelian schools, the one best adapted to a religious revival and best combining the imaginative values of religion with the values of a humane life. Platonism had already long been thoroughly Christianized in the familiar Augustinian tradition, which had dominated medieval thought until well into the thirteenth century and had persisted thereafter side by side with a Christianized Aristotelianism. Duns Scotus had dressed up the essential Augustinian and Platonic theses in an Aristotelian terminology, and Scotism continued as the prevailing conservative, theological, and metaphysical philosophy in the Italian schools. Moreover, Augustine dominates all the various currents of religious revival and reform from the mystics and Cusanus onward. It was but natural for the grammarians of the Renaissance, leading an educational revolt, in behalf of an emerging type of culture, against the vested interests, the complacency and the academic conservatism of the professional intellectuals, to go behind him to his intellectual sources in the Platonic tradition. And it was equally natural that what they found, even when they read Plato's own words, should be still primarily the religious, Neo-Platonic Plato—Plotinus rather than the dialogues as we understand them today, and Augustine rather than Plotinus.

Yet the Renaissance Platonists were now in a position to appreciate something of the humanistic, artistic, and imaginative side of Plato. Intellectually they were indeed left with a theological Neo-Platonism, with the Christian world view minus its Oriental values, its dualism, and its need for magic—with a single Truth, Platonic in philosophy, Christian in theology, and humanistic in values. And yet the Renaissance did manage to make its Platonism an artistic way of life, a this-worldly religion of the imagination—attractive in contour and wistfully reminiscent of another world, like the Platonism of Botticelli's pencil and, like it also, thin and disembodied and ever trembling on the verge of the Christian mystery. With wider horizons, it grew eclectic and universal, embraced the love of perfection wherever it might be discerned, and identified it with the essence of Christian faith.

When Petrarca, combatting the naturalism, the rationalism, and the scientific interests of the Averroists, opposed Plato to the authority of Aristotle and the Commentator, he did not know too much about Plato's philosophy, though he was thoroughly familiar with Augustine. But he at least formulated a program which found its first fulfilment in the translation of certain of Plato's dialogues by the early Humanists. To this was added the influence of Byzantine Platonism, when Pletho and Bessarion came to Italy and made a strong impression on the Italian scholars of their time.

Nicholas of Cusa may in a sense be called the first Western Platonist of the Renaissance. But his influence during the Renaissance, especially during the early period, while suggested by similarities of thought, is very difficult to establish. More specifically, this title belongs to Marsilio Ficino, leader of the Platonic Academy of Florence, which became, after the middle of the fifteenth century, the most important center of Platonic influence in Western Europe. Ficino's Platonism was in many ways a product of the Humanistic movement. Humanistic are his style and the literary form of many of his works, the sources he used and the way he made them available, and even some of the problems that determined his philosophical thought. Yet Ficino was more than a mere Humanist who happened to be interested in Plato. He was a thinker who was attracted by the thought of Plato and of the ancient Neo-Platonists. Consequently, he was not, like most of the Humanists, opposed to the traditions of the medieval schools but was strongly influenced by them. His terminology, his method of arguing, and much of the subject matter of his philosophy are clearly derived from medieval philosophy, theology, and medicine, with which he probably became familiar as a student at the University of Florence. This scholastic heritage is even stronger in Giovanni Pico, the other great representative of the Florentine Academy, who had received part of his training at the universities of Padua and of Paris, and who was also familiar with many of the original sources of medieval Arabic and Jewish philosophy.

Whereas the philosophical thought of the early Humanists was rather amateurish, that of the Florentine Platonists embraced serious if not original metaphysical speculation. Consequently, the influence of Platonism on the later Renaissance, affecting both philosophy and literature, though less extensive was much deeper than that of the Humanistic movement. It consisted not only in the transmission of the works of Plato, Plotinus, and other ancient thinkers, important as this was, but also in an interpretation and restatement of Platonic and Neo-Platonic doctrines which showed originality on many points. This influence can be traced down to the end of the eighteenth century and is still apparent in such thinkers as Berkeley and Coleridge.

The third philosophical current of the Italian Renaissance, the humanistic Aristotelianism of Pomponazzi and Zabarella, sprang from the teaching tradition of the universities and derived in an unbroken line from the academic thinking of the preceding centuries. This Aristotelian tradition, with its central concern for the fields of logic and method, natural philosophy and metaphysics, made its first appearance in Italy toward the end of the thirteenth century. It may have been introduced, together with the writings of John of Jandun, the Latin Averroist, which continued to exert a strong influence on its teachings, from the University of Paris about that time. The physician Pietro d'Abano, early in the fourteenth century, determined the main lines Italian Aristotelianism was to follow. There was a significant difference between the way Aristotle was taken at Paris and in the Italian universities. In Paris the Aristotelian philosophers were either theologians or students of logic and of natural philosophy in the faculty of arts who had to defend themselves against a powerful theological faculty. The Italian universities long had no faculties of theology; and from the beginning Italian Aristotelianism developed as the preparation for medicine rather than for theology. This type of scientifically oriented philosophical thought was elaborated without interruption far into the period of the Renaissance; it did not reach its culmination until the sixteenth century.

Thus, during the entire Renaissance, Aristotle continued to inspire the vigorous intellectual life of the Italian universities and to dominate the professional teaching of philosophy. The new humanistic tendencies appeared almost as early in that living Aristotelianism as in the Florentine Academy; and they were there allied with and not opposed to an already flourishing scientific movement. Pomponazzi, like Ficino, focused attention on man and his destiny; both emphasized individual and personal values, and in this sense both were humanistic. But where Ficino and the Platonists went back to the Hellenistic world and the religious philosophies of Alexandria, the naturalistic humanism, initiated by Pomponazzi and culminating in Zabarella, built on the long tradition of Italian Aristotelianism an original philosophy in accord with the spirit of the emerging natural science and strikingly anticipatory of Spinoza.

Like most of the Schoolmen from Thomas down, the Italian Aristotelians had regarded Averroes as the chief guide and commentator. But, unlike Thomas and the theologians, they had little motive to disagree with him on those points where he followed Aristotle or his Hellenistic commentators rather than the true faith. This version of Aristotle without benefit of clergy is hence known as Latin Averroism. It had accompanied the introduction of Aristotle at Paris in the thirteenth century; when its spokesman, Siger de Brabant, was condemned in 1270 and

1277, and, refuted by the more accommodating modernism of Thomas, it took refuge in the Italian medical schools.

Averroes himself, a physician and judge rather than theologian, had applied a rigid legal method to interpreting Aristotle. But struggling with Arabic texts, and relying on the Neo-Platonic Hellenistic commentators, he found much cosmic mysticism and pantheism in his philosopher. Creation is eternal, by emanations; there is no creation in time, and hence no first man, no Adam and Eve, no Fall. Matter is eternal, and so is that mysterious Intellect of which Aristotle speaks. It is deathless and unremitting, the Intelligence of the lowest sphere, common to all men and particularizing itself in their individual souls, as light illuminates their bodies. These human intellects live on after death only as moments in the single Intellect of mankind. Hence there is no personal immortality, no heaven or hell, and no last judgment.

These views, whether Aristotelian or no, are obviously not Christian; and the earliest Latin Averroists frankly admitted that the conclusions of reason, philosophy, and Aristotle are not the conclusions of faith. Faith is true, but Aristotle is more interesting, held Siger, taking an irrationalist position. But John of Jandun, recognizing no authority save reason in agreement with experience, and meaning thereby Averroes' Aristotle, maintained all these characteristic Averroistic doctrines as an open rationalist, mocked at faith, and called Thomas a compromising theologian. His writings are satirical and ironical in the Voltairean sense. The fifteenth-century Italian Aristotelians maintained on such matters a less defiant and more Christian Averroism. As the Church, thoroughly tamed in Padua, where anticlerical Venice guaranteed liberty of teaching after 1405, offered no menace, they were not enough concerned with Christianity to be violently anticlerical. But the supremacy of natural reason, the denial of creation and personal immortality, with their theological consequences, and the unity of the intellect were taught in the universities and, we are told, accepted by many Venetian gentlemen. Such a philosophy expressed with precision the stage of skepticism toward the religious system, of antisupernaturalism rather than of positive naturalism and humanism, which had been reached by the northern Italian cities in the fourteenth century. It attempted a rational defense of the attitude so well expressed in Boccaccio and so horrifying, as the selection here reveals, to Petrarca.

This was a naturalistic and scientific rather than a Humanistic philosophy; its conception of human nature emphasized man's dependence on the world rather than his freedom and glory. And the unity of the Intellect is a collective and impersonal conception, with little scope for the more individualistic and personal values the Humanists prized. It is small wonder that from Petrarca down the Humanists felt in strong opposition to this professional philosophy of the universities and that their own intellectual defenses and rationalizations were developed in contrast to it. As against its Aristotle, they turned to Plato; as against its prevailing anticlericalism, they turned to a free and modernizing religious gospel; as against its scientific interest, they turned to human nature; and, above all, as against its collectivism, they turned to the dignity and worth of the human personality. The personal immortality of the soul became the banner under which men fought for more individualistic and personal values. And so "spiritual" Florence set out on a crusade against naturalistic Venice. But it was not against medieval asceticism and otherworldliness that their philosophy was aimed; it was against a scientific rationalism in the name of a more personal interpretation of the world. And the answer of the Aristotelians was not to abandon their naturalism but to introduce into it just those individualistic values it had hitherto lacked. Thus the two great philosophic rivals in early sixteenth-century Italy are a naturalistic and an imaginative and religious humanism, with the former widespread and rapidly increasing in strength.

The thinker who opposed the earlier impersonal and collectivistic Averroism, which had received vigorous emphasis during the 1490's, and introduced the humanistic values into Italian Aristotelianism, was Pietro Pomponazzi. He was trained at the University of Padua and published most of his works while a professor of philosophy at the University of Bologna. Even the form of his writings reveals what he has absorbed from the Humanists and the Platonists. He employs the treatise, not the commentary on Aristotle. To the Platonists he owes his quotations from Plato's dialogues and from other ancient philosophers and probably his conception of man as the mean between earth and heaven. He quotes from Pico and in his *Apologia* gives an acute critique of Ficino's argument for immortality based on the *appetitus naturalis*. In the most striking part of his thought, his defense of a thoroughly naturalistic ethics, he is, like all the Humanists, deeply indebted to the Stoics.

During the sixteenth century the Italian Aristotelians maintained a secular rationalism that kept philosophy independent of theology without interfering with its dogmatic teachings. How far any of them subscribed to the notion of a "double truth" is very difficult to determine; this, of course, is the position formally taken in Pomponazzi's treatise. The question of what a man "really believes" who finds a clear contradiction between rational truth and religious truth recurs throughout the whole tradition of Italian Aristotelianism from John of Jandun on. In any event, the rationalism of the Italians inspired the free-thinkers of the seventeenth century, especially in France, though the latter pushed it much further than the Italians did.

In the Italian schools alone the emerging science of nature did not mean a sharp break with reigning theological interests. To them it came rather as the natural outcome of a sustained and co-operative criticism of Aristotelian ideas. Indeed, that mathematical and mechanical development which by the end of the sixteenth century produced Galileo owes very little to the Platonic revival but received powerful stimulus from the critical Aristotelianism of the Italian universities. Pomponazzi, of course, played little part in this major achievement. But Padua remained until the days of Galileo the leading scientific school of Europe, the stronghold of the Aristotelian qualitative physics, and the trainer even of those who were to abandon it. If in the sixteenth century the more original minds were finally led to a formal break with the Padua teaching, we must not forget that even Galileo occupied a chair there from 1592 to 1610 and that he remained in method and in philosophy, if not in physics, close to the tradition of Italian Aristotelianism.

Renaissance Aristotelianism reached its pinnacle in Giacomo Zabarella (1532–89). Heir to both the earlier Averroists and the more recent Humanist reinterpretations, he was able in *De rebus naturalibus* (1590) to discuss each of the problems elaborated by the Italians for over three hundred years and with clarity and lucidity to sum up their collective wisdom in fresh contact with Aristotle's own words. The Scholastic temper remaining in Pomponazzi has disappeared. Zabarella is best known and most original in his logical writings, in which he completed the methodological advances of his predecessors and made them ready for Galileo. But he summed up also the best wisdom of the Humanists about human nature, about its natural destiny and its high estate, combining a sober recognition of its finite conditions with that lingering sense of immortality which is the characteristic stamp of the humanist.

On the soul Zabarella stands much closer to Pomponazzi than to the Averroists; the Mantuan, he judged, came nearer to Aristotle than any other, though he left some questions unresolved. Zabarella is clear and explicit on all points—clearer than Aristotle's statements, though always close to his spirit. And he is both more humanistic and more naturalistic than Pomponazzi: the human soul does more itself, is less dependent on cosmic agencies, but it has ceased to be a "mean" and become frankly a bodily function. No clearer analysis has ever been made of how reason can be a natural life of the body.

The influence of the Renaissance Aristotelians survived far

into the seventeenth and eighteenth centuries. Zabarella's logical writings were long standard; his interpretation of Aristotle remains one of the most accurate of all commentaries. And both Spinoza and Leibniz bear witness to the continuing stimulus of Italian Aristotelianism in the middle of the scientific revolution of the seventeenth century.

Each of the three main trends of early Renaissance thought is represented in this volume by one or two major authors: Humanism by Petrarca and Valla, Platonism by Ficino and Pico, and Aristotelianism by Pomponazzi. We have decided to choose a single comparatively short but complete and characteristic text from each thinker. This has made it impossible to group all the texts around a single idea or doctrine, although we have tried to illustrate at least a few common problems. It is hoped that the lack of unity thus resulting will be outweighed by the greater variety.

The treatise of Petrarca, *De sui ipsius et multorum ignorantia*, is not in the strict sense a philosophical work, but among all the author's writings it offers the greatest interest for the history of philosophy. Offended by a group of former friends, Petrarca launches a strong attack against the contemporary Averroistic Aristotelians. To what seems to him the useless questions of the natural philosophers he opposes Ciceronian eloquence, Platonic wisdom, and Christian piety. At one point he even suggests that the original Aristotle must be freed from the distortions of his medieval translators and commentators. This treatise is supplemented by a few of Petrarca's letters which serve to illustrate some of its major points.

Of the later Italian Humanists, Valla was perhaps the most philosophically minded; but among even his works only three belong to philosophy proper. The shortest of them, *De libero arbitrio*, argues that free will is compatible with divine foreknowledge. The more difficult question of how free will may be reconciled with divine omnipotence is left undecided. The treatise is not very original in its results; but it refutes the common view of Valla as a rationalist, since he rejects the help of reason and philosophy in solving the problems of theology and tries instead to establish a kind of alliance between eloquence and faith.

The *Questiones quinque de mente* belong to a group of short treatises in which Ficino tried to summarize the metaphysical doctrine of his major work, the *Theologia Platonica*, and which he later included in the second book of his *Letters*. The *Questiones quinque* illustrate a number of important ideas, including the doctrine of immortality that lies at the center of Ficino's Platonism. Moreover, it contains the clearest and most explicit account of his theory of "natural appetite." In connection with Pico's *Oration*, it would have been interesting to include a few passages from the *Theologia Platonica* in which Ficino develops his doctrine of the dignity of man. These passages, in the translation of Miss Josephine Burroughs, have been published in the *Journal of the History of Ideas* (V [1944], 227 ff.), where those interested in this problem can easily read them.

Pico della Mirandola is represented by his *Oration*, one of his shortest works, and the most famous. The speech is distinguished by literary elegance. It also illustrates two of Pico's major ideas: the dignity of man founded on man's freedom and Pico's syncretism based on his conception of universal truth.

Pomponazzi's *On the Immortality of the Soul* is the most famous of his philosophical works. It gave rise to a storm of controversy, and it forms the fitting counterpart to the treatise of Ficino. In it Pomponazzi contends that, according to Aristotle, the human soul is absolutely mortal and only relatively immortal. Pomponazzi also goes on to answer the moral and pragmatic arguments for immortality. He holds that virtue is its own reward, as vice is its own punishment. Happiness, the end of human life, is to be found not in contemplation, which is accessible to only a few, but in the life of moral virtue, which may be attained by every human being.

The *Fabula de homine* by Juan Luis Vives, the great Spanish Humanist who spent most of his life in the Low Countries, has been added as a sort of appendix, although the place and time of its composition differ from those of the other texts here collected. Yet the basic idea of this elegant little work is closely related to Pico's *Oration*, and it will thus illustrate the influence which the thought of the Italian Humanists and Platonists exercised in the rest of Europe, especially during the sixteenth century.

Each author and each work should be read and judged primarily on the intrinsic merits of the piece. However, it may be well to note some of the links that connect the various treatises. The Humanistic movement, as we have seen, was primarily a kind of educational revolt and reorientation. Its contempt for medieval philosophy and science, and its emphasis on ancient thought and literature, are well brought out in the works of Petrarca and Valla. The Platonism of Ficino and the syncretism of Pico would not have been possible without this Humanistic revival of other ancient philosophies besides Aristotle's. Yet Ficino, and still more Pico, did not reject the heritage of medieval Aristotelianism but tried to fuse it with the newly discovered thought of the classics. Pomponazzi, it is true, follows closely the dialectical method of the medieval Aristotelians, but he redirects it toward the problems and the values of the Humanists.

The idea of immortality had always played an important part in Platonic and Christian thought, and Thomas had employed some of his most ingenious dialectic in reconciling it with the Aristotelian concepts. In his great controversy with the Latin Averroists, *On the Unity of the Intellect*, he had been chiefly concerned to vindicate the integrity and worth of the individual personality. His most fundamental argument against the idea of a separate and single Intellect for all men is that there would then be no human will, that moral action would be destroyed, "which is contrary to human life." When Ficino came to make the rational defense of personal immortality the major theme of his philosophy, he was arguing in an intellectual environment in which much educated opinion accepted the impersonal immortality of the Averroists. So widespread was this view that the Lateran Council of 1512 found it necessary for the first time to establish the immortality of the soul as a dogma of the Church. What repelled Ficino in the position of the Italian Aristotelians was the conception of human nature that minimized all that was personal and individual. In defending personal immortality against the reigning impersonal immortality, he was at bottom, like Thomas before him, defending the dignity and worth of the individual man.

Pomponazzi accepted these personal and humanistic values and was equally opposed to the impersonal and collectivistic views of the Averroists. But he defended them rather within a more scientific and naturalistic framework of ideas. This is the crux of the agreement as well as of the opposition between the religious humanism of the Platonists and the naturalistic humanism of the Aristotelians. Ficino was, of course, not arguing against Pomponazzi, whose book came out thirty-four years later, but against the Averroists. Nor was Pomponazzi arguing primarily against Ficino, though he does attack him in his *Apologia*. This is a much more revealing and better book than the first treatise of 1516, and it makes clear what Pomponazzi was really trying to do, including his large agreement with Ficino. It is in their devotion to personal values that both belong most clearly to the Renaissance.

The different defenses of these same values are integral parts of the general philosophical views of Ficino and of Pomponazzi. For Ficino, the basic phenomenon of human life is the inward experience of contemplation. This consists in the gradual ascent of the soul toward God and culminates in the immediate vision and enjoyment of God. Since this immediate vision is attained on earth by only a few and then but for a brief moment, we must postulate a future life in which this goal of human existence will be attained by the greatest possible number of men and in permanent fashion. Otherwise the whole of human life, as Ficino understands it, would lose all its meaning.

Pomponazzi starts from an entirely different conception. He denies that there is any direct insight of a spiritual character, since all our knowledge is based on sense. The end of human life is moral virtue. This is its own reward; and it can be attained by every human being during his earthly existence. Hence there is no rational necessity of the immortality of the soul, although in the first treatise Pomponazzi maintains the doctrine as an article of faith. The whole question is there called a "neutral problem," which cannot be decided *intra limites naturales*, "within the limits of natural reason." In the *Apologia* and thereafter Pomponazzi abandons the position that the immortality of the soul is a neutral problem: he insists that it is contrary to all natural principles and can be disproved by rational demonstration. In the light of his passionate and consistent advocacy of a purely secular and this-worldly morality, as well as of his insistence in the *Apologia*, the *Defensorium*, and the *De nutritione* that immortality is contrary to all the principles of natural reason, it remains a moot question how seriously he took his contention that immortality is nevertheless a "religious truth." The opposite conclusions to which reason leads Ficino and Pomponazzi on this issue are a direct result of their very different philosophical principles.

The third problem which links most of the treatises in this volume is the nature of man and of human dignity. In ridiculing the questions of the logicians and natural philosophers of his time, Petrarca insists that they are of no importance for man and his destiny; and, in emphasizing the value of classical learning, he implies that it is of vital concern for man and his proper education—a conception that was soon to find direct expression in the program of the *Studia Humanitatis*. The dignity of man became a favorite theme of Humanistic oratory and served as the starting-point for the speculative idea of human dignity we encounter in both Ficino and Pico. Ficino emphasizes man's skill in the arts and his universality; he assigns to the human soul the central place in the hierarchy of the universe. Pico goes one step further in adding to man's universality his liberty and in making of man a separate world outside the hierarchy in which all other beings have their fixed place. Ficino's conception is echoed in Pomponazzi's idea of man as the "mean"; Pico's view is repeated by Vives, who presents man as the skilful actor who can successfully play the roles of all creatures, from the lowest to the highest, and even that of God himself.

This glorification of man was one of the favorite themes of early Renaissance literature. During the sixteenth century it produced a strong reaction. The emphasis on man's total depravity found in the theology of the early Protestant Reformers may have been an answer to the exaggerated praise of man current in the Humanistic literature of their time. And Montaigne neatly used all the literary and intellectual devices of the Italian Humanists to ridicule that glorification and turn it into its opposite. Though he is too individual a figure to be forced into the mold of any intellectual tradition, it remains true that, on almost all philosophical questions, he repeats the Augustinian distinctions and answers. Montaigne is, philosophically, a representative of a humanized Augustinianism and shares to the full the Augustinian conception of human nature.

For all these reasons, the Renaissance texts collected in this volume should be of considerable intrinsic interest. For the student of intellectual history, this interest is further enhanced by the wide influence these thinkers exercised during the following centuries. The common view that their work was largely superseded, first by the Reformation, and then by the rise of modern science and philosophy, is only superficially true. They continued to be read and studied; and many traces of their influence are to be found in the writings of the seventeenth and eighteenth centuries. This is a subject that deserves much further study. Yet even in the present state of our knowledge it may be confidently asserted that the writers and thinkers of the early Italian Renaissance, by their own ideas as well as by transmitting ancient and medieval doctrines, made a significant contribution to Western literature and philosophy.

I

FRANCESCO PETRARCA
Translated by HANS NACHOD

INTRODUCTION

By HANS NACHOD

PETRARCA'S place in the evolution of the new philosophy which inaugurated the modern era of European civilization is as difficult to determine as is his astoundingly complex personality. We but rarely encounter a similar combination of a lyrical temperament of never slackening intensity with a mental constitution able to grasp reality in a perfectly detached attitude. No wonder that such a propitious blending of seemingly contradictory qualities yielded most fortunate results.

Petrarca's contribution to the forming of the mind of modern man can hardly be overestimated. However, we should not dare to call him a philosopher in the sense of one who conceives new and original philosophical ideas and is willing or at least attempts to organize them into a coherent and harmonious system of his own. He would have been astonished to find himself thus classified. What he thought of himself can be gathered from the charming self-portrait he once drew in a letter to his friend Francesco Bruni (p. 34). He never pretended to be more than an admirer and propagator of the moral teachings he found in the works of ancient philosophers, particularly in those of Latin thinkers who popularized Greek philosophy in the centuries shortly before and after the beginning of the Christian Era.

The great achievements of Scholastic philosophy—as far as they had not become the common property of everyone who received a higher education in Petrarca's time—had no noticeable influence on his thinking. Instinctively he felt a strong aversion for the late Scholastic schools, especially for those which tended toward Arabian Aristotelianism; and Aristotle himself was always more or less suspect to him, however hard he tried to appreciate the greatness of a man he found spoken of with so much reverence by his favorite classical authors.

Many problems which aroused the interest of Petrarca's contemporaries did not touch him at all. As a faithful son of the Church, he was fully satisfied with her teachings and did not need another guide in the labyrinth of this life, in this respect particularly under the spell of his great model Augustine. He used to laugh at vain efforts to penetrate the secrets of nature, and he ridiculed those who pretended to know the answers to problems he thought not worth investigating. Philosophy meant to him an exclusively practical discipline teaching the art of living well and happily, the *ars bene beateque vivendi*, as his beloved Cicero had put it. He did not aspire to be more than a moral philosopher, a man able to show his fellow-men how to learn and to practice this art. As such a philosopher he was willingly acknowledged by his contemporaries, and *philosophus moralis*—even the greatest living moral philosopher—is the predicate given to him in an official Venetian document, when he had declared his intention of leaving his rich library to the Republic of Venice.[1]

There were in the wane of the Middle Ages not a few who endeavored with more or less success to stir up the conscience of their fellow-men. Petrarca's influence was so much greater and more lasting than that of his competitors because he could touch the hearts of his readers more powerfully than most of them. With his unfailing instinct for literary and artistic quality, he had formed his style after the best models of Latin prose and tried to free himself from medieval tradition. His eloquence was long admired by everyone because it was felt how much he had advanced beyond his immediate predecessors in forging the language into an effective instrument for every purpose. When later generations of Humanists turned up their noses at his futile efforts to write an absolutely flawless Ciceronian Latin, they

1. G. Fracassetti, *Lettere di Francesco Petrarca*, V (Florence, 1892), 377.

forgot too rashly that the revival of classical Latin prose in which they took so much pride was largely due to him. He had acquired his very personal style mostly by assiduous reading from his early youth on. A marvelous memory retained for him not only the facts he read, but, what counts more, the form in which they were presented stuck indelibly in his mind. Thus he assimilated the style of his favorites almost without knowing how he achieved it. A student of stylistic problems will easily observe how near he came to his models at times, though he was careful to avoid slavish imitation and shunned what we call plagiarism with an entirely unmedieval conscientiousness.

In another way also Petrarca was able to profit from having read more than any of his contemporaries. He read ancient and medieval literature with a hitherto unheard-of sense for historical interrelations, and his ability to interpret a text critically was just as new. Since he was such a keen observer of actual life and so lovingly devoted to the investigation of the human heart, all the records of the past became a living reality to him, and he felt himself sharing in the drama related as if he had an active part in the cast. It was not just a whim that he, the untiring letter-writer, started to "correspond" with characters of ancient times, as if they could answer him. When he read their works, he almost forgot that they were long since dead. By such intensive reading with a clear comprehension of chronological relations and the inner logic of historical evolution, he developed a conception of history that strikes us very often as thoroughly modern. With all necessary reserve it may be said that the modern way of dealing with historical sources begins with him.

In the fourteenth century quite a number of progressive men in different parts of Europe were trying to widen their knowledge of the glorious past by procuring for themselves and the attentively listening world of scholarly minded friends works of the classical period that had been lying dormant for centuries. Book-hunting became a fashion in many learned circles, and to have found a new manuscript was a feat to boast of. However, no one could make as good a use of what he was lucky enough to discover as Petrarca. He is credited with having been the first to decipher the old codex containing the most important portion of Cicero's letters, those to Atticus and Quintus Cicero. This manuscript was preserved but hardly looked at any longer in the library of the cathedral of Verona. Very probably it had been known to his Humanist friends in that city before him, but only to him did it open a new outlook on the events it touched on and on the character of the man whom he had adored since childhood as the master of Latin prose. He suddenly understood why Cicero had been doomed to fail as a political figure, and he learned that his hero was not free from very tangible blemishes.

The range of Petrarca's knowledge of Roman literature has been described in masterly fashion by Pierre de Nolhac in his classical work on Petrarca and Humanism. Few of the major Latin authors with whom a modern historian and philologist is familiar were unknown to him. Some famous names are still missing in this catalogue, and in several cases strange traditional misconceptions prevented Petrarca from arriving at the conclusions reached by the generations that came after him; but, in general, he was far ahead of the most respected classical scholars of his age. Boccaccio may have known some authors who had escaped the attention of his friend and master, but, lacking Petrarca's imagination, he remained satisfied with the factual knowledge to be derived from classical literature by dry though devoted application.

Since Petrarca's attempts to learn Greek stopped short before they could bear any fruit, his notion of ancient philosophy was almost entirely gathered from Latin writers, mainly from Seneca and Cicero, Lactantius and Augustine. Aristotle's *Metaphysics* and *Ethics* were in his library in thirteenth-century Latin versions, but he did not get more than meager facts and some sententious phrases out of them, because, fascinated as he was by the sonorous rhythm of Ciceronian speech, he disliked the un-

classical style of the medieval translations. This instinctive hor-
ror kept him from understanding the intentions of the philosopher and the real aim of Greek philosophy. Occasionally he
suspected that he would never arrive at a fruitful comprehension of it as long as he had no Greek. It is characteristic of his
still medieval mental attitude that he lacked the energy to penetrate into the difficulties of a foreign language. Thus he could
never fully realize what Plato had contributed to the widening
of the mental horizon of mankind. The codex containing no less
than sixteen of Plato's dialogues in the original language which
he was so proud to possess (see p. 112) remained dumb to him,
and the few works of Plato that were available in Latin at the
time could not enlighten him much in their queer and incomplete translations.

It was therefore of the greatest importance for Petrarca's
philosophical education that he came in contact with Augustine
at a comparatively early age and was overwhelmingly impressed by Augustine's most stirring work, the *Confessions*,
when he reached his maturity. From the moment he devoured
Augustine's spiritual autobiography he was under the Father's
guidance and became as much of an Augustinian as was possible
for a man of the fourteenth century. Augustine appears as his
severe but helpful confessor when he writes his *Dialogues on
the Contempt of the World*, in which he tells the great Saint of
all his inmost feelings and sorrows. His Augustinian thinking
and his almost perfect imitation of Augustine's style are also
manifest in his letter to the Augustinian hermit, Dionigi da
Borgo San Sepolcro (see below).

The selections from Petrarca which are here chosen to represent him among the outstanding Humanist philosophers show
him at different times of his life. Though it was his habit to revise and remodel again and again whatever he had written on
the spur of the moment, these pieces have retained their original
charm almost unimpaired. They will reveal, even in their later

revisions, that they were once written under the inexorable compulsion of actual experience.

The Ascent of Mont Ventoux has long been regarded as one of Petrarca's literary masterpieces and has been translated into English several times. There is no need to relate much of the circumstances which prompted him to write it when he came down from the mountain after a long day's journey. It may be sufficient to point out that Francesco Dionigi de'Roberti from Borgo San Sepolcro (*ca.* 1285–1342), a professor of theology in Paris and later a bishop in the Neapolitan kingdom, was the man who had led him to Augustine. The grateful pupil tells his master of his stirring experiences during a day on which he undertook to reach the top of an isolated and comparatively high peak in the neighborhood of Carpentras, not far from the places connected with the reminiscences of his boyhood. The colorful description of this enterprise has startled many readers who have been amazed to see a man of his epoch venturing to climb a mountain for a view "like a modern alpinist." For many of them this conception of Petrarca has overshadowed the real intentions of the writer, who had much more to tell than the story of a hazardous mountain climb. Throughout the Middle Ages writers and readers had become so familiar with the art of hiding a deeper sense in apparently matter-of-fact reports of actual events that men were accustomed to look for a deeper allegorical sense in almost every work of literature. In this particular case Petrarca has in a masterly way managed to blend together the literal and the allegorical sense. In every sentence of his story of what happened to him on the fateful twenty-sixth day of April, 1336, he records also the phases of the long struggle in his conscience that eventually led to a kind of conversion and elevation to a higher state of mind, suggestive of the tumultuous conversion of his patron saint to the Christian faith almost a thousand years before.

The letter can be regarded as a particularly instructive specimen of what an author trained in medieval tradition could accomplish by filling his writings with quotations from other writers and making them his own by putting them in the right place in his work. This delicate art is brought to a climax toward the end of the letter, where Petrarca, "on the top of the mountain," remembers the crucial moments in the lives of great predecessors and weaves passages from their biographies into his report to indicate in a most solemn manner that the decisive moment in his own life, too, has been reached (p. 45).

The treatise *On His Own Ignorance and That of Many Others* was composed some thirty years later, in a very different phase of Petrarca's career. To understand this work it is necessary to know certain details of Petrarca's life at the time. He was then the most renowned scholar and moral philosopher of his age in the entire Western world. It came therefore as a severe blow to him to learn of a disparaging comment upon his importance pronounced by persons he had believed to be his friends and admirers.

In 1366 four men belonging to the highest social set of Venice had dared to declare in the form of a regular legal sentence that Petrarca was "certainly a good man but a scholar of poor merit." It was, indeed, pronounced after a good dinner which the four had enjoyed in privacy, but it soon became the talk of the town in the literary circles of the city where Petrarca still lived as a much honored guest. It was doubtless discussed with more or less malice among the younger people who could not bear the boundless praise lavished upon the aging celebrity. From a marginal note to a passage in a manuscript copy of the *De ignorantia* in Venice (Codex Marcianus Latinus IV, 86) we know the names of the four "young" men, though young they were only in the eyes of Petrarca, who was then past sixty. They were Leonardo Dandolo (*ca.* 1330–1405), the son of the late doge Andrea, a patrician distinguished by the high title of knight, already proved in the military and diplomatic service of his city; Zaccaria Contarini, also the scion of a very noble house, not knighted and therefore, in the wording of the note "a simple nobleman" but already often employed in important diplomatic missions; Tommaso Talenti (d. 1403), a rich merchant, but compared with the two noblemen only "a simple tradesman"; and Guido da Bagnolo of Reggio-Emilia (*ca.* 1325–70), court physician and resident minister of the king of Cyprus in the metropolis of Levant trade.

The first to break the unpleasant news to Petrarca was his devoted friend, Donato degli Albanzani of Pratovecchio in the Florentine Apennine (*ca.* 1325–1411), who was indignant at the insult inflicted upon his venerated master, all the more since his own reputation as head of a flourishing school rested to some degree upon his intimacy with the great man. Later on, Petrarca believed quite sincerely that he had only laughed at the impudence of the young braggarts, but it is not impossible that the affront hastened his decision to leave "the only haven of liberty," as he had called Venice but a few years before. At first he was sufficiently occupied with moving to Pavia, where Galeazzo Visconti, his generous patron, was about to establish a magnificent court in his marvelous new castle. It took some time before Petrarca was willing to answer in the form of an elaborate refutation. According to what he wrote to Boccaccio some years later, he started the work, reluctantly yielding to the urgent demands of his friends, ultimately because he had nothing better to do on a boresome barge ride on the Po while traveling to Padua late in the year 1367.

It had always been Petrarca's habit to rid himself of annoying and distressing mental burdens by writing. His peculiar temperament as a lyric poet had helped him very effectively on many occasions. So he regained his balance by writing a treatise on human ignorance in the classical form of the invective, a literary genus in which every weapon had been allowed since ancient times. His way of treating his self-appointed judges may, therefore, sometimes look rather shabby and even mean to modern readers who believe in good manners. However, we must remember that such a profusion of direct and hidden insults—queer as it may seem to us—belongs to the invective style. Besides, we see the angry mood slowly evaporating and a certain good-natured humor becoming more and more dominant toward the end of the little book. In the closing passages Petrarca even declares his willingness to make peace with his former friends.

In few other works of his can we so easily notice how far Petrarca has digested the material from which he had gathered his knowledge and understanding of ancient as well as contemporary philosophy.[2] Since the young men claimed to belong to the progressive school of philosophical practice deriving much of its tenets from the Arabian commentators of Aristotle, Petrarca indulges in ridicule of their slavish dependence upon unverified authority in their uncritical admiration of Aristotle and of Averroes, whose commentary had become so popular, though it was so dangerously exposed to misinterpretation in its Latin version. He knew that his opponents, with all their professedly bold and unprejudiced inquiry into truth, had never made more than a halfhearted attempt to risk an investigation on an impartial basis. The form in which he presents his confutation of their verdict is chiefly rhetorical, it is true, but his good common sense and clear judgment break through again and again.

The *Disapproval of an Unreasonable Use of the Discipline of Dialectic* is a product of Petrarca's younger years. He wrote it not long before the great crisis we witness in his letter to Dionigi. The little essay forms a part of the correspondence with one of his companions during the merry, carefree years he spent at the University of Bologna, a Sicilian named Tommaso Caloria of Messina. When the two had to part, never to meet again, they kept in close touch by writing each other about their life and interests until 1341, the date of Tommaso's untimely

2. The reader will have to discover this in the notes. A detailed analysis which would prove to be most revealing cannot be made here, since it would require too much space.

death. Nearly twenty years later, when Petrarca made a selection from his correspondence for his *Letters to Intimates* (*Familiares*),[3] he thought several letters to Caloria worth preserving in this book. It may well be that he chose this one because it demonstrates how an invective can be made in a pleasant manner. For us it is an interesting document of his state of mind at a time when he was fresh from college, still much impressed by what he had learned there. His philosophical attitude is still to a great extent borrowed from Seneca, and the cool and polished style of the Roman courtier-philosopher is used as a model.

Petrarca himself tells what caused him to write on dialectic and its limits. Caloria seems to have told him that an old schoolmaster in Messina, for whom philosophy was equivalent to the pedantic use of dialectic rules, felt offended by remarks on the dialectic methods of the time which Petrarca had made in a previous letter. The old man had even threatened to take revenge on Petrarca by writing against him. This menace offered a good occasion to explain what one ought to think of the discipline of dialectic. For Petrarca it could not do more than prepare beginners for the sound critical handling of more advanced philosophical problems; it could, indeed, furnish the tools of fruitful reading of more important literature, but it was not to be practiced for its own sake. The passage on the dialectic sects infesting the English isles is of documentary interest, since it shows how contemporary English philosophy was looked upon in Petrarca's circle.

Three short fragmentary extracts from other works of Petrarca are added to explain what made him so bitterly hate Averroes, Arab philosophy, and the Arabs in general. In many instances men who wanted to appear learned and profound seem to have discredited an author whose work was far less read than quoted, and usually not read with sufficient criticism. Like his young Venetian friends, many a man hoped to impose upon

3. Hereinafter cited as *Fam.*, while Petrarca's second collection, the *Letters of Old Age* (*Seniles*), are quoted as *Sen.*

others by blasphemously scoffing at whatever was dear to religious-minded men. There is no proof that Petrarca had really begun to compile a refutation of Averroes. Neither did his Augustinian friend, Luigi Marsili (*ca.* 1342–94), whom he invited to take over the task, ever publish a work of this kind. In the later years of the fourteenth century the danger to religion and the Church, with which Petrarca was so much concerned, may have ceased to be so obvious and threatening. Marsili kept Petrarca's tradition alive until the time when a new Humanistic enthusiasm grew up, kindled by the revival of Greek studies on the verge of the fifteenth century.[4]

4. I wish to thank Miss Helen Florence North of Ithaca, N.Y., and Professor John H. Randall, Jr., for their careful revision of my translation.

A SELF-PORTRAIT

From a letter to Francesco Bruni, papal secretary in Avignon. [Milan], October 25, 1362. (*Sen.*, I, 6 [5], in *Opera* [Basel, 1554], p. 824; [1581], p. 745.)

YOU make an orator of me, a historian, philosopher, and poet, and finally even a theologian. You would certainly not do so if you were not persuaded by one whom it is hard to disbelieve: I mean Love. Perhaps you might be excused if you did not extol me with titles so overwhelmingly great: I do not deserve to have them heaped on me. But let me tell you, my friend, how far I fall short of your estimation. It is not my opinion only; it is a fact: I am nothing of what you attribute to me. What am I then? I am a fellow who never quits school,[1] and not even that, but a backwoodsman who is roaming around through the lofty beech trees all alone, humming to himself some silly little tune, and—the very peak of presumption and assurance—dipping his shaky pen into his inkstand while sitting under a bitter laurel tree. I am not so fortunate in what I achieve as passionate in my work, being much more a lover of learning than a man who has got much of it. I am not so very eager to belong to a definite school of thought; I am striving for truth. Truth is difficult to discover, and, being the most humble and feeble of all those who try to find it, I lose confidence in myself often enough. So much do I fear to become entangled in errors that I throw myself into the embrace of doubt instead of truth. Thus I have gradually become a proselyte of the Academy[2] as

1. [In the word *scholasticus* so many meanings are united (schoolboy, student, scholar), that it cannot well be rendered by a single word in a modern language.]

2. [On the skeptical outcome of the New Academy, Petrarca got his information from Cicero's philosophical writings, especially from the

one of the big crowd, as the very last of this humble flock: I do not believe in my faculties, do not affirm anything, and doubt every single thing, with the single exception of what I believe is a sacrilege to doubt.

Academica posteriora. There he found Cicero saying (i. 12. 46) that in Plato's books nothing is firmly stated and much discussed "in both directions" (*in utramque partem*).]

THE ASCENT OF MONT VENTOUX

Letter to Francesco Dionigi de'Roberti of Borgo San Sepolcro, professor of theology in Paris. Malaucène, April 26, 1336. (*Fam.*, IV, 1, in *Le Familiari*, ed. V. Rossi, I, 153–61; *Opera* [Basel, 1581], pp. 624–27.)

To Dionigi da Borgo San Sepolcro, of the Order of Saint Augustine, Professor of Theology, about his own troubles

TODAY I ascended the highest mountain in this region, which, not without cause, they call the Windy Peak.[1] Nothing but the desire to see its conspicuous height was the reason for this undertaking. For many years I have been intending to make this expedition. You know that since my early childhood, as fate tossed around human affairs, I have been tossed around in these parts, and this mountain, visible far and wide from everywhere, is always in your view. So I was at last seized by the impulse to accomplish what I had always wanted to do. It happened while I was reading Roman history again in Livy that I hit upon the passage where Philip, the king of Macedon— the Philip who waged war against the Roman people—"ascends Mount Haemus in Thessaly, since he believed the rumor that you can see two seas from its top: the Adriatic and the Black Sea."[2] Whether he was right or wrong I cannot make out be-

1. [The name of the mountain appears as "Ventosus" in Latin documents as early as the tenth century, though originally it had nothing to do with the strong winds blowing about that isolated peak. Its Provençal form "Ventour" proves that it is related to the name of a deity worshiped by the pre-Roman (Ligurian) population of the Rhone Basin, a god believed to dwell on high mountains (cf. C. Jullian, *Histoire de la Gaule*, VI, 329; P. Julian, "Glose sur l'étymologie du mot Ventoux," in *Le Pélérinage du Mt. Ventoux* [Carpentras, 1937], pp. 337 ff.).]

2. [In his *History of Rome* (xl. 21. 2–22. 7) Livy tells that King Philip V of Macedonia went up to the top of Mount Haemus, one of the highest summits of the Great Balkans (*ca.* 7,800 ft.), when he wanted to reconnoiter the field of future operations before the Third Macedonian War, which he was planning to fight against the Romans (181 B.C.). Since

cause the mountain is far from our region, and the disagreement among authors renders the matter uncertain. I do not intend to consult all of them: the cosmographer Pomponius Mela does not hesitate to report the fact as true;[3] Livy supposes the rumor to be false. I would not leave it long in doubt if that mountain were as easy to explore as the one here. At any rate, I had better let it go, in order to come back to the mountain I mentioned at first. It seemed to me that a young man who holds no public office[4] might be excused for doing what an old king is not blamed for.

I now began to think over whom to choose as a companion. It will sound strange to you that hardly a single one of all my friends seemed to me suitable in every respect, so rare a thing is absolute congeniality in every attitude and habit even among dear friends. One was too sluggish, the other too vivacious; one too slow, the other too quick; this one too gloomy of temper, that one too gay. One was duller, the other brighter than I should have liked. This man's taciturnity, that man's flippancy; the heavy weight and obesity of the next, the thinness and weakliness of still another were reasons to deter me. The cool lack of curiosity of one, like another's too eager interest, dissuaded me from choosing either. All such qualities, however difficult they are to bear, can be borne at home: loving friendship is able to endure everything; it refuses no burden. But on a journey they become intolerable. Thus my delicate mind, craving honest entertainment, looked about carefully, weighing every detail, with no offense to friendship. Tacitly it rejected whatever it could foresee would become troublesome on the projected excursion.

Petrarca knew the exact location of this mountain from Pliny's *Natural History* (iv. 1. 3 and xi. 18. 41), it must have been a slip of his pen that made him substitute "Thessaly" for "Thrace."]

3. [Mela *Cosmographia* ii. 2. 17.]

4. [Cf. Cicero *De imperio Cn. Pompei* 21. 61, where he praises the courage of Pompey, who took over the command of the Roman armies in 77 B.C. though he was then but an "adulescentulus privatus."]

What do you think I did? At last I applied for help at home and revealed my plan to my only brother, who is younger than I and whom you know well enough. He could hear of nothing he would have liked better and was happy to fill the place of friend as well as brother.

We left home on the appointed day and arrived at Malaucène at night. This is a place at the northern foot of the mountain. We spent a day there and began our ascent this morning, each of us accompanied by a single servant. From the start we encountered a good deal of trouble, for the mountain is a steep and almost inaccessible pile of rocky material. However, what the Poet says is appropriate: "Ruthless striving overcomes everything."[5]

The day was long, the air was mild; this and vigorous minds, strong and supple bodies, and all the other conditions assisted us on our way. The only obstacle was the nature of the spot. We found an aged shepherd in the folds of the mountain who tried with many words to dissuade us from the ascent. He said he had been up to the highest summit in just such youthful fervor fifty years ago and had brought home nothing but regret and pains, and his body as well as his clothes torn by rocks and thorny underbrush. Never before and never since had the people there heard of any man who dared a similar feat. While he was shouting these words at us, our desire increased just because of his warnings; for young people's minds do not give credence to advisers. When the old man saw that he was exerting himself in vain, he went with us a little way forward through the rocks and pointed with his finger to a steep path. He gave us much good advice and repeated it again and again at our backs when we were already at quite a distance. We left with him whatever of our clothes and other belongings might encumber us, intent only on the ascent, and began to climb with merry alacrity. However, as almost always happens, the daring attempt was soon followed by quick fatigue.

5. [Virgil *Georgica* i. 145–46; Macrobius *Saturnalia* v. 6.]

Not far from our start we stopped at a rock. From there we went on again, proceeding at a slower pace, to be sure. I in particular made my way up with considerably more modest steps. My brother endeavored to reach the summit by the very ridge of the mountain on a short cut; I, being so much more of a weakling, was bending down toward the valley. When he called me back and showed me the better way, I answered that I hoped to find an easier access on the other side and was not afraid of a longer route on which I might proceed more smoothly. With such an excuse I tried to palliate my laziness, and, when the others had already reached the higher zones, I was still wandering through the valleys, where no more comfortable access was revealed, while the way became longer and longer and the vain fatigue grew heavier and heavier. At last I felt utterly disgusted, began to regret my perplexing error, and decided to attempt the heights with a wholehearted effort. Weary and exhausted, I reached my brother, who had been waiting for me and was refreshed by a good long rest. For a while we went on together at the same pace. However, hardly had we left that rock behind us when I forgot the detour I had made just a short while before and was once more drawing down the lower regions. Again I wandered through the valleys, looking for the longer and easier path and stumbling only into longer difficulties. Thus I indeed put off the disagreeable strain of climbing. But nature is not overcome by man's devices; a corporeal thing cannot reach the heights by descending. What shall I say? My brother laughed at me; I was indignant; this happened to me three times and more within a few hours. So often was I frustrated in my hopes that at last I sat down in a valley. There I leaped in my winged thoughts from things corporeal to what is incorporeal and addressed myself in words like these:

"What you have so often experienced today while climbing this mountain happens to you, you must know, and to many others who are making their way toward the blessed life. This is not easily understood by us men, because the motions of the body lie open, while those of the mind are invisible and hidden. The life we call blessed is located on a high peak. 'A narrow way,'[6] they say, leads up to it. Many hilltops intervene, and we must proceed 'from virtue to virtue' with exalted steps.[7] On the highest summit is set the end of all, the goal toward which our pilgrimage is directed. Every man wants to arrive there. However, as Naso says: 'Wanting is not enough; long and you attain it.'[8] You certainly do not merely want; you have a longing, unless you are deceiving yourself in this respect as in so many others. What is it, then, that keeps you back? Evidently nothing but the smoother way that leads through the meanest earthly pleasures and looks easier at first sight. However, having strayed far in error, you must either ascend to the summit of the blessed life under the heavy burden of hard striving, ill deferred, or lie prostrate in your slothfulness in the valleys of your sins. If 'darkness and the shadow of death'[9] find you there —I shudder while I pronounce these ominous words—you must pass the eternal night in incessant torments."

You cannot imagine how much comfort this thought brought my mind and body for what lay still ahead of me. Would that I might achieve with my mind the journey for which I am longing day and night as I achieved with the feet of my body my journey today after overcoming all obstacles. And I wonder whether it ought not to be much easier to accomplish what can be done by means of the agile and immortal mind without any local motion "in the twinkling of the trembling eye"[10] than what is to be performed in the succession of time by the service

6. [Matt. 7 : 14 (Sermon on the Mount).]

7. [A typical metaphor familiar to ecclesiastical writers; cf., e.g., Anselm of Canterbury *Letters* i. 43 (Migne, *Patrologia Latina*, CLVIII, 1113, etc.), where it is used as a friendly wish in salutations.]

8. [Ovid *Ex Ponto* iii. 1. 35.]

9. [Ps. 106(107) : 10; Job 34 : 22.]

10. [I Cor. 15 : 52; Augustine *Confessions* vii. 1. 1 (cf. Shakespeare, *Merchant of Venice*, Act. II, scene 2, line 183).]

of the frail body that is doomed to die and under the heavy load of the limbs.

There is a summit, higher than all the others. The people in the woods up there call it "Sonny,"[11] I do not know why. However, I suspect they use the word in a sense opposite to its meaning, as is done sometimes in other cases too. For it really looks like the father of all the surrounding mountains. On its top is a small level stretch. There at last we rested from our fatigue.

And now, my dear father, since you have heard what sorrows arose in my breast during my climb, listen also to what remains to be told. Devote, I beseech you, one of your hours to reading what I did during one of my days. At first I stood there almost benumbed, overwhelmed by a gale such as I had never felt before and by the unusually open and wide view. I looked around me: clouds were gathering below my feet, and Athos and Olympus grew less incredible, since I saw on a mountain of lesser fame what I had heard and read about them. From there I turned my eyes in the direction of Italy, for which my mind is so fervently yearning. The Alps were frozen stiff and covered with snow—those mountains through which that ferocious enemy of the Roman name once passed, blasting his way through the rocks with vinegar if we may believe tradition.[12] They looked as if they were quite near me, though they are far, far away. I was longing, I must confess, for Italian air,

11. [Though Petrarca was familiar with the idiom of southern France, he misinterpreted the Provençal word *fiholo*. There is still today a spring just below the summit of Mont Ventoux called "Font-filiole" and a ravine near by by name of "combe filiole," the word meaning a water conduit or a rivulet, but the summit can have received the name only secondarily (P. de Champeville, "L'Itinéraire du poète F. P.," in *L'Ascension du Mt. Ventoux* [Carpentras, 1937], p. 41).]

12. [Hannibal is said to have made his troops burn down the trees on rocks obstructing their way and pour vinegar on the ashes to pulverize the burned material when he crossed the Alps in 218 B.C. (Livy *History of Rome* xxi. 37; cf. Pliny *Nat. Hist.* xxiii. 57). Later authors referred to this incident as an example of Hannibal's ingenuity in overcoming seemingly unsurmountable obstacles (Juvenal *Satire* 10, 153).]

which appeared rather to my mind than my eyes. An incredibly strong desire seized me to see my friend[13] and my native land again. At the same time I rebuked the weakness of a mind not yet grown to manhood, manifest in both these desires, although in both cases an excuse would not lack support from famous champions.

Then another thought took possession of my mind, leading it from the contemplation of space to that of time, and I said to myself: "This day marks the completion of the tenth year since you gave up the studies of your boyhood and left Bologna. O immortal God, O immutable Wisdom! How many and how great were the changes you have had to undergo in your moral habits since then." I will not speak of what is still left undone, for I am not yet in port that I might think in security of the storms I have had to endure. The time will perhaps come when I can review all this in the order in which it happened, using as a prologue that passage of your favorite Augustine: "Let me remember my past mean acts and the carnal corruption of my soul, not that I love them, but that I may love Thee, my God."[14]

Many dubious and troublesome things are still in store for me. What I used to love, I love no longer. But I lie: I love it still, but less passionately. Again have I lied: I love it, but more timidly, more sadly. Now at last I have told the truth; for thus it is: I love, but what I should love not to love, what I should wish to hate. Nevertheless I love it, but against my will, under compulsion and in sorrow and mourning. To my own misfortune I experience in myself now the meaning of that most famous line: "Hate I shall, if I can; if I can't, I shall love though not willing."[15] The third year has not yet elapsed since that perverted and malicious will, which had totally seized me and

13. [Petrarca is referring to Giacomo Colonna, bishop of Lombez, who had gone to Rome in the summer of 1333; cf. *Fam.*, I, 5 (4), and I, 6 (5).]

14. [*Confessions* ii. 1. 1.]

15. [Ovid *Amores* iii. 11. 35.]

reigned in the court of my heart without an opponent, began to encounter a rebel offering resistance. A stubborn and still undecided battle has been long raging on the field of my thoughts for the supremacy of one of the two men within me.[16]

Thus I revolved in my thoughts the history of the last decade. Then I dismissed my sorrow at the past and asked myself: "Suppose you succeed in protracting this rapidly fleeing life for another decade, and come as much nearer to virtue, in proportion to the span of time, as you have been freed from your former obstinacy during these last two years as a result of the struggle of the new and the old wills—would you then not be able—perhaps not with certainty but with reasonable hope at least—to meet death in your fortieth year with equal mind and cease to care for that remnant of life which descends into old age?"

These and like considerations rose in my breast again and again, dear father. I was glad of the progress I had made, but I wept over my imperfection and was grieved by the fickleness of all that men do. In this manner I seemed to have somehow forgotten the place I had come to and why, until I was warned to throw off such sorrows, for which another place would be more appropriate. I had better look around and see what I had intended to see in coming here. The time to leave was approaching, they said. The sun was already setting, and the shadow of the mountain was growing longer and longer. Like a man aroused from sleep, I turned back and looked toward the west. The boundary wall between France and Spain, the ridge of the Pyrenees, is not visible from there, though there is no obstacle of which I knew, and nothing but the weakness of the mortal eye is the cause. However, one could see most distinctly the mountains of the province of Lyons to the right and, to the

16. [Two rival wills are struggling in Petrarca's breast, the old one not releasing him from his amorous servitude and blocking his spiritual progress, the other urging him forward on the way to perfection (cf. Augustine *Confessions* viii. 5. 10; x. 22–23, and Petrarca's Sonnet 52 (68).]

left, the sea near Marseilles as well as the waves that break against Aigues Mortes, although it takes several days to travel to this city. The Rhone River was directly under our eyes.

I admired every detail, now relishing earthly enjoyment, now lifting up my mind to higher spheres after the example of my body, and I thought it fit to look into the volume of Augustine's *Confessions* which I owe to your loving kindness and preserve carefully, keeping it always in my hands, in remembrance of the author as well as the donor.[17] It is a little book of smallest size but full of infinite sweetness. I opened it with the intention of reading whatever might occur to me first: nothing, indeed, but pious and devout sentences could come to hand. I happened to hit upon the tenth book of the work. My brother stood beside me, intently expecting to hear something from Augustine on my mouth. I ask God to be my witness and my brother who was with me: Where I fixed my eyes first, it was written: "And men go to admire the high mountains, the vast floods of the sea, the huge streams of the rivers, the circumference of the ocean, and the revolutions of the stars—and desert themselves."[18] I was stunned, I confess. I bade my brother, who wanted to hear more, not to molest me, and closed the book, angry with myself that I still admired earthly things. Long since I ought to have learned, even from pagan philosophers, that "nothing is admirable besides the mind; compared to its greatness nothing is great."[19]

I was completely satisfied with what I had seen of the mountain and turned my inner eye toward myself. From this hour nobody heard me say a word until we arrived at the bottom. These words occupied me sufficiently. I could not imagine that this had happened to me by chance: I was convinced that what-

17. [The small-sized manuscript codex of Augustine's *Confessions*, a present from Dionigi, accompanied Petrarca wherever he went until the last year of his life, when he could no longer read its minute script and gave the book to Luigi Marsili (see p. 33) as a token of his friendship.]

18. [Augustine *Confessions* x. 8. 15.]

19. [Seneca *Epistle* 8. 5.]

ever I had read there was said to me and to nobody else. I remembered that Augustine once suspected the same regarding himself, when, while he was reading the Apostolic Epistles, the first passage that occurred to him was, as he himself relates: "Not in banqueting and drunkenness, not in chambering and wantonness, not in strife and envying; but put ye on the Lord Jesus Christ, and make no provision for the flesh to fulfil your lusts."[20] The same had happened before to Anthony: he heard the Gospel where it is written: "If thou wilt be perfect, go and sell that thou hast, and give to the poor, and come and follow me, and thou shalt have treasure in heaven."[21] As his biographer Athanasius says, he applied the Lord's command to himself, just as if the Scripture had been recited for his sake. And as Anthony, having heard this, sought nothing else, and as Augustine, having read the other passage, proceeded no further, the end of all my reading was the few words I have already set down. Silently I thought over how greatly mortal men lack counsel who, neglecting the noblest part of themselves in empty parading, look without for what can be found within. I admired the nobility of the mind, had it not voluntarily degenerated and strayed from the primordial state of its origin, converting into disgrace what God had given to be its honor.

How often, do you think, did I turn back and look up to the summit of the mountain today while I was walking down? It seemed to me hardly higher than a cubit compared to the height of human contemplation, were the latter not plunged into the filth of earthly sordidness. This too occurred to me at every step: "If you do not regret undergoing so much sweat and hard labor to lift the body a bit nearer to heaven, ought any cross or jail or torture to frighten the mind that is trying to come nearer to God and set its feet upon the swollen summit of insolence

20. [Rom. 13 : 13–14, quoted by Augustine *Confessions* viii. 12. 29.]

21. [Matt. 19:21, quoted by Athanasius in his *Life of St. Anthony* (Latin version by Euagrius), chap. 2, and from there by Augustine *Confessions* viii. 12. 29.]

and upon the fate of mortal men?" And this too: "How few will ever succeed in not diverging from this path because of fear of hardship or desire for smooth comfort?[22] Too fortunate would be any man who accomplished such a feat—were there ever such anywhere. This would be him of whom I should judge the Poet was thinking when he wrote:

> Happy the man who succeeded in baring the causes of things
> And who trod underfoot all fear, inexorable Fate and
> Greedy Acheron's uproar.....[23]

How intensely ought we to exert our strength to get under foot not a higher spot of earth but the passions which are puffed up by earthly instincts."

Such emotions were rousing a storm in my breast as, without perceiving the roughness of the path, I returned late at night to the little rustic inn from which I had set out before dawn. The moon was shining all night long and offered her friendly service to the wanderers. While the servants were busy preparing our meal, I withdrew quite alone into a remote part of the house to write this letter to you in all haste and on the spur of the moment. I was afraid the intention to write might evaporate, since the rapid change of scene was likely to cause a change of mood if I deferred it.

And thus, most loving father, gather from this letter how eager I am to leave nothing whatever in my heart hidden from your eyes. Not only do I lay my whole life open to you with the utmost care but every single thought of mine. Pray for these thoughts, I beseech you, that they may at last find stability. So long have they been idling about and, finding no firm stand, been uselessly driven through so many matters. May they now turn at last to the One, the Good, the True, the stably Abiding.

Farewell.

On the twenty-sixth day of April, at Malaucène.

22. [Cf. Matt. 7 : 13–15.]
23. [Virgil *Georgica* ii. 490–92.]

ON HIS OWN IGNORANCE AND THAT
OF MANY OTHERS

Opera (Basel, 1554), pp. 1123–68; (1581), pp. 1035–59; L. M. Capelli, *Pétrarque: Le traité De sui ipsius et multorum ignorantia* (Paris, 1906); and P. Rajna, "Il codice Hamiltoniano 493 della R. Biblioteca di Berlino," *Rendiconti dell'Accademia dei Lincei*, XVIII (5a ser., 1909), 479–508. The Dedication, dated January 13, 1368, belongs in Book xiii of the *Seniles*, as No. 5, but is printed before the text in the Basel Editions of the *Opera*.

*To the grammarian Donato the Apennine-born, with a little
book dedicated to him*

HERE at last, my friend, you have the little book long since expected and promised, a little book on a vast matter, namely, "On my own ignorance and that of many others." Had I been allowed to beat it out on the anvil of my inventive genius with the hammer of study, you may believe me, it would have grown into a camel's load. For can there be a wider field, a vaster ground for talking, than a treatise on ignorance and especially on mine? You shall read this book, as you are in the habit of listening to me when I tell tales at the fireside on winter nights, rambling along wherever the impulse takes me. I have called it a book, but it is a talk. It has nothing of a book besides the name: neither the bulk nor the disposition; it has not the style and, above all, not the gravity of a book, since it was written quickly on a hasty journey.

However, I have had the whim to call it a book, because I wanted to win your favor with a small present and a great name. I was convinced that whatever comes from me will please you. Nevertheless, I intended to cheat you. It is customary to cheat another in this manner even among friends. When we send them a few apples or some choice morsel of dainty food, we put these things into a silver vessel and wrap it in pure white linen. What is sent does not then become more. It does not become more valuable but is made more agreeable to him who receives it and more honorable for the sender. Thus I have made a trifling thing more honorable by a beautiful wrapping when I call a book what I might have called a letter.

It will not be the less valuable to you because it is interspersed with countless obliterations and additions and completely crammed with marginals on the borders of its pages.[1] It has lost somewhat of its decorous appearance to the eye, but your mind will surely appreciate that just as much gracefulness has been added. You will realize all the more that you are nearest to my heart, since I write you in such a way that you will regard all these additions and erasures as signs of close friendship and affection.

Moreover, I did not want you to doubt that the book is my work; I have written it in my hand, which has been so familiar to you for years. Almost by intention it comes to you deformed by so many wounds and will remind you that Suetonius Tranquillus has written something similar about the emperor Nero: "There came into my hands some little tablets and small notebooks, in which several well-known verses of his were entered in his own handwriting. It was easy to recognize that they were not copied from elsewhere or written upon dictation, but set down by their inventor or begetter. So much was crossed out, inserted, and written above the lines."[2] So far Suetonius.

I will not write more at present. Farewell and remember me. Goodbye.

Padua, on the thirteenth of January, from the bed of my pains, in the eleventh hour of night.

1. [This is actually the case in both autograph copies.]

2. [Suetonius *Life of Nero* 52.]

THE BOOK OF
FRANCESCO PETRARCA THE LAUREATE
ON HIS OWN IGNORANCE AND THAT OF MANY OTHERS

To the grammarian Donato the Apennine-born

SHALL we never have any respite? Must this pen always needs fight? Shall we never have a holiday? Must we respond every day to praises from our friends, every day make reply to the insults of envious rivals? Will no hiding-place ever protect us from jealousy, will no length of time extinguish envy? Shall I never find quiet repose by fleeing almost everything for which mankind strives and fervently exerts itself? Will my declining and wearied age not at last procure me a release? Envy is a persistent poison. Long since my age would have freed me from duties toward the state;[3] it does not free me from envy. The state, to which I owe so much, gives me a discharge from my obligations; envy, to which I owe nothing, disturbs me. Once, I must confess, the times encouraged a friendlier style. A more serene manner of speaking was always congenial to my nature and would befit my present age. Pardon me, my friends, and you, reader, pardon me, whoever you are. And you above all, my dearest Donato, to whom I tell all this, forgive me. I must speak, not because it is the best thing to do, but because it is so hard to refrain. Reason advises me to keep silent; an indignation which, if I am not mistaken, is proper and dignified, and a just grief extort words from me. Most avidly craving for peace, I am thrust into war. Again, you see, we are driven forward against our will; again we are dragged before a censorious tribunal—I do not know whether I ought to call it the tribunal of envious friendship or of friendly envy.

What is impossible for you, malicious grudge, if you can

3. [At fifty the citizen of the Roman republic reached the age limit of military service, and at sixty he was no longer obliged to accept a public office (Seneca *De brevitate vitae* 20. 4; Livy *History of Rome* xlii. 33; Quintilian *Institutio oratoria* ix. 2. 85. Petrarca had passed even the later limit three years before he began this book.]

inflame even the hearts of friends? Much I have had to experience before; this kind of evil I have never yet experienced. Now for the first time my fate throws into my path this gravest and worst of evils. Clashes with enemies have often a prosperous issue; wrath against an enemy is sweet, as some are pleased to say—sweet at any rate is victory over him. But if you are to fight with friends, it is equally miserable to win or to lose. However, I am at war neither with friends nor with enemies but with envy. It is not a new enemy, though its manner of fighting is new. With bow and quiver it comes to the battlefield; it attacks with arrows and strikes from afar. There is one advantage: it is blind. You can easily evade it if you see it in time. It shoots without aim and often wounds its own ranks. This monster I must now pierce, while friendship must remain unscathed.

It is certainly a precarious task to stab one of two persons while they are clinging closely together without hurting the other. I believe you will remember how Julius Caesar was once engulfed by an unexpected outbreak of fighting in Alexandria.[4] "Then he dragged King Ptolemy with him into all the vicissitudes of battle," determined not to perish without him. This is supposed to have been no small reason for his escape, since those who hated him and loved Ptolemy thought it would be difficult to kill the foe and at the same time save their king. You will also not have forgotten, I guess, how on the day, when the kingdom of Persia was freed from servile tyranny by the shrewdness of the wise Hortanes and the bravery of the seven valiant men, one of the conspirators, "Gophirus, grasped one of the two tyrants in a dark place and bade his companions strike at the man even through his own body, lest, if he himself were spared, the tyrant might escape."[5] Now sacred friendship calls upon me to stab

4. [Lucan *Pharsalia* x. 458–64; Caesar *De bello civili* iii. 109.]

5. [Petrarca knew of the dramatic scenes which happened in 521 B.C., when the Persian nobility revolted against a usurper to the throne, from the summary which Justin (*Historia Philippica* i. 9. 9–23) gives of the extensive account in Herodotus' *History* (iii. 63–79). In the Greek text

with the point of my pen, even through its own breast, the impious grudge it is clutching gently in its bosom in unequal embrace. It is hard to distinguish between two that are clinging together so tightly in such darkness. However, I will try to do so. Then the foe fell, while Gophirus remained unhurt; now bitter envy is to be crushed and dispatched, while sweet friendship is to be saved. If friendship is true friendship—and this can only be accomplished by true virtue[6]—it will rather be hurt while envy is exterminated, if it cannot be done otherwise, than remain unhurt while envy survives and dominates.

But let us now at last come to the matter. It will be known to you no less than to me, as soon as I begin to speak of it—and, if I am not mistaken, even before I begin. Perhaps it will be even better known to you, since a friend is more concerned for the reputation of a friend than for his own.[7] We become more easily and more honorably annoyed when something is said against friends than when it happens to ourselves. Many a man has not minded insults against himself and has been praised for this attitude; nobody has yet been able calmly to witness or hear an affront against a friend. It does not require the same grade of magnanimity to remain unmoved by offenses against others as we must have when we ourselves are insulted.

Besides, how can you fail to know what you yourself made known to me first and what you were grieved to see me treat scornfully and jokingly? I shall, therefore, speak of things known to you, not because I want them to become still better known to you. You shall know how I feel against envy and begin to feel like me and shall not bewail another's wound more vehemently than your own. You shall also learn what kind of

---

the two protagonists were called Otanes and Gobryas. It has not been explained as yet why Petrarca uses the strange variant forms "Hortanes" and "Gophirus."]

6. [Cicero *Laelius, de amicitia* 6, 20.]

7. [*Ibid.* 16. 57.]

weapon I use against it; how, by long practice and diligent application, I have grown deaf to the murmur of those who are barking at me, and how I have been hardened against their envious teeth.

And this is now the gist of the present story:

As had come to be their custom, there called on me these four friends whose names you need not be told, since you know them all. Moreover, an inviolable law of friendship forbids mentioning the names of friends when you are speaking against them, even if they do not behave like friends in a particular case. They came in pairs, as equality of character or some chance bound them together. Occasionally all four of them came, and came with astonishingly winning manners, with a gay expression on their faces, and started an agreeable conversation. I have no doubt they came with good and pious intentions. However, through some cracks an unfortunate grudge had crept into hearts that deserve a better guest. It is incredible, though it is true—if only it were not too true! The man whom they wish not only good health and happiness, whom they not only love but respect, honor by their visit and venerate, to whom they try with greatest effort to be not only kind but obedient and generous—this very same person is the object of their envy. So full of patent and hidden frailties is human nature.

What is it that they envy me? I do not know, I must admit, and I am amazed when I try to find out. Certainly it is not wealth, for every single one of them surpasses me as much in wealth as "the British whale is bigger than the dolphin,"[8] as that man has said. Moreover, they wish me even greater wealth. They know that what I have is moderate, not my own property but to be shared with others. It is not magnificent but very modest without haughtiness and pomp. They know that it really does not deserve any envy. They will not envy me my friends.

8. [Juvenal *Satire* 10. 12. In some cases Petrarca observes a stylistic principle common to medieval writers of not mentioning the name of an author who is quoted. Usually he calls Juvenal "the satyrist"; here he speaks only of "that man" (*ille*).]

The greater part of them death has taken from me, and I have the habit of sharing them willingly, just like everything else, with other friends. They cannot envy me the shapeliness of my body. If there was ever such a thing, it has vanished entirely in the course of the years that vanquish all. By God's overflowing and preserving grace it is still quite satisfactory for my present age, but it has certainly long since ceased to be enviable. And if it were still as it was once, could I forget or could I then have forgotten the poetic sentence I drank in as a small boy: "Shapeliness is a frail possession,"[9] or the words of Solomon in the book in which he teaches the young: "Gracefulness is deceitful and beauty is vain."[10] How should they then envy me what I do not have, what I held in contempt while I had it, and what I would despise now to the utmost were it given back to me, having learned and experienced how unstable it is?

They cannot even envy me learning and eloquence! Learning, they declare, I have absolutely none. Eloquence, if I had any, they despise according to the modern philosophic fashion. They reject it as unworthy of a man of letters. Thus only "infantile inability to speak" and perplexed stammering, "wisdom" trying hard to keep one eye open and "yawning drowsily," as Cicero calls it,[11] is held in good repute nowadays. They do not call to mind "Plato, the most eloquent of all men,"[12] and—let me omit the others—"Aristotle sweet and mild,"[13] but whom they made trite. From Aristotle's ways they swerve, taking eloquence to be an obstacle and a disgrace to philosophy, while he considered it a mighty adornment and tried to combine it with

9. [Ovid *Ars amatoria* ii. 113.]

10. [Prov. 30:31.]

11. [*De oratore* iii. 51. 198; ii. 33. 144–45.]

12. [*Ibid.* i. 11. 47.]

13. [Cicero *Topica* 1. 2; *De oratore* i. 1. 49: cf. *Academica priora* ii. 38. 119; Seneca *Naturales quaestiones* vi. 13. 1; Quintilian *Institutio oratoria* x. 1. 83, a passage missing in Petrarca's Quintilian but known to him from John of Salisbury's *Metalogicon*, 22 (ed. Webb 859a).]

philosophy, "prevailed upon," it is asserted, "by the fame of the orator Isocrates."[14]

Not even virtue can they envy me, though it is beyond doubt the best and most enviable of all things. To them it seems worthless—I believe because it is not inflated and puffed up with arrogance. I should wish to possess it, and, indeed, they grant it to me unanimously and willingly. Small things they have denied me, and this very greatest possession they lavish upon me as a small gift. They call me a good man, even the best of men. If only I were not bad, not the worst in God's judgment! However, at the same time they claim that I am altogether illiterate, that I am a plain uneducated fellow.[15] This is just the opposite of what men of letters have stated when judging me, I do not care with how much truth. I do not make much of what these friends deprive me of, if only what they concede me were true. Most gladly should I divide between me and these brothers of mine the inheritance of Mother Nature and heavenly Grace, so that they would all be men of letters and I a good man. I should wish to know nothing of letters or just so much as would be expedient for the daily praise of God. But, alas, I fear I shall be disappointed in this my humble desire just as they will be in their arrogant opinion. At any rate, they assert that I have a good character and am very faithful in my friendship, and in this last assertion they are not mistaken, unless I am.

This, incidentally, is the reason why they count me among their friends. They are not prevailed upon to do so by my efforts in studying the honorable arts or the hope ever to hear and learn truth from me. Thus it comes plainly to what Augustine tells of his Ambrose, saying: "I began to love him, not as a

---

14. [Cicero *De oratore* iii. 35. 141; *Tusculanae disputationes* i. 4. 7.]

15. [In conformity with classical as well as contemporary custom, Petrarca uses *idiota* for a man without higher education, in contrast to *litteratus*, but the word was already in his time gradually acquiring the meaning of "simpleton," though not yet that of "feeble-minded." This degradation of the term was certainly due to the power of the Humanistic concept of man, of which learning is an essential factor.]

teacher of truth, but as a man who was kind to me";[16] or what Cicero feels about Epicurus: Cicero approves of his character in many passages, while he everywhere condemns his intellect and rejects his doctrine.[17]

Since all this is the case, it may be doubtful what they envy me, though there is no doubt that they do envy me something. They do not well conceal it and do not curb their tongues, which are urged by an inward impulse. In men otherwise neither unbalanced nor foolish this is nothing but a clear sign of undisciplined passion. Provided that they are envious of me as they obviously are, and that there is no other object of their envy—the latent virus is expanding by itself at any rate. For there is one thing, one empty thing, that they envy me, however trifling it may be: my name and what fame I have already won within my lifetime—greater fame perhaps than would be due to my merits or in conformity with the common habit which but very rarely celebrates living men. It is upon this fame that they have fixed their envious eyes. If only I could have done without it both now and often before! I remember that it has done me harm more often than good, winning me quite a few friends but also countless enemies. It has happened to me as to those who go into battle in a conspicuous helmet though with but little strength: they gain nothing from the dazzling brightness of this chimera except to be struck by more adversaries. Such pestilence was once but too familiar to me during my more flourishing years; never was there one so troublesome as that which has now blazed up. I am now an anvil too soft for young men's wars and for assuming such burdens, and this pestilence revives unexpectedly from a quarter from which I do not deserve it and did not suspect it either, at a moment when it should have been

16. [*Confessions* v. 13. 23.]

17. [While Cicero condemns the philosophy of Epicurus wherever he speaks of him (e.g., *De finibus* ii. 30. 98), he frankly acknowledges the unimpeachable character of the great philosopher (*ibid.* 2. 25. 80–81; 30. 96).]

long since overcome by my moral conduct or consumed by the course of time.

But I will go on: They think they are great men, and they are certainly rich, all of them, which is the only mortal greatness nowadays. They feel, although many people deceive themselves in this respect, that they have not won a name and cannot hope ever to win one if their foreboding is right. Among such sorrows they languish anxiously; and so great is the power of evil that they stick out their tongues and sharpen their teeth like mad dogs even against friends and wound those whom they love. Is this not a strange kind of blindness, a strange kind of fury? In just this manner the frantic mother of Pentheus tears her son to pieces[18] and the raving Hercules his infant children.[19] They love me and all that is mine, with the single exception of my name—which I do not refuse to change. Let them call me Thersites[20] or Choerilus,[21] or whatever name they prefer, provided I thus obtain that this honest love suffers not the slightest restriction. They are all the more ablaze and aglow with a blind fire, since they are all such fervent scholars, working indefatigably all night long.

However, the first of them has no learning at all[22]—I tell you only what you know—the second knows a little; the third not much; the fourth—I must admit—not a little but in such confused and undisciplined order and, as Cicero says, "with so much frivolity and vain boasting that it would perhaps be better to know nothing."[23] For letters are instruments of insanity for many, of

18. [Ovid *Metamorphoses* iii. 711–28.]

19. [Seneca *Hercules furens* 987–1023.]

20. [Homer *Iliad* ii. 212–17; Ovid *Ex Ponto* iii. 9. 10; iv. 13. 15.]

21. [About Choerilus, who won a fortune but also the name of a very bad poet by a panegyrical poem on the heroic deeds of Alexander the Great, Petrarca got his information from the pseudo-Acronian scholia to Horace *Epistles* ii. 1. 233–34.]

22. [Cf. the marginal note in Codex Marcianus Lat. IV 86 mentioned on p. 29.]

23. [*Tusculanae disputationes* ii. 4. 12.]

arrogance for almost everyone, if they do not meet with a good and well-trained mind. Therefore, he has much to tell about wild animals, about birds and fishes: how many hairs there are in the lion's mane; how many feathers in the hawk's tail; with how many arms the cuttlefish clasps a shipwrecked man; that elephants couple from behind and are pregnant for two years; that this docile and vigorous animal, the nearest to man by its intelligence, lives until the end of the second or third century of its life; that the phoenix is consumed by aromatic fire and revives after it has been burned; that the sea urchin stops a ship, however fast she is driving along, while it is unable to do anything once it is dragged out of the waves; how the hunter fools the tiger with a mirror; how the Arimasp attacks the griffin with his sword; how whales turn over on their backs and thus deceive the sailors; that the newborn of the bear has as yet no shape; that the mule rarely gives birth, the viper only once and then to its own disaster; that moles are blind and bees deaf; that alone among all living beings the crocodile moves its upper jaw.[24]

24. [Petrarca ridicules the incoherent, incorrect, and often intentionally distorted notions concerning natural history that stuck to the mind of the average man with a Scholastic education. With the exception of the first three items, which he seems to have added on his own in order to give his spirited peroration a more vivid touch, he chose them somewhat at random from reference books then generally considered as trustworthy. Many of these data figure in the big compilation of natural history which Vincent of Beauvais, the Parisian encyclopedist of the preceding century, had published under the title of *Speculum naturale* (no modern edition; *editio princeps ca.* 1478). This learned polymath had indeed not intended to do more than offer a conveniently arranged survey of what older authors had said about various subjects, and Petrarca had read most of them in their own writings too. Besides, he may have consulted other thirteenth-century works that cover the same field, like Alexander Neckam's *De rerum naturis* (ed. Th. Wright in *Rerum Britannicarum medii aevi scriptores* [1863]) and Bartholomaeus Anglicus', *De proprietatibus rerum* (short translated selections published by R. Steele in *Mediaeval Lore* [London, 1907 and 1924]).

A few of the statements cited by Petrarca bear witness to more or less reliable observation and can be traced back to Greek science of the time when Greek scholars had overcome the habit of handing down unchecked assertions. Aristotle speaks in similar terms of the pregnancy and longevity of elephants and their almost human intelligence, the movable upper jaw of the crocodile, and the sterility of the mule (*Historiae*

All this is for the greater part wrong, as has become manifest in many similar cases when animals were brought into our part of the world. The facts have certainly not been investigated by those who are quoted as authorities for them; they have been all the more promptly believed or boldly invented, since the animals live so far from us. And even if they were true, they would not contribute anything whatsoever to the blessed life. What is the use—I beseech you—of knowing the nature of quadrupeds, fowls, fishes, and serpents and not knowing or even neglecting

---

animalium v. 14. 546 *b* 11; x. 46. 630 *b* 18–25; i. 11. 492 *b* 23–24; *De generatione animalium* ii. 8. 747 *a* 24). All this had found its way into Pliny's *Natural History* (viii. 10. 28; 1. 1; 3. 6; x. 45. 128; viii. 25. 89; xi. 37. 159) and Isidore's *Origins* (xii. 2. 16; 2. 15; 6. 20). However, Aristotle was also responsible for the wrong notion of the blindness of the mole, whose small eyes he believed to be completely covered by its fur (*Metaphysics* iv. 22. 1022 *b* 26; *De anima* iii. 1. 425 *a* 11). The deafness of the bees he had stated in a very conspicuous place—in the Introduction to the *Metaphysics* (i. 1. 980 *b* 23). He seems, indeed, to have doubted it later on, as the more cautiously chosen words in his *History of Animals* (ix. 40. 627 *a* 15) would suggest. However, those who read the *Metaphysics* during their university years remembered too well what the philosopher said there; and the better tradition to be found in Pliny (*Nat. Hist.* x. 20. 63) did not leave a lasting impression in their memory.

Statements which annoyed Petrarca particularly as being bold lies and impudent inventions we know to be the product of the poetical imagination of various ancient nations who lived around the eastern Mediterranean and in the Near East. One is the fable of the Arimasps, of whom Greek legends told that they had but one eye in their forehead and were incessantly struggling with the griffin birds that guarded the gold of the Scythian mines in the farthest northeastern corner of the inhabited world (Pliny *Nat. Hist.* vii. 2. 10). The beautiful myth of the phoenix cremating itself and reviving from the ashes after having outlived all other animated beings on earth (*ibid.* x. 2. 2–3; Isidore *Origins* xii. 7. 22) had originally been told of the holy sun-bird of Egyptian Heliopolis and had become popular in Christian literature as an allegory of the Resurrection.

Old pseudo-scientific learning is preserved in the story of the abnormal birth of vipers, which were believed to bite their way through the womb of their mothers, thus revenging their fathers who had been cruelly murdered by their wives (Pliny *Nat. Hist.* x. 62. 170; Isidore *Origins* xii. 4. 10–11). This story was nowhere supported in Aristotle's genuine works but was readily accepted in the Latin-speaking West, since a queer etymology helped to interpret the word "viper" as "giving birth in violence" (*vipera —vi pariens*). A similar etymological trick made people swallow the grotesque nonsense that the little sucker fish (*echeneis* in Greek, *remora* in Latin), which is equipped with a suction plate enabling it to cling to

man's nature, the purpose for which we are born, and whence and whereto we travel?[25]

These and like matters I have often discussed with these "scribes"[26] who are most learned, not in the Law of Moses and the Christian Law, but, as they flatter themselves, in the Aristotelian law. I did so more frankly than they were accustomed to hear and perhaps with less caution: talking with friends, I did not think of any harm that might derive from it. At first they were astonished, then they became angry, and, as they felt that

---

smooth surfaces, had the miraculous power of stopping ships in their course; and this had even been transferred to the sea urchin because of the similarity of the names (*echinus:* Pliny *Nat. Hist.* xxxii. praef. 1–9; Isidore *Origins* xii. 6. 34). In an interesting article (*Speculum* XXII [1947], 205 ff.), Professor Pauline Aiken proves that this "telescoping" of two different animals, like many other amusing misinterpretations of ancient sources, must be debited to Thomas de Cantimpré.

The belief that the she-bear licks her newborn cubs into shape had its roots in a passage of Aristotle's *Historia animalium* (vi. 30. 579 *a* 18), where a group of mammals including the bear are said to be born disproportionately small and not yet fully developed in all their limbs. This correct statement had not yet become absurd in the form reported by Pliny (*Nat. Hist.* viii. 36. 116), where we learn that the bear must warm its cubs by pressing them to its womb, but the apparent identity of vulgar Latin *orsus* = "bear," Latin *orsus* = "beginning," and *ore suo* = "with its mouth," seems to have produced the ridiculous story before the second century A.D., when it appears even in the Greek text of Aelian's *History of Animals.*

A typical Munchausen yarn is preserved in the stories of how hunters evaded the fury of a tigress after having stolen her brood from her lair: on their flight they let the pursuing tigress see her own image in a mirror and mistake it for one of her lost cubs running toward her (somewhat differently related by Pliny *Nat. Hist.* viii. 18. 66; cf. Isidore *Origins* xii. 6. 34). To the same category belongs the often-repeated account of the exciting adventure which happened to seafarers who landed on a whale and took it for an island, until it turned over and dived into the sea, a popular "true story" that has, for instance, been inserted into the legend of the westward voyage of the Irish St. Brandan.]

25. [The distinction between unprofitable knowledge and learning that spurs a man to a decent and happy mode of living is characteristic for Petrarca's Augustinian attitude: Augustine *Confessions* x. 8. 15 (see p. 44); cf. also Cicero *Tusculanae disputationes* ii. 412.]

26. [The word "scribe," by which the title of the learned Jewish record-keepers is rendered in the New Testament, has become equivalent to hypocrite, because of Christ's grim words against them and the Pharisees in the Gospels, particularly in Matthew, chap. xxiii.]

my words were directed against their sect and the laws of their father, they set up a council among themselves to condemn for the crime of ignorance—not me whom they undoubtedly love—but my fame which they hate. If only they had called others to this court! Then there would perhaps have been opposition to the sentence they intended to pronounce. However, to keep the verdict harmonious and unanimous, only these four convened. They discussed many different matters concerning the absent and undefended defendant—not because they disagreed in their opinions, for they all felt the same way and intended to say the same thing, but they were arguing with each other and against their own sentence after the manner of expert judges. Thus they wanted to render a decision with more color by sifting and squeezing the truth through the narrow sieve of contradictions.

As the first point, they said that public renown supported me, but replied that it deserved little faith. So far they did not lie, since the vulgar mass very rarely sees the truth. Then they said that friendship with the greatest and most learned men, which has adorned my life—as I shall boast before the Lord—stood against their verdict. For I have enjoyed close friendship with many kings, especially with King Robert of Sicily, who honored me in my younger years with frequent and clear testimonials of my knowledge and genius.[27] They replied—and here I will not say their iniquity but their vanity evidently made them lie—that the king himself enjoyed great fame in literary matters but had no knowledge of them; and the others, however learned they were, did not show a sufficiently perspicacious judgment concerning me, whether love of me or carelessness was the cause. They then made another objection against themselves, saying that the last three Roman popes had vied with each other in inviting me—in vain, it is true—to a high rank in their intimate

27. [King Robert "the Wise" of Sicily had been Petrarca's generous sponsor for his coronation as poet laureate on the Roman Capitol in 1341 (cf. E. H. Wilkins, "The Coronation of Petrarch," *Speculum,* xviii [1943], 180–85).]

household;[28] and that Urban himself, who is now at the head, was wont to speak well of me and had already bestowed on me a most affable letter. Besides, it is known far and wide and doubted by no one that the present Roman emperor—for there has been no other legitimate emperor at this time—counts me among his dear familiars and has been wont to call me to him with the weight of daily requests and repeated messages and letters.[29] In all this they feel that some people find some proof that I must have a certain value. However, they resolve this objection too, maintaining that the popes went astray together with the others, following the general opinion about me, or were induced to do so by my good moral behavior and not by my knowledge; and that the emperor was prevailed upon by my studies of the past and my historical works, for in this field they do not deny me some knowledge.

Furthermore, they said, another objection against them was my eloquence. This I do not acknowledge altogether, by God not. They pretend that it is a rather effective means of persuasion. It might be the task of a rhetor or an orator to speak oppositely in order to persuade for a purpose, but many people without knowledge had succeeded in persuading by mere phrases. Thus they attribute to luck what is a matter of art and bring forth the widespread proverb: "Much eloquence, little wisdom."[30] They do not take into account Cato's definition of the orator,[31] which contradicts their false charge. Finally, it was

28. [Three predecessors of Urban V wanted Petrarca for the important office of apostolic secretary, which he three times refused, though it would have opened the highest ecclesiastical career to him.]

29. [Since 1351 Petrarca had tried to urge Charles IV into a vigorous intervention in Italian affairs (*Fam.*, x. 1; xii. 1; xviii, 1). The emperor was at no time willing to accept Petrarca's advice in political matters but received him most graciously when he came to Italy in 1354 and invited him to his court repeatedly at later times.]

30. [Sallust *Catilina* 5. 4.]

31. [In the definition of the perfect orator attributed to Cato the Elder (Seneca Rhetor *Controversiae* i. praef. 9; Quintilian *Institutio oratoria* i. praef. 1. 9; xii. 1. 44) irreproachable moral goodness is included as an essential quality.]

said that the style of my writing is in opposition to their statement. They did not dare to blame my style, not even to praise it too reservedly, and confessed that it is rather elegant and well chosen but without any learning. I do not understand how this can be, and I trust they did not understand it either. If they regain control of themselves and think over again what they have said, they will be ashamed of their silly ineptitude. For if the first statement were true—which I for my part would neither assert nor make myself believe—I have no doubt that the second is wrong. How could the style of a person who knows nothing at all be excellent, since theirs amounts to nothing, though there is nothing they do not know? Do we so far suspect everything to be fortuitous that we leave no room for reason?

What else do you want? Or what do you believe? I think you expect to hear the verdict of the judges. Well, they examined each point. Then, fixing their eyes on I know not what god— for there is no god who wants iniquity, no god of envy or ignorance, which I might call the twofold cloud-shrouding truth— they pronounced this short final sentence: I am a good man without learning. Even if they have never spoken the truth and never shall speak it, may they have spoken it at least this once! O bounteous, O saving Jesus, true God and true Giver of all learning and all intelligence, true "King of Glory" and "Lord of all powers of virtue,"[32] I now pray to Thee on the knees of my soul: If Thou dost not wish to grant me more, let it be my portion at least to be a good man. This I cannot be if I do not love Thee dearly and do not adore Thee piously. For this purpose I am born, not for learning. If learning happens to come along, it inflates, it tears down; it does not build up. It is a glittering shackle, a toilsome pursuit, and a resounding burden for the soul. Thou knowest, O Lord, before whom all my desire and all my sighs are expanded: Whenever I have made a sober use of learning, I have sought in it nothing but to become good. It was

32. [Pss. 23(24):7–10; 45:8 and 12(46:7 and 10; 68:7; 69:6); 79:20-(80:19); 83:2, 4, 9, 13(84:1, 3, 8, 12).]

not that I was confident that learning can achieve this or that anyone can achieve it beside Thee, although Aristotle and many others have promised just this.[33] I believed that the road on which I made my way would become more honorable and more clearly marked, and at the same time more pleasant with the aid of literary erudition, under the guidance of Thee and no one else. "Thou who lookest into the hearts and reins,"[34] Thou knowest that it is as I say. I never was such a youth, never eager for fame to such a degree—though I do not deny I coveted it occasionally—that I should not have wished to be good rather than learned. I desired to be both, I confess, since human longing is boundless and insatiable until it comes to rest in Thee, above Whom there is no place to which it could still rise. I desired to be both good and learned. Now that the latter is wrenched from me or denied me, I am grateful to my judges for leaving me the better of the two, provided they have not lied on this point also and granted me what they are not, intending to rob me of what they wanted to have. I was to find a comfort for my loss, though an empty one. They dealt with me after the fashion of envious women. When a woman is asked whether the woman next door is beautiful, she says that she is good and has good and decent manners. All good qualities—just such as are not true—she allows her, because she wants to spoil her of the single and perhaps even true title, beauty. But Thou, my God, "Lord of Learning," "besides Whom there is no other god,"[35] Thou Whom I must and will prefer to Aristotle and all the philosophers and poets and all those who "boastingly make many haughty words,"[36] to learning and doctrines and to all things whatsoever: Thou canst grant me the true name of a good man

33. [*Ethica Nicomachea* ii. 2. 1103 *b* 24. Petrarca owned and read this book in the *translatio vetus* made about 1250 under the supervision of Robert Grosseteste, bishop of Lincoln (Paris, Bibl. Nat., fonds Latin, Codex 6458).]

34. [Ps. 7 : 10(9).]

35. [I Kings (I Sam.) 2 : 2–3.]

36. [*Ibid.*]

which these four grant me untruly. I pray to Thee, grant it to me. I do not ask so much for the good name which Solomon prefers to "precious ointments";[37] I ask for the thing itself. I want to *be* good, to love Thee, and to deserve to be loved by Thee—for no one repays his lovers like Thee—to think of Thee, to be obedient to Thee, to set my hope in Thee, and to speak of Thee. "Let all that is obsolete, shrink back from my mouth; let all my thoughts be prepared unto Thee." For it is true: "The bow of the mighty man has been overcome and the weak have been girded with strength."[38] Happier by far is one of these feeble ones who believe in Thee, than Plato, Aristotle, Varro, and Cicero, who with all their knowledge did not know Thee. "Brought before Thee and put next to Thee Who art the Rock, their judges are overthrown and their learned ignorance has become manifest."[39]

Therefore, let learning be the portion of those who take it away from me, or since it cannot be their portion, unless I am mistaken, let it be the portion of those who may have it. Let them keep their exorbitant opinion of everything that regards them, and the naked name Aristotle which delights many ignorant people by its four syllables.[40] Moreover, let them have the vain joy and the unfounded elation which is so near to ruin; in short, let them have all the profit people who are ignorant and

37. [Eccles. 7:2.]

38. [Ps. 140(141):6, combined with I Cor. 10:4 in Augustine's *Enarratio in psalmum CXL* (Migne, *Pat. Lat.*, XXXVII, 1828); cf. *Fam.*, XVII, 2, 41–42.]

39. [These words from Augustine's *Epistle* 130. 15. 28 ("Corpus Scriptorium Ecclesiasticorum Latinorum" = *CSEL*, XLIV, 72) are famous as the title of the epoch-making book *On Learned Ignorance* by Nicolaus Cusanus. It is perhaps not a mere coincidence that the philosopher-cardinal owned a copy of Petrarca's *De ignorantia* made from one of the two autograph copies (Cues on the Mosel, Bibliotheca Cusana, Codex 200). Petrarca uses the words here to convey that his opponents do not possess the blessed ignorance which Augustine calls enlightened by the teachings of the Holy Spirit.]

40. [In the Latin original the word "Aristoteles" has five syllables.]

puffed up earn from their errors in vague and easy credulity. My portion shall be humility and ignorance, knowledge of my own weakness, and contempt for nothing except the world and myself and the insolence of those who are condemning me, and, furthermore, distrust in myself and hope in Thee. Finally, may God be my portion and what they do not envy me, illiterate virtue. They will burst into loud laughter when they hear this and will say that I speak piously without learning like any old woman. People of their kind, tumid as they are with the fever of literary erudition, know nothing so vile as piety; truly and soberly literate men love it above all things. For them it is written, "Piety is wisdom."[41] However, my talking will confirm the others more and more in their opinion that I am "a good man without learning."

What shall we say now, my most faithful Donato? I speak to you, since the sting of their grudge has wounded you more than myself, whom it actually stung. What shall we do, my friend? Shall we appeal to fairer judges or shall we keep silent and confirm their decision by our silence? I prefer the latter course. I want you to know that I do not in the least refuse to await the tenth day.[42] This very moment I acquiesce in the verdict of any judge whomsoever. I implore you and everyone whom it may concern, all you who have passed a quite different sentence on me, to hold your hands up as I do and let their verdict become right by patiently accepting it. I wish it were right on the point they concede me. Willingly I confess and freely I declare their verdict is right in what they deprive me of, though I emphatically deny that they are the right judges. Perhaps they will seek support in the law of which their god Aristotle speaks when he says: "Everybody judges well of what he knows and is a good

41. [Cf. Eccles. 1:22, 25; 19:18.]

42. [In *Novella* xxiii. 1 the emperor-legislator Justinian determined that an appeal was to be considered valid if made within ten days after a sentence had been passed.]

judge in that matter; it would not seem likely that anything can be better known than that in which he that judges abounds."[43] Under such a pretext the most ignorant men would be best able to judge of ignorance. But it is not so. It is the wise man who is entitled to judge of ignorance as well as of wisdom and of anything whatsoever—wise, of course, he must be in the specific matter of which he is judging. Not as musicians judge of music and grammarians of grammar do the ignorant judge of ignorance. There are things of which it is extreme destitution to have plenty. Such things are better judged by anyone else than by him who is most affluent in them. None understands less of deformity than the deformed, who has become intimate with it and does not see what must offend the eye of the beautiful. The same is true with all other defects. Nobody judges worse of ignorance than the ignorant. This I do not say because I intend to reject the court but because I want those who are ignorant to be ashamed of having pronounced a verdict—provided they can be ashamed. As for the rest, I accept the sentence in this matter, not only the verdict of friendly envy, but just as readily that of hatred. To sum up: Whoever calls me ignorant shares my own opinion. Sorrowfully and tacitly I recognize my ignorance, when I consider how much I lack of what my mind in its craving for knowledge is sighing for. But until the end of the present exile has come and terminated this our imperfection by which "we know in part,"[44] I console myself with the consideration that this belongs to our common nature. I suppose it happens to all good and modest minds that they learn to know themselves and then find just this same consolation. It will certainly happen even to those who have obtained a vast knowledge—vast according to the character of human knowledge, which in itself is always trifling small and becomes vast only when we take into account in what straits it is conceived and compare it with the knowledge of others. How infinitely small, I beseech you, is the

43. [*Eth. Nic.* i. 1. 1094 *b* 27.]
44. [I Cor. 13:9.]

greatest amount of knowledge granted to one single mind! Indeed, what a man knows, whosoever he may be, is nothing when compared—I will not say with God's knowledge—but with his own ignorance. The very men who know most and understand most possess, I presume, in the highest degree this knowledge of themselves and of their own imperfection, this knowledge which I have called their consolation. My judges are happy in their errors; they do not need such a consolation. They are happy, I say, not in their knowledge, but in their error and arrogant ignorance. They believe they lack nothing of having angelic knowledge, while without doubt much of human knowledge is lacking to everyone, and to many it is entirely lacking.

But let me now return to myself. Alas, my friend, is there an evil that does not happen to a man who lives too long? Who has ever enjoyed a prosperity so permanent that it did not at some time suffer a change and become old, so to speak, by sheer living? Men grow old, so does fortune, so does man's fame: every human thing grows old, and—there was a time when I did not believe it—finally even souls grow old, though they are immortal, and the Cordovan's words become true: "Too long a life undoes vast souls."[45] This does not mean that the old age of the soul is followed by its death. What actually follows is its separation from the body and that dissolution we observe, which is commonly called death and actually is the death of the body and not of the soul. But, look, my soul has become old and cold. As an old man I now experience what I sang in my pastoral poem when I was an inexperienced youth: "What does not long life bring to a man?"[46] In what mood should I have borne this but a few years ago? How should I have opposed it with all my strength? It must certainly have been a foreboding of what I still had before me that never did I read without compassion the

45. [Lucan *Pharsalia* viii. 27–28. Lucan, a native of Cordova in Spain, is one of the classical authors whom Petrarca rarely quotes by name (see n. 8).]

46. [*Eclogue* ix. 37–38.]

story of Laberius.[47] This man lived all his life in honest knighthood. When he was sixty years old, he was at last put on the stage, persuaded by Julius Caesar's flatteries and requests, such as come forth in full armor from the mouth of a prince, and was thus changed from the status of a Roman knight to that of a mimic actor. He himself did not suffer this disgrace in silence. He deplored it in many words, among others in the following: "Thus I lived twice thirty years without reproach as a Roman knight, and as a Roman knight I left my house today, to come back an actor. Certainly I have lived one day longer than I ought to have lived."

And I—let me boast before you—I left my home as a boy and do not even return there as an old man. Never have I been truly a learned man, but sometimes I was believed to be one, and almost all my life was devoted to studying. Rarely ever was there a day I spent in idleness when I was well; rarely was there a day on which I was not reading or writing or meditating on scholarly matters or listening to people who read, or questioning them, if they were quiet. I went not only to learned men, but to learned cities too, anxious to return more learned and a better man. First I went to Montpellier, because I was living so near to that place in the years of my boyhood, soon afterward to Bologna, later to Toulouse and Paris, to Padua and Naples. There at Naples—I know I shall offend the ears of many a man—Robert resided, the greatest of all the kings and philosophers of our age, whose erudition was not inferior to the glory of his kingdom. My judges call him ignorant, and I think my disgrace is almost glorious for me, since I have it in common with such a great king, though we both might share it with others who are greater in fame and age. Of these I shall speak at the end of this book. Of this king the whole world and truth itself at any rate had a dif-

47. [Caesar prevailed upon the Roman knight Laberius, a successful author of mimic plays, to appear on the stage in one of them at a very generous fee. Laberius accepted the offer but started his part in the play with an address to the audience, deploring his degradation, because he feared to have forfeited his knighthood (Macrobius *Saturnalia* ii, 7. 2–3).]

ferent opinion. Then I was young and he was old; I had the greatest respect for him, not so much because he was a king—for of kings there is a plenty everywhere. I esteemed him so highly as a rare miracle of genius and a venerable sanctuary of learning. I, who was so unequal to him in fortune and years, was particularly dear to him, as many in that city still remember. I did not deserve it by any merits or by military or courtly arts, of which I knew none at all, but by my genius, as he said, and by my literary erudition. Either he was a bad judge or I a bad keeper, since with all my studying and hard work I must have constantly forgotten what I learned.

Besides, I spent the greatest, and for my studies the most prosperous, part of my life at the court they call the Roman Curia—I do not know why they do so.[48] It was then residing on the left bank of the Rhone, where it remained fifty and more years and whence it departed recently—even in this very year—let us hope never to return, under the leadership and auspices of Urban the Fifth, the Saint, if he will persevere in his purpose.[49] It went back to the Venerable City and Peter's most holy See—let us hope to stay there forever. It was in this Curia, and not far from it, in my Helicon beyond the Alps,[50] where the Sorgue, the king of springs, has his source,[51] that I lived many years. Almost all the men of letters of our world gathered there constantly and were accessible to me. In my Helicon I found solitude and silence and quiet peace most fit for meditation. There at the Curia

48. [Petrarca often feigned to be astonished that the papal Curia could be called Roman, as long as it was in exile.]

49. [Urban V brought the Curia back to Rome on October 16, 1367, but was forced to return to Avignon in September, 1370.]

50. [Petrarca calls the rustic little country place he owned in the Vaucluse near Avignon after 1337 his "Helicon beyond the Alps" in contrast to his Italian summer houses.]

51. [The Sorgue, which streams through the Vaucluse, has been celebrated in many of Petrarca's poems and lovingly mentioned in various passages of his prose writings. He believed it to be the river "Orga" described by Pliny (*Nat. Hist.* xviii. 22. 190).]

I spent my time almost entirely dedicated to scholarly work, studying, attending schools and masters, and reciting to friends what I had learned or written; around my Helicon I also roamed and meditated often—though I am a sinner—praying and cogitating, rarely on anything else than the liberal studies. Meanwhile I became known to a thousand learned and respectable old men and won their good graces. If I went on to enumerate them all, the remembrance would be sweet, but the list of their names would certainly not be short. All these men liked me exclusively or particularly because then, as a young man, I had the reputation in learned cities of being a man of erudition. Now that I am old, four young men in a maritime city tear it away from me. Thus it happened to me as it did to Laberius: having completed my sixtieth year, I lost my status. I did not lose it like Laberius by acting in a mimic play—such a performance requires only a single artist, but at least a skilled and intelligent one, and holds its place among the mechanical crafts. I lost it from ignorance, and that is the lowest of all grades. But so things go.

This is now the result of our studies and pains and our hard night work. In my younger years some used to call me a scholar. Now that I am old, it has been discovered by a more profound judgment that I am an illiterate fellow. This may perhaps be difficult to bear, but it must be borne, just as everything else that happens to men: damage, poverty, laborious toil, pain, disgust, exile, and ill fame. Let us scorn such fame if it is not truly deserved. For it will encounter opponents and collapse by itself when it has run its course. If it is truly deserved, we should not oppose it as we should not other punishments that have been devised for human offenses. Therefore, I shall laugh if the truly deserved glory of knowledge is torn from me by mere words. If it is false glory, I shall not only bear the loss; I shall rejoice, relieved of a burdensome load which does not belong to me and released from the trouble of keeping undeserved fame. It is better for a robber to be deprived of his unjust spoil than to use it unpunished. If a man despoils another of what he owns unjustly, he can be unjust; in itself such despoiling is perfectly just.

As far as I am concerned, as I have already said, I declare that I approve of the verdict, not only if it is just, but even if it is unjust. I do not reject any judge or any robber. Fame is certainly a thing hard to win and hazardous to possess, especially the fame of being learned. Everybody is on armed guard against it. Those, too, who cannot hope to obtain such fame try to tear it away from those who possess it. You must always have your pen in your hand; with vigilant and attentive ears you must always stand in the line of battle. I do not care who will relieve me of these sorrows and this burden. I am grateful to any man who as my champion brings me such relief whatever may be his purpose in doing so. Whether my title as a man of erudition is true or false, it is loaded with toil and care. In my avid desire for peace and leisure I readily lay it down, remembering Annaeus Seneca's words: "This praise is obtained at great expense of time and by greatly troubling other people's ears. A man of letters! Let us be content with the more rustic title: a good man."[52] I follow your advice, my excellent preceptor of morals; I am content with the more rustic title, as you call it, though according to me it is the better and holier and therefore nobler title. I do so all the more, as it is the very title my judges leave me. I fear only that even this title is false, but I will try hard to make it a true one. I will not desist from exerting all my energy and shall not tire until my last breath and last sigh. You once said elsewhere that I must have will-power to be good. If the will accomplishes this task, it will be good; if it makes only a start, then desiring to become good is at least a part of being good. And thus far, I hope, my title is true.

I come back to my censors, of whom I have said so much already and must say more now; for I want nothing to remain hidden from you. I should not like to be called silly and stupid

52. [*Epistle* 88. 38.]

after having been called illiterate. Learning is an adventitious ornament; reason an inborn part of man. I should not be so much ashamed of lacking erudition as of lacking reason. I had enough reason to have avoided their snares. It would not have been so easy for them to catch me by their tricks. I was trapped in my own purity and caught in the most decent veil of friendship, which I believed to be true. It is but too easy to deceive one who is confiding in you.

I have told you before and now repeat it: Like many other citizens of that very beautiful and very great city, they used to come and see me, very often two at a time, occasionally also all four of them together. I was delighted and received them as though they were angels of God. I forgot everything besides them, since they occupied my mind entirely, cheering me up wonderfully. Without delay we started long and various talks, as is the custom among friends. I paid no attention to what I said or how I said it. I had nothing else in mind than to show a joyful face and a still more joyful heart at the arrival of such guests. At times it was joy that forced me to keep silent; at times it was also a kind of reverence which told me not to block their strong desire to speak by interrupting them, as happens in such cases, and from joy I said either nothing or mere commonplaces. I have not been taught to dress up or dissemble or feign anything in the company of friends. I am wont to carry my mind on my tongue and face and never to speak to friends in any other way than I would to myself. "Nothing is more pleasant," as Cicero says.[53]

Why ought we to display ostentatiously our eloquence or our learning before friends who see our hearts, our affection, and our entire personality, provided they do not question us with the intention of putting us to the test but of learning from us? In the latter case no ostentation or embellishment is needed but a trustful sharing of knowledge and all other things, free from reserve and envy. I therefore often wonder why so great a

53. [*Laelius, de amicitia* 6. 22.]

prince as the Emperor Augustus could take so much pains with trifles, amid such concern for important matters, that he never said a word without thorough deliberation and frequently preferred to address in written form, not only the people and the Senate, but even his wife and friends.[54] Perhaps he did so in order to avoid letting slip by chance from his mouth a superfluous or foolish word for which his heavenly speech could be denounced or criticized. He may have been justified in so acting when from the highest peak he was addressing his subjects in written form, in oracles as it were. I prefer a casual way of talking with friends and no elaborate sentences. Goodbye to eloquence if it must be obtained with such constant effort! I had rather not be eloquent than always on my guard and pedantic. This was always my intention when with dear friends and intimates, especially when they were familiar with my powers.

Lately I have practiced it more than ever in the company of these four friends, and in my friendly faith I inadvertently fell into the trap of hostile calumny. I said nothing that was carefully polished, nothing that was anxiously prepared. Whatever came to my mind sprang from my mouth before it even got there. They trapped me according to a preconcerted plan and tested every single word of mine, taking whatever I said as if I had nothing better to say and could not say it more elegantly. This they did once and again and again, until they found themselves easily confirmed in a sentence they wished to be true. Nothing is easier than to persuade people who want to be persuaded and already believe. This made them speak to me all the more confidently as to an ignorant fellow and to laugh at my ignorance, as I now believe. At the time I did not suspect it in the least. As I took no precautions and was but a single man, I was entangled by the artifices of many and herded into the crowd of the ignorant without being aware of it.

They used to raise an Aristotelian problem or a question concerning animals. Then I was either silent or made a joke or be-

54. [Suetonius *Life of Augustus* 84.]

gan another subject. Sometimes I smiled and asked how on earth
Aristotle could have known something for which there is no
reason and which cannot be proved by experience. They were
amazed and felt angry at me in silence. They looked at me as
though I were a blasphemer to require anything beyond his authority in order to believe it. Thus we clearly ceased to be philosophers and eager lovers of wisdom and became Aristotelians,
or, more correctly, Pythagoreans. They revived the ridiculous
habit of allowing no further question if "he" had said so. "He,"
as Cicero tells us, "was Pythagoras."[55] I certainly believe that
Aristotle was a great man who knew much, but he was human
and could well be ignorant of some things, even of a great many
things.

I should say more if those who are as much friends of truth
as they are of sects permitted. By God, I am convinced and I
have no doubt that "he went astray," as the saying goes, "the
whole length of the way,"[56] not only in what is of little weight,
where an error is unimportant and by no means dangerous, but
in matters of the greatest consequence, and precisely in those
regarding supreme salvation. Of happiness he has indeed said a
good deal in the beginning and at the end of his *Ethics*.[57] However, I will dare to say—and my censors may shout as loud as
they please—he knew so absolutely nothing of true happiness
that any pious old woman, any faithful fisherman, shepherd or
peasant is—I will not say more subtle but happier in recognizing
it. I am therefore all the more astonished that some of our Latin
authors have so much admired that Aristotelian treatise as to
consider it almost a crime to speak of happiness after him and
that they have borne witness of this even in writing.

It may perhaps be daring to say so, but it is true, unless I am
mistaken: It seems to me that he saw of happiness as much as
the night owl does of the sun, namely, its light and rays and not

55. [*De natura deorum* i. 5. 10.]
56. [Terence *Eunuchus* ii. 2. 4(245).]
57. [Aristotle *Eth. Nic.* 1. 2–13. 1095 *a* 15; x. 7–10. 1177 *a* 14 ff.]

the sun itself. For Aristotle did not establish happiness within its own boundaries and did not found it on solid ground, as a high building ought to be founded, but far away in foreign territory on a trembling site, and consequently did not comprehend two things, or, if he did, ignored them.[58] These are the two things without which there can be absolutely no happiness: Faith and Immortality.[59] I already regret saying that he did not comprehend them or ignored them. For I ought to have said only one of the two phrases. Faith and immortality were not yet comprehended: he did not know of them, nor could he know of them or hope for them. The true light had not yet begun to shine,[60] which lights every man who comes into this world. He and all the others fancied what they wished and what by his very nature every man wishes and whose opposite no one can wish: a happiness of which they sang as one sings of the absent beloved, and which they adorned with words. They did not see it. Like people made happy by a dream, they rejoiced in an absolute nothing. In fact, they were miserable and to be roused to their misery by the thunder of approaching death, to see with open eyes what that happiness really is like, with which they had dealt in their dreams.[61]

Some may believe that I have said all this out of my own imagination and therefore but too frivolously. Let them then read Augustine's thirteenth book on the Trinity. There they will find many weighty and acute discussions on this subject against those philosophers who—I use his words:—"shaped their happy lives for themselves, just as it pleased each of them."[62] This, I confess, I have said often before, and I will say it as long

58. [Cf. Lactantius *Divinae institutiones* vi. 14. 6 (*CSEL* XIX, 535).]

59. [Augustine *De Trinitate* xiii. 7. 10–8. 11 (Migne, *Pat. Lat.*, XLII, 1020–21).]

60. [John 1 : 9.]

61. [Cf. Lactantius *Divinae institutiones* v. 13. 15 (*CSEL*, XIX, 441–42); Augustine *Enarratio in psalmum CXL* 19. v. 6 (Migne, *Pat. Lat.*, XXXVII, 1328).]

62. [*De Trinitate* xiii. 7 (Migne, *Pat. Lat.*, XLII, 1021).]

as I can speak, because I am confident that I have spoken the truth and shall speak it in the future, too. If they consider it a sacrilege, they may accuse me of violating religion, but then they must accuse Jerome too, "who does not care what Aristotle but what Christ said."[63] I, on the contrary, should not doubt that it is they who are impious and sacrilegious if they have a different opinion. God may take my life and whatever I love most dearly before I change this pious, true, and saving conviction or disown Christ from love of Aristotle.

Let them certainly be philosophers and Aristotelians, though they are neither, but let them be both: I do not envy them these brilliant names of which they boast, and even that wrongly. In return they ought not to envy me the humble and true name of Christian and Catholic. But why do I ask for this? I know they are willing to comply with this demand quite spontaneously and will do what I ask. Such things they do not envy us; they spurn them as simple and contemptible, inadequate for their genius and unworthy of it. We accept in humble faith the secrets of nature and the mysteries of God, which are higher still; they attempt to seize them in haughty arrogance. They do not manage to reach them, not even to approach them; but in their insanity they believe that they have reached them and strike heaven with their fists. They feel just as if they had it in their grip, satisfied with their own opinion and rejoicing in their error. They are not held back from their insanity—I will not say by the impossibility of such an attempt, as is expressed in the words of the Apostle to the Romans: "Who has known the mind of the Lord, or who has been His counselor?"[64] Not even by the ecclesiastical and heavenly counsel: "Seek not what is above thee and search not out things above thy strength; the things that God hath commanded to thee, think thereupon always and be not inquisitive in His many works; for it is not necessary for thee to behold what is hidden."[65] Of all this I will

63. [*Adversus Pelagianos* i. 19 (Migne, *Pat. Lat.*, XXIII, 512c).]
64. [Rom. 11 : 34.]   65. [Eccles. 3 : 22.]

not speak: indiscriminately they despise whatever they know
has been said from Heaven—yea, let me say, what is actually
true—whatever has been said from a Catholic point of view.
However, there is at least a witty word not ineptly said by
Democritus: "No one looks at what is before his feet," he said;
"it is the regions of the sky they scrutinize."[66] And there are
very clever remarks Cicero made to ridicule frivolous dispu-
tants who are heedlessly arguing and arguing about nothing,
"as if they just came from the council of the gods"[67] and had
seen with their eyes what was going on there. And, finally,
there are Homer's more ancient and sharper words, by which
Jupiter deters in grave sentences not a mortal man, not any one
of the common crowd of the gods, but Juno, his wife and sister,
the queen of the gods, from daring to investigate his intimate
secret or presumptuously believing it could be known to her
at all.[68]

But let us return to Aristotle. His brilliance has stunned many
bleary and weak eyes and made many a man fall into the ditches
of error. I know, Aristotle has declared himself for the rule of
one, as Homer had done before him. For Homer says thus, as
far as it has been translated for us into our prose: "Multidomin-
ion is not good; let one be the lord, one the supreme commander";[69] and Aristotle says: "Plurality of rule is not good; let
therefore one be the ruler."[70] Homer meant human rulership,
Aristotle divine dominion; Homer was speaking of the princi-

66. [Petrarca could not know that this line, here referred to as a saying
of Democritus because of Cicero De divinatione ii. 13. 30, was in fact
taken from Ennius' drama Iphigenia, as we now know from the same
Cicero's De republica i. 8. 30, a work recovered in 1820.]

67. [De natura deorum i. 8. 18.]

68. [Iliad i. 544–50; 560–67.]

69. [Ibid. ii. 204. Translating the Homeric word polykoiranie, Petrarca's
Greek interpreter, Leontius Pilatus, used a Latin word of his own invention: "multidominium."]

70. [Metaphysics xii. 9. 1076 a 4. Though Petrarca does not mention it
here, he knew that this line, which he read in William of Moerbeke's version, is but another translation of the Homeric hexameter. Cf. Petrarca's
marginal note in his Iliad: "Hinc Ari(stotiles)."]

pate of the Greeks, the other of that of all men; Homer made Agamemnon the Atride king and ruler, Aristotle God—so far had the dazzling brightness of truth brought light to his mind. He did not know who this king is, I believe, nor did he know how great He is. He discussed the most trifling things with so much curiosity and did not see this one and greatest of things, which many illiterate people have seen, not by another light, but because it shed a very different illumination. If these friends of mine do not see that this is the case, I see that they are altogether blind and bereft of eyesight; and I should not hesitate to believe that it must be visible to all who have sound eyes, just as it can be seen that the emerald is green, the snow white, and the raven black.

Our Aristotelians will bear my audacity in a more balanced mood when I say that this is not merely my opinion of a single man, though I mention him alone. However ignorant I am, I do read, and I thought I understood something, before these people discovered my ignorance. I say, I do read; but in my more flourishing years I read even more assiduously. I still read the works of poets and philosophers, particularly those of Cicero, with whose genius and style I have been particularly delighted since my early youth. I find much eloquence in them and the greatest elegance and power of words. What he says regarding the gods themselves, on whose nature he has published books under this title, and religion in general, sounds to me all the more like an empty fable the more eloquently it is presented. I thank God in silence that He gave me sluggish and moderate gifts and a mind that does not saunter wantonly and "does not seek things above itself,"[71] not curious in scrutinizing what is difficult to investigate and pestiferous when discovered. I am grateful that I love Christ all the more and become all the firmer in the faith in Him, the more I hear sneering at His faith. My experience has been like that of one who has been rather lukewarm in his love for his father and hears people now raise their

71. [Eccles. 3 : 22.]

voice against him. Then the love which seemed to be lulled to sleep flames up immediately; and this must necessarily happen if the son is a true and genuine son. Often, I call Christ Himself to witness, blasphemies uttered by heretics have turned me from a Christian into a most ardent Christian. For while the ancient pagans may tell many fables about their gods, they do not, at any rate, blaspheme; they have no notion of the true God; they have not heard of Christ's name—and faith results from hearing. The voices of the Apostles were heard all over the earth, and their words spread unto the end of the world; but, when their words and doctrines were resounding all over the globe, these men were already dead and buried. Thus they are to be pitied rather than culpable. Then envious soil had obstructed their ears, through which they might have drunk in the saving faith.

Of all the writings of Cicero, those from which I often received the most powerful inspiration are the three books which, as I said before, he entitled *On the Nature of the Gods.*[72] There the great genius speaks of the gods and often ridicules and despises them—not too seriously, it is true. It may be that he was afraid of capital punishment,[73] which even the Apostles feared, before the Holy Ghost came to them.[74] He ridicules them with very effective jokes, of which he has always so many at hand, to make it clear to everyone who understands how he feels with regard to what he has undertaken to discuss. When I read these passages, I often have compassion for his fate and grieve in silent sorrow that this man did not know the true God. He died only a few years before the birth of Christ. Death had closed his eyes when, alas, the end of the error-stricken night and darkness, the first rise of truth, the dawn of true light and

72. [In the following chapter Petrarca has inserted entire passages from this work of Cicero, which was one of the main sources for his knowledge of Greek philosophy.]

73. [Cf. Cicero *De natura deorum* i. 22. 60–23. 63; Lactantius *Divinae institutiones* ii. 3. 1–6 (*CSEL,* XIX, 104).]

74. [John 20 : 19–23 : "for fear of the Jews."]

the sun of justice were so near. In the countless books he wrote, Cicero, indeed, often falls short and speaks of "gods," engulfed by the torrent of vulgar error, as I said before; but at least he ridicules them, and even in his youth, when he wrote his book *About Invention,* he said that "those who have devoted their energies to philosophy do not believe there are gods."[75] Now it is a fact that it is true and supreme philosophy to know God, not "the gods"—always provided that such knowledge is accompanied by piety and faithful worship.

When the same Cicero in his later years, in the books he wrote *About the Gods*—not about God—gains control of himself, how is he lifted up by the wings of genius! At times you would think you were hearing not a pagan philosopher but an Apostle. Thus he says, for instance in the first book, opposing Velleius, who is defending the doctrine of Epicurus: "You have censured those who beheld the world and its limbs: heaven, earth, the seas, and their insignia—the sun, the moon, and the stars—and found out how the seasons bring about maturation, alteration, and all kind of vicissitudes, and who thereupon began to suspect from the magnificent and wonderful works produced that there is some excellent and outstanding nature that makes, moves, rules, and governs all this."[76]

In the second book he says: "When we look at the sky and behold the heavenly bodies, what can be so manifest and perspicuous as that there is a Divine Being of most outstanding mind, by whom all this is ruled?" And in the same book: "Chrysippus has a most acute mind, but, when he says all this, it seems that he has learned it from nature and did not discover it by himself." "If there is anything in the nature of things," he says, "which the mind and reason of man and human might and power cannot produce, the being that has produced it is cer-

75. [*De inventione* i. 29. 46.]

76. [*De natura deorum* i. 36. 100: words spoken by C. Aurelius Cotta, whom Cicero presents as the opponent of both the Epicurean and the Stoic participants in the discussion.]

tainly better than man. All the heavenly things, and all that has an everlasting order, cannot be made by man. Therefore, that which has made all this is better than man. Yet how should you call it, if not God?"[77] And afterward, not much later: "Since all the parts of the world are so made up that they could not be better fitted for use or more beautiful to behold, let us see whether they are fortuitous or such as could by no means remain together in their condition unless they were under the control of a Divine Providence that acts reasonably. If then what has been wrought by nature is better than what has been produced by art, and if art does not make anything without reason, nature cannot well be regarded as being without reason. If you know that art has been employed when you look at a statue or a painted panel; if you do not doubt that a ship is moved by reason and art, when from a distance you see it on its course; if you understand that a sun-dial or a water-clock indicates the hours by art and not by chance—then it is not consistent to assume that the world, which comprises all these arts and artisans and everything else, is bare of counsel and reason. Suppose somebody brought into Scythia or into Britain the globe recently constructed by our friend Posidonius, in which various revolutions make the sun and the moon and the five planets do just what they do in the sky every day and night—who in these barbarian countries would doubt that this globe was made by reason? These thinkers, however, are not sure whether our world, from which everything originates and comes to be, is the product of chance or of necessity or of Divine Reason and Intellect. They believe Archimedes was more efficient in imitating the revolutions of the sphere than Nature in effecting them, although in many parts these revolutions are so much more cunningly contrived than the others are imitated."[78]

77. [*Ibid.* ii. 2. 4. Here and in most of the following passages Lucilius Balbus, the defender of the Stoic tenets, is speaking.]

78. [*Ibid.* 6. 16.]

All this is written in Cicero's book, just as you hear it. And, having told it, he soon afterward takes over that "rude shepherd" from the poet Accius and exploits for his purpose the ship in which the Argonauts fared to Colchis. When the shepherd saw this ship from a distant mountain, he was stupefied and terrified by the novelty of the miracle and made various conjectures: whether a mountain or a rock thrown out from the bowels of the earth was driven along by the winds and hurled over the sea, or whether "black whirlwinds were conglutinated by a collision of the waves,"[79] or something of this kind. Then he saw young men who helped the vessel move by their efforts, he "heard their sailor's song"[80] and saw the faces of the heroes, pulled himself together, shook off his error and amazement, and began to understand what the thing was. After having told the story so far, Cicero goes on immediately: "This man believed at first sight he was beholding an inanimate object void of sense. Then he began to suspect from clearer indications what it was about which he was in doubt. In such a manner the philosophers may perhaps have been confused when they first beheld the world. However, as soon as they saw that its motions are finite and equable and every single one organized in a precisely calculated order and in immutable consistency, they were compelled to understand that there is someone in this heavenly and divine mansion who is not merely an inmate but the ruler and supervisor and, as it were, the architect of this huge work and monument."[81]

And the same is put by Cicero almost in the same words into the first book of his *Tusculan Disputations*. There he says: "When we behold all these and countless other things, can we doubt that ruling them there is some being that either has created them, if they were born, as it seems to Plato, or, if they

79. [*Ibid.* 34. 87–88.]

80. [*Ibid.* 35. 89–36. 90, with long quotations from the *Medea* by the tragic poet Accius, who was about three generations older than Cicero.]

81. [*Ibid.*]

have always been, as it pleases Aristotle, is the supervisor of this huge work and monument?"[82]

You see Cicero describing everywhere in this passage one single God as the governor and maker of all things, not in a merely philosophical but almost in a Catholic manner of phrasing it. I therefore approve of what he says here more than of what follows in the same book on the *Nature of the Gods*, where the author, it is true, is Aristotle. Although the meaning is the same, mention is there made of "the gods." Wherever gods are named, an investigation into truth is subject to suspicion. The passage runs thus: "Aristotle puts it excellently when he says: 'Let us suppose that somebody had always lived beneath the earth in a well-built and brightly lighted mansion that was adorned with statues and pictures and furnished with everything of which those have plenty who are considered to be fortunate. He had never come above ground, had, however, learned from rumor and hearsay that there were gods of might and power. After a while the jaws of the earth opened and he could come forth and emerge from these hidden places to those where we live. Suddenly he saw the earth, the seas, and the heavens and came to know the vastness and beauty of the clouds and the power of the winds, beheld the sun and saw its greatness and beauty, and learned to know from its operations, too, that it brings about the day by spreading its light all over the sky. When, then, night covered the earth in darkness, he saw all the sky spangled and adorned with stars, the varying light of the moon, now waxing now waning, and all the risings and settings of the stars and their immutable courses, as they are determined for all eternity. When he saw all this, he surely believed that there are gods and that all these marvels are the work of the gods.' Thus far he," namely, Aristotle.[83]

82. [*Tusculanae disputationes* i. 28. 70.]

83. [*De natura deorum* ii. 37. 95, where portions from Aristotle's lost dialogue *About Philosophy* are quoted—passages that made a deep impres-

This example may have appeared to Cicero too far-fetched and remote from experience. Therefore, he refers to an actual event, not a fictitious one, recent enough to be remembered: "Let us now for our part," he says, "imagine a darkness as dense as that which is said to have obscured the neighborhood during a flaming eruption of Mount Etna, so dense that for two days no man recognized an other. When on the third day the sun began to shine, they felt as if they had come to life again. If the same happened to us outsiders, that we suddenly saw the light, how beautiful would the aspect of the sky appear? By daily recurrence and by the adaptation of our eyes our minds become accustomed to it and no longer wonder or require a reason for the things they see all the time. It is just as if the novelty of things more than their greatness had to rouse them to inquire into their causes. Imagine that a man saw how exactly the motions of the sky are determined, how accurately the order of the stars is calculated, and how all things are so harmoniously connected with and adapted to each other. This man might believe that there were no reason in all this and say that everything of which we by no means succeed in finding out, with how much prudent counsel it is managed, came to be rather by chance. Should we call such a man human? We see something moved by machinery, for instance, a sphere, a clock, and a great many other things. Are we not convinced by such a sight that they are works contrived by reason? When we see the moving impulse of the sky rotating around and revolving with admirable swiftness, most constantly producing the annual alterations for the most perfect welfare of everything, do we then doubt that all this comes to be not merely by reason but by some outstanding and Divine Reason? For we may now put aside all subtle discussion and behold to a certain degree with

sion on Petrarca, since he could read them in Ciceronian Latin. He inserted a free paraphrase of them in the chapter "Things Wisely Said and Done" of his *Rerum memorandarum liber*.]

our eyes the beauty of everything of which we say that it has
been brought into existence by Divine Providence."[84]

As I said before, my friends, you hear Cicero speak not like
a philosopher but like an Apostle. Does not all this, every single
word, sound to you like the apostolic message to the Romans:
"God has made it manifest unto them. For the invisible things
of Him since the creation of the world are understood and
clearly seen by the things that are made, even His everlasting
power and divinity. Thus they are without excuse, because that,
when they knew God, they glorified Him not as God, neither
were thankful, but became vain in their thoughts."[85] What else,
I beseech you, does Cicero intend to accomplish when he so
often repeats that the world is established by Divine Providence
and likewise governed by Divine Providence, and when he
hammers it, so to say, into everybody's tongue and eyes? This
is what he wants to achieve: ingenious men, to whom the
Author and Maker of all things has become known, should feel
ashamed of having turned their back to the Source of true Happiness and of having been whirled around in vain and barren
thoughts through the devious paths of opinions.

You might be astonished, if you did not know me, that I can
hardly tear myself away from Cicero, so much am I fascinated
by this genius. Even now I am carried along by the no longer
unfamiliar charm of the subjects he treats and the way he treats
them, and let myself do what I am not used to do: I cram my
little works with what belongs to someone else, and it is not
only you that I beg to have patience with me but my readers
too. As long as I seemed to possess something of my own, I
wore clothes of my own. Now I am a poor peddler of learning,

84. [*De natura deorum* ii. 38. 96–98. Only in a group of corrupt manuscripts, to which Petrarca's copy (Municipal Library of Troyes, France)
belongs, do we read the strange phrase: "If the same happened to us outsiders" (*externis*). Cicero had written: "If the same happened to us after
emerging from eternal darkness" (.... *ex aeternis tenebris*).]

85. [Rom. 1 : 21.]

robbed by these four highwaymen who are looting my knowledge and fame. There is nothing left that would belong to me, and my poverty must be an excuse for my importunity and impudence if I am cadging other people's property. If you ask what kind of poverty I am suffering from, ignorance is the mind's great poverty; there is no greater except vice. But I will not squeeze all these three Ciceronian books into this little booklet here. I will transcribe no more from Cicero today, though he has often treated a great many of these problems with much care in laborious argumentation, elsewhere, and particularly in these books, in order to make us understand from all we see that there is a God, the Maker and Ruler of all.

His argument can be summed up more or less in this way: he puts before us almost all heavenly and earthly things, the spheres of heaven and the stars, the stability and fertility of the earth, the usefulness of the sea and the streams, the variety of the seasons and the winds, herbs, plants, and trees and animate beings, the wonderful nature of birds, quadrupeds, and fishes, the manifold advantages derived from all these things, like food, handicraft, transportation, remedies against illness, hunting and fowling, architecture and navigation, and innumerable arts—and all this devised either by ingenious minds or by nature. Furthermore, he points out the miraculously coherent structure and disposition of body, sense and limbs, and finally reason and sedulous activity. Everything he displays with great care and eloquence. I wonder whether any writer ever treated these matters with greater heed and keener insight. And all this he does merely to lead us to this conclusion: whatever we behold with our eyes or perceive with our intellect is made by God for the well-being of man and governed by divine providence and counsel.[86] And even when he descends to individuals, when he mentions, if I am right, fourteen outstanding Roman leaders, Cicero adds: "We must believe that without the aid of God none of them was the man he was," and soon afterward:

86. [A brief summary of the speech delivered by Balbus (see n. 77).]

"Without divine inspiration no one was ever a great man."[87] And by inspiration a pious man can doubtless understand nothing but the Holy Ghost. Therefore, not to speak of his eloquence, which was unequaled among men, what would any Catholic author change in this sentence?

What shall we conclude from all this? Shall I count Cicero among Catholics? I wish I could. Were I but allowed to do so, if He who gave him such gifts had but permitted him also to know Himself, as He granted permission to seek Him! Though the true God does not need our praise and mortal speech, we should now have hymns to the glory of God in our churches that would not be more true and holy, I presume—for this can neither be nor is it to be hoped for—but perhaps more melodious and more resounding.

However, far be it from me to espouse the genius of a single man in its totality because of one or two well-formulated phrases. Philosophers must not be judged from isolated words but from their uninterrupted coherence and consistency. This I have learned from Cicero himself and from inborn reason. Who is so uncouth that he does not occasionally say a graceful word? But is that enough? Often one word hides for the moment much ignorance; often bright eyes and fair hair veil ugly defects of the body. He who wants to be safe in praising the entire man must see, examine, and estimate the entire man. It happens that, side by side with what is pleasing, something else is hidden that offends as much or even more. Thus Cicero himself returns to his "gods" to the point of nausea, in the very same book in which he has discussed many subjects most seriously and in a manner very closely resembling piety. He gives an account of the names and qualities of each of these gods, no longer intent on dealing with the providence of "God" but with that of "the gods." Listen, please, what he puts in: "We must venerate and worship these gods," he says, "and the best and at the same time the most chaste form of worshiping the

87. [*De natura deorum* ii. 66. 165–67.]

gods, that which is overflowing with piety, is adoring them with unabatedly pure, unpolluted, and uncorrupted mind and voice."[88]

Alas, my dear Cicero, what did you say? So quickly have you forgotten the one God and yourself. Where did you leave that "outstanding Nature" and "that Divine Being of most outstanding mind"? Where is now "the God who is better than man," and "the Maker of whatever cannot be made by human reason," "the Maker of all that is in heaven, and of the everlasting order we behold"? Where did you leave "the Inmate of the heavenly and divine mansion," moreover "the Ruler and Supervisor and, as it were, Architect of this huge work"? You have almost driven Him out of the starry mansion you had allotted Him in that beautiful confession by giving Him such mean and unworthy companions, though He disdains them and proclaims through the voice of a prophet: "See ye that I alone am, and there is no other god besides me."[89] Who are these new, these recent and infamous gods whom you try to smuggle into the house of the Lord? Are they not those of whom another prophet says: "All gods of the nations are demons; it is the Lord who makes the heavens."[90] Just now you spoke of that Maker and Creator of the heavens and all things, pleasing with good reason the ears and heart of a pious hearer. Thus quickly you group Him with rebellious creatures and impure spirits. With one word you tear down whatever you seemed to say wisely' and soberly.

But what am I saying? With one word? No, with many words. Often, yes everywhere, you stumble back with staggering steps like a sleeper and adore the gods you have just ridiculed. Even sun and moon and stars, and finally this whole tangible world we behold and touch, and on which we tread, you make an animated being with sense, and—the very silliest thing

88. [*Ibid.* 28. 71.]
89. [Deut. 32 : 39.] 90. [Ps. 95 (96) : 5.]

you can think of—a god. It is true that you allot these words not to yourself but to Balbus, who speaks in your book.[91] This is perhaps an Academic caution.[92] However, at the end of the book, not daring to say that the discussion we hear from Balbus is more true, you have called it "more like unto truth,"[93] for fear of sinning against the laws of the Academy. Thus it must seem that you have approved and made your own whatever he has brought forth in his disputation. In this manner what you prefer to allot to another is actually your own property, while you let your opinions rather be pronounced by the fictitious mouth of another according to the Platonic method.

It is true that in one passage Balbus himself seems to introduce one god, though in manifold names.[94] This is the shield to protect errors the Stoics used to employ in order to excuse the mad belief in the existence of a crowd of gods. They claim that but one and the same god is meant and must be understood by different names. Thus there would be, for instance, one god, and he would be called "Ceres on earth, Neptune in the sea, Jupiter in the ether,"[95] and Vulcanus in the fire. However, everyone must see how frivolous this excuse and semblance of truth really is when he observes how in the writings of pagan authors one god enjoys a pre-eminence above others, how they are at variance and war with each other, and—let me omit the rest—how different their rites are. There can be no true God, unless He is one. He is not anywhere greater or smaller, for He is always the same, and cannot be or have been occasionally in con-

91. [Lactantius *Divinae institutiones* ii. 3. 1–2 (CSEL, XIX, 103), where a lost passage of Cicero's *De natura deorum* is preserved.]

92. [The precept of the Academic sect never to make a statement regarding ambiguous matters (cf. Cicero *De natura deorum* i. 1. 1).]

93. [*Ibid.* ii. 40. 95.]

94. [*Ibid.* 30. 77, quoted by Lactantius *Divinae institutiones* i. 5. 24 (CSEL, XIX, 17), where he tries to prove that Cicero occasionally professed faith in the one God.]

95. [*De natura deorum* ii. 28. 71; i. 15. 40.]

necessities of one God

flict with Himself. He does not take His delight at one time with a sheep and at another with a bull: He takes it always in the offerings of praise and justice of the contrite spirit and of tears. He is one in heaven and on earth; in both places He has "one Substance and one Name." "Philosophers who are called theologians"—that is, theologians of gods, not of the one God—have seen that what is told of Jupiter is not becoming to the god Jupiter, and speak, therefore, of "two Jupiters," as Lactantius reports, "one natural, the other fabulous," or of "three Jupiters," as Cicero tells us.[96]

He who wants to know how much weight such evasive aberrations and such subterfuges of fiction carry and how much they are to be valued will find it explained by Lactantius of Formiae[97] himself in the second book of his *Institutions*. It is disgusting to mention even with few words that some speak of five suns and just as many Mercuries, Dionysuses, and Minervas, of four Vulcans, four Apollos, and four Venuses, of three Aesculapiuses, three Cupids, and three Dianas,[98] of six Herculeses according to Cicero and forty-three according to Varro.[99] They are not ashamed to say such things; we should be ashamed to hear, far more to believe, them. Who, I should like to know, would not become enraged at such silly talk? Who could bear such trickery? All this is so full and so completely crammed with empty dreams that sometimes I feel compassion

96. [Lactantius *Divinae institutiones*, i. 11. 37 (*CSEL*, XIX, 43); Cicero *De natura deorum* iii. 21. 53.]

97. [Petrarca believed that Lactantius was a native of Formiae near Naples, because Firmianus, the family name of this author, who almost certainly came from North Africa, was sometimes corrupted into Formianus.]

98. [Cicero *De natura deorum*. iii. 21. 54–23. 60, rearranged according to the number of divine individuals bearing the same name.]

99. [*Ibid.* 16. 42. In his *Commentary on the Aeneid* (viii. 564) Servius quotes Varro as his authority for the statement that all strong and brave heroes were once called Hercules. Reading this in his copy of Servius, Petrarca wrote a passage from Augustine's *City of God* (xviii. 19) on the margin, since he found told there that Samson, the judge of the Hebrews, was believed to be Hercules because of his miraculous strength.]

and indignation that the noble Latin idiom is employed and wasted on such cares. Of other things everybody may think as he pleases. But is it not an awful circling-around, a revolting play, and a loathsome fable to invent five suns? It has been said that "the sun is called Sol, because it shines solely."[100] When, on the other hand, it has been at times reported as a miracle that several suns seemed to be visible simultaneously—not that they were really seen—this was probably due to a defect of the eyes or a disturbance of the mind.[101] The ancients, and particularly Cicero, may pardon me if I say: this great man devoted much energy to compiling what, as it seems to me, ought not to have been written and, as I think, ought not to be read either, unless such futile stories are to be read and become known in order that love of the True Deity and the One God, contempt for superstition imported from abroad, and reverence for our religion are to be roused in the hearts of those who read it. There is no way of learning to understand a thing more clearly except by comparing it to its contrast. Nothing makes light so deserving to be loved as hatred of darkness.

If I have said all this of my Cicero, whom I admire in many ways, what do you expect me to say of others? Many men have written many things in a subtle manner, some even in grave, pleasant, and eloquent form. But they have blended some false, dangerous, and ridiculous things with their words, as if they were mixing poison with honey. A discussion of all this would take too much time and is not to the point here. Not in every case should I have the excuse Cicero had: not everyone is so alluring; and, though their subjects may also be sublime, they have not all his sweetness of speech. It happens often that one and the same song sounds pleasant or annoying according to the different persons who sing it, and a different voice produces the same song very differently.

I will not leave the matter without an example: Who does not

100. [*De natura deorum* iii. 21. 54; ii. 27. 68.]
101. [*Ibid.* ii. 5. 14.]

know that Pythagoras was a man of exalted genius? However, we also know his Metempsychosis.[102] I am amazed beyond belief that this idea could spring up in the brain, not of a philosopher, but even of any human being. But it sprang up, and, since it originated with a great genius, other men of great genius—as we find reported—have also been infected. I should like to say something about it here if I dared. Since I do not dare, Lactantius of Formiae will speak through me more boldly. In the books of the *Institutions* he is not afraid to call this very same Pythagoras of whom we are speaking "a vain and foolish old man" and "a most frivolous man, full of ridiculous vanity." With generous freedom of style and mind he despises and rejects the whole fabulous and empty lie and especially his deceitful pretense of "having been Euphorbus in an earlier life."[103] This is the choicest of all Pythagorean tenets, and by this very doctrine this man has won such a name among the credulous people of "Metapontum, where he closed his days," that "his house there was held in pious respect as a temple and he himself worshiped and regarded as a god,"[104] though he was a foreigner in that city. He did not put his doctrine into writing himself;[105] for we are told that he did not write anything, but he expounded it in his conversations, and after him others wrote it down.

Who has not heard of the crowd of atoms and their chance combinations? Democritus and his follower Epicurus try to make us believe that heaven and earth, and all things in general

---

102. [In his two autograph copies of the *De ignorantia* (and in some other places also) Petrarca wrote this Pythagorean term very proudly, but not too correctly, in Greek letters. Of the transmigration of souls according to Pythagoras, Petrarca knew from Lactantius *Divinae institutiones* iii. 18 (*CSEL*, XIX, 239) and also from Ovid *Metamorphoses*. xv. 160–61.]

103. [*Divinae institutiones* iii. 18. 15–17.]

104. [Justin *Historia Philippica*, xx. 4. 16.]

105. [Augustine *De consensu evangelistarum* i. 12 (*CSEL*, XLIII, 12).]

consist of atoms which have gathered in one spot.[106] Both these men, wishing to leave not a single bit of madness untold, established "the innumerable worlds."[107] When Alexander the Macedonian heard of them, "he broke into tears," as we are told, "and exclaimed that he had not yet subjugated a single one of these innumerable worlds"[108]—indeed, the complaint of a vain and vast soul. The two philosophers who were the founders of this philosophical sect had certainly not explored the thousandth part of this one world when they dreamed of the innumerable worlds. You will surely not deny that they were not only learned, sober, and discreet men but most evidently idle men also, since they found the leisure to imagine such things.

What shall I say of the others who did not propound the innumerability of the worlds and the infinity of space, like the last-named, but the eternity of this world of ours? Nearly all the philosophers, except Plato and the Platonists, incline to this opinion, and with them my judges too, who wish to appear as philosophers rather than as Christians. Intending to defend the very famous or rather infamous little line of Persius: "Nothing comes out of nothing, and nothing can return to nothing,"[109] they would not shrink from assailing not only the fabric of the world of Plato in his *Timaeus*[110] but the Genesis of Moses and the Catholic Faith and the whole most holy and saving dogma of Christ, which is impregnated with the sweet honey of celestial dew. Only the fear of human rather than of divine punishment keeps them from doing so. As soon as this punishment is no longer to be feared and the judges are removed, they attack

---

106. [Cicero *De natura deorum* i 24. 66; *Academica posteriora* i. 2. 6.]

107. [Cicero *De natura deorum* i. 26. 73; *Academica priora* ii. 17. 55; 40. 155; Lactantius *De ira Dei* 10. 10 (*CSEL*, XXVII, 86).]

108. [Valerius Maximus *Facta et dicta memorabilia* viii. 14, ext. 2; cf. Seneca *Epistle* 91. 17 (apparently referring to another version of the story). Cf. Gautier of Châtillon *Alexandreis* x. 320–21.]

109. [Persius *Satira* 3. 83.]

110. [In the incomplete Latin version by Chalcidius.]

truth and piety and sneer at Christ stealthily at every street corner, adoring Aristotle, whom they do not understand. They ascribe to ignorance what actually appertains to Faith.

Not daring to run against Faith itself, they attack the adherents of Faith. They call them dull and ignorant and pay no attention to what others know or do not know but concentrate their interest at the point on which they agree or disagree with them. Any dissent they call ignorance, though it is supreme wisdom to dissent from those who err. Stubbornly they stick to their purpose, and, since it is impossible for anything in nature to originate from nothing, they ascribe the same impotence to God Himself. Blind and deaf as they are, they do not even listen to Pythagoras, the most ancient of all natural philosophers, who asserts that "it is the virtue and power of God alone to achieve easily what Nature cannot, since He is more potent and efficient than any virtue or power, and since it is from Him that Nature borrows her powers." No wonder they do not listen to Christ, the Apostles and the Doctors of the church, all of whom they despise; I only wonder why they do not listen to this philosopher or why they despise him. We have no right to suspect that these great judges of others have not read these words. However, it may be that they actually have not read them. Then let them read them in the second book of the commentary which Chalcidius wrote on Plato's *Timaeus*,[111] if any shame is left with them.

However, my advice will be without avail. With a temerity that equals their impiety, they scorn all that tends to piety, without regard to who may have said it. Wishing to keep up the appearance of scholars, they are mad enough to assume that what is denied to the humble handmaid is forbidden to the omnipotent master too. You could, furthermore, observe in their tumultuous gatherings that, as soon as a public disputation is started, they are in the habit of declaring emphatically that during the debate they intend to lay aside faith and store it

111. [Chalcidius *Commentary on Plato's Timaeus* xiii. 295.]

away for the moment; and they declare this because they do not dare to spit out their errors. However, I beseech you, is this anything else than seeking the truth after having rejected the truth? Is it not abandoning the sun and, as it were, forcing a way into the deepest pitch-dark fissures of the earth in order to find the light in the darkness there? Nothing more insane can be imagined. Do not believe that they are not doing anything of the kind or that they do not know what they are doing.[112] They deny faith in a clandestine protestation, not daring to do it in an open profession. Sometimes they do it in sophistical blasphemies, sometimes in ludicrous, wickedly false and stinking impious jokes.

In Cicero's book Balbus says amid much applause from his audience: "It is a bad and impious habit to dispute against the gods, whether it be from one's heart or in pretense."[113] For a worshiper of the gods he speaks piously, though his piety is but impious and pestiferous. How bad and impious must then appear to those who worship the true God this habit of disputing by any means against their God, the one true living God of Heaven? If they do it from the heart, it is an enormous crime and impiety; if they do it just for fun, it is most silly fun and deserves censorious rebuke. However, this is just what my judges do not understand. I would not appear in their court as such an ignorant person if I were not a Christian. How can a Christian appear as a man of literary culture to those who call Christ, our Master and Lord, an uneducated fellow? The pupil of an uncultured master does not easily acquire erudition unless he swerves from his master's footsteps. Eagerly, boldly, and impudently they defy their preceptor and his disciples, bark at them, and insult them. Their greatest pride is to say something confused and perplexingly entangled which they themselves and others do not understand. For who, I beseech you, will understand one who himself does not understand?

112. [Cf. Luke 23 : 34.]
113. [Cicero *De natura deorum* ii. 67. 168.]

And these men do not listen to Caesar Augustus, who was among other accomplishments of heart and intellect a most eloquent prince. As is written of him, he made use of an elegant and moderate form of eloquence and took particular pains to express the sentiments of his heart as openly as possible. He laughed at friends who hunted up unfamiliar and obscure words; he scolded an enemy and called him crazy for writing what the audience was supposed to admire rather than understand.[114] They are indeed queer who thus earn ill fame from their learning. The strongest argument for genius and learning is clarity. What a man understands clearly, he can clearly express and thus he can pour over into the mind of a hearer what he has in the innermost chamber of his mind. In this respect it is true what Aristotle, whom they love but do not understand, says in the first book of the *Metaphysics:* "It is a mark of one who knows that he can teach."[115] There is no teaching, it is true, without knowing; for, as Cicero says in the second book *On the Laws:* "It requires a certain skill not only to know something but also to teach it."[116]

However, this skill has its foundations doubtless in the clarity of intellect and knowledge. For though there is need for such skill besides knowledge, no such skill will get clear speech out of an obscure intellect if it comes to expressing the conceptions of the mind and imprinting them on others. Our friends are looking down from their heights on us who enjoy the light and do not stagger on in darkness as they do. They think we have no confidence in our knowledge and take us for ignorant of everything, because we do not discuss everything in all the public streets and squares. They are full of tricks which are unheard of and are pleased with themselves for that reason, because they have learned to have an opinion on everything and make a great noise about all topics without knowing anything.

114. [Suetonius *Life of Augustus* 86.]
115. [Aristotle *Metaphysics* i. 1. 981 *b* 7.]
116. [Cicero *De legibus* ii. 19. 47.]

Neither shame nor modesty nor consciousness of badly concealed ignorance makes them refrain from doing so. I will not say that the line from the mimic farce by Publius ought to curb them: "In too much altercation truth is lost";[117] but the authentic words of Solomon certainly ought: "There are too many words that would have much vanity in disputing";[118] and these words of the Apostle too: "But if any man seem to be contentious, we have not the custom nor has the Church of God";[119] or these words of the same Apostle: "Beware lest any man cheat you by philosophy and vain deceit doing so according to the tradition of men, according to the rudiments of the world, and not according to Christ."[120]

However, why am I saying all this? Or how shall I ever hope they will have faith in Paul? Is not this disciple of Christ all the more repulsive to them the dearer he is to his Master? Who has ever lent an ear to an odious adviser? They will not keep peace when a friend tightens the rein, not even when Aristotle does it. So vehemently are they pushed by their instincts, so great is the temerity of their minds, so big their boasting with the name of a philosopher, so great and vain the ostentation of their opinions, and so wicked are their foreign dogmas and windy disputations.

In this category of pretenses one is particularly damnable: the claim, which I have already mentioned, that the world is coeternal with God. Not without great anger am I used to hearing these profane little tunes which our friends repeat at all corners, and which Velleius, the defender of the faction of Epicurus, puts forth in Cicero's book, where he asks the following question: "With what kind of eyes of the soul could Plato wit-

---

117. [Macrobius *Saturnalia* ii. 7. 10. In most of the manuscripts of this book the name of the playwright Publilius Syrus, who was a successful rival of Laberius (see n. 47), is corrupted into "Publius."]

118. [Eccles. 6:11 (here according to the Douai Version).]

119. [I Cor. 11:16.]

120. [Coloss. 2:8 (quoted by Augustine *Confessions* iii. 4. 9).]

ness the framing of this great and mighty work in which he makes God construct and build the world?"[121] Such a question may be tolerated to a certain extent, though the answer is already given in the question itself. With what kind of eyes did Plato behold it? He saw it with the eyes of the soul, with which we see invisible things and with which he, a philosopher, saw much, trusting to their immense sharpness and clarity, though men of our creed came nearer to this sight, not that their eyes were clearer but that the light shone brighter.

But who can bear what follows? "What equipment did he employ," Velleius continues; "what were his toils and levers? What machinery did he use? Who were the workmen for this great and mighty monument? How could air, fire, water, and earth obey and execute the will of the architect?[122] This is a question asked by an unbelieving and irreligious soul. Velleius puts it as if it concerned a carpenter or a blacksmith, not Him of whom is written: "For He spake and it was done."[123] He did not speak a volatile word, or ought it to be fancied, as many have done, that He even took the pains to command. He spoke through the "Word in Him" and "coeternal with Him," which "was in the beginning with God, true God from true God, consubstantial with the Father by whom all was made."[124] It was truly He who made the world out of nothing, or if the world, as some philosophers claim, was made out of the unformed matter which the Greeks call "Yle," some others "Silva"[125]—then it was "this unformed matter, which was made

121. [Cicero *De natura deorum* i. 8. 19.]

122. [*Ibid.*]

123. [Ps. 32 (33) : 9.]

124. [John 1 : 1, combined with a passage from the Credo of the Mass.]

125. [Chalcidius *Commentary on Plato's Timaeus* vii. 123; xiii. 268; 351, etc. The Scholastic term for "unformed matter" was preserved in its Greek form in most medieval texts, and especially in the Old Latin version of Aristotle, probably due to the importance of Augustine's philosophical terminology (e.g., *Contra Faustum Manichaeum* 20. 14 [*CSEL*, XXV, 554]). The Latin translation of this term as presented by Chalcidius never became popular.]

out of the absolute nothing," as Augustine says. God made the world by the Word which Epicurus and his followers could not know and our Aristotelian philosophers do not deign to know, in an attitude that makes them but more "inexcusable"[126] than these ancient thinkers. Even a lynx cannot see in the darkness; he who does not see with open eyes in bright daylight is completely blind.

However, further on in Cicero's disputation Velleius asks not unreasonably, "How a man having introduced the world as born and made could say that it would be sempiternal."[127] We, too, say that the world had a beginning and will have an end. The question that follows is rather futile, but it is a common one. "I want to know," says Velleius, "why the builders of the world woke up so suddenly after having slept innumerable ages?"[128] Those who ask thus do not notice that the same question might be asked if the world had been made a hundred thousand years ago or—since we find it written by Cicero too that the Babylonians counted 470,000 years[129]—before this period or even many more thousands of years before. A thousand times a thousand years, compared with the infinite, are no more than just so many days according to the Psalmist, who says: "For a thousand years are before Thy eyes as yesterday which is past."[130] They are even much less, or, more correctly, they are absolutely nothing. The relation of one day or of one hour to a thousand years or to a thousand times a thousand years is similar to that between one small drop that has fallen as rain and the entire ocean and all the seas. The drop is enormously small, it is true, but a comparison is possible, and there is even some kind of proportion. The relation that holds between many

126. [Rom. 1 : 20.]

127. [Cicero De natura deorum i. 8. 20.]

128. [Ibid. 1. 9. 21.]

129. [De divinatione i. 39. 86; ii. 46. 97; Lactantius Divinae institutiones vii. 14. 4 (CSEL, XIX, 628); cf. Cicero De natura deorum ii. 20. 51.]

130. [Ps. 89(90) : 4.]

thousand years—as many as you like, until the number has no longer a name—and eternity is absolutely null. In the first case there is a number great beyond all measure on one side and a number small beyond all measure on the other. However, both are certainly finite. In the other case there is an infinite number here and a finite one there, which, however great, must not be judged small but null in comparison to it, as the great Augustine says when he is discussing the problem so effectively in the twelfth book of his *City of God*.[131]

And this is the perplexity which forced philosophers to propound the eternity of the world, since they wanted to avoid God appearing to have been idle so long. To this opinion which is held by many, Theodosius Macrobius refers in a few words in the second book of his commentary on the sixth book of Cicero's *Republic*. "Philosophy is the authority," he says, "that the world has been always, founded by God, it is true, but outside the range of time. For time could not be before the world was, since it is nothing else than the course of the sun which makes time."[132] This, however, is ruled out by Cicero himself in these words: "It does not follow that there were no ages, if there were no world—ages I call here not those which are made up by a number of days and nights in the annual courses, for I admit, that these ages could not be without the rotation of the world. There was, however, from infinite times an eternity measured not by any limit of time; but in terms of space it can be understood how it was. For it does not enter in the least into our thoughts that there was a time when there was none."[133] These words Augustine inserts into the passage mentioned above, almost to the letter. It is to that eternity of which we are told in the preceding passage that ingenious rather than pious men add various changes caused by "conflagrations and inundations of the earth"[134] which were inflicted upon the

131. [xii. 13.]   132. [Macrobius *Scipio's Dream* ii. 10. 9.]
133. [Cicero *De natura deorum* i. 9. 21.]
134. [Plato *Timaeus* 22 C–E; cf. Macrobius *Scipio's Dream* ii. 10. 19.]

[100]

world. Accordingly, it might appear temporal and, so to speak, new, being actually eternal.

But let me now at last, though late enough, return to where I started. For I have been driven off my course by the chain of related subjects. In this whole field Aristotle must be most carefully avoided, not because he committed more errors, but because he has more authority and more followers.

Forced by truth or by shame, they will perhaps confess that Aristotle did not see enough of divine and eternal things, since they are far removed from pure intellect. However, they will contend that he did foresee whatever is human and temporal. Thus we come back to what Macrobius says when he is disputing against this philosopher either jokingly or in earnest. "It seems to me that there was nothing this great man could not know."[135] Just the opposite seems to me true. I would not admit that any man had knowledge of all things through human study. This is why I am torn to pieces, and though envy has another root; this is what is claimed to be the reason: I do not adore Aristotle.

But I have another whom to adore. He does not promise me empty and frivolous conjectures of deceitful things which are of use for nothing and not supported by any foundation. He promises me the knowledge of Himself. When He grants this to me, it will appear superfluous to busy myself with other things that are created by Him—one will see that it is easy to grasp them and, consequently, ridiculous to investigate them. It is He in whom I can trust, whom I must adore; it is He whom my judges ought to worship piously. If they did, they would know that philosophers have told many lies—those I mean who are philosophers by name, for true philosophers are wont to say nothing but what is true. However, to their number Aristotle does not belong, nor even Plato, of whom our Latin philosophers have said that "he came nearer to truth than any one of the entire set of ancient philosophers."[136]

135. [*Scipio's Dream* ii. 15. 18.]   136. [Augustine *City of God* viii. 9.]

These friends of ours, I have already said, are so captivated by their love of the mere name "Aristotle" that they call it a sacrilege to pronounce any opinion that differs from his on any matter. From this position they derive their crucial argument for my ignorance, namely, that I said something of virtue—I do not know what—otherwise than he did and did not say it in a sufficiently Aristotelian manner. It is very possible that I said something not merely different but even contradictory. I should not necessarily have said it badly, for I am "not bound to swear to the words of any master," as Horace says of himself.[137] It is possible, too, that I said the same thing he said, though in other words, and that these friends of mine who judge of everything without understanding everything, had the impression that I said something else. The majority of the ignorant lot clings to words, as the shipwrecked do to a wooden plank, and believe that a matter cannot be better said and cannot be phrased otherwise: so great is the destitution of their intellect or of their speech, by which conceptions are expressed. I must confess, I have not too much delight in that man's style, as we have it; though I have learned from Greek witnesses and from Cicero's authority, long before I was condemned by the verdict of ignorance, that it is sweet[138] and rich and ornate in his own tongue. It is due either to the rudeness or to the envious disposition of his interpreters that his style has come down to us so harsh and shabby. It cannot fully please our ears and does not stick to our memory. For this reason it is occasionally more agreeable for the hearer and more convenient for the speaker to express Aristotle's mind not in the words he used but in one's own.

Moreover, I do not dissemble what I have said very often to friends and must now write down here. I am well aware of the great danger threatening my fame and of the great new charge

137. [*Epistles* i. 1. 14.]
138. [See p. 53.]

of ignorance brought against me. Nevertheless, I will write it down and will not fear the judgment of men: Let all hear me who are Aristotelians anywhere. You know how easily they will spit at the lonely stranger, this tiny little booklet; they are a lot prone to insult. But for this the little book may take care itself. Let it look for a linen cloth to wipe itself clean; I shall be content if they do not spit at me. Let all the Aristotelians hear, I say, and since Greece is deaf to our tongue, let all those hear whom all Italy harbors and France and contentious Paris with its noisy Straw Lane.[139]

I have read all Aristotle's moral books if I am not mistaken. Some of them I have also heard commented on. I seemed to understand something of them before this huge ignorance was detected. Sometimes I have perhaps become more learned through them when I went home, but not better, not so good as I ought to be; and I often complained to myself, occasionally to others too, that by no facts was the promise fulfilled which the philosopher makes at the beginning of the first book of his *Ethics*, namely, that "we learn this part of philosophy not with the purpose of gaining knowledge but of becoming better."[140] I see virtue, and all that is peculiar to vice as well as to virtue, egregiously defined and distinguished by him and treated with penetrating insight. When I learn all this, I know a little bit more than I knew before, but mind and will remain the same as they were, and I myself remain the same. It is one thing to know, another to love; one thing to understand, another to will. He teaches what virtue is, I do not deny that; but his lesson lacks the words that sting and set afire and urge toward love of virtue and hatred of vice or, at any rate, does not have enough of such power. He who looks for that will find it in our Latin writers, especially in Cicero and Seneca, and, what may be

139. [Most of the classrooms of the medieval Parisian university were located on Straw Street (Rue de Fouarre); cf. Dante *Paradiso* 10. 137, a line familiar to Petrarca.]

140. [*Eth. Nic.* i. 1. 1094 *b* 23–1095 *a* 6.]

astonishing to hear, in Horace, a poet somewhat rough in style but most pleasing in his maxims.[141]

However, what is the use of knowing what virtue is if it is not loved when known? What is the use of knowing sin if it is not abhorred when it is known? If the will is bad, it can, by God, drive the lazy wavering mind toward the worse side, when the rigidity of virtue and the alluring ease of vice become apparent. Nor ought we to be astonished. Aristotle was a man who ridiculed Socrates, the father of this kind of philosophy, calling him—to use his own words—"a peddler in morals, and despised him," if we believe Cicero, "though Socrates despised him no less."[142] No wonder that he is slow in rousing the mind and lifting it up to virtue. However, everyone who has become thoroughly familiar with our Latin authors knows that they stamp and drive deep into the heart the sharpest and most ardent stings of speech, by which the lazy are startled, the ailing are kindled, and the sleepy aroused, the sick healed, and the prostrate raised, and those who stick to the ground lifted up to the highest thoughts and to honest desire. Then earthly things become vile; the aspect of vice stirs up an enormous hatred of vicious life; virtue and "the shape, and as it were, the face of honesty," are beheld by the inmost eye "and inspire miraculous love" of wisdom and of themselves, "as Plato says."[143] I know but too well that all this cannot be achieved outside the doctrine

141. [Petrarca mentions Horace together with the two moral philosophers, because the Roman poet was admired much more for the sound moral advice his satirical sermons offered the reader than for the artistic quality of his poetry.]

142. [Aristotle *Metaphysics* i. 6. 987 *b* 1. The rendering in the *translatio vetus* can easily mislead one to believe that Aristotle speaks here disrespectfully of Socrates. Moreover, the passage which Petrarca quotes from Cicero's *De officiis* (i. 1. 4) has the reading "Socrates" instead of "Isocrates" in his copy. It seems that Petrarca, who in most cases is an astonishingly critical reader of classical texts, did not recall to his memory that Socrates, having been dead for sixteen years when Aristotle was born, could not well despise him (the same error is found in Petrarca's *Fam.*, X, 5, 15).]

143. [Cicero *De officiis* i. 5. 14.]

of Christ and without His help: no one can become wise and good who has not drunk a large draught—not from the fabulous spring of Pegasus in the folds of Mount Parnassus[144]—but from the true and unique source which has its origin in heaven, the source of the water that springs up in eternal life. Those who drink from it no longer thirst. However, much is achieved also by the authors of whom I have just spoken. They are a great help to those who are making their way to this goal.

This is what many a man has thought of many of their writings, and Augustine professes such an opinion, explicitly naming Cicero's *Hortensius*, in grateful remembrance of what he experienced while reading it.[145] For though our ultimate goal does not lie in virtue, where the philosophers locate it, it is through the virtues that the direct way leads to the place where it does lie; and these virtues, I must add, must be not merely known but loved. Therefore, the true moral philosophers and useful teachers of the virtues are those whose first and last intention is to make hearer and reader good, those who do not merely teach what virtue and vice are and hammer into our ears the brilliant name of the one and the grim name of the other but sow into our hearts love of the best and eager desire for it and at the same time hatred of the worst and how to flee it. It is safer to strive for a good and pious will than for a capable and clear intellect. The object of the will, as it pleases the wise, is to be good; that of the intellect is truth. It is better to will the good than to know the truth. The first is never without merit; the latter can often be polluted with crime and then admits no excuse. Therefore, those are far wrong who consume their time in learning to know virtue instead of acquiring it, and, in a still higher degree, those whose time is spent in learning to know God instead of loving Him. In this life it is impossible to know God in His fulness; piously and ardently to love Him is possible. This love is a blessing at all times whatsoever; this knowl-

144. [Ovid *Metamorphoses* v. 250–67.]
145. [Augustine *Confessions* iii. 4. 7; viii. 7. 17.]

edge sometimes makes us miserable—as does that knowledge the demons have, who tremble below in hell before Him they have learned to know. Things that are absolutely unknown are not loved; but, for those to whom more is not granted, it is sufficient to know God and virtue so far as to know that He is the most lucid, the most fragrant, the most delectable, the inexhaustible source of all that is good, from which, through which, and in which we are as good as we are, and to know that virtue is the best thing next to God Himself. When we know this, we shall love Him for His sake with our heart and marrows, and virtue we shall love for His sake too. We shall revere Him as the unique author of life; virtue we shall cultivate as its foremost adornment.

Since this is the case, it is perhaps not reprehensible, as my judges think, to trust our own philosophers, although they are not Greek, particularly in matters of virtue. If following them, and perhaps my own judgment too, I said something, even if Aristotle has said it otherwise or said something different, I hope not to lose my good reputation before fairer judges. Well known is the Aristotelian habit, as it is expressed by Chalcidius in Plato's *Timaeus:* "In a manner peculiar to him he picks out from a complete and perfect dogma what appears to him to be right and neglects the rest in disdainful lack of interest."[146] I may therefore have said that he disdained to treat or neglected some matters or perhaps did not think of them. I may really have said so; it is not incompatible with human nature, though, if we follow our friends, that it does not agree with the fame of the great man—provided I said something of the kind—for I do not remember well what it was, and these men assail me with accusations that are not all too sincere and not definite enough and make use of suspicions and murmured hints instead. Is this, then, a sufficient reason for plunging me so deep into the floods of ignorance and charging me with every error, because I was mistaken on one single point—on a point on which I was per-

146. [Chalcidius *Commentary on Plato's Timaeus* xi. 250.]

haps not even wrong while they were? Must I be condemned as always in error and knowing nothing whatever?

Here someone might say: What does all this mean? Do you snarl at Aristotle too? At Aristotle not in the least but in behalf of the truth which I love though I do not know it. I snarl at the stupid Aristotelians, who day by day in every single word they speak do not cease to hammer into the heads of others Aristotle whom they know by name only. He himself, I suppose, and their audience will at last become sick and tired of it. For recklessly these people distort his words into a wrong sense, even those which are right. Nobody loves and respects illustrious men more than I. To genuine philosophers and particularly to true theologians I apply what Ovid says: "Whenever poets were present, I believed gods were there in person."[147] I would not say all this of Aristotle if I did not know him to be a very great man. He was a very great man, I know, but, as I have said, he was human. I know that much can be learned from his books, but I am convinced that outside of them much can be learned also; and I do not doubt that some men knew a great deal before Aristotle wrote, before he studied, before he was born. I will mention only Homer, Hesiodus, Pythagoras, Anaxagoras, Democritus, Diogenes, Solon, and Socrates,[148] and the prince of philosophy, Plato.

And who, they will say, has assigned this principate to Plato? I answer, not I, but truth, as is said—that truth which he saw and to which he came nearer than all the others, though he did not comprehend it. Moreover, there are many authorities who assign this highest rank to him: first of all Cicero[149] and Virgil —who does not mention his name, it is true, but was a follower

147. [*Tristia* iv. 10. 42.]

148. [Homer: cf. Horace *Satirae* i. 10. 50; *Ars poetica* 401; Hesiodus: Cicero *Cato maior, de senectute* 15. 54; Pythagoras: *ibid.* 7. 23, etc.; Anaxagoras: *De naturum deorum* i. 11. 26, etc.; Democritus: *De divinatione* i. 3. 5; Diogenes of Apollonia: *De natura deorum* i. 12. 29; Solon: Augustine *City of God* xviii. 25, etc.; Socrates: Cicero *Academica posteriora.* i. 4. 15–16.]

149. [*De oratore* i. 11. 47; *De finibus* v. 3. 7.]

of his[150]—then Pliny[151] and Plotinus,[152] Apuleius[153] and Macrobius,[154] Porphyry[155] and Censorinus,[156] Josephus,[157] and among our Christian authors Ambrose,[158] Augustine,[159] and Jerome,[160] and many others still. This could easily be proved if it were not known to everybody.

And who has not assigned this principate to him except the crazy and clamorous set of Scholastics? That Averroes prefers Aristotle to all others comes from the fact that he undertook to comment upon his works and made them, as it were, his own property. These works deserve much praise, but the man who praises them is suspect. For it comes back to the old adage: "Every tradesman praises his own merchandise." There are people who do not dare to write anything of their own. Eager to write, they become interpreters of the works of others. Like those who have no notion of architecture, they make it their profession to whitewash walls. They attempt to obtain the praise they cannot hope to acquire by themselves, not even with the help of others, unless they praise above everyone else those authors and their books—the objects of their efforts—in an excited and at the same time immoderate tone and always with great exaggeration. There are a great many people who comment upon the works of others—or, should I say, devastate them?— especially nowadays. More than any other work the *Book of*

150. [Augustine *City of God* x. 30. 22–26.]

151. [*Nat. Hist.* vii. 30. 110.]

152. [*Enneads* iii. 5. 1; cf. Augustine *City of God* ix. 10; Macrobius *Scipio's Dream* i. 8. 5.]

153. [*De deo Socratis*, p. 691; *De Platonis dogmate, passim.*]

154. [*Scipio's Dream* ii. 15. 18.]

155. [Augustine *City of God* vii. 25; x. 9–11.]

156. [*De die natali* 14. 12.]

157. [*Contra Apionem* (in the version attributed to Rufinus) ii. 31. 37 (*CSEL*, XXXVII, 124).]

158. [*De Abraham* ii. 7. 37 (*CSEL*, XXXII, 593).]

159. [*City of God* viii. 4; ii. 14; *Contra Academicos* iii. 17. 37 (*CSEL*, LXIII, 75).]

160. [*Adversus Pelagianos* i. 14 (Migne, *Pat. Lat.*, 506 D).]

Sentences would bear witness to such devastation in a clear and complaining voice if it could speak: it has been the victim of thousands of such craftsmen.[161] And was there ever a commentator who did not praise the work he had adopted as though it were his own, or even more profusely than he would have extolled his own, since it is a token of refined manners to praise the work of another, while it betrays vanity and haughtiness to praise one's own product?

Let me omit those who chose entire books: one of them, or the most prominent of them, is Averroes. It is well known what Macrobius, an eminent commentator, but an eminent writer too, added at the end of his commentary, in which it was his purpose to interpret not even all the books of Cicero's *Republic* but only a part of one of them: "I must indeed declare," he says, "that there is nothing more perfect than this work: it contains the whole philosophy in its complete and perfect state."[162] Imagine, now, he spoke not of a part of a book but of all the books of all philosophers. Even with more words he could not have said more, for to a complete and perfect state only superfluous things can be added. Can therefore more than this complete perfection be contained in all the books that ever have been or will be written by philosophers—always provided that even all books taken together could ever contain or will contain this perfection and that something is not missing in the first of them just as it will be missing in the very last?

So much for this matter. I know—as I have said before—that I am striking the hard rock of fame in not only mentioning such great philosophers but attempting to compare them with one

161. [Peter Lombard, the great theologian of the University of Paris (d. 1160 as bishop of Paris), wrote the most authoritative textbook for a general course in theology, which was commented upon again and again by later theologians (e.g., by Thomas Aquinas). Petrarca mentions his countryman with marked national pride as one of the outstanding foreign scholars who contributed to the fame of French civilization (*Invectiva contra Gallum* 18. 71 [ed. Cocchia, *Atti della R. Acc. di Archeologia, etc.* (Napoli), VII (new ser., 1920), 184]).]

162. [*Scipio's Dream* ii. 17. 17 (the concluding sentence of this book).]

another. The ignorance laid to my charge and never rejected will excuse my style, for ignorance is in the habit of making people bold and loquacious. Orators are usually kept in check by the fear of losing their reputation or seeing it belittled. Of such fear I am relieved by the verdict of my friends. What should I still fear? What I have lost cannot be lost a second time and can no longer be diminished. However I appraise it, it will amount to just what my friends figure it in their decision, or perhaps to a little bit more: nothing can be less than nothing.

Having reached this point under the impulse of whatever kind of inspiration it may be, I shall at last try to find my way out as well as I can. I shall say what I remember having answered often enough to great men who asked me. If the question is raised, "Who was the greater and more brilliant man, Plato or Aristotle?" my ignorance is not so great—though my friends attribute to me so much of it—that I should dare to pronounce a hasty judgment. We ought to keep our judgment under control and ponder it scrupulously even in matters of minor importance. Moreover, it does not slip from my memory how often a great dispute has broken out among learned men about learned men, for instance, about Cicero and Demosthenes, or the same Cicero and Virgil, about Virgil and Homer, or Sallustius and Thucydides;[163] finally about Plato and his schoolfellow Xenophon,[164] and many others. In all these cases an inquiry is difficult to make and an appraisal would be questionable. Who will then sit in court and pass a judgment in the case Plato versus Aristotle? However, if the question is asked, "Which of the two is more praised?" I would state without hesitation that in my opinion the difference between them is like that between two persons of whom one is praised by princes and nobles, the other

163. [Disputes regarding Cicero and Virgil, Sallust, etc., are reflected in statements made by authors like Seneca Rhetor (e.g., *Controversiae* iii. praef. 8). Homer's superiority over Virgil is treated pro and contra in great detail by the participants in the discussion in Book v of the *Saturnalia* of Macrobius.]

164. [John of Salisbury *Policraticus* ii. 2 (ed. Webb 460b).]

by the entire mass of common people. Plato is praised by the greater men, Aristotle by the bigger crowd; and both deserve to be praised by great men as well as by many, even by all men. Both have come as far in natural and human matters as one can advance with the aid of mortal genius and study. In divine matters Plato and the Platonists rose higher, though none of them could reach the goal he aimed at. But, as I have said, Plato came nearer to it. No Christian and particularly no faithful reader of Augustine's books will hesitate to confirm this, nor do the Greeks deny it, however ignorant of letters they are in our time; in the footsteps of their forebears they call Plato "divine" and Aristotle "demonious."[165]

On the other hand, I know quite well how strongly Aristotle has the habit of disputing against Plato in his books. Let him look to it, how honestly he does so and how remote from suspicion of envy he is. It is true that in some passage he asserts that "Plato is his friend, but truth his better friend still,"[166] but at the same time he ought to take to himself particularly the saying:

165. [In the Athenian Academy, Plato was worshiped as the founder-hero by many later generations of disciples. Therefore, not only Greek authors of all ages but Roman admirers too call him "divine" (Antistius Labeo in Augustine *City of God* ii. 14; Cicero *De legibus* iii. 1. 16; cf. also *Letters to Atticus* xiv. 16. 3, where Cicero calls him "his god," and *De natura deorum* ii. 12. 32, where he makes Balbus call Plato "almost a god of philosophers." "Divinus Plato" and "Daemonius Aristoteles" occur side by side in Proclus *De providentia et fato et eo quod est in nobis* (preserved only in Moerbeke's Latin version of 1280; cf. V. Cousin, *Procli philosophi opera inedita* [Paris, 1864], p. 150). In *De divinatione* i. 25. 53 Cicero has translated Aristotle's epithet as "almost divine" (*paene divinus*).]

166. [For Aristotle's disapproval of Plato's theory of ideas the most conclusive passages are found in *Metaphysics* (i, x, xiii, xiv). It is in one of the many other passages in which Aristotle is attempting to justify his different point of view, that he recalls the advice of Socrates in Plato's *Phaedon* (91 C), not to care too much for his person but rather for truth, and continues: "Being philosophers, we must undo what is nearest to us (*ta oikeia*), that we may save the truth. If both are our friends, it is our duty (*hosion*) to prefer truth" (*Eth. Nic.* i. 4. 1096 *a* 16). The pregnant wording of the sentence as we read it in Petrarch's text here has become common property as early as the fourteenth century, though it is generally said that it cannot be traced back before the Renaissance period.]

"It is easy to quarrel with a dead man."[167] Moreover, many very great men took up the defense of Plato after his death, especially on account of his Ideas, against which this eminently passionate disputant exerted every nerve of his genius so powerfully. Best known and very effective is the defense made by Augustine.[168] I should believe that a pious reader will agree with him no less than with Aristotle or Plato.

Here I should like to insert only a word to refute the error of my judges and whoever agrees with them. It is their habit to form an opinion following closely the footsteps of the vulgar mass and insolently and ignorantly as well claiming that Aristotle wrote much. Not that they are wrong in saying this. There is no doubt that he wrote much, even more than they think; for there are some works which the Latin language does not possess as yet. However, they assert that Plato, whom they hate, whom they do not know, and whom they dislike, did not write anything except one or two small little books. This they would not say if they were as learned as they declare me to be unlearned. I am not versed in letters and am no Greek. Nevertheless, I have sixteen or more of Plato's books at home, of which I do not know whether they have ever heard the names.[169] They will be amazed when they hear this. If they do not believe it, let them come and see. My library, which I left in your hand, is not illiterate, though it is the library of an illiterate man. It is not unknown to them. When they were testing me, they often set foot in it. Let them enter it now and test Plato, whether he, too, is famous without letters. They will find that it is as I say and will confess that I may be ignorant but am no liar, I expect. These most literate men will see not only several Greek writings of his but also some which are translated into Latin, all of which they

167. [Cf. Pliny *Nat. Hist.* preface 31 (citing Plancus).]
168. [*De diversis quaestionibus LXXXIII* 46. 2 (Migne, *Pat. Lat.*, XL, 30).]
169. [Petrarca owned a Greek codex of Plato's dialogues as early as 1354 (see R. Sabbadini, *Rendiconti del R. Institutio Lombardo*, XLIX [1906], 313).]

have never seen elsewhere. They are free to judge of their value; of their number they will not dare to judge otherwise than I say and will not dispute it, however litigious they are. And how small a portion of Plato is this? I have seen many other works of his with my own eyes, especially in the hands of Barlaam the Calabrian, that modern example of Greek wisdom, who once began to teach me Greek,[170] though I am ignorant of Latin learning, and would perhaps have made me make good progress if death had not enviously bereaved me of him, thus obstructing the honest beginnings as is its custom.

Much too vagrantly am I rambling along at the heels of my ignorance, much too much am I indulging my mind and my pen. It is time to return. These and similar reasons brought me before the friendly and nevertheless unfair court of my friends—a strange combination of attributes! As far as I understand, none has so much weight as the fact that, though I am a sinner, I certainly am a Christian. It is true, I might well hear the reproach once launched at Jerome, as he himself reports: "Thou liest, thou art a Ciceronian. For where thy treasure is, there is thy heart also."[171] Then I shall answer: My incorruptible treasure and the superior part of my soul is with Christ; but, because of the frailties and burdens of mortal life, which are not only difficult to bear but difficult merely to enumerate, I cannot, I confess, lift up, however ardently I should wish, the inferior parts of my soul, in which the irascible and concupiscible appetites are located,[172] and cannot make them cease to cling to earth. I call upon Christ as witness and invoke Him: He alone knows how often I have tried again and again, sadly and indignantly

170. [On the Basilian monk Barlaam of Seminara in Calabria (d. 1348 as bishop of Gerace), who had begun to teach Petrarca the elements of Greek, see Lo Parco, *Petrarca e Barlaam* (Reggio Calabria, 1905).]

171. [Jerome *Epistle* 6. 22. 30 (*CSEL*, LIV, 190) with a quotation from Matt. 6:21.]

172. [The threefold division of the soul into the rational, irascible, and concupiscent parts is ultimately based on Plato and appears quite frequently in ancient and medieval Latin writers.]

and with the greatest effort, to drag them up from the ground and how much I suffer because I have not succeeded. Christ will perhaps have compassion on me and lend me a helping hand in the sound attempt of my frail soul, which is weighed down and depressed by the mass of its sins.

In the meantime I do not deny that I am given to vain and injurious cares. But among these I do not count Cicero. I know that he has never done me harm; often has he brought me benefit. Nobody will be astonished to hear this from me, when he hears Augustine assert that he has had a similar experience. I remember discussing this a little while ago and even more explicitly. Therefore, I shall now be content with this simple statement: I do not deny that I am delighted with Cicero's genius and eloquence, seeing that even Jerome—to omit countless others—was so fascinated by him that he could not free his own style from that of Cicero, not even under the pressure of the terrible vision and of the insults of Rufinus.[173] It always retained a Ciceronian flavor. He feels this himself, and in one place he apologizes for it.[174]

Cicero, read with a pious and modest attitude, did no harm to him or to anybody else at any time. He was profitable to everybody, so far as eloquence is concerned, to many others as regards living. This is especially true in Augustine's case, as I have already said. Augustine filled his pockets and his lap with the gold and silver of the Egyptians when he was about to depart from Egypt.[175] Destined to be the great fighter for the

173. [The terrible vision: cf. n. 171; the insults of Rufinus: Rufinus, *Apologia in Hieronymum* ii. 7 (Migne, *Pat. Lat.*, XXI, 588). Petrarca knew this story from a long quotation in a late biographical compilation preceding the text of his Cicero (Codex Troyes; cf. n. 84).]

174. [Jerome *Apologia adversus Rufinum* i. 30–31 (Migne, *Pat. Lat.*, XXIII, 423).]

175. [Augustine never returned from Egypt, where he never was in his life; but he took over into his Christian life what he had learned from his pagan teachers and from pagan authors, to enrich and adorn Christian literature, just as the Jews, when they left Egypt, took with them the silver and golden vessels they had borrowed upon Moses' command: Exod. 3 : 21–22; 11 : 2; 12 : 35–36.]

eloquence
existence of God

Church, the great champion of Faith, he girded his loins with the weapons of the enemy, long before he went into battle. When such weapons are in question, especially when eloquence is concerned, I confess, I admire Cicero as much or even more than all whoever wrote a line in any nation. However, much as I admire him, I do not imitate him. I rather try to do the contrary, since I do not want to be too much of an imitator of anybody and am afraid of becoming what I do not approve in others.

If to admire Cicero means to be a Ciceronian, I am a Ciceronian. I admire him so much that I wonder at people who do not admire him. This may appear a new confession of my ignorance, but this is how I feel, such is my amazement. However, when we come to think or speak of religion, that is, of supreme truth and true happiness, and of eternal salvation, then I am certainly not a Ciceronian, or a Platonist, but a Christian. I even feel sure that Cicero himself would have been a Christian if he had been *wrong* able to see Christ and to comprehend His doctrine. Of Plato, Augustine does not in the least doubt that he would have become a Christian if he had come to life again in Augustine's time or had foreseen the future while he lived.[176] Augustine relates also that in his time most of the Platonists had become Christians and he himself can be supposed to belong to their number.[177] If this fundament stands, in what way is Ciceronian eloquence opposed to the Christian dogma? Or how is it harmful to consult Cicero's writings, if reading the books of heretics does no harm, nay, is profitable, according to the words of the Apostle: "There must be heresies that they which are approved may be made manifest to you."[178] Besides, any pious Catholic, however unlearned he may be, will find much more credit with me in this respect than Plato or Cicero.

176. [*City of God* xxii. 27.]

177. [*De vera religione* 4. 7 (Migne, *Pat .Lat.*, XXXIV, 126); *Epistle* 118. 33 (CSEL, XXXIV, 2, 697).]

178. [I Cor. 11 : 19; Augustine *De vera religione* 8. 15 (Migne, *Pat. Lat.*, XXXIV, 199).]

These, then, are the more valid arguments for our ignorance. By God, I am so glad they are true that I wish them to become more true every day. Indeed, I agree perfectly with what certain eminent men have said—that these arrogant and ignorant people will charge any philosopher, however famous, and even their god Aristotle, with being rude and ignorant, as soon as they hear that one of them has come to life again and has become a Christian. In their arrogant ignorance they will look down on the same man to whom they before looked up in reverence, as if he had forgotten what he had learned just because he had turned away from the beclouded and loquacious ignorance of this world to the wisdom of God the Father: so rare is truth and so much is it hated. "Victorinus" was reputed to be such a brilliant man that he "deserved and got a statue in the Roman Forum,"[179] while he was still teaching rhetoric. I have no doubt that as soon as he professed Christ and the true Faith with clear and saving voice, he was considered dull and downright delirious by those arrogant demon-worshipers whom he feared so much to offend that, as Augustine reports in his *Confessions*, he delayed his conversion for quite a while. Just the same I suspect Augustine did himself. I suspect it all the more, because he was a more brilliant figure and his conversion was more conspicuous. The enemies of Christ and His Church were the more exasperated and grieved the more propitious and gratifying it was for the faithful when he resigned his chair of rhetoric in Milan—as he mentions in his same *Confessions*—grasped the heavenly wisdom under the guidance of Ambrose, that most faithful and holy herald of truth, and, ceasing to be a commentator of Cicero, was about to become a preacher of Christ.[180]

Here let me tell what I once heard said of him, for I want you to understand how grave, how pestiferous, how deeply rooted this disease is. It happened that I once quoted some maxim of Augustine's to a man with a great name, and he took a deep

179. [Augustine *Confessions* viii. 2. 3.]
180. [*Ibid*. ix. 5. 13.]

breath and said, "What a pity that a genius like him was so deeply entangled in empty fables!"

I replied: "How miserable are you to say such a thing; most miserable if you really believe it."

But he smiled and retorted: "On the contrary, it is you who are stupid, if you believe what you say, though I hope better for you." What else might he hope for me than that I should silently agree with him in his contempt of piety?

By all faith in God and men, in the judgment of such people nobody can be a man of letters unless he is also a heretic and a madman besides being impertinent and impudent, a two-legged animal disputing about four-legged animals and beasts everywhere in the streets and squares of every city. No wonder my friends declare me not only ignorant but mad, since they doubtless belong to that sort of people who despise piety without regard to the attitude in which it is practiced and take diffidence to be a religious habit. They believe that a man has no great intellect and is hardly learned unless he dares to raise his voice against God and to dispute against the Catholic Faith, silent before Aristotle alone. The more boldly a man ventures to attack Faith—for he will not be able to seize this fortress by the power of intelligence or by violence—the more these men think him highly gifted and learned. The more faithful and pious he proves to be when defending Faith, the more he is supposed to be slow of perception and unlearned, the more he is suspected of using Faith as a veil to cover and mask himself, in consciousness of his ignorance. They act just as if the old fables they tell were not inconsistent and shaky and their silly talk empty and void; as if there could be had certain knowledge of ambiguous and unknown matters and not merely vague, loose, and uncertain opinions; as if knowledge of the true Faith were not the highest, most certain, and ultimately most beatifying of all knowledge. If one deserts it, all other knowledge is not a path but a road with a dead end, not a goal but a disaster, not knowledge but error. However, these friends of ours have a strange mentality and a peculiar way of forming their judgments. I am not sure whether the two philosophers of whom I have just now spoken, or others like them, would—I will not say: "have begun to displease the Jews, whom they had pleased all the while before,"[181] as Jerome tells us in his interpretation of Paul's *Epistle to the Galatians*, but appear to these our friends just as raving mad as Paul appeared to the Pharisees and priests, since he had become a lamb instead of a wolf, an Apostle of Christ instead of a persecutor of the Christian name.[182]

Therefore, it can be a comfort to me to be charged with ignorance. Even were I charged with madness, it would be a comfort—since such great men are my companions. And it *is* a comfort to me: sometimes I am even delighted in my heart and happy to be accused, for honorable reasons, not only of ignorance, but even of madness.

Thus I am happy for myself but feel sorry for my friends. Still other arguments were brought before their court. They are perhaps of lighter weight, though they are not free from crime and impiety. To them they are deadly and infamous; for me they are so glorious that I would suffer with perfect peace of mind to be deprived not only of fame but above all of life, if it came to it. It is exceedingly painful that a grudge is the true reason for their biased judgment, the only true reason, or at any rate the most prominent of all. A grudge has infected many a man's eyes and made him see things distorted, though to sound and clear eyes this could never happen. It is something new to me, amazing and unheard of, that, much against my will, I have had to experience in my own case that an envious grudge may dwell in the hearts of friends. Of friends, I say, but not of those whose friendship is perfect and complete: such friendship means to love a friend as one's self. These friends of mine love me, but not with all their hearts. I should rather say that they love me

181. [*Comment. in epistulam ad Galatas* i. 1: 10 (Migne, *Pat. Lat.*, XXVI, 321 C).]

182. [Acts 9:21.]

with all their hearts but not all of me. They certainly love my life, my body and soul, and whatever is mine, except my fame, and this so far as it is literary fame. This fame I would hand over confidently and without reluctance to all of them, every single one of them. And this exception is caused not by hatred or luke-warm friendship but, as I have said, by envy, such as dwells even in the midst of friendship.

This may be hard to hear, and I had better say that it is an ex-ception caused not by any grudge but by grief. They are per-haps grieved, indeed they are surely grieved, that in the esti-mate of learned men they are neither men of letters nor known at all, while they hear me called by that name which, rightly or wrongly, I have acquired. Therefore, they wish to tear from me what they lack and what they cannot hope to acquire if they are reasonable. It must lead to great conflict and discordance of wishes if you wish a person all that is good, even the best, and begrudge him the most trifling thing. They do so, I believe, out of deep regret, which they feel not so much because I enjoy fame but because they do not. They wish to be equal in friend-ship, and this, I admit, is not unjust; but they are trying to achieve it in such a way that we are to be equally obscure, all of us, because they believe this to be the easier way, since we can-not all be brilliant and famous. I do not deny that equality among friends is something extremely beautiful. As soon as one party is noticeably preponderant, the souls of the friends seem to be not well teamed under the yoke of friendship, like unequal young bullocks. However, this parity ought to be a parity of love and confidence, not necessarily of fortunes and fame. This is proved by unequal pairs of friends like Hercules and Philoc-tetes, Theseus and Pirithous, Achilles and Patroclus, Scipio and Laelius,[183] not to mention those that remain unknown.[184] There-

183. [Cicero Laelius, de amicitia 19. 69.]

184. [The classical examples of unequal pairs of friends: Hercules and Philoctetes (Servius Commentary on the Aeneid iii. 402); Theseus and Piri-thous (Virgil Aeneid vi. 393–97; cf. Servius); Achilles and Patroclus (Homer Iliad); Scipio and Laelius (Cicero Laelius).]

fore, it is up to these friends of mine to see how they are disposed toward my fame. For, if I am not mistaken, they are most kindly disposed toward me.

I do not want you to lack knowledge of anything that concerns me, my friend. You shall know where and in what mood I am writing you this. Know then that I am sitting in a small boat amid the whirling waves of the Po. Thus you shall not wonder when you find both the hand and the speech of the writer fluctuating: I am driving against the current of this huge river with all my ignorance. Once when I was still young, I wrote much on its banks and meditated a good deal, all of which was destined to please the old men of those days, long before these youths trapped my senile ignorance. The fate of men is indeed unstable. The Po himself seems to feel compassion for me somehow, remembering as it were my studies and conscious of my ancient sorrows, since he saw me—if it can be said without arrogance—glorified by fame when I was young and now sees me as an old man inglorious and despoiled of the brilliantly shining attire of fame. With all the might of his current he urges me incessantly back to demand my right from my unfair judges.

However, I am tired of the toilsome burden of my fame, which arouses the envy of those from whom I do not in the least expect it. I flee from quarrels and lawsuits and despise contempt. Therefore, I leave my spoils to these dear robbers. They may have them; willingly I give my spoils up to them, if fame can be handed over to a robber in the way money can when it is snatched from its owner. Let them have learning or, what is the same in the opinion of the stupid mass, the confidence that they have it. I shall get along without both or, at any rate, without the latter, that is to say, without this confidence. Happier and richer I shall be in my humble nakedness than they in the superb spoils, which in my view do not belong to them. I proceed onward, glad enough that I am relieved of a brilliant but heavy burden. With oars, sails, and ropes I master the Po that resists me on my way home to Padua, this old city of studies. There, if I care to, I shall get back the old robe of fame I have lost among the seafaring people, for I can never get rid of it, however intensely I may want to. It shall always be my aim and wish to be called illiterate, as long as I am a good man or, at any rate, not a bad one, and therein I wish to find repose at last. Nothing is more gratifying to a weary man than repose. My literary fame had deprived me of this quiet rest, and, as I now hear, it was lying all the time. This repose will be restored to me by the reputation of being ignorant, whether it is true or untrue. Thus, late but still in time, everything will turn out all right.

But I am afraid my endeavors and wishes will be in vain. There are so many whose opinions are so much opposed to those of my judges. Not only in the city to which I am now traveling, but wherever they make this their verdict public all over our world it will return upon their heads by the judgment of more and greater men, although with me it has become a settled case by now, as you have already heard. One single exception will perhaps be that most noble and good city where they dare sit in court. Because of its large population and its manifold variety, there are many in that city who practice philosophy and pass judgment without any knowledge. Much freedom reigns there in every respect, and what I should call the only evil prevailing—but also the worst—far too much freedom of speech. Confiding in this freedom, the extremely inept often insult famous men, much to the indignation of the good. Of this latter kind there are there so many that I do not know whether as many good and modest people live in any other city. However, the horde of stupid fellows is everywhere so much greater that the indignation of the wise is of no avail. So sweet does the word Freedom sound to everyone that Temerity and Audacity please the vulgar crowd, because they look so much like Freedom. Thus the night owls insult the eagle with impunity; so do the ravens the swan and the monkeys the lion; thus the nasty rend the honest to pieces, the ignorant the learned, the cowards the brave, the bad the good. And the good do not oppose the licentiousness of the bad, because the bad are the greater number and more in favor with the public, which believes it to be expedient to let everyone talk as he likes. So deeply fixed in the mind is that word of Tiberius Caesar: "In a free state tongue and mind ought to be free."[185] They ought to be free, of course, but so that freedom remains free from injustice and injuriousness.

Do you see how I am hurrying toward the end and never reach it? There are so many things that interfere with the course of my speech and obstruct it. It is not that I did not know how much wiser and more composed it would have been to pass over in silence all these and similar matters; but it is difficult to remain unmoved when you are stung from all sides. Often I have had to crush or shake off such fleas. I should have taken it easily had I seen that you took it easily too. In all this affair I am not so much grieved because of my ignorance, which I am willing to accept, but because of their insolence. However, if it had not been for you, I should have borne it in silence as I have said before. Therefore, it is your indignation I have satisfied in my long discourse, not mine. I have written you not a letter but a book on my ignorance. I have added whatever came my way while I was hurrying along concerning the ignorance of many others and of almost everyone. One could compose huge books on this matter, not such a tiny little booklet, if one had the leisure to think it over more thoroughly. For what, I beseech you, is so common as ignorance? What is more abundant and more widespread? Wherever I turn my eyes, I find it: in me and in others, but nowhere in such affluence as in my judges. Had they known ignorance as well as I do, they would perhaps have refrained from pronouncing a verdict on the ignorance of others, and this most iniquitous and inept court would have taken recess all the year round. For who condemns in another what he sees in himself, unless he is indiscreet to the last degree? There is but one excuse: they seem learned to themselves and seemed so especial-

185. [Suetonius *Life of Tiberius* 28.]

ly at the given moment. For it is certain that they passed their judgment after dinner.

The title *On My Own Ignorance* might appear novel at first sight had I not added something. However, it will not appear amazingly new to one who recalls to his memory that Anthony the triumvir wrote a book *On His Drunkenness*.[186] This title is all the more ignominious, since vices of the will are more shameful than those of the intellect. Ignorance might be the consequence of laziness or inborn slowness; drunkenness is a vice of the will and the perverted mind. Anthony confesses in his book that he is the greatest of all drunkards and excepts—for shame!— only great Cicero's son. I do not deny that I am the greatest of all the ignorant, but I will not except only one other man—there are perhaps four others.

However, this is enough for the present, even more than enough. Still in turbulent waters, as it were, I see the port before me. Let us then bear this false infamy or true reputation of ignorance with an unruffled mind. No one fears what is false, unless he has little confidence in truth; it will soon fade away, even among those who started it, as soon as they are seized by shame, when they come to ponder what they have said. Among others it will not even set forth nor will it find an open door at the house of a learned man, where it might stay. If the reputation is founded on truth, why do we try to evade it or attempt to overthrow solid truth from love of an empty name? There is nothing in such infamy that can greatly torture a generous soul that knows the condition of man and ardently desires what is in heaven. It cannot torture anyone who thinks over and weighs how insignificant, how nearly nothing at all, is that which—I will not say this or that philosopher knows or those know who enjoy greatest fame for their knowledge, but what all men together know. A generous soul will realize how meager

186. [Pliny *Nat. Hist.* xiv. 22. 148; cf. Petrarca's marginal note to this passage in his Pliny (Paris, Bibl. Nat. 6802), in which he expresses his amazement that his beloved Cicero's son had so far degenerated.]

a portion of knowledge is that which is allotted to all men combined, if we compare it to human ignorance and to divine wisdom.

You will lend me a willing ear, my friend, and will believe me. You will not think that what I am saying is a thought formed recently or now come for the first time to my lips. Often have I said, and even more often have I thought, choose whom you please among those who enjoy great fame for their knowledge; take any one of the number of illustrious men and splendid names of the ancient as well as the modern world and examine them diligently. If you gaze upon actual truth and disregard the noisy talk of men, you will find that they had a moderate portion of knowledge and an enormous mass of ignorance. I am convinced that they themselves would frankly confess it, if they were present and ingenuous shame were not absent. According to what some authors report, the dying Aristotle said with a deep sigh, "No one ought to flatter himself or take pride in the belief that he has knowledge. He ought rather to thank God if he has by some chance received more than the common measure. Even this he ought not to believe too quickly; he ought to use his own judgment regarding himself rather than that of others, and ought not to flatter and admire himself, but to be a rigid censor of his own person."[187] In fact, everyone who gets rid of the favorable inclination by which we deceive ourselves and are in turn deceived, everyone who looks with open eyes at his own affairs, will find in himself much to be deplored and little to be applauded.

But let us not speak of what is to be lamented more deeply—I mean what regards the virtues—let us return to knowledge. What should a poor man fear to lose in the case where those who are considered extremely rich are in truth so extremely poor? It is with this small portion of what can be known that, inflated by presumption, we practice philosophy, that we are at variance

187. [Probably taken from a medieval writer who remembered Cicero *Tusculanae disputationes* iii. 28. 69.]

with each other in utter restlessness and boast arrogantly of that little bit, as though it were a shining glory of knowledge. The very greatest minds are in the same straits: they know little, and what they do not know is much. If they have not lost their mental balance, they are not unaware that they have no knowledge, and what Cicero says is entirely true: every serious philosopher knows that he lacks much of knowledge.[188] The less he comprehends his deficiency, the less he feels it and the less he cares for it. Therefore, look at the most learned men who most avidly crave knowledge and most intensely realize their own ignorance.

No wonder human arrogance meets countless rugged cliffs when it unfolds its unfledged wings to the wind in this penury of knowledge. How copious and how ridiculous are the vanities of philosophers, how many contradicting opinions show up; how great is their obstinacy, how great their impudence! Innumerable are the sects, innumerable the differences. How many quarrels break out, how ambiguous are all matters, how great and entangled is the confusion of words! Deep and inaccessible are the caverns where truth is hidden, and sophists lay countless ambushes which completely obstruct the road to truth, as it were, with briars and thorns, so as to make it impossible to distinguish which way leads straight to truth. It was for this reason that Cato the Elder, as we have learned, voted for the expulsion of Carneades from Rome.[189] And, lastly, how great is the rashness even of very great men and, on the other hand, their self-distrust and their despair that truth can be grasped by all! Pythagoras says that "you can dispute about everything with equally convincing arguments on both sides, even about the problem whether everything is disputable on both sides."[190] There are men who pretend that truth is buried in the depths and, as it were, sunk into a profound pit, as if it were to be dug

188. [Petrarca refers to *ibid.* 68.]   189. [Pliny *Nat. Hist.* vii. 30. 112.]

190. [Seneca *Epistle* 38. 43, where Petrarca's copy, like many others of an inferior class, has "Pythagoras" instead of "Protagoras."]

up from the innermost hiding-place in the earth and not rather brought down from the highest summit of heaven; as if it were to be extracted with grappling hooks and hauled up with ropes and not rather approached with the steps of genius on the ladder of grace.

Socrates says: "This one thing I know, that I know nothing."[191] This most humble confession of ignorance Arcesilas blames as still too bold, asserting that "even this knowing nothing cannot be known."[192] A glorious philosophy that either confesses ignorance or precludes even the knowledge of this ignorance! It is a vicious circle and a play impossible to disentangle. "Gorgias of Leontini, the very ancient rhetor, held the opinion," as Cicero tells us, "that an orator could speak of all matters in the best manner imaginable,"[193] though he himself certainly could not. However, he would have been unable to speak of all matters in the best manner, unless he knew them in that manner. This was also what Hermagoras felt when he said that the orator must master not only rhetoric but the whole of philosophy and all knowledge of everything.[194] Great confidence indeed for a mediocre genius! By far the most confident of all was Hippias, who dared to declare that he knew everything, thus usurping the full glory not only of the liberal studies and all philosophy but even of the mechanic arts.[195] This man I should call divine if I did not believe he was mad. It is by now a well-known fact that man cannot know everything, not even many things. On the other hand, the Academy is disapproved and rebutted long since, and it is established that something can be known when God reveals it. Therefore, it may be sufficient to know as much as is necessary for salvation. Many people who knew more than they ought to know have perished, and those who "professed to be wise became fools and their foolish heart

191. [Cicero *Academica posteriora* i. 4. 16; *Academica priora* ii. 23. 74.]
192. [*Academica posteriora* i. 12. 45.]
193. [*De inventione* i. 5. 7.]
194. [*Ibid.* 6. 8.]   195. [Cicero *De oratore* iii. 32. 127.]

was darkened," as the Apostle says.[196] It will be enough if I succeed in being wise within the limits of sobriety; and this can be achieved without much learning, even without any, as is clearly shown by the long line of illiterate saints of both sexes. I shall believe that a happy lot has fallen to me and shall never regret my studious efforts. I shall feel compassion for these loquacious simpletons who in their swollen pride are pleased to be falsely called men of letters, which they are not; or shall be angry and laugh at them, since they argue on matters void of sense and unknown. I shall feel envy neither for their arrogance and pestiferous presumption nor for anything whatsoever, certainly not for their wealth. For they fail to find their way back to themselves, frittering away their powers incessantly in caring for things outside of them and seek themselves there.[197]

To sum up: Willingly I lay down the name of a man of letters —I have done so already—in case I do not deserve it. For I want to satisfy truth and conscience or else to satisfy envy. How the matter actually stands posterity shall see if I shall come down to it on the steps of fame; otherwise oblivion will take care of it. Leave it to uncorrupted posterity, I say, whom no perturbation of mind, no hatred or anger, no love or grudge, these enemies of truth, will encumber. Posterity will look to it, provided it knows me; for doubtlessly it will not know or acknowledge my judges. Not even the present age knows them, for they are hardly known to their immediate neighbors. Posterity shall look to it and pass its judgment. If it approves the verdict of these judges, I shall calmly submit; if it rescinds it, I shall nevertheless not be angry with them, since I know how strong the power of the passions is in the souls of men. For passions have dictated the sentence passed on me—but no, I am wrong: it was but a single passion, that which I have mentioned so often today: It was Grudge. Grudge wrote the verdict with its own hand, and nei-

196. [Rom. 1 : 21–22.]

197. [A paraphrase of Augustine *Confessions* x. 8. 15, the words Petrarca read on Mont Ventoux (see p. 44).]

ther Love nor Reason could change it. Why should I then be angry with my friends for what has been committed by one of their enemies? A father is not responsible for the wickedness of his son nor is the son for that of his father. Much less should the wickedness of an enemy be prejudicial to a friend, particularly when he is kept in fetters in an enemy's custody. Once he is his own master again, he will revenge the insults he and his friend have suffered.

There would be still much more that could quench and calm my anger if I were angry. Many examples from literature could be employed as remedies. For was there ever learning or saintliness or virtue so eminent that it did not lie open to envious adversaries? Indeed, as Livy says, "the greater the fame, the nearer it is to envy."[198] And so it is. Envy is an inert evil; it does not rise into exalted souls but "creeps on the ground like a viper," as Naso puts it.[199] Nevertheless, it has learned to harass with special eagerness the roots of high fame and to inject its poison into brilliant and famous names, not unlike some worms that live underground and gnaw at the roots of slender trees with clandestine bites and silent infection. Thus envy often rages tacitly but at times boils up with greater violence when the passions of the soul break silence and burst into loud shouting. Homer's *Iliad* tells of Thersites, the man who is "limping on one foot with distorted legs, a hunchback with a hollow breast" and "a bald and scurfy head," how he slanders in public Agamemnon the king of the Greeks and Achilles the bravest of all Greek heroes;[200] and Virgil's *Aeneid* tells of Drances, how he insulted Turnus with scandalous words.[201] But this is not to be wondered at. There is a natural hatred between contrasts. How much has been said against the deified Julius and Caesar Augustus by friends as well as by foes? I am amazed beyond belief that "Pescennius Niger,

198. [*History of Rome* xxxv. 10. 5–6.]
199. [Ovid *Ex Ponto* iii. 3. 102.]
200. [*Iliad* ii. 212–17.]
201. [Servius *Commentary on the Aeneid* xi. 122.]

a very brave man, used to say that the descendants of the Scipios," which were so prominent all over the Roman world, "were fortunate rather than brave."[202] The reason for such a statement was doubtless not a grudge but inconsiderate freedom of judgment. However, these stories and others of like kind are taken from foreign history that is far away from us. Let us turn to what is nearer to our parts.

I could mention saints, particularly Jerome, but the matter that concerns us is profane, and we are speaking only of learning. I will therefore briefly refer to some, not to all those who are nearer to our complaint. Who has not heard of Epicurus, how he more than anyone else reviled everybody in intolerable arrogance or envy or both? He did so to Pythagoras, Empedocles, and Timocrates, whom, it is told, he tore to pieces in entire volumes, although Timocrates was his friend, merely because Timocrates disagreed but slightly with him and his crazy opinions. However, these three and others whom he has plucked have reason to be patient, since Epicurus, strangely enough, disdains Plato also and insults Aristotle and Democritus most injuriously.[203] From Democritus he had learned whatever he knew of philosophical matters, and he followed him closely with slightly altered words everywhere. Nevertheless, he speaks ill of Democritus, all the more acrimoniously because he wanted to boast of not having had any master and to appear without one.[204] Metrodorus and Hermarchus followed their teacher in this eagerness to defame. They too tore to pieces the above-named philosophers, without sparing the greatness and fame of any of them. Zeno also was a bad tongue and a scoffer. When he spoke of Chrysippus, that very acute-minded man, who belonged to the same philosophical sect, "he did not call him Chrysippus but always Chrysippa."[205] Not only contemporaries but

202. [Spartianus (Scriptores Historiae Augustae), *Life of Pescennius* 12. 2; 4. 4.]

203. [Cicero *De natura deorum* i. 33. 93.]

204. [*Ibid.* 26. 73; 43. 120.]   205. [*Ibid.* 34. 93.]

"even the father of philosophy, Socrates, he insulted with invective and abusing words: he called him the Attic buffoon, using the Latin word *scurra*," I believe in order to make the joke more pungent by borrowing a word from a foreign tongue.[206] This mordant pun—whether it ought to be called a pun and not rather a libel—was later on turned against Cicero, in whose writings it is reported. His rivals called him "the consular buffoon,"[207] on account of the uncommon wittiness of his tongue, a joke not worthy of Cicero's ears and character but rather of the mouths and the waggishness of the jokers.

Well known are the invectives of Annaeus Seneca against Quintilian and those of Quintilian against Seneca.[208] Both these men were outstanding figures and both Spaniards. However, they snap at each other with bites and condemn each other's style in mutual altercations—a behavior altogether amazing in men of such great genius. Learned men are usually the object of hatred and amazement on the part of unlearned people. The latter gnaw at their fame as soon as an opportunity comes to light. On the other hand, scholars, even such as do not know each other face to face, feel very congenial to each other, so long as grudges and the desire to surpass the other do not disrupt this sympathy. We may believe that this happened to be the case with the last two named and with others of whom we have spoken before.

Sometimes grudges and the desire to surpass cease to rage; then some kind of rivalry seems to remain still active between brilliant men, just as the sea is still swollen when the storm has

206. [*Ibid.*]

207. [Macrobius *Saturnalia* ii. 1. 12.]

208. [Seneca Rhetor, whose writings were not yet distinguished from those of his son by Petrarca and his contemporaries, speaks of the short-lived fame of a certain Quintilian, who may have been the father of the author of the *Institutio* (*Suasoriae* x. praef. 2). Quintilian criticizes the rhetorical style of the elder Seneca (*Instituto oratoria* x. 1. 125; 128; 130).]

calmed down. I find two reasons for this in some authors. One is the favor such men find with their disciples and followers. These drag their masters into combat by their contrasting views, though the masters would rather remain silent. The other reason is the very parity of such men, which drives spectators into different camps of judgment while those who are compared with each other are not even aware of it. The two men themselves may be in harmony with each other and free from passions, but one gets the impression that they are fighting tacitly for the greater eminence and excellence, like two neighboring mountains or lofty towers. If my memory does not deceive me, the above-mentioned pair, Plato and Xenophon,[209] can serve as an example. Sometimes it is not envy for the great learning of the rival but deeply rooted hatred that has made much sharper strife flare up than in the cases just mentioned and the earlier ones. In the *Invectives* of Sallustius against Cicero[210] and those of Aeschines against Demosthenes[211] and vice versa, the insults are launched against the character of the attacked, not against his genius or style. They are full of bitterness and hostility and show not the slightest hint of a peaceful mood. There is no room in them for facetiousness or joke. It is a struggle of quite another kind that is usually fought in literary matters or for fame. Compared to such combats, all the stings of my judges are but a play which is to be borne with a serene mind. Apart from those of whom you have heard, I remember thousands more who have grappled with others for mere matters of literary erudition, the Homerics Aristarchus[212] and Zoilus,[213] the Virgilians

209. [John of Salisbury *Policraticus* 2. 26 (Webb 460*b*).]

210. [These literary exercises of an anonymous rhetor of the Augustan age were available to Petrarca in his Cicero codex.]

211. [Cicero *De oratore* 31. 111; Valerius Maximus *Facta et dicta memorabilia* viii. 10. ext. 1.]

212. [Cicero *In Pisonem* 30. 73; *Letters to Atticus* i. 14; Ovid *Ex Ponto* iii. 9. 24.]

213. [Ovid *Remedia amoris* 365–66.]

Cornificius[214] and Evangelus[215], the Ciceronians Asinius[216] and Calvus.[217] And Gaius comes to mind, a savage prince, I admit, though not at all an uneducated man, who, as the story goes, "thought of doing away with the Homeric epics. 'Why,' he said, 'was he not allowed to do what Plato had been entitled to perform when he drove Homer out of the state he had built up?' It nearly came to such a point that Gaius removed the works of Virgil and Livy and their portraits from all libraries, blaming the former for having no intelligence and very little learning, the other for being loquacious and careless in his history. Annaeus Seneca found as much favor then as he does now; but Gaius called him 'sand without lime.' "[218] And we speak of men, when a Greek woman, Leontium, even "a little prostitute," as Cicero says, dared to write against a philosopher like Theophrastus.[219] Who will then be indignant that a few words are said against himself, when such insults have been hurled against such men by such people?

Now nothing remains to be done besides entreating and imploring—I would not say you and those few who do not need to

214. [In late versions of Virgil's biography that are derived from the commentaries on Virgil's works by the fourth-century grammarians Aelius Donatus and Servius and enlarged by notes taken from similar works of their successors (cf. J. J. Savage, "Aelius Donatus and the Virgilian Tradition," *Folia*, I [1946], 65–70), Cornificius is mentioned as a man who "due to his perverse nature" could not abide the gentle poet ("Donatus auctus," in *Vitae Vergilianae*, ed. E. Diehl [Bonn, 1915], p. 35).]

215. [One of the fictitious partners in the conversations held in Macrobius' *Saturnalia* (i. 7. 2; 5. 21) who indulges in passionate criticism of Virgil.]

216. [C. Asinius Pollio (76 B.C.–A.D. 5), a famous man of ancient times to whom Petrarca wrote one of his letters to such "correspondents" (*Fam.*, XXIV, 9; M. E. Cosenza, *Petrarca's Letters to Classical Authors* [Chicago, 1910], pp. 112–24), was known as a severe critic of many of his contemporaries and especially of Cicero (Seneca Rhetor *Suasoriae* vi. 14–15; 24; 27).]

217. [C. Licinius Macer Calvus (82–47 B.C.), a man of literary ambitions who, according to Seneca Rhetor (*Controversiae* vii. 4. 6), dared to compete even with Cicero in his speeches.]

218. [Suetonius *Life of Caligula* 34 and 54.]

219. [Cicero *De natura deorum* i. 33. 92.]

be urged to love me, but my other friends and among them my censors—to love me from now on, not as a man of letters, but as a good man, and if not as such, then as a friend—and finally, if I do not deserve the name of a friend, being so poor in virtues—at least as a benevolent and loving soul.

Explicit.

This little book was composed two years ago and written down by me elsewhere. I have re-written it, again with my own hand, and have brought it to an end at Arquà in the Euganean Hills, on the twenty-fifth of June of the year 1370, when the day was declining toward sunset.[220]

220. [The postscript in Petrarca's second autograph copy, the Codex Vaticanus 3359, "completed on June 25, 1370" (L. M. Capelli, *Pétrarque: Le traité de sui ipsius ignorantia* [Paris, 1906]), refers to the two preceding stages of the work: the first draft of December, 1367, written on the river barge on the Po, which is not preserved (cf. p. 120), and the autograph presentation copy for Donato degli Albanzani, the Codex Hamiltonianus 493 in the State Library of Berlin, which Petrarca wrote early in 1370 (cf. P. Rajna, *Rendiconti dell'Accademia dei Lincei*, XVIII [5a ser., 1909], 479–508).]

A DISAPPROVAL OF AN UNREASONABLE USE OF THE DISCIPLINE OF DIALECTIC

Letter to Tommaso Caloria in Messina. Avignon, March 12, *ca.* 1335. (*Fam.*, I, 7 [6], in *Le Familiari*, ed. V. Rossi, I, 35–38; *Opera* [Basel, 1581], pp. 579–80.)

To Tommaso of Messina, against old dialectic cavilers

IT IS a risky task to contend with an enemy who is not so eager to win as to fight. You tell me of an old dialectician who has been violently annoyed by my letter, as though I had condemned his profession. He is raging in public, you say, and threatens to assail our field of studies in a letter of his; and you have been waiting for this letter in vain for months. Do not expect it any longer. Believe me, it will never come. That much good sense is left in him. He is evidently ashamed of his stylistic capacities, or else his silence is a confession of his ignorance. Those who are implacable with their tongues do not battle with the pen. They do not like to let men know how frail their armor is. They fight after the Parthian manner, while they are fleeing; they cast their volatile words into the air, as if they were committing their darts to the wind.

As I said before, it is risky to fight with such people after their fashion, especially because they so much enjoy the combat itself. They are not set to find the truth—they want the struggle. But there is a Varronian maxim: "In too much altercation truth is lost."[1] Do not be afraid that they will come out to the open battleground of written words and solid discussion. It is of such people that Quintilian has said in his *Instruction of Speech-making:* "You will find certain people miraculously

1. [This maxim is not preserved among the fragments which have come down to us of Varro's work but among excerpts from plays by Publilius Syrus in Macrobius *Saturnalia* ii. 7. 11. Later in his life Petrarca knew that the author was Publilius, whom he calls Publius because of a corrupt reading in his Macrobius (see p. 97).]

clever in disputing. However, as soon as they must do without this kind of caviling, they are no more efficient in any serious operation than certain animals which are very nimble in narrow straits but easily caught in the open field."[2] Therefore, they are quite right if they fear to come out. For it is true what the same Quintilian says: "The weak have recourse to crooked ways and evasive tricks, for those who do not achieve much in running away escape adroitly by their flexibility."[3]

There is one thing, my friend, that I want to tell you: If you aim at virtue and truth, avoid this sort of men. But where can we find refuge from such mad folk if even islands are not safe from them? Not even Scylla and Charybdis prevent this pest from swimming across to Sicily. This kind of misfortune is evidently peculiar to islands, since a horde of new Cyclopes has gathered near Mount Etna, to match the host of dialectic fighters in Britain.[4] Did I not read in Pomponius Mela's *Cosmography* that Britain resembles Sicily very much?[5] I believed, it is true, that this resemblance consisted in the geographical situation and the almost triangular shape of the two islands and perhaps also in the ceaseless breaking of the sea against the shores of both. I had not thought of the dialecticians. I had heard that the Cyclopes were the first to live there, then the tyrants, and that both were ferocious people. However, I did not know that a new kind of monster had arrived there, armed with double-edged enthymemes,[6] a gang more insolent than the wild

2. [*Instituto oratoria* xii. 2. 14.]

3. [*Ibid.* ix. 2. 78.]

4. [Petrarca seems to refer to a recently increasing dialectic tendency among men of philosophical interests in Sicily and places it beside that of contemporary English philosophers.]

5. [Mela *Cosmographia* iii. 50.]

6. [Remembering the "well-rounded enthymeme" from Juvenal's Sixth Satire (vs. 449–50), Petrarca apparently invents a new class of syllogisms with contradicting premises, "enthymemata bisacuta," which are sharpened at both ends.]

breakers on the shore of Taormina. One thing I had not noticed before you brought it to my attention: They shield their sect with the splendid name of Aristotelians and pretend that Aristotle was wont to discuss in their manner. It is a kind of excuse to stick to the footsteps of famous leaders. Marcus Tullius, too, says that "not unwillingly he would commit an error," if necessary, "together with Plato."[7] But they are mistaken: Aristotle, who was a man of fervent spirits, discussed problems of the highest order and wrote about them. How else would he have managed to write so many volumes that are composed with so much application in so many sleepless nights amid so many other occupations, particularly with his fortunate pupil, and during a life that did not last long? For we hear about him from ancient authors that he died in the ill-famed sixty-third year of his age.[8] However, why are these people straying so far away from their leader, why are they so eager to be called Aristotelians, why are they not rather ashamed of this name? No greater contrast can be imagined than that between this great philosopher and a man who does not write anything, understands but little, and shouts much and without consequence. Who does not laugh at the insignificant little conclusions in which these highly educated people fatigue themselves and others? They waste their whole lives in such conclusions, since they are not good for anything else and especially destructive in this particular case.

Such syllogisms are very often ridiculed by Cicero and Seneca. Well known also is a repartee which Diogenes made, when a quarrelsome dialectic debater assailed him in the fol-

7. [Cicero *Tusculanae disputationes* i. 17. 40.]

8. [Ancient medical theory considered every seventh and ninth year in the life of an individual as critical, and consequently the sixty-third year as the most critical of all (Firmicus Maternus *Matheseos* iv. 20. 3). On his own sixty-third birthday (July 20, 1367), Petrarca told Boccaccio of the strange feelings with which he began this suspicious year (*Sen.*, VIII, 1), and exactly a year later, in another letter to Boccaccio (*ibid.*, p. 9), he felt relieved because he had passed it without serious trouble.]

lowing manner: "What I am you are not," he began. When Diogenes admitted this statement, he went on: "But I am a man." When Diogenes did not deny this either, the caviler smuggled in the conclusion: "Thus you are not a man." It was then that Diogenes replied: "This is a wrong conclusion, and if you want it to become right, you must start with me."[9] Many most ridiculous conclusions are like this one. These people will perhaps know what they intend to achieve by them: whether they hope to win fame or to have a pleasant time or to get counsel on how to lead a decent and happy life. I certainly do not know what they want. To noble minds profit should not appear to be a dignified reward for studies. It fits a craftsman to seek profit; generous arts know a nobler goal.

These friends of dialectic get angry when they hear what I say, for the ceaseless talking of quarrelsome persons is always liable to degenerate into an angry mood. "Thus you disapprove of the discipline of dialectic," they say. Not in the least. I know how much it was appreciated by the Stoics, this strong and masculine sect of philosophers that is so often cited by Cicero, particularly in his book *About the Ultimate Ends.*[10] I know that it is one of the liberal arts and a stepping-stone for those who want to rise to higher grades. It is not a useless weapon in the hands of those who try to find a way through the thickets of philosophy. It sharpens the intellect, marks off the path toward truth, and teaches how to avoid fallacies. If it does not achieve anything else, it certainly gives a man a ready wit and makes him most resourceful. All this I do not deny. But where we pass with honor, we do not stay with praise. A wayfarer who forgets the goal he has set to himself because the road is so pleasant is not sound of mind. A traveler is praised if he completes a long journey quickly without ever stopping before its end. And who among us is not a traveler? All of us must cover

9. [Gellius *Noctes atticae* xviii. 13. 78.]
10. [*De finibus* Books iii-iv.]

a long and difficult road in a short set time in bad weather, almost as it were on a rainy winter day. Occupation with dialectic may cover a part of this road; it ought never to be the goal. It may be on the morning schedule but never on that of the evening. At one time we were completely right in doing many things that would turn out to be most disgraceful for us if we still did them. If we do not succeed in our old age in leaving the dialectic schools behind us, because we played in them while we were boys, we might just as well not feel ashamed to continue "playing odd and even and using a shaky reed"[11] as a hobby horse or to start again rocking in a baby cradle.

Things are strangely different and times are changing. With most vigilant art Nature has thought out how to prevent man from being bored. Do not believe that such changes happen only within the course of a single year; many more of them will happen during a long life. Spring is charming for its blossoming flowers and trees; summer is rich in all kinds of grain, autumn in fruit, and winter brings abundance of snow. All this is not just tolerable but pleasant and agreeable. If you change one for the other, the laws of Nature will break down and everything becomes hard to bear. Just as no one would endure icy January frost all summer with even temper, or torrid summer heat if it raged in months where it does not belong, everybody without exception would become angry and laugh at an old man who did nothing else than play with little children, and everybody would be amazed at a gray-haired, gouty boy. Can you imagine anything, I ask you, that is so useful or even so necessary as the first notion of letters? They are the foundation on which all our studies rest. However, vice versa, is there anything so ridiculous as an old man who is still occupied with these elements? Therefore, stir up the pupils of that old man, quoting my words: Do not deter them, rather encourage them, not indeed to throw themselves in all haste into the study of dialectic, but to pass

11. [Horace *Satires* ii. 3. 247.]

quickly through this discipline to better ones. And tell your old man that I do not condemn the liberal arts, but childish old people. For as there is nothing more disgraceful than "an old man in a first-grade class," as Seneca says,[12] so there is nothing so ugly as an old man who is a dialectic debater. And if he starts to spit out syllogisms, this is my advice: Run away and let him dispute with Encheladus.[13]

Farewell.

Avignon, March 12.

12. [*Epistle* 36. 4.]

13. [The ferocious giant of the ancient myth whom Jupiter buried under the flaming masses of Mount Etna (cf. Virgil *Aeneid* iii. 595) is so to say a neighbor of the old man in Messina.]

AN AVERROIST VISITS PETRARCA

From a letter to Boccaccio. Venice, August 28, 1364. (*Sen.*, V, 2 [3], in *Opera* [Basel, 1554], p. 880; [1581], p. 796.)[1]

I WONDER from where these new theologians sprout up who do not spare the Doctors of the Church. Soon they will not respect the Apostles either, nor the Gospel, and eventually they will let loose their frivolous talk against Christ Himself, unless He whom it must concern comes to our aid and tightens the reins of these untamed animals. By now it has become almost a habit with them to strike out with a silent gesture or even with an impious word whenever these venerable and holy names are pronounced. They say: "Your Augustine saw a lot, but he did not know much." And of others they speak no more respectfully.

Some days ago there was[2] here in my library one of these "religious" men[3] (not the habit alone, but to be Christian is the highest form of religion).[4] He belonged to that sect of men who practice philosophy after the modern fashion and think they are not efficient enough if they do not bark at Christ and His heavenly doctrine. When I happened to mention some passage from the Scriptures—I forget which—he began to foam with rage and a hideous native anger. His face was distorted, and he made an ugly grimace of haughty contempt. "You may

1. [The text is badly corrupted in some sentences in the Basel editions. The corrections indispensable for its restitution are mentioned in the following notes.]

2. [*Fuit*, not *fui* (correct in the Venice editions of 1501 and 1503).]

3. [*Religiosum*, not *religiosius* (Basel) or *religiosus* (Venice, 1501). The sentence is elliptic.]

4. [The unidentified visitor belonged to a religious order. Petrarca wants to say that taking orders does not necessarily raise a man to a higher moral order, but being a true Christian is the highest way of being religious.]

keep your petty Doctors of the Church to yourself," he said. "I know whom to follow and whom to believe."[5]

"You used the words of the Apostle," I replied; "so you had better use his faith too."

"Your Apostle," was his answer, "was 'a word-sower' and 'a madman.'"

"You speak[6] excellently," I said, "my worthy philosopher. The first phrase you used was hurled at him in reproach by other philosophers,[7] and the second was said to him by Festus, the governor of Syria.[8] Indeed, he was a sower of the most useful word. We see before us the abundant harvest of faith that grew up from this seed, when it had been cultivated with the saving plow of his successors and irrigated with the blood of the martyrs."

Here he burst into a disgusted laughter and exclaimed: "Well, you are surely a good Christian. I, for my part, do not believe in such things. Your Paul and Augustine, and all the others you preach and extol, were awfully loquacious fellows. If you could only bear Averroes, you would see how much greater he is than these silly babblers of yours."

I must confess, I flared up, hardly able to keep from slapping him in his impure and blasphemous face: "This is an argument of long standing. I have had such disputes with other heretics too. Be gone and never come back, neither you nor your heresy!" Saying this, I seized him by his coat and pushed him out of my house, more insultingly than my manners, though not his, would have required. . . . .

5. [II Tim. 2 : 12.]

6. [*Loqueris*, not *sequeris*.]

7. [Acts 17 : 18. The famous word *seminiverbius* is here rendered according to the Reims-Douai New Testament of 1582.]

8. [Acts 26 : 24.]

PETRARCA'S AVERSION TO ARAB SCIENCE

From a letter to his physician and friend Giovanni de'Dondi dell'Orologio in Padua. Arquà, November 17, 1370. (*Sen.*, XII, 2, in *Opera* [Basel, 1554], p. 1010; [1581], p. 913.)

BEFORE I close this letter, I implore you to keep these Arabs from giving me advice about my personal condition. Let them stay in exile. I hate the whole lot. I know that the Greeks were once most ingenious and eloquent men. Many very excellent philosophers and poets; outstanding orators and mathematicians have come from Greece. That part of the world has brought forth princes of medicine. You know what kind of physicians the Arabs are. I know what kind of poets they are. Nobody has such winning ways; nobody, also, is more tender and more lacking in vigor, and, to use the right words, meaner and more perverted. The minds of men are inclined to act differently; but, as you used to say, every man radiates his own peculiar mental disposition. To sum up: I will not be persuaded that any good can come from Arabia.....

A REQUEST TO TAKE UP THE FIGHT
AGAINST AVERROES

From a letter to Luigi Marsili in Paris (*ca.* 1370). (*Sen.*, XV [XIV], 6 = sine nomine 22, in *Opera* [Basel, 1554: sine titulo XVIII], p. 812; [1581], p. 734.)

FINALLY, this is what I beg you to do. As soon as you have gained the position you are longing for[1]—and I trust this will speedily come to pass—set all your strength and all your nerves to the fight against that frantic dog Averroes, who is prompted by an undescribable fury to bark at his Lord and Master Jesus Christ and the Catholic Faith. For this purpose gather his blasphemies from all sources. You know that I have already begun such a collection. However, I have always been enormously busy, and I am now busier than ever. Lack of time no less than of learning has prevented me from completing the collection. It is a task that has been impiously neglected by many great men. Therefore, do write a little book and dedicate it to me, whether I am then still living or have meanwhile departed. There is always the right moment for every man, and for me too, to think at last of departing. And do not think that your faculties or your stylistic abilities will not be sufficient, though they were lacking in some of your brothers. Christ will aid you while you are doing His work, He who has been at your side since the very hour of your birth.

1. [Marsili seems to have expected promotion to a higher position in his order. Though still a young man, he was evidently already a prominent figure. A few years after Petrarca's death he had become a famous preacher in Florence, where his popularity grew so high that he was twice proposed for appointment as bishop of that diocese and received an honorary tomb in the cathedral when he died in 1394.]

I I

LORENZO VALLA

ON FREE WILL TO GARSIA, BISHOP OF LERIDA

Translated by CHARLES EDWARD TRINKAUS, JR.

INTRODUCTION

By CHARLES EDWARD TRINKAUS, JR.

LORENZO VALLA (1405–57) has usually been regarded as among the most original and influential Italian Humanists. Perhaps because of that very originality, he must also be regarded as unique and atypical of the Humanists in many aspects of his thought. Although "singularity" might conceivably be regarded by some scholars as "typical" of the Humanists, nevertheless, it is clear today that there were certain broad patterns of attitude and behavior that characterized numerous groups of these writers.[1] While Valla shared many of the Humanists' antipathies to Aristotle, dialectic, and the Scholastics,[2] and while he subscribed to the general interest in classical philology (making, of course, one of the outstanding Humanist contributions to that discipline)[3] and manifested the same general taste for the dialogue and informal modes of presentation,[4] his hostility to the ancient schools of philosophy (except for some aspects of Epicureanism) was general, so that he neither participated in the revival of Stoic philosophy among the Humanists of the first half of the *quattrocento* nor anticipated the later Neo-Platonism.[5] His appreciation of the ancients was al-

---

1. Cf., e.g., the translator's *Adversity's Noblemen* (New York, 1940).

2. He elaborated on his antipathies in *Dialectice Laurentii Vallae libri tres seu ejusdem Reconcinnatio totius dialectice et fundamentorum universalis philosophiae; ubi multa adversus Aristotelem, Boetium, Porphyrium* etc......*disputantur*, etc...... (Paris, 1509). Cf. the present work, below, pp. 155 ff. and pp. 179–80.

3. His *De linguae latinae elegantia libri sex* appearing in many editions.

4. This present work on *Free Will* is a good example of his use of dialogue, polite padding of the argument, and witty byplay. Hardly more than half the space consumed is taken up with the actual argument.

5. He condemned the Stoics and Epicureans in *De voluptate ac vero bono libri tres* (Basel, 1519); the Aristotelians as above, n. 2. He seems to have shown no interest in the Platonists either favorable or critical.

most exclusively confined to their linguistic and rhetorical contributions.

On the positive side Valla identified himself with Latin patristic thought.[6] In this respect it might very plausibly be claimed that he belongs rather with the Christian Humanists or with the Pre-Reformers than with the nominally orthodox Catholic Humanists who dallied with pagan philosophy. This is a rather extreme claim to make in view of the persistent tendency to regard Valla as an outstanding proponent of anti-Christian, particularly sensualist Epicurean, views, who for this reason drew upon himself the disfavor of the papacy, with which he subsequently sought to ingratiate himself. Nevertheless, there is far more logic in the view that Valla's pietism and antirationalist and antiphilosophical tendencies found an unsought target in the Church, which both in doctrine and in practice had far more in common with Humanists who favored different classical philosophic schools.

It is well known by now that the Italian Humanists differed from their Scholastic rivals less in essential doctrines than in stylistic predilections, forms of presentation, and classical mentors. Medieval Catholic thought had long made its peace with Greek logic and psychology, and the view that there was any hostility between medieval thinkers and the pagan classics (Christianly interpreted, of course) is a figment of some modern imaginations.[7] To a certain extent Humanism was Scholasti-

6. Cf. his affirmation of the Greek and Latin Fathers, but especially the latter, in his *Encomium Sancti Thomae Aquinatis*, a work of his later years, published by Johannes Vahlen in *Vierteljahrschrift für Kultur- und Litteraturgeschichte der Renaissance*, I (1886), 387–96.

7. These assertions are reinforced from opposite sides, as it were, by both the modern Catholic scholars who have shown the generally enlightened, rational, and Humanistic qualities of the medieval theologians and philosophers (e.g., Father Gerald G. Walsh, *Medieval Humanism* [New York, 1942]), and the Protestant writers who have tried to re-emphasize the orthodoxy of the Reformation and have therefore sought to show the contrasts between patristic and Reformation thought, on the one hand, and pagan classical, medieval Catholic, and Italian Renaissance thought, whose affinities they emphasize, on the other (e.g., Anders Nygren, *Agape*

cism without the complexities and subtleties; hence the main interest of the Humanists was in simplification and purification of "barbarisms." Similarly the elaborate care with which the Scholastics, in particular Thomas Aquinas, had reconciled Aristotelian classical philosophy with Catholic doctrine had its influence in the fact that the Humanists, for the most part, simply took it for granted that there was no conflict between Catholicism and the classics; that the latter were pagan in form but Christian in content; that the Greek mythology and pantheon might legitimately be employed as a vehicle for expressing thoughts about Christian holy persons and saints. Furthermore, on the crucial moral question of the capacities and potentialities of man, the Humanist notions of man as a microcosm and theories of ethical freedom rested on the same metaphysical foundations as the orthodox views of man's place in the scale of being and his capacity for continuous regeneration; Scholastic emphasis on free will and its rationalistic-moral approach to psychology were matched by both the Stoic and Neo-Platonic schools of Humanist thought.

Valla, on the other hand, broke decisively with these endeavors of both high Scholastic and Humanist thought to create a synthesis of paganism and Christianity. Quite apart from the question of where his own loyalties lay (and it does seem quite conclusive that they were Christian) is the fact that he consistently and comprehensively emphasized the irreconcilability of reason and faith, of philosophy and theology, of paganism and Christianity. It is important to emphasize this, despite the fact that it frequently was more of a formally reiterated position than something Valla consistently carried out in practice. Although his own unfortunately feeble essay in the field of dialectic,[8] trying to improve on Aristotle and the Scholastics, and his classical philological studies[9] show that he certainly did not

---

and Eros [New York, 1932, 1939]; and Reinhold Niebuhr, *The Nature and Destiny of Man* [New York, 1941 and 1943]).

8. *Dialectice, etc.*   9. *De linguae latinae elegantia.*

believe in keeping himself entirely unsullied by these aspects of paganism, it might be said in extenuation that these were conceived as strictly secular, nonreligious activities. In his essays in moral philosophy, moreover (among which the present *Dialogue on Free Will* is no exception), he makes strong protestations against philosophy,[10] and this must be claimed as the essential bearing of the argument. He is not, however, above using figures of classical mythology to represent Christian personages and members of the Deity,[11] nor is he too much of a rhetorician to abjure logical argumentation (superficial though at times it may be).[12]

Indeed, in these works he broke with rationalistic medieval and Renaissance Catholicism on the same grounds that the reformers later took.[13] In his treatise on *Pleasure and True Good*[14] he denied the general validity of good works as a Chris-

10. Cf. below, pp. 155 ff. and pp. 179–80.

11. As his use of Apollo and Jupiter below, pp. 170 ff.

12. Ernst Maier (*Die Willensfreiheit bei Laurentius Valla* [Bonn, 1911]) shows (pp. 22–35) the contradictory and superficial quality of Valla's reasoning when compared to the subtlety and acuteness of Boethius and the Scholastics, who followed Boethius on free will (pp. 18–25). Such criticism, however, does not meet Valla's arguments, as his major contention is that free will is mystically and paradoxically consistent with divine predestination and consequently is inaccessible to human reason, however acute and subtle (cf. below, pp. 175 ff.).

13. In general, it might be suggested that medieval thinkers and Humanists tended to give divine attributes to man and human attributes to God. The reformers, and, like them, Valla, tended to emphasize the difference between the divine and the human and to abandon the hierarchical modes of thought so prominent in Aquinas, e.g., or in Pico della Mirandola or Marsilio Ficino. The difference may be seen by comparing the following remark of Aquinas with Valla's argument below, pp. 175 ff.: "Now the last end of every creature is to attain God's likeness.....It would therefore be inconsistent with divine providence if anything were deprived of that whereby it attains to a likeness to God. But the voluntary agent attains to God's likeness in that he acts freely: for we have proved that there is free will in God. Therefore providence does not deprive the will of liberty" (*Summa contra Gentiles* iii. lxxiii).

14. Especially Book iii.

tian goal, and in *The Profession of the Religious*[15] he denied that institutionalized monastic virtue had superior validity and asserted that spontaneous good actions were higher. In *The Donation of Constantine*[16] he attacked the historical validity of the papal claims to temporal sovereignty. And in this present work on *Free Will* he attacked the Aristotelian and Scholastic reconciliation of free will and divine providence and asserted the irrationality of any attempt to understand the paradox that God by hardening or showing mercy allowed free will to men.[17]

It would be wrong to claim that for these reasons Valla thought of himself as a heretic[18] or even a reformer. In fact, he seemed to take some comfort out of his views by feeling more orthodox than the orthodox. He was also very persistent in his views and very determined. After having had sufficient difficulty with the accusations of heresy so freely used against him by his enemies to know the dangers, and after he had cleared himself sufficiently with the papal Curia to secure a position there, he was willing to preach a sermon before the Congregation of the Dominican Order in Rome supposedly *In Praise of St. Thomas Aquinas.*[19] Despite the title, he, nevertheless, reasserted his distaste for the Saint's use of dialectics and his preference especially for Paul and for the early Fathers, in particular Augustine, Ambrose, Gregory, and Jerome.[20] "This is a slip-

15. *De professione religiosorum*, ed. J. Vahlen (*Laurentii Vallae opuscula tria*, in "Sitzungsberichte der Kaiserlichen Akademie der Wissenschaften, Philos. und Hist. Kl.," Nos. 61 and 62 [Wien, 1869]).

16. *De falso credita et ementita Constantini donatione declamatio* (Leipzig, 1928); English trans. by Christopher B. Coleman (New Haven, 1922).

17. Cf. below, esp. pp. 175 ff.

18. Cf. his *Apologia adversus calumniatores quando super fide sua requisitus fuerat* (Basel, 1518). Poggio's accusation that Valla was condemned as a confessed heretic and imprisoned by the inquisitor of Naples seems to have been a libel prompted by his personal hostility to Valla (cf. Girolamo Mancini, *Vita di Lorenzo Valla* [Florence, 1891], pp. 186–88). In view of Valla's criticism of and lack of sympathy for the use of rationalism and philosophy in theology, it is not surprising that he had some trouble on the question of his orthodoxy.

19. *Encomium Sancti Thomae Aquinatis.*   20. *Ibid.*, pp. 394–95.

pery and dangerous place for me," he said there,[21] "not only on account of the saint whose praises we speak, but also because of the habitual view of many persons that no one can practice theology without the precepts of dialectics, metaphysics, and the other philosophers. What may I do about it? Reform, reverse, conceal what I believe? But the tongue would disagree with the heart."

In spite of the fact that Valla's views on these matters were well known in his own day and in the succeeding two centuries, the tendency persists to try to make of him another Renaissance prophet of man's newly grasped rational freedom. Reinhold Niebuhr in reference to Pomponazzi's *On Fate, Free Will and Predestination*[22] and Valla's *Free Will* (the dates of which he incidentally interchanges) remarks[23] that "the Renaissance concept of individuality, rooted in the idea of the greatness and the uniqueness of man, naturally implies his liberty. It was therefore one of the primary interests of Renaissance thinkers to prove that divine foreknowledge does not circumscribe human liberty of action or invalidate man's creative role in history."

There is, however, less justification for Ernst Cassirer to claim that what raised Valla's work on *Free Will* far above the level of medieval treatises was that "for the first time since the days of the ancients the problem of freedom was cited before a pure worldly forum, before the judgment chair of 'natural reason.' . . . . And still one traces above all in his work the power of the new critical-modern spirit which begins to become conscious of its might and its intellectual tools."[24]

Just how far these estimates correspond to Valla's actual views may be left to the readers of the present translation. That

21. *Ibid.*, p. 393.

22. Pietro Pomponazzi, *De fato, libero arbitrio, praedestinatione, et providentia Dei, libri v* (1525) (Basel, 1567).

23. Niebuhr, *op. cit.*, I, 64, and n. 6.

24. *Individuum und Kosmos in der Philosophie der Renaissance* ("Studien der Bibliothek Warburg," Vol. X [Leipzig and Berlin, 1927]), p. 82.

they clash with the early modern view, the following citations make clear. Erasmus, for example, in his first attack on Luther, the *Diatribe on Free Will*,[25] asserts: "From Apostolic times to this day there was no writer hitherto who totally denied the force of free will save Manichaeus and John Wyclif alone. For Lorenzo Valla, who almost seems to agree with them, has little authority among theologians of weight."[26] Erasmus later remarks on Valla's distinction between foreknowledge and divine will.[27]

Luther claimed Valla as a complete partisan of his own views in his reply on *The Enslaved Will*,[28] and in *The Table Talks*[29] he praises him on three occasions much as the following: "Lorenzo Valla is the best Italian that I have seen or discovered. He disputes ably on free will. He sought simplicity in piety and letters at the same time. Erasmus seeks him as much in letters as he contemns him in piety."

Calvin also refers to Valla's distinction between foreknowledge and will. "But Valla, a man otherwise not much versed in theology, appears to me to have discovered superior acuteness and judiciousness by showing that this controversy is unnecessary, because both life and death are acts of God's will rather than of his foreknowledge."[30]

A century and a half later, Leibniz, it is true, as Cassirer

25. *De libero arbitrio diatriba sive collatio*, in *Opera omnia* (Leyden, 1706), Vol. IX, cols. 1215–48.

26. *Ibid.*, col. 1218. Cf. also his *Hyperaspistes diatribae adversus servum arbitrium Martini Lutheri*, in *Opera omnia* Vol. X, cols. 1314–15.

27. *De libero arbitrio diatriba sive collatio, ibid.*, col. 1231. Cf. below, pp. 173 ff.

28. *De servo arbitrio*, ed. A. Freitag (*Werke*, WA, Band XVIII [1908]), pp. 600–787. Luther remarks (p. 640): "Indeed, for my part, one, Wyclif, and another, Lorenzo Valla, as well as Augustine, whom you (Erasmus) omit (*praeteris*), is my entire authority."

29. *Tischreden*, Band I (WA, 1912), No. 259; cf. also Band II (1913), No. 1470, and Band III (1919), No. 5729.

30. *Institutes of the Christian Religion* (6th ed.; Philadelphia, 1932), Book iii, chap. 23, sec. 6.

states,[31] called Valla, "no less a philosopher than a Humanist."[32] However, he points out that, while Valla succeeded in "reconciling liberty with foreknowledge, he does not dare to hope to reconcile it with providence,"[33] and Leibniz found it necessary to extend Valla's argument in such a way as to reach a quite different position.[34]

Among modern commentators on Valla, perhaps Luciano Barozzi[35] comes closest to a just estimate of this work. He rightly sees that Valla's attitude is nearer to modern positivist and statistical methods of proof than to rationalism,[36] and, like the positivist philosophers, Valla was concerned with the problem of human liberty,[37] which he solved by a psychological determinism.[38] Just as Valla anticipated Erasmus, Ulrich von Hutten, and Luther in his philological, critical, and exegetical work, "so also in this doctrine of free will he has many points of contact with what was expressed on this question by Luther and by Calvin."[39]

31. *Op. cit.,* p. 84.

32. *Essais de theodicée sur la bonté de Dieu, la liberté de l'homme, et l'origine du mal* (Amsterdam, 1710). References to *Opera philosophica .... omnia,* ed. J. E. Erdmann (Berlin, 1839–40), pars altera, pp. 468–629: *Essais sur la bonté de Dieu,* Vol. III, § 405.

33. *Ibid.,* § 365.

34. *Ibid.,* § § 413–17. Leibniz actually takes the position of rational freedom Cassirer sees in Valla, but not Valla.

35. *Lorenzo Valla,* printed with Remigio Sabbadini, in *Studi sul Panormita e sul Valla* ("R. Istituto di studi superiori ... in Firenze, Sezione di filosofia e filologia, Pubblicazioni," No. 25 [Florence, 1891]), esp. chap. vii: "La Dottrina del Libero Arbitrio di Lorenzo Valla e i moderni positivisti."

36. *Ibid.,* p. 218.

37. *Ibid.,* p. 220.

38. *Ibid.,* p. 219, referring to Valla's passage on the fierce wolf, etc., below, p. 173.

39. *Ibid.,* p. 220.

DIALOGUE ON FREE WILL[1]

I WOULD prefer, O Garsia,[2] most learned and best of bishops, that other Christians and, indeed, those who are called theologians would not depend so much on philosophy or devote so much energy to it, making it almost an equal and sister (I do not say patron) of theology. For it seems to me that they have a poor opinion of our religion if they think it needs the protection of philosophy. The followers of the Apostles, truly columns in the temple of God, whose works have now been extant many centuries, used this protection least of all. In fact, if we look carefully, the heresies of those times, which we understand were many and not insignificant, derived almost entirely from philosophic sources, so that philosophy not only profited our most sacred religion little but even violently injured it.[3] But they of whom I speak consider [philosophy] a tool for weeding out heresies, when actually it is a seedbed of heresy. They do not

1. [*Laurentii Vallae De libero arbitrio edidit Maria Anfossi* ("Opusculi filosofici: testi e documenti inediti o rari pubblicati da Giovanni Gentile," Vol. VI [Firenze, 1934]), was used for the following translation. Anfossi's edition, based on Codices Monacensis 3561, 78, and 17523 and on the editions of Louvain, 1483, and Basel, 1543, seemed clear and reliable. For the most part the variations, deriving from two families of texts (Clm 3561, 78 and Louvain: Clm 17523 and Basel), are in spelling, word order, and grammatical form; rarely is meaning involved. Valla's style is relatively direct, and, for a Humanist, not too intricate. There are very few places where his meaning is obscure. The aim in the translation was to secure a simple, clear, informal rendering of the Latin. Where this has succeeded, it is in keeping with the spirit of Valla's own efforts to treat serious matters on a familiar level.]

2. [Garzia Asnarez de Añon was bishop of Lerida from 1435 to 1449 (Girolamo Mancini, *Vita di Lorenzo Valla* [Florence, 1891], p. 111, and Gams, *Series episcoporum*, p. 44). As Valla was secretary to Alfonso in Gaeta from 1435 to 1443, and his contact with Garzia was through the Aragonese connection, the dialogue would seem to have been written between the latter dates.]

3. [An allusion to the early Fathers' war against classicism consistent with remarks in the Introduction.]

realize that the most pious antiquity, which lacked the arm of philosophy in combating heresies, and which often fought bitterly against philosophy itself—driving it forth like Tarquin into exile, never to allow its return—is thus accused of ignorance. Were those men ignorant and weaponless? And how did they reduce so much of the world to their authority? You who are fortified by such armament are not able to guard what they have left you as a patrimony, ah, lamentable and unworthy thing!

Why, therefore, do you not walk in the footsteps of your ancestors? If not their reason, certainly their authority and example ought to persuade that they should be followed instead of your entering upon some new path. I consider the physician who tries out new and experimental medicines on the sick rather than time-tested ones to be mean and contemptible. So is the sailor who prefers to hold an uncharted course to one upon which others safely sail their ships and cargoes. You have likewise reached such a degree of insolence that you believe no one can become a theologian unless he knows the precepts of philosophy and has learned them, most diligently and thoroughly, and you also suppose those of former times who either did not know or did not wish to know them to be stupid. O times! O customs! Formerly neither citizen nor stranger was allowed to speak in a foreign tongue in the Roman state, and only the dialect of that city could be used. However, you who could be called senators of the Christian commonwealth are better pleased to hear and employ pagan speech than ecclesiastical.

As time will be given to criticism of others elsewhere, in this present work we have wished to show that Boethius (for no other reason than that he loved philosophy excessively) argued incorrectly about free will in the fifth book of his *Consolation of Philosophy*.[4] We have replied to the first four books in our

4. [Anicii Manlii Severini Boethii, *Philosophiae consolationis libri v*, with the English translation of "I.T." (1609) revised by H. F. Stewart

work on *True Good*.[5] Now I will exert myself as far as possible in the discussion and solution of this problem, and, so that it will not seem purposeless after so many other writers have held forth on this subject, I shall add something of my own.[6] Although I was anxious myself to do this, I was further driven by an argument I recently held with Antonio Glarea,[7] a very well-read and keen man, long dear to me both because of his habits and because he is a countryman of San Lorenzo. I have reported the words of our argument in this little book, recounting them as if the affair were proceeding and not narrated, so that "I said" and "he said" does not need to be so frequently interpolated. I fail to see why Marcus Tullius, that man of immortal genius, claims to have done this in his book the *Laelius*,[8] for where an author does not report what he himself said, but what was reported by others, how, pray, can he interpose "I said"? Such is the case in the *Laelius* of Cicero, which contains a debate held by Laelius with two sons-in-law, Gaius Fannius and Quintus Scaevola. It is related by Scaevola, himself, with Cicero and some of his friends listening, and because of his youth he scarcely dares to argue and contend with Scaevola, who inspired a certain veneration either of age or of dignity.

But let us return to our subject. Antonio, therefore, had come to visit me at midday and finding me unoccupied and sitting

---

("Loeb Classical Library" [New York, 1926]). The fifth book of the *Consolations* also takes up in its first section the question of the relation of chance to providence.]

5. [*De voluptate ac vero bono libri tres* (Basel, 1519).]

6. [The "something of my own" apparently is Valla's distinction between the operation of divine foreknowledge and divine will below, pp. 169 ff.]

7. [Mancini (*op. cit.*, p. 111) thinks that Glarea was a native of Huesca in Aragon, one of the birthplaces claimed for San Lorenzo.]

8. [The *Laelius* or *De amicitia* of Cicero begins with a description of the setting and personages as Valla describes it, and continues with some remarks about the impressiveness of the dialogue form. Cf. the translation by W. Melmoth in the Everyman's edition, pp. 167–69.]

with some servants in the hall, made a few introductory remarks concerning the subject and then continued as follows:

Ant. To me the question of free will seems very difficult and extremely arduous; on it depends all human action, all right and wrong, all reward and punishment, in this life and in the future as well. It is not easy for us to say whether any question either needs more understanding or is less understood than this. I repeatedly inquire about it, by myself and with others, and have not so far been able to find any way out of its ambiguity. So much so that I am sometimes disturbed, as well as confused, within myself because of it. Nevertheless, I never shall weary of wondering about it, nor shall I despair of being able to perceive, although I know many were frustrated in the same hope. Therefore I should also like to hear your opinion on this question, because by thorough investigation and survey I may perhaps arrive at that which I seek, and also because I have known how sharp and exact you are in judgment.

Lor. As you say, this question is very difficult, and I scarcely know whether it has been understood by anyone. But that is no reason for you to be disturbed or confused, even if you never understand it. For what just complaint is there if you do not measure up to that which you see none has come up to? Even if others may have much that we have not, nevertheless we should bear it gladly and calmly. One may be endowed with nobility, another with high office, another with wealth, another with genius, another with eloquence, another with many of these, another with all. Nevertheless, no levelheaded person who is aware of his own efforts would think of mourning because he himself does not have those things. Besides, how much less ought he to mourn because he lacks the wings of a bird, which no one has? For if we were sorrowed by all we do not know, we would make life hard and bitter for ourselves. Would you like me to list for you how many things are unknown to us, not only divine and supernatural things such as this of which we are talking, but also the human ones which can enter our knowledge? In brief, there are many more things which are unknown. For this reason the Academics, though wrongly, nevertheless said nothing is fully known to us.[9]

Ant. To be sure, I admit that what you say is true, but somehow I am so impatient and greedy that I cannot control the impulse of my mind. For I hear what you have said about the wings of a bird, that I should not regret it if I don't have them; yet why should I forswear wings if I could possibly obtain them by Daedalus' example? And indeed how much finer wings do I long for? With them I might fly not from the prison of walls but from the prison of errors and fly away and arrive not in the fatherland, which breeds bodies as did Daedalus, but in the one where souls are born. Let us dismiss the Academics with their point of view, who, although they would put all in doubt, certainly could not doubt of their own doubts; and, although they argued nothing is known, nevertheless they did not lose their zeal for investigation. Furthermore, we know that later thinkers added much to what was previously found out; their precept and example ought to spur us to discovering other things also. Wherefore, I pray, do not wish to take this worry and burden from me, for, having removed the burden, you will at the same time have removed desire for inquiry, unless, perhaps, as I hope and would prefer, you will satisfy my greedy appetite.

Lor. Might I satisfy what no one else could? For what should I say about books? Either you agree with them, then nothing further is demanded; or you do not agree with them, and then there is nothing which I can put better. Yet you will see how pious and tolerable it is for you to declare war on all books, including the wisest, and not to side with any of them.

Ant. Of course I know it seems intolerable and almost a sacri-

9. [This counsel of humility and the succeeding passage where Antonio expresses a wish for wings of knowledge and praises the stimulating effects of the pursuit of the unknown symbolize the new and old attitudes. Valla, however, in contrast to Pico on the *Dignity of Man* (cf. pp. 176 ff.) seems definitely on the conservative side both in his own statement and in the disbelief of Antonio in any possible solution to his question.]

lege not to agree with books already tested by custom, but you also mark that in many things it is usual for them to differ among themselves and to support divergent views and that there are very few whose authority is too great for their sayings to be questioned. Indeed, on other questions I do not completely reject writers, thinking now this one, now that one, speaks with greater probability. Yet in this question on which I am about to speak with you, with your leave and that of others, I agree absolutely with no one. For what might I say of the others when Boethius, to whom all give the palm in explaining this question, is himself unable to complete what he undertakes and at certain points takes refuge in the imaginary and fictitious? For he says God, through an intelligence which is beyond reason, both knows all things for eternity and holds all things present.[10] But can I, who am rational and know nothing outside of time, aspire to the knowledge of intelligence and eternity? I suspect Boethius himself did not understand them, even if the things he said were true, which I do not believe. For he should not be thought to speak truly whose speech not he himself or anyone else understands. And so although he began this argument correctly, he did not correctly conclude it. If you agree with me on this, I shall rejoice in my own opinion; if not, because of your humanity [i.e., eloquence and culture of language], you will not refuse

---

10. [Boethius, *op. cit.* "Wherefore, since every judgment comprehendeth those things which are subject unto it, according to its own nature, and God hath always an everlasting and present state, His knowledge also surpassing all notions of time, remaineth in the simplicity of His presence, and comprehending the infinite spaces of that which is past and to come, considereth all things in his simple knowledge as though they were now in doing. So that, if thou will weigh His foreknowledge with which He discerneth all things, thou wilt more rightly esteem it to be the knowledge of a never fading instant than a foreknowledge as of a thing to come" (pp. 403 and 405). "But God beholdeth those future things which proceed from free will present. These things, therefore, being referred to the divine sight are necessary by the condition of the divine knowledge, and considered by themselves, they lose not absolute freedom of their own nature. Wherefore doubtless all those things come to pass which God foreknoweth shall come, but some of them proceed from free will ...." (p. 407). Cf. also pp. 396 and 397, ll. 46–56.]

to express more lucidly what he said obscurely; in either case, you will reveal your opinion.

Lor. See what a fair demand you make, ordering me, either by damning or amending, to insult Boethius!

Ant. But do you call it an insult to have a true opinion about another or to interpret his obscure statements more clearly?

Lor. Well, it is unpleasant to do this to great men.

Ant. It is certainly more unpleasant not to show the way to the erring and to him who asks you to show it.

Lor. What if I do not know the way?

Ant. To say "I do not know the way" is to have no desire to show the way; therefore, do not refuse to reveal your opinion.

Lor. What if I should say that I agree with you about Boethius, that I do not understand him, and that I have nothing else by which I might explain this question?

Ant. If you say this truly, I am not such a fool that I would ask for more than you are able to give; but beware lest you discharge poorly the office of friendship and show yourself begrudging and false to me.

Lor. What do you ask me to explain to you?

Ant. Whether the foreknowledge of God stands in the way of free will and whether Boethius has correctly argued this question.

Lor. I shall attend to Boethius later; but if I satisfy you in this matter, I want you to make a promise.

Ant. What sort of a promise?

Lor. That if I serve you splendidly in this luncheon, you will not want to be entertained again for dinner.

Ant. What do you mean as lunch for me and what as dinner, for I do not understand?

Lor. That contented after discussing this one question, you will not ask for another afterward.

Ant. You say another? As if this one will not be sufficient and more! I freely promise that I will ask no dinner from you.

Lor. Go ahead then and get into the very heart of the question.

Ant. You advise well. If God foresees the future, it cannot happen otherwise than He foresaw. For example, if He sees that Judas will be a traitor, it is impossible for him not to become a traitor, that is, it is necessary for Judas to betray, unless—which should be far from us—we assume God to lack providence. Since He has providence, one must undoubtedly believe that mankind does not have free will in its own power; and I do not speak particularly of evil men, for as it is necessary for these to do evil, so conversely it is necessary for the good to do good,[11] provided those are still to be called good or evil who lack will or that their actions are to be considered right or wrong which are necessary and forced. And what now follows you yourself see: for God either to praise this one for justice or accuse that of injustice and to reward the one and punish the other, to speak freely, seems to be the opposite of justice, since the actions of men follow by necessity the foreknowledge of God.[12] We should therefore abandon religion, piety, sanctity, ceremonies, sacrifices; we may expect nothing from Him, employ no prayers, not call upon his mercy at all, neglect to improve our mind, and, finally, do nothing except what pleases us, since our justice or injustice is foreknown by God. Consequently, it seems that either He does not foresee the future if we are endowed with will or He is not just if we lack free will. There you have what makes me inclined to doubt in this matter.

11. [The moral (or psychological) determinism raised by Antonio here as an obstacle to foreknowledge may be compared with the speech Lorenzo attributes to Apollo when he tells Sextus that his evil nature, created by Jupiter, will make him sin. Cf. p. 173.]

12. [Cf. Boethius, *op. cit.*, p. 379: "For in vain are rewards and punishments proposed to good and evil, which no free and voluntary motion of their minds hath deserved. And that will seem most unjust which now is judged most just, that either the wicked should be punished or the good rewarded, since their own will leadeth them to neither, but they are compelled by the certain necessity of that which is to come," etc.]

Lor. You have indeed not only pushed into the middle of the question but have even more widely extended it. You say God foresaw that Judas would be a traitor, but did He on that account induce him to betrayal? I do not see that, for, although God may foreknow some future act to be done by man, this act is not done by necessity because he may do it willingly. Moreover, what is voluntary cannot be necessary.

Ant. Do not expect me to give in to you so easily or to flee without sweat and blood.

Lor. Good luck to you; let us contend closely in hand-to-hand and foot-to-foot conflict. Let the decision be by sword, not spear.

Ant. You say Judas acted voluntarily and on that account not by necessity. Indeed, it would be most shameless to deny that he did it voluntarily. What do I say to that? Certainly this act of will was necessary since God foreknew it; moreover, since it was foreknown by Him, it was necessary for Judas to will and do it lest he should make the foreknowledge in any way false.

Lor. Still I do not see why the necessity for our volitions and actions should derive from God's foreknowledge. For, if foreknowing something *will be* makes it come about, surely knowing something *is* just as easily makes the same thing *be*. Certainly, if I know your genius, you would not say that something *is* because you *know* it is. For example, you know it is now day; because you know it is, is it on that account also day? Or, conversely, because it is day, do you for that reason know it is day?[13]

Ant. Indeed, continue.

Lor. The same reasoning applies to the past. I know it was night eight hours ago, but my knowledge does not make that it was night; rather I know it was night because it was night. Again, that I may come closer to the point, I know in advance that after eight hours it will be night; and will it be on that account? Not at all, but because it will be night, for that reason I

13. [Cf. *ibid.*, pp. 387 and 405, where a parallel argument is employed.]

foreknew it; now if the foreknowledge of man is not the cause of something occurring, neither is the foreknowledge of God.

Ant. Believe me, that comparison deceives us; it is one thing to know the present and past, another to know the future. For when I know something is, it cannot be changed, as that day, which now is, cannot be made not to be. Also the past does not differ from the present, for we did not notice the day when it was past but while it was occurring as the present; I learned it was night not then when it *had passed* but when it was. And so for these times I concede that something *was*, or *is*, not because I know it but that I know it because it *is* or *was*. But a different reasoning applies to the future because it is subject to change. It cannot be known for certain because it is uncertain. And, in order that we may not defraud God of foreknowledge, we must admit that the future is certain and on that account necessary; this is what deprives us of free will. Nor can you say what you said just now that the future is not preordained merely because God foresees it but that God foresees it because the future is preordained; you thus wound God by implying that it is necessary for him to foreknow the future.

Lor. You have come well armed and weaponed for the fight, but let us see who is deceived, you or I. First, however, I would meet this latter point where you say that, if God foresees the future because it is to be, He labors under the necessity to foresee the future. Indeed this should not be attributed to necessity but to nature, to will, to power, unless it is an attribute of weakness perchance that God cannot sin, cannot die, cannot give up His wisdom rather than an attribute of power and of divinity. Thus, when we said He is unable to escape foresight, which is a form of wisdom, we inflicted no wound on Him but did Him honor. So I shall not be afraid to say that God is unable to escape foreseeing what is to be. I come now to your first point: that the present and the past are unalterable and therefore knowable; that the future is alterable and therefore not capable of being foreknown. I ask if it can be changed that at eight hours from now night will arrive, that after summer there will be autumn, after autumn winter, after winter spring, after spring summer?

Ant. Those are natural phenomena always running the same course; I speak, however, of matters of the will.

Lor. What do you say of chance things? Can they be foreseen by God without necessity being imputed to them? Perchance today it may rain or I may find a treasure, would you concede this could be foreknown without any necessity?[14]

Ant. Why should I not concede it? Do you believe I think so ill of God?

Lor. Make sure that you do not think ill when you say you think well. For if you concede in this case, why should you doubt in matters of the will, for both classes of events can happen in two different ways?

Ant. The matter is not that way. For these chance things follow a certain nature of their own, and for this reason doctors, sailors, and farmers are accustomed to foresee much, since they reckon consequences out of antecedents, which cannot happen in affairs of the will.[15] Predict which foot I will move first, and, whichever you have said, you will lie, since I shall move the other.

Lor. I ask you, who was ever found so clever as this Glarea? He thinks he can impose on God like the man in Aesop who consulted Apollo whether the sparrow he held under his coat was dead for the sake of deceiving him. For you have not told

14. [Boethius (pp. 367 and 369, citing Aristotle *Physics* ii. 4) makes use of the same example of a buried treasure to prove that providence and chance events are compatible.]

15. [Valla has thus classified events into "natural phenomena always running the same course," "chance things" which "follow a certain nature of their own," and "affairs of the will." Since he later argues that human action follows man's individual nature (p. 173), he would seem to be a natural determinist, leaving freedom as a gift of grace. This is what Barozzi, *Lorenzo Valla* .... (Florence, 1891), meant when he called Valla a positivist.]

me to predict, but God. Indeed, I have not the ability to predict whether there will be a good vintage, such as you ascribe to farmers. But by saying and also believing that God does not know which foot you will move first, you involve yourself in great sin.

Ant. Do you think I affirm something rather than raise the question for the sake of the argument? Again you seem to seek excuses by your speech and, giving ground, decline to fight.

Lor. As if I fought for the sake of victory rather than truth! Witness how I am driven from my ground; do you grant that God now knows your will even better than you yourself do?

Ant. I indeed grant it.

Lor. It is also necessary that you grant that you will do nothing other than the will decides.

Ant. Of course.

Lor. How then can He not know the action if He knows the will which is the source of the action?

Ant. Not at all, for I myself do not know what I shall do even though I know what I have in my will. For I do not will to move this foot or that foot, in any case, but the other than He will have announced. And so, if you compare me with God, just as I do not know what I will do, so He does not know.

Lor. What difficulty is there in meeting this sophism of yours? He knows that you are prepared to reply otherwise than He will say and that you will move the left first if the right is named by Him; whichever one He should say therefore, it is certain to Him what will happen.

Ant. Yet which of the two will He say?

Lor. Do you speak of God? Let me know your will and I will announce what will happen.

Ant. Go ahead, you try to know my will.

Lor. You will move the right one first.

Ant. Behold, the left one.

Lor. How have you shown my foreknowledge to be false, since I knew you would move the left one?

[166]

Ant. But why did you say other than you thought?

Lor. In order to deceive you by your own arts and to deceive the man willing to deceive.

Ant. But God Himself would not lie nor deceive in replying, nor did you do rightly in replying for Another as He would not reply.

Lor. Did you not tell me to "predict"? Therefore, I should not speak for God but for myself whom you asked.

Ant. How changeable you are. A little while ago you were saying I told God to "predict," not you; now on the contrary you say the opposite. Let God reply which foot I will move first.

Lor. How ridiculous, as if He would answer you!

Ant. What? Can He not indeed reply truly if He wishes?

Lor. Rather He can lie who is the Truth itself.

Ant. What would He reply then?

Lor. Certainly what you will do, but, you not hearing, He might say to me, He might say to one of those other people, He might say it to many; and, when He has done that, do you not think He will truly have predicted?[16]

Ant. Yea, indeed, He will have truly predicted, but what would you think if He predicted it to me?

Lor. Believe me, you who thus lie in wait to deceive God, if you should hear or certainly know what He said you would do, either out of love or out of fear you would hasten to do what you knew was predicted by Him. But let us skip this which has nothing to do with foreknowledge. For it is one thing to foreknow and another to predict the future. Say whatever you have in mind about foreknowledge, but leave prediction out of it.

Ant. So be it, for the things that I have said were spoken not

16. [Boethius, *op. cit.*, p. 409, also uses this argument: "But thou wilt say, 'If it is in my power to change my purpose, shall I frustrate providence if I chance to alter things which she foreknoweth?' I answer that thou mayest indeed change thy purpose, but because the truth of providence, being present, seeth that thou canst do so or not, and what thou purposest anew, thou canst not avoid the divine foreknowledge. . . . ."

so much for me as against you. I return from this digression to where I said it was necessary for Judas to betray, unless we entirely annul providence, because God foresaw it would be thus. So if it was possible for something to happen otherwise than it was foreseen, providence is destroyed; but if it is impossible, free will is destroyed, a thing no less unworthy to God than if we should cancel His providence. I, in what concerns me, would prefer Him to be less wise rather than less good. The latter would injure mankind; the other would not.

Lor. I praise your modesty and wisdom. When you are not able to win, you do not fight on stubbornly but give in and apply yourself to another defense, which seems to be the argument of what you set forth a while back. In reply to this argument, I deny that foreknowledge can be deceived as the consequence of the possibility that something might turn out otherwise than as it has been foreseen. For what prevents it from also being true that something can turn out otherwise than it will immediately happen? Something that can happen and something that will happen are very different. I can be a husband, I can be a soldier or a priest, but will I right away? Not at all. Though I can do otherwise than will happen, nevertheless I shall not do otherwise; and it was in Judas' power not to sin even though it was foreseen that he would, but he preferred to sin, which it was foreseen would happen. Thus foreknowledge is valid and free will abides. This will make a choice between two alternatives, for to do both is not possible, and He foreknows by His own light which will be chosen.

Ant. Here I have you. Are you unaware of the philosophical rule that whatever is possible ought to be conceded as if it were? It is possible for something to happen otherwise than it is foreknown; it may be granted it will happen that way, through which it is now manifest that foreknowledge is deceived since it happens otherwise than foreknowledge had believed.

Lor. Are you using formulas of philosophers on me? Indeed, as if I would not dare to contradict them! Certainly I think that precept you mention, whose ever it is, most absurd, for I can concede it to be possible to move the right foot first, and we may concede it will be so, and I can also concede it possible for me to move the left foot first, and we may concede this will be as well; I will move therefore both the left before the right and the right before the left, and through your concession of the possible I arrive at the impossible. Therefore, know that it is not to be conceded that whatever is possible will likewise happen. It is possible for you to do otherwise than God foreknows, nevertheless you will not do otherwise, nor will you therefore deceive Him.

Ant. I will not object further, nor, since I smashed all my weapons, will I fight with tooth and nail as is said; but, if there is any other point through which you can explain it to me more amply and plainly persuade, I wish to hear it.[17]

Lor. You covet the praise of wisdom and modesty again, since you are your true self. And so I will do as you ask because I was doing it anyway of my own will. For what has been said so far is not what I had decided to say but what need of defense itself demanded. Now attend to what persuades me and perhaps it will even persuade you that foreknowledge is no impediment to free will. However, would you prefer me to touch on this subject briefly or to explain it more clearly at greater length?

Ant. It always seems to me, indeed, that those who speak lucidly speak most briefly, while those who speak obscurely, though in the fewest words, are always more lengthy. Besides, fulness of expression has itself a certain appropriateness and aptness for persuasion. Wherefore, since I asked you from the start that this matter be more lucidly stated by you, you should not doubt my wishes; neverthelesss, do whatever is more agree-

17. [Valla breaks off at this point from where he was essentially reworking Boethius' arguments to begin the "something of my own" he mentioned above, p. 157.]

able to you. For I would never put my judgment ahead of yours.

Lor. Indeed, it is of importance to me to follow your wish, and whatever you think more convenient I do also. Apollo, who was so greatly celebrated among the Greeks, either through his own nature or by concession of the other gods, had foresight and knowledge of all future things, not only those which pertained to men but to the gods as well; thus, if we may believe the tradition, and nothing prevents our accepting it just for the moment, Apollo rendered true and certain prophecies about those consulting him. Sextus Tarquinius consulted him as to what would happen to himself. We may pretend that he replied, as was customary, in verse as follows:

> An exile and a pauper you will fall,
> Killed by the angry city.

To this Sextus: "What are you saying, Apollo? Have I deserved thus of you that you announce me a fate so cruel, that you assign me such a sad condition of death? Repeal your response, I implore you, predict happier things; you should be better disposed toward me who so royally endowed you." In reply Apollo: "Your gifts, O youth, certainly are agreeable and acceptable to me; in return for which I have rendered a miserable and sad prophecy, I wish it were happier, but it is not in my power to do this. I know the fates, I do not decide them; I am able to announce Fortune, not change her; I am the index of destinies, not the arbiter; I would reveal better things if better things awaited. Certainly this is not my fault who cannot prevent even my own misfortune that I foresee. Accuse Jupiter, if you will, accuse the fates, accuse Fortune whence the course of events descends. The power and decision over the fates are seated with them; with me, mere foreknowledge and prediction. You earnestly besought an oracle; I gave it. You inquired after the truth; I was unable to tell a lie. You have come to my temple from a far-distant region, and I ought not to send you away without a reply. Two things are most alien to me: false-hood and silence." Could Sextus justly reply to this speech: "Yea, indeed, it is your fault, Apollo, who foresee my fate with your wisdom, for, unless you had foreseen it, this would not be about to happen to me"?

Ant. Not only would he speak unjustly but he should never reply thus.

Lor. How then?

Ant. Why do you not say?

Lor. Should he not reply in this way: "Indeed, I give thanks to you, holy Apollo, who have neither deceived me with false-hood nor spurned me in silence. But this also I ask you to tell me: Why is Jupiter so unjust, so cruel, to me that he should assign such a sad fate to me, an undeserving, innocent wor-shiper of the gods"?

Ant. Certainly I would reply in this way if I were Sextus, but what did Apollo reply to him?

Lor. "You call yourself undeserving and innocent, Sextus? You may be sure that the crimes that you will commit, the adulteries, betrayals, perjuries, the almost hereditary arrogance are to blame." Would Sextus then reply this way: "The fault for my crimes must rather be assigned to you, for it is necessary for me, who you foreknow will sin, to sin"?

Ant. Sextus would be mad as well as unjust if he replied in that way.

Lor. Do you have anything that you might say on his behalf?

Ant. Absolutely nothing.

Lor. If therefore Sextus had nothing which could be argued against the foreknowledge of Apollo, certainly Judas had noth-ing either which might accuse the foreknowledge of God. And, if that is so, certainly the question by which you said you were confused and disturbed is answered.

Ant. It is indeed answered and, what I scarcely dared to hope, fully solved, for the sake of which I both give you thanks and have, I would say, an almost immortal gift. What Boethius was unable to show me you have shown.[18]

Lor. And now I shall try to say something about him because I know you expect it and I promised to do it.[19]

Ant. What are you saying about Boethius? It will be agreeable and pleasant to me.

Lor. We may follow the line of the fable we started. You think Sextus had nothing to reply to Apollo; I ask you what would you say to a king who refused to offer an office or position to you because he says you would commit a capital offense in that function.

Ant. "I would swear to you, King, by your most strong and faithful right hand that I will commit no crime in this magistracy."

Lor. Likewise perhaps Sextus would say to Apollo, "I swear to you, Apollo, that I will not commit what you say."

Ant. What does Apollo answer?

Lor. Certainly not in the way the king would, for the king has not discovered what the future is, as God has. Apollo therefore might say: "Am I a liar, Sextus? Do I not know what the future is? Do I speak for the sake of warning you, or do I render a prophecy? I say to you again, you will be an adulterer, you will be a traitor, you will be a perjurer, you will be arrogant and evil."

Ant. A worthy speech by Apollo! What was Sextus able to muster against it?

Lor. Does it not occur to you what he could argue in his own defense? Is he with a meek mind to suffer himself to be condemned?

Ant. Why not, if he is guilty?

Lor. He is not guilty but is predicted to be so in the future.

18. [Thus foreknowledge is relieved of responsibility for human actions, but, in so doing, Valla has conceived of human nature as acting according to predetermined conditioning rather than as possessed of free will. The succeeding passage will make this even more clear.]

19. [What follows seems to have little relation to Boethius.]

Indeed, I believe that if Apollo announced this to you, you would flee to prayer, and pray not to Apollo but to Jupiter that he would give you a better mind and change the fates.

Ant. That I would do, but I would be making Apollo a liar.

Lor. You speak rightly, because if Sextus cannot make him a liar, he employs prayers in vain. What should he do? Would he not be offended, angered, burst forth in complaints? "Thus, Apollo, am I unable to restrain myself from offenses, am I unable to accept virtue, do I not avail to reform the mind from wickedness, am I not endowed with free will?"

Ant. Sextus speaks bravely and truly and justly. What does the god reply?

Lor. "That is the way things are, Sextus. Jupiter as he created the wolf fierce, the hare timid, the lion brave, the ass stupid, the dog savage, the sheep mild, so he fashioned some men hard of heart, others soft, he generated one given to evil, the other to virtue, and, further, he gave a capacity for reform to one and made another incorrigible. To you, indeed, he assigned an evil soul with no resource for reform. And so both you, for your inborn character, will do evil, and Jupiter, on account of your actions and their evil effects, will punish sternly, and thus he has sworn by the Stygian swamp it will be."[20]

20. [To Setus' question, "Am I not endowed with free will?" Valla has Apollo reply, "You, for your inborn character, will do evil." It is interesting to compare this treatment with Leibniz' extension of the fable, *Opera*, ed. Erdmann, ¶¶ 413–17. "This dialogue of Valla is fine," he said, "although there is something to revise here and there. The principal fault, however, is that . . . . he seems to condemn providence under the name of Jupiter whom he makes almost the author of sin." Leibniz goes on to say, contrary to what Valla left possible, that Sextus had the choice of reforming or going his way and chose the latter. Thereafter continuing the fable he shows all of the possible futures open to Sextus through the additional figure of Pallas. This point of view is more like the doctrine of multiple possibility and rational freedom that is usually expected in the Humanists and is found in the case of Pico, certainly. But it is very different from that of Valla, who views man as a much less flexible creature. Leibniz goes on (¶ 417): "It seems to me that this continuation of the fiction can clear up the difficulty which Valla did not at all want to touch on. If Apollo has well represented the divine knowledge of vision (which concerns existences), I hope Pallas would not badly make

Ant. At the same time that Apollo neatly excuses himself, he accuses Jupiter the more, for I am more favorable to Sextus than Jupiter. And so he might best protest justly as follows: "And why is it my crime rather than Jupiter's? When I am not allowed to do anything except evil, why does Jupiter condemn me for his own crime? Why does he punish me without guilt? Whatever I do, I do not do it by free will but of necessity. Am I able to oppose his will and power?"

Lor. This is what I wished to say for my proof. For this is the point of my fable, that, although the wisdom of God cannot be separated from His power and will, I may by this device of Apollo and Jupiter separate them. What cannot be achieved with one god may be achieved with two, each having his own proper nature—the one for creating the character of men, the other for knowing—that it may appear that providence is not the cause of necessity but that all this whatever it is must be referred to the will of God.

Ant. See, you have thrown me back into the same pit whence you dug me; this doubt is like that which I set forth about Judas. There necessity was ascribed to the foreknowledge of God, here to the will; what difference is it how you annul free will? That it is destroyed by foreknowledge, you indeed deny, but you say it is by divine will, by which the question goes back to the same place.

Lor. Do I say that free will is annulled by the will of God?

Ant. Is it not implied unless you solve the ambiguity?

Lor. Pray who will solve it for you?

Ant. Indeed I will not let you go until you solve it.

Lor. But that is to violate the agreement, and not content with luncheon you demand dinner also.

Ant. Is it thus you have defrauded me and coerced me through a deceitful promise? Promises in which deceit enters do

---

the personage called the knowledge of simple intelligence (which concerns all possibilities) where it is ultimately necessary to search for the origin of things."]

not stand, nor do I think I have received luncheon from you if I am forced to vomit up whatever I have eaten, or, to speak more lightly, you send me away no less hungry than you received me.

Lor. Believe me, I didn't want to make you promise in such a way that I would cheat you, for what advantage would there have been to me, since I not even have been allowed to give you luncheon? Since you received it willingly and since you gave me thanks for it, you are ungrateful if you say you were forced by me to vomit it or that I send you away as hungry as you came. That is asking for dinner, not luncheon, and wanting to find fault with luncheon and to demand that I spread before you ambrosia and nectar, the food of the gods, not men. I have put my fish and fowl from my preserves and wine from a suburban hill before you. You should demand ambrosia and nectar from Apollo and Jupiter themselves.

Ant. Are not ambrosia and what you call nectar poetic and fabulous things? Let us leave this emptiness to the empty and fictitious gods, Jupiter and Apollo. You have given luncheon from these preserves and cellars; I ask dinner from the same.

Lor. Do you think I am so rude that I would send away a friend coming to me for dinner? But since I saw how this question was likely to end, I consulted my own interests back there and compelled you to promise that afterward you would not exact from me anything besides the one thing that was asked. Therefore, I proceed with you not so much from right as from equity. Perhaps you will obtain this dinner from others which, if friendship can be trusted, is not entirely in my possession.

Ant. I will give you no further trouble lest I seem ungrateful to a benefactor and distrustful of a friend; but, still, from whom do you suggest I seek this out?

Lor. If I were able, I would not send you away for dinner, but I would go there for dinner together with you.

Ant. Do you suppose no one has these divine foods, as you call them?

Lor. Why should I not think so.[21] Have you not read the words of Paul about the two children of Rebecca and Isaac? There he said:

> For the children being not yet born, neither having done any good or evil, that the purpose of God according to election might stand, not of works, but of him that calleth; it was said unto her, The elder shall serve the younger. As it is written, Jacob have I loved, but Esau have I hated. What shall we say then? Is there unrighteousness with God? God forbid. For he saith to Moses, I will have mercy on whom I will have mercy, and I will have compassion on whom I will have compassion. So then it is not of him that willeth, nor of him that runneth, but of God that showeth mercy. For the scripture saith unto Pharaoh, Even for this same purpose have I raised thee up, that I might show my power in thee, and that my name might be declared throughout all the earth. Therefore hath he mercy on whom he will have mercy, and whom he will he hardeneth. Thou wilt say then unto me, Why doth he yet find fault? For who hath resisted his will? Nay but, O man, who art thou that repliest against God? Shall the thing formed say to him that formed it, Why hast thou made me thus? Hath not the potter power over the clay, of the same lump to make one vessel unto honor, and another unto dishonor? [Rom. 9:11–21 (King James Version)].

And a little later, as if the excessive splendor of the wisdom of God darkened his eyes, he proclaimed (Rom. 11:33): "O the depth of the riches both of the wisdom and knowledge of God! how unsearchable are his judgments, and his ways past finding out!" For if that vessel of election who, snatched up even to the third heaven, heard the secret words which man is not permitted to speak, nevertheless was unable to say or even to perceive them, who at length would hope that he could search out and comprehend? Carefully notice, however, free will is not said to be impeded in the same way by the will of God as by foreknowledge, for the will[22] has an antecedent cause which is seated in the wisdom of God. Indeed the most worthy reason

---

21. [In the preceding passage, and the succeeding citations from Paul, Valla seems to be stating his position as essentially agnostic. He thus limits his conception of human powers even further.]

22. [It is unclear whether this is divine or human will, but it seems to make better sense as divine.]

may be adduced as to why He hardens this one and shows mercy to that, namely, that He is most wise and good. For it is impious to believe otherwise than that, being absolutely good, He does rightly. Yet, in foreknowledge there is no antecedent or any cause at all of justice and goodness. We do not ask: Why has He foreknown this or why does He wish it? We rather ask this only: How is God good if He takes away free will? For He would take it away if it were not possible for something to happen otherwise than is foreknown. Now, indeed, He brings no necessity, and His hardening one and showing another mercy does not deprive us of free will, since He does this most wisely and in full holiness.[23] He has placed the hidden reason of this cause in a certain secret sort of treasury. I will not hide the fact that certain men have dared to inquire into this purpose, saying, those who are hardened and reprobated are justly hardened and reprobated, for we come out of that lump polluted and converted into clay by the guilt of the first parent. Now, if I may cut across much and reply by one argument, why was Adam, made of unpolluted matter as he was, himself hardened for sin and why did he make the universal lump of his offspring of clay?

What was done to the angels was similar. Some of them were hardened, some obtained mercy, although all were of the same substance, from the same unpolluted lump which up to this point, if I may say so boldly, remained in the nature of a substance and in the quality of a material that is, so to speak, golden. Neither were some changed into better matter through election nor others into worse by reprobation. Some, as if chosen vessels for ministering to the divine table, received grace; others indeed could be thought vessels hidden from sight because, more des-

23. [This would seem to leave it that man does have free will, but not only can God's wisdom not be questioned, but free will itself is left in an ambiguous situation if we are either hardened and, therefore, unable not to sin, or shown mercy and thereby enabled to do good. The latter state would seem to be the nearest to freedom, which becomes in this way not a natural possession of man but a gift of grace—a position extremely close to Luther.]

picable than if they became clay, they caught up every collection of obscenity! For that reason their damnation is more to be mourned than men's. For gold, from which angels are made, receives more outrage than silver, from which men are made, if filled with filth. Therefore the silver, or if you prefer to call it clay, matter in Adam is not changed but remained the same as it was before. And so, just as it was with him, so is it with us. Does not Paul say that from the same lump of clay one vessel was made unto honor and the other indeed unto dishonor? Nor ought it to be said that the vessels of honor were made of polluted matter. We are, therefore, vessels of silver, I would say, rather than of clay, and we have long been vessels of dishonor, damnation, and of death rather than hardness. For God poured into us, on account of the disobedience of the first parent in whom all of us have sinned, the penalty of death, not the guilt which comes from hardening. Paul says the same (Rom. 5:14): "Nevertheless death reigned from Adam to Moses, even over them that had not sinned after the similitude of Adam's transgression."

If we really had been hardened because of Adam's sin, then freed by the grace of Christ, we would no longer be hardened, which is not the case, for many of us are hardened. Therefore, all who are baptized in the death of Christ are freed from that original sin and from that death. Baptism not having been sufficient, some of them receive mercy; and others are hardened just as Adam and the angels were hardened. Let him who wishes reply why He hardens one and shows mercy to the other, and I will confess he is an angel rather than a man, if this is even known to angels, which I do not believe, since it was not known to Paul (see how much I attribute to him). If the angels, therefore, who always see the face of God, do not know this, how great is our boldness to wish to know it at all? But before we conclude we should say something of Boethius.

Ant. You have opportunely mentioned him. In truth I was concerned about the man who hoped that he knew this matter himself and could teach others, not along the same road as Paul, yet tending in the same direction.

Lor. He not only trusted himself more than ought to be, and attempted things too great for his capacities, but he does not pursue the same road or complete the path entered upon.

Ant. Why is that?

Lor. Listen, for this is what I wished to say: Paul first said, "So then it is not of him that willeth, nor of [man] that runneth, but of God that showeth mercy." But Boethius in his whole argument concludes, not actually in words but in substance: It is not of God who forseeth, but of man who willeth and runneth.[24] Thence it is not enough to dispute about the providence of God unless the will (of God) is also discussed. This in short can be proved from your behavior. Not content with the explanation of the first question, you thought also to ask about the next.

Ant. If I consider your arguments deeply, you have expressed a most true opinion of Boethius from which not even he should appeal.

Lor. And what cause was there for a Christian man to depart from Paul and never remember him when dealing with the same matter he had dealt with? What is more, in the entire work of *Consolation* nothing at all is found about our religion—none of the precepts leading to a blessed life, no mention and hardly a hint of Christ.

Ant. I believe it was because he was too ardent an admirer of philosophy.

Lor. You are of a good opinion, or rather of understanding, for I also think that no such ardent admirer of philosophy can please God. And therefore Boethius, sailing north instead of south, did not bring the fleet laden with wine into the port of the fatherland but dashed it on barbarian coasts and on foreign shores.

24. [A clear enough repudiation of the doctrine of human independence.]

Ant. You prove all that you say.

Lor. Let us therefore come to the conclusion and make some sort of finish, since I judge I have satisfied you on the foreknowledge, the will of God, and Boethius. I say what remains for the sake of exhortation rather than teaching, although, as you have a well-constituted soul, you do not need exhortation.

Ant. Indeed, go ahead. Exhortation is always fitting and useful, and I am accustomed to accept it gladly both from others and the most intimate and serious friends, such as I have always regarded you.

Lor. Indeed, I shall exhort not you alone but the others present here and myself among the first. I said that the cause of the divine will which hardens one and shows mercy to another is known neither to men nor to angels. If because of ignorance on this matter and on many others the angels do not lose their love of God, do not retreat from their service, and do not consider their own blessedness diminished on that account, should we for this same reason depart from faith, hope, and charity and desert as if from a commander? And if we have faith in wise men, even without reason, because of authority, should we not have faith in Christ who is the Power and Wisdom of God? He says He wishes to save all and that He does not wish the death of the sinner but rather that he be converted and live. And if we loan money to good men without a surety, should we require a guarantee from Christ in Whom no fraud may be found? And if we intrust our life to friends, should we not dare to intrust it to Christ, who for our salvation took on both the life of the flesh and the death of the cross? We do not know the cause of this matter; of what consequence is it? We stand by faith not by the probability of reason. Does knowledge do much for the corroboration of faith? Humility does more. The Apostle says (Rom. 12:16): "Mind not high (wise) things, but condescend to men of low estate." Is the foreknowledge of divine things useful? Charity is more useful. For the Apostle likewise says (I Cor. 8:1): "Knowledge puffeth us, but charity edifieth." And lest you think so much was said about the knowledge of human affairs, he says (II Cor. 12:7): "And lest I should be exalted above measure through the abundance of the revelations, there was given to me a thorn in the flesh." Let us not wish to know the height, but let us fear lest we become like the philosophers who, calling themselves wise, are made foolish; who, lest they should appear ignorant of anything, disputed about everything. Raising their own mouths to heaven, and wishing to scale it—I do not say tear it apart—like proud and rash giants, they were hurled to earth by the strong forearm of God and buried in Hell as Typhoeus in Sicily. Among the chief of these was Aristotle, in whom the best and greatest God revealed and at length damned the arrogance and boldness of not only this same Aristotle but of the other philosophers as well. For when he (Aristotle) could not discover the nature of Euripus, throwing himself into its depth, he was swallowed up, but before that he testified with this sentence:

Ἐπειδὴ Ἀριστοτέλης οὐχ εἵλετο Εὔριπον Εὔριπος εἵλετο Ἀριστοτέλην
("Since Aristotle did not grasp Euripus, Euripus grasped Aristotle").[25] What is more arrogant or mad than this, or how could God by more manifest judgment condemn his cleverness and that of others like him than by letting him be turned into a madman by immoderate greed for knowledge and thus bring his own death on himself, a death, I say, far more horrible than that of the most wicked Judas? Let us therefore shun greedy knowledge of high things, condescending rather to those of low estate. For nothing is of greater avail for Christian men than to feel humble. In this way we are more aware of the magnificence of God, whence it is written (I Pet. 5:5): "God resisteth the proud and giveth grace to the humble." To attain this grace I will no longer be anxious about this question lest by investigating the majesty of God I might be blinded by His light. I hope you also will do this. Here you have what I had to say by way

25. Gregory Nazianzen, *Oratio IV, Contra Iulianum* (Migne, *Patrologia Graeca*, XXXV, 597), refers to this same legend.]

of an exhortation, which I said not so much that I might move you and them as that I might show my own disposition of mind.

Ant. Indeed, this exhortation both showed the persuasion of your mind very well and, if I may reply for the others, has deeply moved us. Will you not commit this debate which we have had between us to writing and make a report of it so that you may have others share this good?

Lor. That is good advice. Let us make others judges in this matter, and, if it is good, sharers. Above all, let us send this argument, written and, as you say, made into a report, to the Bishop of Lerida, whose judgment I would place before all I know, and if he alone approves, I would not fear the disapproval of others. For I attribute more to him than Antimachus to Plato or Cicero to Cato.

Ant. You could say or do nothing more correct, and I beg you to do this as soon as possible.

Lor. So it will be done.

THE END OF THE "DIALOGUE ON FREE WILL"

III

MARSILIO FICINO
Translated by JOSEPHINE L. BURROUGHS

INTRODUCTION

By JOSEPHINE L. BURROUGHS

AS THE most influential exponent of Platonism in Italy during the fifteenth century, Marsilio Ficino belongs both to the history of the diverse fortunes of that ancient philosophy and to the evolution of those ideas and attitudes which we term "modern." He was born near Florence in 1433, and the Humanistic influences of this environment did much to shape both the style of his writings and the problems with which he was concerned. Under the patronage of Cosimo de' Medici, he devoted himself to the task of reviving Platonism in Italy, not only as a distinct philosophical doctrine, but also as an intellectual movement with the same vitality and community of interest which characterized the ancient school. The first part of this task consisted in making the source material of Platonism easily accessible through Latin translations. Of these, the translation of the *Corpus Hermeticum* was completed in 1463, that of Plato's dialogues in 1468, some writings of Porphyry and Proclus in 1489, and those of Dionysius the Areopagite and Plotinus in 1492.

In 1462 Cosimo established what has since been called the Platonic Academy of Florence. Although "academy" only in name, the villa at Careggi gave Ficino an opportunity to promote the study of Platonism among a congenial group of thinkers, artists, and literary men and also to present the fruits of his own thought to a sympathetic and enthusiastic audience. Through this "teaching" at Careggi and through his own writings, particularly his major work, the *Theologia Platonica*, and the short treatises which comprise the *Letters*, Ficino was able to inspire a new attitude toward the Platonic material as a comprehensive framework within which the dominant ideas of

Humanism might be expressed and its dominant problems resolved. It is this attitude and the character of the doctrine which resulted from it, rather than the revival of Platonism as such, which accounts for the popularity and diverse influence of Ficino's work.

What, then, are the distinguishing characteristics of Ficino's Platonic philosophy? According to his own statements, the choice of Platonism as source and framework for a philosophic system was determined by the harmony he believed to exist between it and the Christian faith. The use of Platonic concepts and arguments to support and develop religious beliefs was, of course, not an innovation but rather a return to the tendency of the early Church Fathers. Ficino himself cites Augustine as his guide in judging Platonism to be superior to all other philosophies. However, the earlier writers had either used particular Platonic doctrines divorced from their context or absorbed Platonic ideas in a diluted form from others. Ficino deliberately set out to combine the Platonic doctrine as a whole with the Christian doctrine, itself the result of centuries of incremental development. Such an attempt was possible only after the recovery of the complete and original texts of the Platonic writers. Furthermore, it depends upon a fundamental difference between the earlier evaluation of Platonism and that which is characteristic of Ficino. For instance, in *De doctrina Christiana* Augustine advises that if the Platonists have "by chance" taught anything that is "true and in harmony with our faith," this part of their teaching should be appropriated by the Christian, who must, nevertheless, "separate himself in spirit from the miserable company of these men."[1] Ficino, on the other hand, regards the Platonic doctrine as an authority comparable to that of the divine law and contrasts it, like the latter, to independent philosophical reasoning. Not only is the Platonic tradition itself divinely inspired; its revival is necessary

1. *De doctrina Christiana* ii. 40.

in order that the Christian religion may be confirmed and rendered sufficiently rational to satisfy the skeptical and atheistical minds of the age.

This change reveals a new conception of the unity and universality of human aspiration, a conception in terms of which certain important characteristics of Ficino's thought may be stated. First, philosophy is no longer taken to be an activity separated from religion, whether as rival or "handmaid." Both are manifestations of spiritual life and, as such, have a single aim—the attainment of the highest good. Each is required by the other, for religion saves philosophy from an inferior notion of this highest good, while philosophy saves religion from ignorance, and without knowledge the goal cannot be reached. Thus for Ficino philosophy must be religious, religion philosophical. Being philosophical, Ficino's system is constructed through the application of universal principles to all levels of being. At the same time, being religious, it is ultimately concerned with a system of the universe only because in that system the glorification of the human soul can be justified and its ability to attain the *summum bonum* can be demonstrated. This concentration of interest upon the unique nature and destiny of the human soul is inherent in the religious tradition. The desire to develop this notion in relation to nature as a whole springs from the tendencies of the new Humanism. The insistence that this be substantiated by rational arguments, as part of a system of speculative thought, shows that in Ficino the religious heritage and the new Humanism have together taken on philosophic form.

Second, the assertion that Platonism is of divine origin is related to the Humanistic belief in the universal ability of man to envision and attain the highest good. The truth and superiority of the Christian religion is not questioned in Ficino's writings, but this truth and superiority does not depend upon a unique revelation. Rather, Christianity could not be regarded as the true religion unless all men in all times had a desire for and a capacity to attain that same goal, the pursuit of which it defines as the only way to salvation. It could not be regarded as superior unless it perfected and facilitated the attainment of such a natural aim. Therefore Ficino must find in the nature of man himself a basis for the identification of the highest good with the knowledge and enjoyment of God. The assertion that there is such a basis may then obtain support from the opinions of thinkers of other cultures and of other times. For instance, in the treatise here translated Ficino uses the agreement of the Hermetic, Peripatetic, Platonic, and Persian writers as an argument. In accordance with this, it cannot be said that Ficino as Humanist and Platonist opposes either the Scholastic thinkers or Aristotle and the Aristotelian school. On the contrary, he does not hesitate to use the methods of the former and the ideas of both.[2] For example, the principles of *primum in aliquo genere* and *appetitus naturalis* are directly related to the medieval Aristotelian tradition. Many of his technical terms are taken from the Scholastic writers without substantial change in signification, and a number of his treatises, including the present one, preserve the form of *quaestiones*.

In *Five Questions concerning the Mind*[3] Ficino sets out to demonstrate that the ultimate end of all human desire and activity can be no other than "boundless truth and goodness," that is, God; and that the soul must be able to reach this end and enjoy it forever. The assertion that the soul must be directed toward some end peculiar to it, and be able to attain that end, depends upon the theory of natural movement, or natural desire, *appetitus naturalis*. The assertion that this end of the soul

2. See P. O. Kristeller, "Florentine Platonism and Its Relations with Humanism and Scholasticism," *Church History*, VIII, (1939), 201 ff.

3. Written in 1476, two years after the completion of *Theologia Platonica*, this treatise was incorporated into a collection called *Five Keys of Platonic Wisdom* in 1477, and also into the second book of Ficino's letters, which was first printed in 1495. See *Supplementum Ficinianum*, ed. P. O. Kristeller (Florence, 1937), I, xcv ff.

is infinite truth and goodness and that it can be attained only in the after-life depends upon the unique nature of the soul, its universality and dual inclination.

The theory of *appetitus naturalis*[4] is, for Ficino, both a necessary explanation of the observed facts of orderly change and a consequence of the perfection of God and of His relation to the universe. The observed order of created things results from a tendency or desire inherent in the essence characteristic of each species, a tendency to proceed toward a particular end identified with the good of that species. The origin of any motion is thus found in the essence of the moving thing; the end, in the perfection of that thing. These tendencies are called "natural" because they are directly dependent upon the essence and common to all members of a species at all times. Further, as dependent upon essence, every natural tendency is ultimately related to God. The relation between particular goods and the highest good and that between the order found in particular things and God as the one source of order illustrates the general ontological principle of *primum in aliquo genere*.

According to this principle,[5] there is in every genus a highest member, or *primum*, which contains through itself the essence characteristic of that genus, whereas all other members must be referred back to the *primum* as cause and source of the attributes they share. The members of every genus are thus organized into a definite hierarchy, from the *primum* which is pure and complete, through descending degrees which participate in the defining essence only partially, and contain other qualities which are alien to that essence. This principle is applied to any plurality of entities which share certain attributes and differ in the possession of others. For instance, the five degrees of Ficino's order of Being are related successively as cause and

4. See P. O. Kristeller, *The Philosophy of Marsilio Ficino* (New York, 1943), chap. x.

5. *Ibid.*, chap. ix.

effect, so that each degree below God resembles the one above it in some way, differs from it in another; and each is passive in respect to those above it and active in respect to those below it.

Since the totality of Being is conceived as a kind of genus, God, as Being itself and Goodness itself, may be called the *primum* of that genus. Thus all things below God receive being and goodness from Him. From this it follows that all natural desires are related to God, both with respect to origin and to end. God as the cause of all being is the source of the essence upon which the desire of each created thing is based. The end of every desire is a good, and God is Goodness itself, so that all desire "takes its beginning" from God as the highest end. Finally, since order is the result of natural desire, order of any kind is derived from God.

The attainment of the appropriate end is guaranteed by this relationship between God and created being. Just as the order and goodness found in particular things is ultimately dependent upon God, so the perfection of the whole order is a necessary consequence of the perfection of God. No created thing can exist which does not contribute to the order and good of the whole. A natural desire unaccompanied by the power to achieve its proper end would be worthless in this respect and therefore contrary to the "order of nature."

Since all less perfect things are directed toward ends in which they are perfected, the soul must likewise possess a natural desire for an end identified with its good. This desire, like all others, must be grounded in the nature of the desiring thing. Therefore, the specification of the ultimate end and good of the soul is based upon the doctrine of the unique metaphysical position of the soul, and the characteristics which result from this position. In Ficino's hierarchy of Being the soul is the third or middle essence[6] and the "fountain of motion." Because

6. Cf. *Theologia Platonica* iii. 2, trans. in *Journal of the History of Ideas*, V (1944), 227 ff.

of its central position, it has an affinity with all things above and below it; because of its self-motion, it is able to move in either direction. Therefore, through the intellect the soul strives to know all things; through the will it strives to enjoy all things. This desire for all truth and goodness cannot be satisfied except by the possession of that infinite truth and goodness which is the source of all others, that is, God.

Like all other things, the soul must be able to attain this desired end. Unlike all others, its attainment of this end does not follow inevitably from the presence of its natural desire. By virtue of its central position, the soul of man is of a dual nature. With lower forms of life man shares the powers of generation, nutrition, and sensation, and these comprise the lower or irrational soul. The higher soul includes both the power of contemplation ("mind" in the strict sense), which man shares with the angels and God, and the discursive power of reason which is peculiar to him alone. In accordance with this, the soul itself has two tendencies, one toward the body and associated with sense, the other toward God and associated with the rational soul. Because human reason is free, it can either oppose the senses or be misled by them; but in neither case can it attain its own end and good or let the lower soul find satisfaction. The result of this is the paradox which Ficino expresses through the Humanistic interpretation of the myth of Prometheus.[7] Because of reason, the nature or essence of man is more perfect than that of all other beings below God and the angels, that is, of all things characterized by motion, and thus possessing some determinate desire. Also because of reason, man is unable to attain happiness, that is, final perfection. This conclusion not only compromises the perfection of man but also contradicts the general ontological principle that no natural desire can be

7. For similar interpretations of the Prometheus myth in literature and painting see Erwin Panofsky, *Studies in Iconology* (New York, 1939), pp. 50–51, esp. n. 53.

in vain. Therefore, referring to this principle, Ficino asserts that the human soul must attain knowledge and enjoyment of God, if not in this life, then in the after-life. However, in thus attaining the end of one inclination, that toward God, the soul cannot abandon the other, that toward the body, for this is also "natural." The final end, therefore, can be attained only when this second inclination is satisfied through the possession of its own body "made everlasting." In this most natural condition the soul finds eternal rest.[8]

8. This argument for the resurrection of the body is reminiscent of that of Thomas Aquinas *Summa contra Gentiles* iv. lxxix.

FIVE QUESTIONS CONCERNING
THE MIND*

FIVE questions concerning the mind: first, whether or not the motion of the mind is directed toward some definite end; second, whether the end of this motion of the mind is motion or rest; third, whether this [end] is something particular or universal; fourth, whether the mind is ever able to attain its desired end; fifth, whether, after it has obtained the end, it ever loses it.

MARSILIO FICINO TO HIS FELLOW-PHILOSOPHERS
SENDS GREETING

Wisdom, sprung from the crown of the head[1] of Jove, creator of all, warns her philosophical lovers that if they truly desire ever to gain possession of their beloved, they should always seek the highest summits of things rather than the lowest places; for Pallas, the divine offspring sent down from the high heavens, herself frequents the high citadels which she has established.[2] She shows, furthermore, that we cannot reach the highest summits of things unless, first, taking less account of the inferior parts of the soul, we ascend to the highest part, the mind. She promises, finally, that if we have concentrated our powers in this most fruitful part of the soul, then without doubt

*Epistolae, Book ii, No. 1 (ed. Venice, 1495 [Hain 7059]), fols. xxxviii ff. Cf. Opera (ed. Basel, 1576), pp. 675 ff.

1. [Summum caput. Literally, the "highest part of the head," this phrase is also used frequently to refer to the highest part or summit of a mountain. Thus Ficino applies it to the head of Jove and, by implication, to the summit of Mount Cellano, also figuratively, to the highest realm of being, and the highest part of the soul.]

2. ["Pallas enim Divina progenies quae coelo demittitur alto: Altas ipsa colit quas et condidit arces." Cf. Virgil, Eclogue IV, l. 7: "iam nova progenies caelo demittitur alto"; and Eclogue II, l. 61: "Pallas quas condidit arces ipsa colat").]

by means of this highest part itself, that is, by means of mind, we shall ourselves have the power of creating mind;[3] mind which, I say, is the companion of Minerva herself and the foster-child of highest Jove. So then, O best of my fellow-philosophers, not long ago on Monte Cellano I may perhaps have created, in a night's work, a mind of this kind, by means of mind; and this mind I would now introduce among you in order that you yourselves, who are far more fruitful than Marsilio, prompted by a kind of rivalry, as I might say, may at some time bring forth an offspring more worthy of the sight of Jove and Pallas.

THE MOTION[4] OF EACH NATURAL SPECIES, BECAUSE IT IS DRIVEN IN A CERTAIN ORDERLY MANNER, IS KNOWN TO BE DIRECTED AND TO PROCEED FROM SOME DEFINITE ORIGIN TO SOME CERTAIN END

The motion of each of all the natural species proceeds according to a certain principle. Different species are moved in different ways, and each species always preserves the same course in its motion so that it always proceeds from this place to that place and, in turn, recedes from the latter to the former, in a certain most harmonious manner. We inquire particularly from what source motion receives order of this kind.

According to the philosophers, the limits of motion are two, namely, that from which it flows and that to which it flows. From these limits motion obtains its order. Therefore, a motion

---

3. [*Mente mentem procreaturos.* Mind, as the highest faculty of the soul, creates the contemplative or highest state of the soul. This is here figuratively identified with the philosophical treatise produced by mind. Cf. Plotinus *Ennead III* viii. 5 and Ficino's Latin translation iii. viii 4: "[The higher soul's] contemplation and natural disposition, which is desirous for learning and eager for inquiry, and further, the present birth pangs caused by those things of which it has gained knowledge, and its complete fruitfullness, bring it about that, itself completely made into a thing contemplated (*contemplamen*), it may produce another thing contemplated."]

4. [Motion in the sense of change from one condition to another as well as from one place to another.]

does not wander from one uncertain and disorderly state to another but is directed from a certain and orderly state [its origin] to a certain and orderly state [its end], harmonizing with that origin. Certainly, everything returns to its own place rather than to that which belongs to another. If this were not so, different species of things would sometimes move in the same manner, and the same species in a different manner; and, similarly, the same species would be set in motion in different ways at different times, and different species often in the same way. Further, if this were not the case, the orderly sequence of motion would have been destroyed—the sequence by which a motion gradually flows forth at a certain time through many appropriate steps and seemly forms and, by turns, flows back after a definite interval of time. Add to this that, if each motion did not proceed according to a certain principle, it would not be directed to one determined region, or quality, or substance, rather than to any other whatsoever.

THE MOST ORDERLY MOTION OF THE COSMOS IS DIRECTED BY DIVINE PROVIDENCE TO A DETERMINED END

If individual motions are brought to completion according to such a wonderful order, then certainly the universal motion of the cosmos itself cannot be lacking in perfect order. Indeed, just as the individual motions are derived from and contribute to universal motion, so from the order of universal motion they receive order and to the order of universal motion they contribute order. In this common order of the whole, all things, no matter how diverse, are brought back to unity according to a single determined harmony and rational plan. Therefore, we conclude that all things are led by one certain orderer who is most full of reason. Indeed, a supremely rational order flows from the highest reason and wisdom of a mind; and the particular ends to which single things are directed have been prescribed by that mind; certainly, the common end of the whole to which the single ends are led must also be prescribed by that mind.

CONCERNING THE ENDS OF THE MOTION OF THE
ELEMENTS, OF PLANTS, AND OF BRUTES

We are not in doubt concerning the ends of the motion of the elements and plants and irrational animals. Certainly, some elements, because of a certain heaviness, descend to the center of the universe; while others, because of their lightness, ascend to the vault of the superior sphere. It is clear also that the motion of plants originates from the powers of nutrition and generation and is terminated in the sufficient nourishment of the plant itself and reproduction of its kind. The same is true of the powers which we and the brutes have in common with the plants. The motion of irrational animals, which characteristically pertains to sense, arises from the sensible form and the need of nature and, by means of that which is perceived from without, moves toward the fulfilment of bodily needs. The same is true of that nature which we ourselves have in common with all animals. Certainly, it must be recognized that all these motions which we have just mentioned, because they strive toward some particular thing, are the result of a particular power and, further, that in those ends which we have described they achieve sufficient rest and are perfected as much as their natures require.

FIVE QUESTIONS CONCERNING THE MOTION OF THE MIND

It remains for us to inquire concerning the motion of the human mind: first, whether or not the mind strives toward some end; second, whether the end of its motion is motion or rest; third, whether this good [toward which the mind strives] is something particular or something universal; fourth, whether the mind is strong enough eventually to attain its desired end, that is, the highest good; fifth, whether, after it has attained the perfect end, it ever loses it.

THE MOTION OF THE MIND LOOKS TOWARD A CERTAIN END

If other things do not wander upward and downward in a foolish accidental way but are directed according to a certain

[196]

rational order toward something which is in the highest degree peculiar and appropriate to them and in which they are entirely perfected, then certainly mind,[5] which is the receptacle of wisdom,[6] which comprehends the order and ends of natural things, which orders its daily affairs in a rational manner to a certain end, and which is more perfect than all the others we have mentioned; mind, I say, must be directed in a far greater degree to some ordered end in which it is perfected according to its earnest desire. Just as the single parts of life[7] [of man], that is, deliberations, choices, and abilities, refer to single ends (for any one of these looks toward its own end, as it were, its own good); so in like manner the whole life [of man] looks toward the universal end and good. Now, since the parts of anything serve the whole, it follows that the order which is inherent in them in relation to each other is subordinate to their order in relation to the whole.[8] It follows further that their order in relation to particular ends depends upon a certain common order of the whole —an order which especially contributes to the common end of the whole. Indeed, if any mover whatsoever moves for its own benefit, then it is reasonable to suppose that mind brings any of its own [parts] to their proper ends only because they contribute to the common end and good of the mind. Finally, who is so weak in mind that he believes it possible for the mind to strive, both by nature and by plan, to give diverse and single things an order in relation to one thing, without the mind itself having an order in relation to one thing? Furthermore, the ultimate common end moves the rest everywhere (for all other things are desired for the sake of that which is desired first).

5. ["Mind" here is used in the broader sense, meaning the rational soul, and its achievements are listed in order of perfection, according to the familiar threefold division of knowledge into *scientia divina, scientia naturalis,* and *scientia humana.*]

6. [For *spīae* read *sapientiae.*]

7. [*Singulae vitae partes* and *universa vita,* the parts and whole of human life, considered as the activity of the soul.]

8. [The order immanent in the parts, being lower and less perfect, depends upon the order of the whole which transcends the parts.]

Therefore, it would not be extraordinary if, the ultimate and common end itself being absent, the rest could not be present at all. In the same way, unless the perfect form of an edifice is prescribed by the architect, the different workmen will never be moved to particular tasks which accord with the plan of the whole itself. Nay, truly, by no means will they be moved to their prescribed occupations by anyone who does not first possess the common prescribed end of the whole work.

THE END OF INTELLECTUAL MOTION IS NOT MOTION BUT REST

If the end of intellectual motion is itself motion, then certainly the intellect is moved in order that it may be further moved, and again is moved in order that it may be moved yet further, and so on without end. From this it is brought about that, persevering in its own motion, the intellect does not cease to be moved and on that account does not at any time cease to live and to know. Perhaps this is that continuous motion of the soul by which, in the opinion of some Platonists, the soul is always set in motion and always lives. I believe, however, that the mind, because it knows rest and judges rest itself to be more excellent than change, and because it naturally desires rest beyond motion, desires and finally attains its end and good in a certain condition of rest rather than of motion. For this there is the following evidence: the mind makes more progress at rest than in motion; the familiar objects of the mind are the eternal reasons of things, not the changeable passions of matter; just as the characteristic power or excellence of life,[9] namely, intelligence and will, proceeds beyond the ends of mobile things to those things which are stable and eternal, so life itself certainly reach-

9. [*Virtus.* The active potentiality intrinsic to the *essentia* or nature of a given substance. Then intelligence proper and will which is a parallel function of intelligence comprise the *operatio* or action of the thinking being, and this *operatio* must be referred to the *essentia.* Since *operatio* in this case is internal or self-returning activity, it includes as a prior element, external or outgoing activity which Ficino calls *vita,* "life." In this way, reflective action, *intelligentia,* is dependent upon *vita,* and both ultimately upon *essentia.*]

es beyond any temporal change to its end and good in eternity; indeed the soul could never pass beyond the limits of mobile things, either by understanding or by willing, unless it could transcend them by living; finally, motion is always incomplete and strives toward something else, while the nature of an end, especially the highest, is above all such that it is neither imperfect nor proceeds toward some other thing.

THE OBJECT AND END OF THE MIND IS UNIVERSAL TRUTH AND GOODNESS

Now it is asked whether the end of intelligence and will is some particular truth and goodness or universal truth and goodness. It is universal, certainly, for the following reasons. The intellect grasps a certain fullest notion of that which the philosophers call being and truth and goodness, a notion under which everything that either is or is possible is completely comprehended. That which is itself called being and truth and goodness, and which contains all things, the Peripatetics think is the common object of the human intellect, because just as the object of sense is said to be the sensible, so the object of intellect itself is the intelligible. The intelligible, moreover, comprehends all in its fulness. Again, the intellect is prompted by nature to comprehend the whole breadth of being; in its notion it perceives all, and, in the notion of all, it contemplates itself; under the concept of truth it knows all, and under the concept of the good it desires all. The Peripatetics refer both of these to the concept of being, while the Platonists think that goodness is fuller than being. This question, however, clearly has no bearing on the problem in hand, and we shall for the present use these three names, that is, being and truth and goodness, as if they were synonymous. (In the commentary on the *Philebus* we have discussed this very matter more diligently.)

The first question appears to be whether or not the intellect can attain a clear understanding of everything which is included under being. Certainly it can. The intellect divides being into ten most universal genera, and these ten by degrees into as many subordinate genera as possible. It then arranges certain ultimate species under the subordinate genera; and, finally, it places single things, without end, as it were, under the species in the manner we have described. If the intellect can comprehend being itself as a definite whole, and, as it were, divide it by degrees into all its members, diligently comparing these members in turn both to each other and to the whole, then who can deny that by nature it is able to grasp universal Being itself? Surely that which sees the form of the whole itself, and which, from any point, beholds the limits of the whole, and the gradations through which it extends, can comprehend as middle points the particular things which are included under these limits. Now, it goes without saying that since the intellect, according to the Platonists, can devise the one and the good above being and below being, how much more will it be able to run discursively through the broad whole of being! Certainly, next to the notion of being (the name of which we have already repeated many times), the intellect can at its pleasure think of that which is most different from being, that is, nonbeing. If it can go from being to that which is infinitely far from being, then how much more must it be able to run through those things which are contained under being as middle points! For this reason Aristotle says: just as matter, which is the lowest of natural things, can put on all corporeal forms and by this means become all corporeal things, so the intellect, which is, as it were, the lowest of all supernatural things and the highest of natural things, can take on the spiritual forms of all things and become all. In this manner the universe, under the concept of being and truth, is the object of the intellect; and similarly, under the concept of goodness, it is the object of the will. What, then, does the intellect seek if not to transform all things into itself by depicting all things in the intellect according to the nature of the intellect? And what does the will strive to do if not to transform itself into all things by enjoying all things according to the nature of each? The former strives to bring it about that the universe, in a certain manner, should become intellect; the latter, that the will should become the universe. In both respects therefore, with regard to the intellect and with regard to the will, the effort of the soul is directed (as it is said in the metaphysics of Avicenna) toward this end: that the soul in its own way will become the whole universe. Thus we see that by a natural instinct every soul strives in a continuous effort both to know all truths by the intellect and to enjoy all good things by the will.

THE ORIGIN AND END OF THE SOUL IS NONE OTHER THAN INFINITE TRUTH AND GOODNESS

It is indeed necessary to remember that the universe, which we say is the end of the soul, is entirely infinite. We reckon to be peculiar and proper to each thing an end for which that thing characteristically feels a very strong desire, as if this end were the highest good for it; an end, moreover, for whose sake it desires and does everything else; and in which at length that thing rests completely, so much so that it now puts an end to the impulses of nature and desire. Surely, the condition natural to our intellect is that it should inquire into the cause of each thing and, in turn, into the cause of the cause. For this reason the inquiry of the intellect never ceases until it finds that cause of which nothing is the cause but which is itself the cause of causes. This cause is none other than the boundless God. Similarly, the desire of the will is not satisfied by any good, as long as we believe that there is yet another beyond it. Therefore, the will is satisfied only by that one good beyond which there is no further good. What can this good be except the boundless God? As long as any truth or goodness is presented which has distinct gradations, no matter how many, you inquire after more by the intellect and desire further by the will. Nowhere can you rest except in boundless truth and goodness, nor find an end except in the infinite. Now, since each thing rests in its own especial origin, from which it is produced and where it is perfected, and since our soul is able to rest only in the infinite, it follows that that which is infinite must alone be its especial origin. Indeed, this should properly be called infinity itself and eternity itself rather than something eternal and infinite. Certainly, the effect nearest to the cause becomes most similar to the cause. Consequently, the rational soul in a certain manner possesses the excellence of infinity and eternity. If this were not the case, it would never characteristically incline toward the infinite. Undoubtedly this is the reason that there are none among men who live contentedly on earth and are satisfied with merely temporal possessions.

AT SOME TIME THE SOUL CAN ATTAIN ITS DESIRED END AND GOOD

Surely the rational soul can at some time reach its perfect end. If those things which are less perfect in nature attain their natural perfection in the possession of their desired ends, how much more will the soul, which is both most perfect and the end of all natural things! If those things which do not prescribe an end either to themselves or to others, at some time attain an appropriate end, how much more will the mind, which seeks and discovers its own end and, further, determines the end of many things, foreknows the end of many, and sees the end of all! If natural power is not ineffectual in the lowest things, certainly it is not ineffectual in the soul, for the soul is so great a thing that it can accurately measure by how great an interval every smallest thing is exceeded by the greatest things. Moreover, the soul would never naturally follow a certain end unless it were able to attain it, for by what[10] other power is it moved to it [a certain end] except by that by which it can attain it? Further, we see that when it [the soul] strives very eagerly, in motion toward a certain end, it makes great progress; assuredly, in so far as it makes progress by a certain power, by that same power it is at some time perfected. Finally, we see that the soul is gradually moved more and more rapidly, just as any element moves faster and faster toward its natural goal the closer it comes to it. Therefore,

10. [For *quae* read *qua*.]

the mind, like the element, does not forever proceed in vain from one point to another without end but at some time or other attains an end which is desired for the sake of itself alone.

Further, there are in things and actions, both natural and human, certain beginnings and ends. It is contrary to nature itself and to the rationality of a beginning for anything to ascend continually from one beginning to another without a [first] beginning. It is contrary to the rationality of an end for anything to descend successively from one end to another without a [last] end. All action takes its beginning from the highest agent. All desire takes its beginning from the highest end. All things which have a certain characteristic because of something else are necessarily related to that very thing which has that characteristic through its own nature. Therefore, if there were no extremes on both sides [i.e., a first beginning and a last end], absolutely no action would commence nor any appetite be aroused. Finally, since any mover moves for its own benefit, where the highest mover is, there is also found the highest end. This is the case in every order of things. Truly, this is the case in the order of the universe.

But it might be well to expand further the above argument concerning the mind. If someone asks us which of these is more perfect, intellect or sense, the intelligible or the sensible, we shall promise to answer promptly if he will first give us an answer to the following question. You know, my inquiring friend, that there is some power in you which has a notion of each of these things—a notion, I say, of intellect itself and of sense, of the intelligible and of the sensible. This is evident, for the same power which compares these to each other must at that time in a certain manner see both. Tell me, then, whether a power of this kind belongs to intellect or to sense. Tell me, I entreat you, without hesitation, so that with the help of what you say I may soon answer the question which you asked. Now, then, I hear you answering thus: a power of this kind does not belong to sense. Certainly we all continually make very active use of the senses. If, then, sense were able to perceive both itself and these other things, all men, or at least most men, would clearly and easily know the very power of perceiving and of knowing, and intelligible and sensible things. Since, however, those who know all these are very few in number, and indeed those few gain this knowledge only with effort and after a long, hard process of logical reasoning on the part of intelligence, it is certain that sense has no power to know either itself or intellect and the objects of intellect. Nay, indeed, all this remains for the intellect to know. Further, the power which inquires earnestly concerning both intellect and sense is the same as that which discovers these by argumentation, and which by reason decides which is more perfect. Because this power inquires by reasoning and assigns a reason for its decision, it is reason, not sense. Therefore, intellect alone is that which knows all things.

To that original question of yours I now give the following answer. Intellect is at least as much more perfect than sense, as its power is extended in its action more widely and more perfectly than that of sense. Sense, as you yourself have shown, can perceive neither itself nor intellect and the objects of intellect; whereas intellect knows both. Moreover, another certain degree of perfection may be attributed to intellect. Certainly, when intellect successively compares itself and sense and the rest with respect to their degrees of perfection, it has the highest form of perfection itself, before its eyes, as it were; and, bringing each near to this form, it judges that one which comes nearest to it to be the more perfect. If intellect thus touches upon the highest form of perfection, it does so undoubtedly because of a certain highest affinity between that highest form and itself. Therefore, intellect is not only more perfect than sense but is also, after perfection itself, in the highest degree perfect. I see, in addition, a third degree of perfection belonging to intelligence. Since the intellect inquires into and judges itself, it is certainly reflected into itself. Moreover, that which has this characteristic [of being reflected into itself] exists and remains within itself. It is, furthermore, entirely incorporeal and simple. Finally, since it goes forth from itself to itself in a circular motion, it can be perpetually moved, that is, it can always act and be alive. It goes without saying that intellect, as if more perfect, is characteristic of fewer men and is perfectly employed much later in life and much more seldom. Indeed, as if it were an end, it is granted [to us] only after the vegetable powers and senses have been exercised. To sense the intellect gives guidance and laws, and for sense it prescribes an end. Intellect, when it argues and ponders, guides its own motion according to free choice. Sense, however, when reason does not resist, is always driven by the instinct of nature. It goes without saying that reason often chooses in a way different from that which sense and the need of the body demand, for clearly the beginning of the choice does not depend on the body. Otherwise, the end of the choice would always have a regard for the body. It is seen from this that reason is never subjected to bodily things in its motion, because in its speculations it transcends bodily things, in its pondering it extends itself to things diverse and opposite, and in its choice it often opposes the inclination of the body. Therefore, we say that intellect is much less subjected to any corporeal substance, in essence and in life. Moreover, sense seems to be dulled in a certain manner by advancing age, whereas intellect is certainly by no means dulled. Intellect can, however, be diverted from its speculative intention when it occupies itself excessively with the care and cultivation of the body. Moreover, when the object of sense is very violent, it injures sense at once, so that sense, after its occurrence,[11] cannot immediately discern its weaker objects. Thus extreme brightness offends the eye, and a very loud noise offends the ears. Mind, however, is otherwise; by its most excellent object it is neither injured nor ever confused. Nay, rather, after this object is known, it distinguishes inferior things at once more clearly and more truly. This indicates that the nature of the mind is exceedingly spiritual and excellent. Moreover, sense is limited to corporeal objects; the intellect, in its inmost action, frees itself

11. [For *obscursum* read *occursum*.]

from all corporeal things, seeing that in its essence and life it has not been submerged.[12] It separates the corporeal forms from the passions of matter. It also distinguishes from the corporeal forms those which through their own nature are completely incorporeal. Certainly it has itself been separated from the passions of matter and the conditions of corporeal forms. Further, sense is satisfied with particular objects alone, whereas the familiar objects of the intellect are the universal and everlasting reasons of things. With these it could never become familiar unless it were in a peculiar way similar to them. In this way, intellect shows itself, also, to be absolute and everlasting.

Finally, we say this especially because it [intellect] reaches reasons of such a kind through certain species which it both makes and receives itself. These must necessarily be unconditioned by the passions of matter, otherwise they could not refer to those reasons and ideas. Furthermore, unless intellect itself were free from the passions of matter, it could neither create species of this kind nor receive them in this way.

THE MIND IS MUCH BETTER ABLE THAN SENSE TO
ATTAIN ITS DESIRED END

Reason is certainly peculiar to us. God has not bestowed it upon the beasts, otherwise he would have given[13] them discourse which is, as it were, the messenger of reason. [He also would have given them] the hand, the minister and instrument of reason. [If the beasts possessed reason,] we would also have seen in them some indications of deliberation and of versatility. On the contrary, we now observe that they never act except in so far as they are driven by a natural impulse toward a necessity of nature. Thus all spiders weave their webs in a similar manner; they neither learn to weave nor become more proficient through practice, no matter how long. Lastly, if the beasts possessed reason, definite indications and works of religion manifest to all would have appeared among them. Where intellect is present, in-

12. [See above, n. 9.]   13. [For *dedisse* read *dedisset*.]

tellect which is, as it were, a kind of eye turned toward the intelligible light, there also the intelligible light which is God shines and is honored and loved and worshiped.

As intellect is more perfect than sense, man is more perfect than the brutes. Because of this very thing, he is more perfect: he has a characteristic not shared by the beasts. Thus on account of his intelligence alone man is judged to be more perfect, especially since, by means of the function of intelligence, he approaches the infinite perfection which is God, through love, thought, and worship. Moreover, the especial perfection of each thing consists in the possession of its appropriate end. The attainment of this end is easier and more abundant in proportion to the richness of the innate perfection of that thing; for where that formal perfection which is innate from the beginning is more strong, at that very place final perfection, according to the order of nature, is granted more easily, more abundantly, and with greater felicity, for the latter [final perfection] obeys the former [formal perfection] yet does not result from its obedience. From this we conclude that reason can attain its wished-for and appropriate end more easily than sense; man, more easily than the beasts.

THE IMMORTAL SOUL IS ALWAYS MISERABLE IN ITS MORTAL BODY

We know by experience that the beast in us, that is, sense, most often attains its end and good. This is the case, for instance, when sense, so far as pertains to itself, is entirely satisfied with the attainment of its adequate object. We do not, however, know by experience that the man in us, that is, reason, attains its desired end. On the contrary, when sense itself, in the greatest delights of the body, is as much satisfied as is possible to it, reason is still violently agitated and agitates sense. If it chooses to obey the senses, it always makes a conjecture about something; it invents new delights; it continually seeks something further, I know not what. If, on the other hand, it strives to resist the senses, it renders life laborious. Therefore, in both cases reason not only is unhappy but also entirely disturbs the happiness of sense itself. Yet if reason tames sense, and concentrates itself in itself, then, driven by nature, it searches eagerly for the reasons and causes of things. In this search it often finds what it does not want, or does not find what it does want, or, by chance, does not understand as much as it desires and is able to. Truly, reason is always uncertain, vacillating and distressed; and since it is nowhere at rest while thus affected, it certainly never gains possession of its desired end or permits sense to take possession of its proper end which is already present.

Nothing indeed can be imagined more unreasonable than that man, who through reason is the most perfect of all animals, nay, of all things under heaven, most perfect, I say, with regard to that formal perfection which is bestowed upon us from the beginning, that man, also through reason, should be the least perfect of all with regard to that final perfection for the sake of which the first perfection is given. This seems to be that most unfortunate Prometheus. Instructed by the divine wisdom of Pallas, he gained possession of the heavenly fire, that is, reason. Because of this very possession, on the highest peak of the mountain, that is, at the very height of contemplation, he is rightly judged most miserable of all, for he is made wretched by the continual gnawing of the most ravenous of vultures, that is, by the torment of inquiry. This will be the case, until the time comes when he is carried back to that same place from which he received the fire, so that, just as he is now urged on to seek the whole by that one beam of celestial light, he will then be entirely filled with the whole light.

MAN, THE MORE LABORIOUSLY HE FOLLOWS HAPPINESS WHEN HE IS PLACED OUTSIDE HIS NATURAL CONDITION, THE MORE EASILY HE REACHES IT WHEN RESTORED TO THAT NATURAL CONDITION

The reasons we previously offered for the facility with which human happiness may be attained plainly seemed to show the truth itself according to a certain natural order. For what reason then is so much difficulty, as experience teaches, placed in the way of our strivings, so that we seem to be rolling the great stone of Sisyphus up the steep slopes of the mountain? What wonder? We seek the highest summits of Mount Olympus. We inhabit the abyss of the lowest valley. We are weighted down by the burden of a most troublesome body. Panting toward the steep places, we often slide back to a sudden precipice because of this burden itself and because of the overhanging rocks on both sides. Moreover, from one side as many dangers and obstacles as possible detain us, while from the other the harmful blandishments of certain meadows delay us. Thus, alas, outside the sublime fatherland, we, unhappy people, are confined to the lowest places, where nothing presents itself which is not exceedingly difficult, where nothing happens which is not lamentable.

How, then, shall we reply to a contradiction of this kind? On the one hand, the argument promised the greatest ease; on the other, experience shows in an equal degree, the greatest difficulty. Only the law of Moses will solve this conflict for us. Indeed, we have been placed outside the order of first nature, and —O sorrow!—live and suffer contrary to the order of nature. The more easily the first man was able to receive happiness when in the beginning he was entirely devoted to God, the more easily he has lost ease itself when thereafter he turned against God. Therefore, the greater the difficulty with which all the descendants of the first parent receive blessedness when placed outside the order of nature, the greater the ease with which they would receive it if restored to that very order.

What do the philosophers say to these things? Certainly the Magi, followers of Zoroaster and Hostanes, assert something similar. They say that, because of a certain old disease of the human mind, everything that is very unhealthy and difficult befalls us; but, if anyone should restore the soul to its previous condition, then immediately all will be set in order. Neither does the opinion of the Pythagoreans and Platonists disagree with this. They say that the soul is manifestly afflicted in the sensible world by so many ills because, seduced by an excessive desire for sensible goods, it has imprudently lost the goods of the intelligible world. The Peripatetics perhaps will say that man wanders from his appropriate end more than the brutes because he is moved by free will. For this reason, as he makes use of various conjectures in deliberating, man subsequently strays on this side or on that side. The irrational animal, on the contrary, is not led by its own will but is directed to the end appropriate for it by the very providence of nature, which never strays, just as the arrow is directed to the target. However, since our error and violation of duty result not from a defect of nature but rather from the variety of the opinions of reason and the divergence of resolution from the straight way, they by no means destroy the natural power but rather throw the will into turmoil. Just as, even when an element is situated outside its proper location, its power and natural inclination toward that natural place are preserved together with its nature, in so far as it is able at some time to return to its own region; so, they think, even after man has wandered from the right way, the natural power remains to him of returning first to the path, then to the end.

Finally, the most precise investigations of the theologians briefly sum up the whole matter in the following way. There can be no inclination toward any motion greater than the moving power. Since the inclination of the soul is clearly directed toward the infinite, it undoubtedly depends solely upon the infinite. If, on the contrary, the inclination of the soul had resulted immediately from some limited cause which moved the soul besides God, then it would also have been directed in like measure to a limited end. The reason for this is that, however much the power of moving were infinite in its infinite origin, it would be limited in a subsequent cause which is limited. Motion follows the quality of the most immediate rather than of the remote moving power. The mover which alone turns the soul toward the infinite is therefore none other than infinite power itself. This power, conformably with the free nature of the will, moves the mind in a certain manner which is in the highest degree free toward the paths to be chosen; while conformably with the infinite power of the moving cause, it urges the mind toward the desired end, so much so that the mind cannot fail to strive after that end. If motion of this kind could not reach the end to which it is directed, certainly none could. Where infinite power is active, in that very place infinite wisdom and goodness rule. This power, moreover, neither moves anything in vain nor denies to anything a good which that thing could and should receive. Accordingly, since man, on the one hand, because of the use of reason and contemplation, comes much nearer to the blessed angels than do the brutes, and, on the other hand, because of divine worship, comes much nearer than they to God, the fountain of blessedness, it is necessary that he can at some time be much more blessed than they in the possession of his desired end. This is necessary in order that he who is more similar to the celestial beings, both because of the ardor of the will and because of the light of intelligence, may be, in like manner, more similar to them in happiness of life, for the power and excellence of thinking and willing originate from the power of life.

Now, in the body the soul is truly far more miserable, both because of the weakness and infirmity of the body itself and its want of all things and because of the continual anxiety of the mind; therefore, the more laborious it is for the celestial and immortal soul continually to follow its happiness, while fallen into an intemperate earthly destructible body, the more easily it obtains it when it is either free from the body or in a temperate immortal celestial body. The natural end itself, moreover, seems to exist only in a natural condition. The condition of the everlasting soul which seems to be in the highest degree natural is that it should continue to live in its own body made everlasting. Therefore, it is concluded by necessary reasoning that the immortality and brightness of the soul can and must at some time shine forth into its own body and that, in this condition alone, the highest blessedness of man is indeed perfected. Certainly, this doctrine of the prophets and theologians is confirmed by the Persian wise men and by the Hermetic and the Platonic philosophers.

THE MIND WHICH HAS ATTAINED BLESSEDNESS NEVER LOSES IT

When, indeed, the soul attains the infinite end, it certainly attains it without end, for it attains it in the same manner in which it is influenced, drawn along, and led by it [the end]. If the soul has been able at some time to rise up again to immensity from a certain finite condition infinitely distant from immensity, then certainly it can remain infinitely steadfast in immensity itself. This must indeed be true, for the same infinite power which attracted the soul to itself from afar will, when close by, hold it fast within itself with indescribable power. Finally, in the infinite good nothing evil can be imagined, and whatever good can be imagined or desired is most abundantly found there. Therefore, at that place [shall be found] eternal life and the brightest light of knowledge, rest without change, a positive condition free from privation, tranquil and secure possession of all good, and everywhere perfect joy.

THE END OF FIVE QUESTIONS CONCERNING THE MIND

I V

GIOVANNI PICO DELLA MIRANDOLA
Translated by ELIZABETH LIVERMORE FORBES

INTRODUCTION

By PAUL OSKAR KRISTELLER

GIOVANNI PICO, count of Mirandola, thanks to his social position and to his early death, has always appealed strongly to the popular imagination, while his learning and his thought have earned him the admiration of serious scholars, both in his own time and ever since.[1] The circumstances of his life and death did not permit him to develop his ideas into a mature system of thought. Yet his extant writings display a remarkable wealth of knowledge and erudition and contain brilliant suggestions that were both fruitful and characteristic.

The range of Pico's learning is not only extensive; it assumes additional interest from the fact that he was able to absorb many different ideas and traditions that most of his contemporaries would have considered incompatible.[2] Having enjoyed a thorough classical education, he was familiar with the major works of Latin and Greek literature and philosophy; he cultivated the friendship of some of the leading Humanists of his time; and was able to write letters and treatises in a style which satisfied their meticulous standard of literary elegance. At the universities of Padua and Paris he became acquainted with the logical and philosophical tradition of the Middle Ages and with the writings of the Schoolmen. Pico was not only able to handle their technique of argument and their terminology; he was ready to defend their reputation against the attacks of his Humanist friends. Through his extended stay in Florence and through his friendship with Ficino, he became exposed to the influence of Platonic and Neo-

1. The best and most complete monograph on Pico is E. Garin's *Giovanni Pico della Mirandola: Vita e dottrina* (Florence, 1937).

2. For the extent of Pico's learning see P. Kibre, *The Library of Pico della Mirandola* (New York, 1936).

Platonic doctrines emanating from the Florentine Academy. At the same time, because of his different background and ideas, he was able to enrich the thought and influence of that distinguished circle. Adding the study of Hebrew and Arabic to the more common Latin and Greek, he not only gave an impulse to oriental studies but also came into direct contact with the heritage of medieval Arabic and Jewish philosophy. Strongly shaken by his unexpected conflict with the Church authorities over his disputation, in his later years Pico showed an increasing concern for religion and finally became a friend and follower of Savonarola. If we add to this his interest in vernacular Italian poetry and literature, we have the picture of a many-sided if not "universal" intellectual activity that corresponded to the best traditions and ideals of his time.

No less significant are the direct contributions which Pico made to the thought of the Renaissance. His attack on astrology, though prompted by religious and moral rather than by scientific considerations, remains a remarkable episode that made an impression on Kepler himself. Pico's interest in the Cabala led to a broad current of Christian Cabalism which includes, among others, John Reuchlin, and which remained important throughout the sixteenth century.[3]

Even more important are Pico's conception of the dignity of man and his ideal of a universal harmony among philosophers. Both find eloquent expression in the short treatise known as the *Oration on the Dignity of Man*. Since the *Oration* is one of Pico's most famous writings, it seems strange that it has not been translated into English long ago,[4] for the little work fully de-

3. Joseph L. Blau, *The Christian Interpretation of the Cabala in the Renaissance* (New York, 1944).

4. An English translation by Charles Glenn Wallis was recently published in the magazine *View* (fall, 1944, pp. 88–90, 100–101; December, 1944, pp. 134–35; 146–51). However, the present translation has been ready for publication for many years, and several passages from it were published as early as 1942 (*Journal of the History of Ideas*, III [1942], 347–54).

serves its reputation, as its content is both instrinsically interesting and characteristic of its author and of its time. A recent attempt to dismiss this work as a merely rhetorical exercise is not convincing; its characteristic ideas are confirmed by Pico's other writings, and a rhetorical form of expression is no proof that the author does not mean to indorse the ideas he is setting forth in that fashion.[5]

In order to understand the content and significance of the *Oration*, it is important to recall the circumstances of its composition. In December, 1486, Pico published in Rome his nine hundred theses, inviting all scholars interested to a public disputation in January, 1487. The disputation never took place. Pope Innocent VIII suspended it and appointed a commission to examine the theses. The commission condemned some of them as heretical; and, when Pico tried to defend the incriminated theses in an *Apologia*, he made things even worse and became involved in a conflict with the papal authorities that was to last for several years. Pico's *Oration* was written as an introductory speech for this projected disputation, probably in 1486. Apparently it was not usual to furnish this kind of rhetorical introduction for a disputation. Yet introductory speeches at the beginning of the school year or at the opening of particular courses were an established custom of medieval schools and universities—a custom further developed by the Humanists of the Renaissance. Pico's disputation speech was obviously patterned after such examples of academic eloquence. Especially typical is the scheme of the two parts, the first dealing with a general philosophical theme, the second announcing and justifying the topics of the disputation that is to follow. The above-mentioned events explain why the speech was never delivered and why its text was not published during Pico's lifetime. It may be added that the second half was incorporated almost verbally in the *Apologia*.

5. See Avery Dulles, *Princeps concordiae: Pico della Mirandola and the Scholastic Tradition* (Cambridge, Mass., 1941).

The *Oration* was printed only after Pico's death, when his nephew, Gian Francesco, included it in a posthumous edition of his uncle's collected works. After the *Oration*, especially its first part, had become famous, some of the later editions added to the simple original title "Oration" the now familiar words "On the Dignity of Man." The criticism often voiced that the *Oration* does not correspond to its title except at the outset is hence without foundation.

The first part of the *Oration* attempts a general justification of the study of philosophy. Pico begins with a praise of man. But he rejects as unsatisfactory the traditional views that man owes his distinction to his place in the center of things or to his character as a microcosm. The true distinction of man consists rather in the fact that he has no fixed properties but has the power to share in the properties of all other beings, according to his own free choice. Yet since man has this power of choosing what form and value his life shall acquire, it is his lot and duty to make the best possible choice and to elevate himself to the life of the angels. In this ascent toward the highest form of life he is assisted by philosophy and its various parts. The second part of the *Oration* explains Pico's own interest in philosophy and the plan of his disputation. He is proposing to defend so great a number of theses because he does not follow the teachings of any particular thinker or school but wants to support propositions drawn from many different sources. This leads to a survey of his nine hundred theses, in which he discusses the various thinkers from whom most of them are taken and then emphasizes the original contribution he is trying to make with some of the others. This survey follows on the whole the arrangement of the *Conclusiones* as they appear in the printed editions. The speech ends with an appeal to the supposed audience to begin the disputation.

The general scheme of the *Oration* is obviously adapted to the occasion for which it was written, yet within this setting there stand out two major ideas which give significance to the little work: the dignity of man and the unity of truth.

The idea of the dignity of man has a long and rather complex history. The praise of man as the inventor of the arts and crafts, as a microcosm, as a being distinguished by speech and by reason, is a common theme of ancient thought and literature. The notion that man is closer to God than any other earthly creature appears in Genesis and pervades all the Old Testament. Early Christian emphasis on the salvation of mankind and on the incarnation of Christ also implied a special position of man in the world, and some of the Church Fathers developed this notion and fused it with the conceptions inherited from pagan antiquity. All these ideas were repeated with new emphasis during the Renaissance. Giannozzo Manetti composed a treatise *On the Excellency and Dignity of Man* as a counterpart to Innocent III's work *On the Misery of Man*. Ficino, in his *Theologia Platonica*, gave an additional philosophical importance to the conception by stressing man's universality and his central position in the universe. Pico, who was undoubtedly familiar with most of these previous statements, introduced, however, an important new element. He emphasized not so much man's universality as his liberty. Man is the only creature whose life is determined not by nature but by his own free choice; and thus man no longer occupies a fixed though distinguished place in the hierarchy of being but exists outside this hierarchy as a kind of separate world.[6]

The notion of the unity of truth which dominates the second part of the *Oration* is an attempt to solve a problem that has puzzled many thinkers since ancient times: the variety and contrast between different philosophers and philosophical schools. Ancient skeptics and modern relativists have used the fact to prove

6. G. Gentile, "Il concetto dell'uomo nel Rinascimento," in his *Il Pensiero italiano del Rinascimento* (3d ed.; Florence, 1940), pp. 47–113; P. O. Kristeller, *The Philosophy of Marsilio Ficino* (New York, 1943), pp. 407 ff., and "Ficino and Pomponazzi on the Place of Man in the Universe," *Journal of the History of Ideas*, V (1944), 220–26.

that there is no truth or certainty. Another and more satisfying answer to the problem has been the assumption that the opposing schools of philosophy do not merely have a common share in error but that they rather share in a common truth. This assumption was held in antiquity by the so-called eclectics and by the Neo-Platonists; it was reasserted on different grounds by Hegel; and it still underlies the better part of the studies devoted to the "history of ideas." Pico's notion of a universal truth in which the various thinkers and schools all have a part obviously belongs to this same tradition. It has been suggested that Pico's conception may have had some connection with the Averroistic doctrine of the unity of the intellect. On the other hand, Pico may have tried to give a broader application to Ficino's doctrine of natural religion and to his attempt to reconcile Platonic philosophy and Christian theology. However this may be, Pico's "syncretism" differs from ancient "eclecticism" and modern "perspectivism" on one characteristic point which seems to reflect his Scholastic background: He does not believe with the ancient eclectics that the major philosophers all agree in their doctrines and merely disagree in their words. Nor does he believe with the modern "perspectivists" that every system of thought taken as a whole represents a particular aspect of universal truth. For Pico, truth consists in a number of true statements; and the various philosophers participate in truth in so far as their writings contain, besides numerous errors, a number of specific statements that are true and hence must be accepted. In this sense, his syncretism is exclusive as well as inclusive and further removed from skepticism than its modern counterparts.

The great influence Pico's ideas of the dignity of man and of the unity of truth were destined to exercise in the Renaissance and afterward was due not only to their intrinsic merits but also to their prominent place in the thought of Pico and of his contemporaries. The notion that man owes his distinction to his freedom and that he is emancipated from the hierarchy of being is further developed and emphasized in Pico's *Heptaplus;* the concern for man's freedom is the underlying cause for his attack on astrology, which is the subject of his major extant work.[7] On the other hand, the unity of truth is the underlying conception of Pico's nine hundred theses; and one particular aspect of this unity —the harmony between Plato and Aristotle—was to be the subject of a large work he planned to write, of which the treatise *De ente et uno* is the only extant fragment.[8] It is hence understandable that some scholars consider this syncretism as the central conception of Pico's thought.[9]

Less obvious but equally significant are the links that connect these two conceptions with the Humanistic movement of the early Renaissance. The early Italian Humanists were primarily concerned not with philosophical speculation but rather with the development of a cultural and educational ideal that was based on the study and imitation of classical antiquity. Yet when they were driven to justify that ideal and the significance of their classical studies, they claimed that these studies contribute to the formation of a desirable human being and are hence of particular concern for man as man. This argument is reflected in such expressions as *studia Humanitatis*, the "Humanities," and the "Humanists." This emphasis on man is one of the few ideas— perhaps the only philosophical idea—contained in the program of the early Humanists. When Pico, and Ficino before him, worked out a philosophical theory of the dignity of man in the universe, they were merely giving a more systematic and speculative development to a vague idea that had dominated the thought and aspirations of their Humanist predecessors for several generations. Pico's syncretism is likewise related to the eclecticism of the early Humanists. In their opposition to the exclusive Aristotelianism of the medieval philosophers, the Humanists

7. Ernst Cassirer, "Giovanni Pico della Mirandola," *Journal of the History of Ideas*, III (1942), 123–44, 319–46.

8. Victor M. Hamm, *Pico della Mirandola: On Being and Unity, Translated from the Latin, with an Introduction* (Milwaukee, Wis., 1943).

9. E. Anagnine, *G. Pico della Mirandola: Sincretismo religioso-filosofico* (Bari, 1937).

liked to quote and make use of the teachings of all the different ancient thinkers and schools accessible to them. They did it often in a rather haphazard and superficial manner, but they broadened the horizon and enriched the source material on which profounder thinkers could afterward draw. Pico's syncretism was a philosophical justification of this Humanist procedure and for the first time gave to it something like a positive method and dignity.

Thus the *Oration on the Dignity of Man* is not merely a piece of rhetoric; it contains ideas that are of major importance in the thought of Pico and in the thought of the Renaissance.

ORATION ON THE DIGNITY OF MAN

I HAVE read in the records of the Arabians, reverend Fathers, that Abdala the Saracen,[1] when questioned as to what on this stage of the world, as it were, could be seen most worthy of wonder, replied: "There is nothing to be seen more wonderful than man." In agreement with this opinion is the saying of Hermes Trismegistus: "A great miracle, Asclepius, is man."[2] But when I weighed the reason for these maxims, the many grounds for the excellence of human nature reported by many men failed to satisfy me—that man is the intermediary between creatures, the intimate of the gods, the king of the lower beings, by the acuteness of his senses, by the discernment of his reason, and by the light of his intelligence the interpreter of nature, the interval between fixed eternity and fleeting time, and (as the Persians say) the bond, nay, rather, the marriage song of the world, on David's testimony but little lower than the angels.[3] Admittedly great though these reasons be, they are not the principal grounds, that is, those which may rightfully claim for themselves the privilege of the highest admiration. For why should we not admire more the angels themselves and the blessed choirs of heaven? At last it seems to me I have come to understand why man is the most fortunate of creatures and consequently worthy of all admiration and what precisely is that rank which is his lot in the universal chain of Being—a rank to be envied not only by brutes but even by the stars and by minds beyond this world. It is a matter past faith and a wondrous one. Why should it not be? For it is on this very account that man is rightly called and judged a great miracle and a wonderful creature indeed.

2. But hear, Fathers, exactly what this rank is and, as friendly

1. [Abdala, that is, Abd Allah, probably the cousin of Mohammed.]
2. [*Asclepius* i. 6 (*Hermetica*, ed. W. Scott, I, 294).]   3. [Ps. 8:5.]

auditors, conformably to your kindness, do me this favor. God the Father, the supreme Architect, had already built this cosmic home we behold, the most sacred temple of His godhead, by the laws of His mysterious wisdom. The region above the heavens He had adorned with Intelligences, the heavenly spheres He had quickened with eternal souls, and the excrementary and filthy parts of the lower world He had filled with a multitude of animals of every kind. But, when the work was finished, the Craftsman kept wishing that there were someone to ponder the plan of so great a work, to love its beauty, and to wonder at its vastness. Therefore, when everything was done (as Moses and Timaeus bear witness), He finally took thought concerning the creation of man. But there was not among His archetypes that from which He could fashion a new offspring, nor was there in His treasure-houses anything which He might bestow on His new son as an inheritance, nor was there in the seats of all the world a place where the latter might sit to contemplate the universe. All was now complete; all things had been assigned to the highest, the middle, and the lowest orders.[4] But in its final creation it was not the part of the Father's power to fail as though exhausted. It was not the part of His wisdom to waver in a needful matter through poverty of counsel. It was not the part of His kindly love that he who was to praise God's divine generosity in regard to others should be compelled to condemn it in regard to himself.

3. At last the best of artisans ordained that that creature to whom He had been able to give nothing proper to himself should have joint possession of whatever had been peculiar to each of the different kinds of being. He therefore took man as a creature of indeterminate nature and, assigning him a place in the middle of the world, addressed him thus: "Neither a fixed abode nor a form that is thine alone nor any function peculiar to thyself have we given thee, Adam, to the end that according to thy longing and according to thy judgment thou mayest have and possess what abode, what form, and what functions thou thyself shalt

4. [Cf. Plato *Protagoras* 321c ff.]

desire. The nature of all other beings is limited and constrained within the bounds of laws prescribed by Us. Thou, constrained by no limits, in accordance with thine own free will, in whose hand We have placed thee, shalt ordain for thyself the limits of thy nature. We have set thee at the world's center that thou mayest from thence more easily observe whatever is in the world. We have made thee neither of heaven nor of earth, neither mortal nor immortal, so that with freedom of choice and with honor, as though the maker and molder of thyself, thou mayest fashion thyself in whatever shape thou shalt prefer. Thou shalt have the power to degenerate into the lower forms of life, which are brutish. Thou shalt have the power, out of thy soul's judgment, to be reborn into the higher forms, which are divine."

4. O supreme generosity of God the Father, O highest and most marvelous felicity of man! To him it is granted to have whatever he chooses, to be whatever he wills. Beasts as soon as they are born (so says Lucilius)[5] bring with them from their mother's womb all they will ever possess. Spiritual beings, either from the beginning or soon thereafter, become what they are to be for ever and ever. On man when he came into life the Father conferred the seeds of all kinds and the germs of every way of life. Whatever seeds each man cultivates will grow to maturity and bear in him their own fruit. If they be vegetative, he will be like a plant. If sensitive, he will become brutish. If rational, he will grow into a heavenly being. If intellectual, he will be an angel and the son of God.[6] And if, happy in the lot of no created thing, he withdraws into the center of his own unity, his spirit, made one with God, in the solitary darkness of God, who is set above all things, shall surpass them all. Who would not admire this our chameleon? Or who could more greatly admire aught else whatever? It is man who Asclepius of Athens, arguing from his mutability of character and from his self-transforming nature, on just grounds says was symbolized by Proteus in the mysteries.

5. [Frag. 623 (Marx).]

6. [Cf. Ficino *Theologia Platonica* xiv. 3.]

Hence those metamorphoses renowned among the Hebrews and the Pythagoreans.

5. For the occult theology of the Hebrews sometimes transforms the holy Enoch into an angel of divinity whom they call "Mal'akh Adonay Shebaoth," and sometimes transforms others into other divinities.[7] The Pythagoreans degrade impious men into brutes and, if one is to believe Empedocles, even into plants. Mohammed, in imitation, often had this saying on his tongue: "They who have deviated from divine law become beasts," and surely he spoke justly. For it is not the bark that makes the plant but its senseless and insentient nature; neither is it the hide that makes the beast of burden but its irrational, sensitive soul; neither is it the orbed form that makes the heavens but their undeviating order; nor is it the sundering from body but his spiritual intelligence that makes the angel. For if you see one abandoned to his appetites crawling on the ground, it is a plant and not a man you see; if you see one blinded by the vain illusions of imagery, as it were of Calypso, and, softened by their gnawing allurement, delivered over to his senses, it is a beast and not a man you see. If you see a philosopher determining all things by means of right reason, him you shall reverence: he is a heavenly being and not of this earth. If you see a pure contemplator, one unaware of the body and confined to the inner reaches of the mind, he is neither an earthly nor a heavenly being; he is a more reverend divinity vested with human flesh.

6. Are there any who would not admire man, who is, in the sacred writings of Moses and the Christians, not without reason described sometimes by the name of "all flesh," sometimes by that of "every creature," inasmuch as he himself molds, fashions, and changes himself into the form of all flesh and into the character of every creature? For this reason the Persian Euanthes, in describing the Chaldaean theology, writes that man has no semblance that is inborn and his very own but many that are external and foreign to him; whence this saying of the Chaldaeans:

7. [Book of Enoch 40 : 8.]

"Hanorish tharah sharinas," that is, "Man is a being of varied, manifold, and inconstant nature."[8] But why do we emphasize this? To the end that after we have been born to this condition— that we can become what we will—we should understand that we ought to have especial care to this, that it should never be said against us that, although born to a privileged position, we failed to recognize it and became like unto wild animals and senseless beasts of burden, but that rather the saying of Asaph the prophet should apply: "Ye are all angels and sons of the Most High,"[9] and that we may not, by abusing the most indulgent generosity of the Father, make for ourselves that freedom of choice He has given into something harmful instead of salutary. Let a certain holy ambition invade our souls, so that, not content with the mediocre, we shall pant after the highest and (since we may if we wish) toil with all our strength to obtain it.

7. Let us disdain earthly things, despise heavenly things, and, finally, esteeming less whatever is of the world, hasten to that court which is beyond the world and nearest to the Godhead. There, as the sacred mysteries relate, Seraphim, Cherubim, and Thrones hold the first places; let us, incapable of yielding to them, and intolerant of a lower place, emulate their dignity and their glory. If we have willed it, we shall be second to them in nothing.

8. But how shall we go about it, and what in the end shall we do? Let us consider what they do, what sort of life they lead. If we also come to lead that life (for we have the power), we shall then equal their good fortune. The Seraph burns with the fire of love. The Cherub glows with the splendor of intelligence. The Throne stands by the steadfastness of judgment. Therefore if, in giving ourselves over to the active life, we have after due consideration undertaken the care of the lower beings, we shall be strengthened with the firm stability of Thrones. If, unoccupied by deeds, we pass our time in the leisure of contemplation, con-

8. [The source of this quotation could not be discovered.]
9. [Cf. Ps. 82:6.]

sidering the Creator in the creature and the creature in the Creator, we shall be all ablaze with Cherubic light. If we long with love for the Creator himself alone, we shall speedily flame up with His consuming fire into a Seraphic likeness. Above the Throne, that is, above the just judge, God sits as Judge of the ages. Above the Cherub, that is, above him who contemplates, God flies, and cherishes him, as it were, in watching over him. For the spirit of the Lord moves upon the waters, the waters, I say, which are above the firmament[10] and which in Job praise the Lord with hymns before dawn. Whoso is a Seraph, that is, a lover, is in God and God in him, nay, rather, God and himself are one. Great is the power of Thrones, which we attain in using judgment, and most high the exaltation of Seraphs, which we attain in loving.

9. But by what means is one able either to judge or to love things unknown? Moses loved a God whom he saw and, as judge, administered among the people what he had first beheld in contemplation upon the mountain. Therefore, the Cherub as intermediary by his own light makes us ready for the Seraphic fire and equally lights the way to the judgment of the Thrones. This is the bond of the first minds, the Palladian order, the chief of contemplative philosophy. This is the one for us first to emulate, to court, and to understand; the one from whence we may be rapt to the heights of love and descend, well taught and well prepared, to the functions of active life. But truly it is worth while, if our life is to be modeled on the example of the Cherubic life, to have before our eyes and clearly understood both its nature and its quality and those things which are the deeds and the labor of Cherubs. But since it is not permitted us to attain this through our own efforts, we who are but flesh and know of the things of earth, let us go to the ancient fathers who, inasmuch as they were familiar and conversant with these matters, can give sure and altogether trustworthy testimony. Let us consult the Apostle Paul, the chosen vessel,[11] as to what he saw the hosts of

10. [Gen. 1 : 2.]   11. [Acts 9 : 15.]

Cherubim doing when he was himself exalted to the third heaven. He will answer, according to the interpretation of Dionysius,[12] that he saw them being purified, then being illuminated, and at last being made perfect. Let us also, therefore, by emulating the Cherubic way of life on earth, by taming the impulses of our passions with moral science, by dispelling the darkness of reason with dialectic, and by, so to speak, washing away the filth of ignorance and vice, cleanse our soul, so that her passions may not rave at random nor her reason through heedlessness ever be deranged.

10. Then let us fill our well-prepared and purified soul with the light of natural philosophy, so that we may at last perfect her in the knowledge of things divine. And lest we be satisfied with those of our faith, let us consult the patriarch Jacob, whose form gleams carved on the throne of glory. Sleeping in the lower world but keeping watch in the upper, the wisest of fathers will advise us. But he will advise us through a figure (in this way everything was wont to come to those men) that there is a ladder extending from the lowest earth to the highest heaven, divided in a series of many steps, with the Lord seated at the top, and angels in contemplation ascending and descending over them alternately by turns.[13]

11. If this is what we must practice in our aspiration to the angelic way of life, I ask: "Who will touch the ladder of the Lord either with fouled foot or with unclean hands?" As the sacred mysteries have it, it is impious for the impure to touch the pure. But what are these feet? What these hands? Surely the foot of the soul is that most contemptible part by which the soul rests on matter as on the soil of the earth, I mean the nourishing and feeding power, the tinder of lust, and the teacher of pleasurable weakness. Why should we not call the hands of the soul its iras-

12. [Dionysius the Areopagite. The writings current under that name, composed by an unknown author probably about A.D. 500, were long attributed to Dionysius, the disciple of Paul, and hence enjoyed an enormous authority.]

13. [Gen. 28 : 12.]

cible power, which struggles on its behalf as the champion of
desire and as plunderer seizes in the dust and sun what desire will
devour slumbering in the shade? These hands, these feet, that is,
all the sentient part whereon resides the attraction of the body
which, as they say, by wrenching the neck holds the soul in
check, lest we be hurled down from the ladder as impious and
unclean, let us bathe in moral philosophy as if in a living river.
Yet this will not be enough if we wish to be companions of the
angels going up and down on Jacob's ladder, unless we have first
been well fitted and instructed to be promoted duly from step to
step, to stray nowhere from the stairway, and to engage in the
alternate comings and goings. Once we have achieved this by the
art of discourse or reasoning, then, inspired by the Cherubic
spirit, using philosophy through the steps of the ladder, that is,
of nature, and penetrating all things from center to center, we
shall sometimes descend, with titanic force rending the unity like
Osiris into many parts, and we shall sometimes ascend, with the
force of Phoebus collecting the parts like the limbs of Osiris into
a unity, until, resting at last in the bosom of the Father who is
above the ladder, we shall be made perfect with the felicity
of theology.

12. Let us also inquire of the just Job, who entered into a life-
covenant with God before he himself was brought forth into
life, what the most high God requires above all in those tens of
hundreds of thousands who attend him. He will answer that it is
peace, in accord with what we read in him: "He maketh peace in
his high places."[14] And since the middle order expounds to the
lower orders the counsel of the highest order, let Empedocles the
philosopher expound to us the words of Job the theologian. He
indicates to us a twofold nature present in our souls, by one side
of which we are raised on high to the heavenly regions, and by
the other side plunged downward into the lower, through strife
and friendship or through war and peace, as he witnesses in the
verses in which he makes complaint that he is being driven into

14. [Job 25:2.]

the sea, himself goaded by strife and discord into the semblance of a madman and a fugitive from the gods.[15]

13. Surely, Fathers, there is in us a discord many times as great; we have at hand wars grievous and more than civil,[16] wars of the spirit which, if we dislike them, if we aspire to that peace which may so raise us to the sublime that we shall be established among the exalted of the Lord, only philosophy will entirely allay and subdue in us. In the first place, if our man but ask a truce of his enemies, moral philosophy will check the unbridled inroads of the many-sided beast and the leonine passions of wrath and violence. If we then take wiser counsel with ourselves and learn to desire the security of everlasting peace, it will be at hand and will generously fulfil our prayers. After both beasts are felled like a sacrificed sow, it will confirm an inviolable compact of holiest peace between flesh and spirit. Dialectic will appease the tumults of reason made confused and anxious by inconsistencies of statement and sophisms of syllogisms. Natural philosophy will allay the strife and differences of opinion which vex, distract, and wound the spirit from all sides. But she will so assuage them as to compel us to remember that, according to Heraclitus, nature was begotten from war, that it was on this account repeatedly called "strife" by Homer, and that it is not, therefore, in the power of natural philosophy to give us in nature a true quiet and unshaken peace but that this is the function and privilege of her mistress, that is, of holiest theology. She will show us the way and as comrade lead us to her who, seeing us hastening from afar, will exclaim "Come to me, ye who have labored. Come and I will restore you. Come to me, and I will give you peace, which the world and nature cannot give you."[17]

14. When we have been so soothingly called, so kindly urged, we shall fly up with winged feet, like earthly Mercuries, to the embraces of our blessed mother and enjoy that wished-for peace, most holy peace, indivisible bond, of one accord in the friendship

15. [Frag. 115. 13–14. (Diels).]
16. [Cf. Lucan *Pharsalia*. i. 1.]   17. [Matt. 11:28 and John 14:27.]

through which all rational souls not only shall come into harmony in the one mind which is above all minds but shall in some ineffable way become altogether one. This is that friendship which the Pythagoreans say is the end of all philosophy. This is that peace which God creates in his heavens, which the angels descending to earth proclaimed to men of good will,[18] that through it men might ascend to heaven and become angels. Let us wish this peace for our friends, for our century. Let us wish it for every home into which we go; let us wish it for our own soul, that through it she shall herself be made the house of God, and to the end that as soon as she has cast out her uncleanness through moral philosophy and dialectic, adorned herself with manifold philosophy as with the splendor of a courtier, and crowned the pediments of her doors with the garlands of theology, the King of Glory may descend and, coming with his Father, make his stay with her. If she show herself worthy of so great a guest, she shall, by the boundless mercy which is his, in golden raiment like a wedding gown, and surrounded by a varied throng of sciences, receive her beautiful guest not merely as a guest but as a spouse from whom she will never be parted. She will desire rather to be parted from her own people and, forgetting her father's house and herself, will desire to die in herself in order to live in her spouse, in whose sight surely the death of his saints is precious[19]—death, I say, if we must call death that fulness of life, the consideration of which wise men have asserted to be the aim of philosophy.[20]

15. Let us also cite Moses himself, but little removed from the springing abundance of the holy and unspeakable wisdom by whose nectar the angels are made drunk. Let us hearken to the venerable judge in these words proclaiming laws to us who are dwellers in the desert loneliness of this body: "Let those who, as yet unclean, still need moral philosophy, live with the people outside the tabernacle under the sky, meanwhile purifying them-

18. [Luke 2 : 14.]
19. [Cf. Ps. 116 : 15.]   20. [Cf. Plato *Phaedo* 81a.]

selves like the priests of Thessaly. Let those who have already ordered their conduct be received into the sanctuary but not quite yet touch the holy vessels; let them first like zealous Levites in the service of dialectic minister to the holy things of philosophy. Then when they have been admitted even to these, let them now behold the many-colored robe of the higher palace of the Lord, that is to say, the stars; let them now behold the heavenly candlestick divided into seven lights; let them now behold the fur tent, that is, the elements,[21] in the priesthood of philosophy, so that when they are in the end, through the favor of theological sublimity, granted entrance into the inner part of the temple, they may rejoice in the glory of the Godhead with no veil before his image." This of a surety Moses commands us and, in commanding, summons, urges, and encourages us by means of philosophy to prepare ourselves a way, while we can, to the heavenly glory to come.

16. But indeed not only the Mosaic and Christian mysteries but also the theology of the ancients show us the benefits and value of the liberal arts, the discussion of which I am about to undertake. For what else did the degrees of the initiates observed in the mysteries of the Greeks mean? For they arrived at a perception of the mysteries when they had first been purified through those expiatory sciences, as it were, moral philosophy and dialectic. What else can that perception possibly be than an interpretation of occult nature by means of philosophy? Then at length to those who were so disposed came that ΕΠΟΠΤΕΙΑ,[22] that is to say, the observation of things divine by the light of theology. Who would not long to be initiated into such sacred rites? Who would not desire, by neglecting all human concerns, by despising the goods of fortune, and by disregarding those of the body, to become the guest of the gods while yet living on earth, and, made drunk by the nectar of eternity, to be endowed with the gifts of immortality though still a mortal being? Who would not wish to

21. [Cf. Exod. 26:14; 36:19; 39:33.]
22. [Initiation in the Eleusinian mysteries.]

be so inflamed with those Socratic frenzies sung by Plato in the *Phaedrus*,[23] that, by the oarage of feet and wings escaping speedily from hence, that is, from a world set on evil, he might be borne on the fastest of courses to the heavenly Jerusalem? Let us be driven, Fathers, let us be driven by the frenzies of Socrates, that they may so throw us into ecstasy as to put our mind and ourselves in God. Let us be driven by them, if we have first done what is in our power. For if through moral philosophy the forces of our passions have by a fitting agreement become so intent on harmony that they can sing together in undisturbed concord, and if through dialectic our reason has moved progressively in a rhythmical measure, then we shall be stirred by the frenzy of the Muses and drink the heavenly harmony with our inmost hearing. Thereupon Bacchus, the leader of the Muses, by showing in his mysteries, that is, in the visible signs of nature,[24] the invisible things of God to us who study philosophy, will intoxicate us with the fulness of God's house, in which, if we prove faithful, like Moses, hallowed theology shall come and inspire us with a doubled frenzy. For, exalted to her lofty height, we shall measure therefrom all things that are and shall be and have been in indivisible eternity; and, admiring their original beauty, like the seers of Phoebus, we shall become her own winged lovers. And at last, roused by ineffable love as by a sting, like burning Seraphim rapt from ourselves, full of divine power we shall no longer be ourselves but shall become He Himself Who made us.

17. If anyone investigates the holy names of Apollo, their meanings and hidden mysteries, these amply show that that god is no less a philosopher than a seer; but, since Ammonius has sufficiently examined this subject, there is no reason why I should now treat it otherwise. But, Fathers, three Delphic precepts may suggest themselves to your minds, which are very necessary to those who are to go into the most sacred and revered temple, not of the false but of the true Apollo, who lights every soul as it enters this world.[25] You will see that they give us no other advice

23. [245*b* ff.]   24. [Cf. Rom. 1 : 20.]   25. [John 1:9.]

than that we should with all our strength embrace this threefold philosophy which is the concern of our present debate. For the saying μηδὲν ἄγαν, that is, "Nothing too much," prescribes a standard and rule for all the virtues through the doctrine of the Mean, with which moral philosophy duly deals. Then the saying γνῶθι σεαυτόν, that is, "Know thyself," urges and encourages us to the investigation of all nature, of which the nature of man is both the connecting link and, so to speak, the "mixed bowl." For he who knows himself in himself knows all things, as Zoroaster first wrote, and then Plato in his *Alcibiades*.[26] When we are finally lighted in this knowledge by natural philosophy, and nearest to God are uttering the theological greeting, εἶ, that is, "Thou art," we shall likewise in bliss be addressing the true Apollo on intimate terms.

18. Let us also consult the wise Pythagoras, especially wise in that he never deemed himself worthy the name of a wise man. He will first enjoin us not to sit on a bushel, that is, not by unoccupied sloth to lose our rational faculty, by which the soul measures, judges, and considers all things; but we must direct and stimulate it unremittingly by the discipline and rule of dialectic. Then he will point out to us two things particularly to beware of: that we should not make water facing the sun or cut our nails while offering sacrifice. But after we have, through the agency of moral philosophy, both voided the lax desires of our too abundant pleasures and pared away like nail-cuttings the sharp corners of anger and the stings of wrath, only then may we begin to take part in the holy rites, that is, the mysteries of Bacchus we have mentioned, and to be free for our contemplation, whose father and leader the Sun is rightly named. Finally, Pythagoras will enjoin us to feed the cock, that is, to feast the divine part of our soul on the knowledge of things divine as if on substantial food and heavenly ambrosia. This is the cock at whose sight the lion, that is, all earthly power, trembles and is filled with awe. This is that cock to whom, we read in Job, intelligence was given.

26. [133c ff.]

When this cock crows, erring man comes to his senses. This cock in the twilight of morning daily sings with the morning stars as they praise God. The dying Socrates, when he hoped to join the divinity of his spirit with the divinity of a greater world, said that he owed this cock to Aesculapius, that is, to the physician of souls, now that he had passed beyond all danger of illness.[27]

19. Let us review also the records of the Chaldeans, and we shall see (if they are to be trusted) the road to felicity laid open to mortals through the same sciences. His Chaldaean interpreters write that it was a saying of Zoroaster that the soul is winged and that, when the wings drop off, she falls headlong into the body; and then, after her wings have grown again sufficiently, she flies back to heaven. When his followers asked him in what manner they could obtain souls winged with well-feathered wings, he replied: "Refresh ye your wings in the waters of life." Again when they asked where they should seek those waters, he answered them thus by a parable (as was the custom of the man): "God's paradise is laved and watered by four rivers, from whose same source ye may draw the waters of your salvation. The name of that in the north is Pischon, which meaneth the right. The name of that in the west is Dichon, which signifieth expiation. The name of that in the east is Chiddikel, which expresseth light, and of that in the south, Perath, which we may interpret as piety."

20. Turn your attention, Fathers, to the diligent consideration of what these doctrines of Zoroaster mean. Surely nothing else than that we should wash away the uncleanness from our eyes by moral science as if by the western waves; that we should align their keen vision toward the right by the rule of dialectic as if by the northern line; that we should then accustom them to endure in the contemplation of nature the still feeble light of truth as if it were the first rays of the rising sun, so that at last, through the agency of theological piety and the most holy worship of God, we may like heavenly eagles boldly endure the

27. [Cf. *Phaedo* 118a.]

most brilliant splendor of the meridian sun. These are, perhaps, those ideas proper to morning, midday, and evening first sung by David and given a broader interpretation by Augustine. This is that noonday light which incites the Seraphs to their goal and equally sheds light on the Cherubs. This is that country toward which Abraham, our father of old, was ever journeying. This is that place where, as the doctrines of Cabalists and Moors have handed down to posterity, there is no room for unclean spirits. And, if it is right to bring into the open anything at all of the occult mysteries, even in the guise of a riddle, since a sudden fall from heaven has condemned the head of man to dizziness, and, in the words of Jeremiah, death has come in through our windows and smitten our vitals and our heart,[28] let us summon Raphael, celestial physician, that he may set us free by moral philosophy and by dialectic as though by wholesome drugs. Then, when we are restored to health, Gabriel, "the strength of God," shall abide in us, leading us through the miracles of nature and showing us on every side the merit and the might of God. He will at last consign us to the high priest Michael, who will distinguish those who have completed their term in the service of philosophy with the holy office of theology as if with a crown of precious stones.

21. These, reverend Fathers, are the considerations that have not only inspired but compelled me to the study of philosophy. I should certainly not set them forth were I not answering those who are wont to condemn the study of philosophy, especially among men of rank or even of a mediocre station in life. For this whole study of philosophy has now (and it is the misfortune of our age) come to despise and contumely rather than to honor and glory. Thus this deadly and monstrous conviction has come to pervade the minds of well-nigh all—that philosophy either must be studied not at all or by few persons, as if it were absolutely nothing to have clearly ascertained, before our eyes and before our hands, the causes of things, the ways of nature, the

28. [Jer., 9:21.]

plan of the universe, the purposes of God, and the mysteries of heaven and earth; unless one may obtain some favor, or make money for one's self. Rather, it has come to the point where none is now deemed wise, alas, save those who make the study of wisdom a mercenary profession, and where it is possible to see the chaste Pallas, who was sent among men as the gift of the gods, hooted, hissed, and whistled off the stage; and not having anyone to love or to befriend her, unless by selling herself, as it were, she repays into the treasury of her "lover" even the ill-gained money received as the poor price of her tarnished virginity.

22. I speak all these accusations (not without the deepest grief and indignation) not against the princes of this time but against the philosophers, who both believe and openly declare that there should be no study of philosophy for the reason that no fee and no compensation have been fixed for philosophers, just as if they did not show by this one sign that they are no philosophers, that since their whole life is set either on profit or on ambition they do not embrace the very discovery of truth for its own sake. I shall grant myself this and blush not at all to praise myself to this extent that I have never studied philosophy for any other reason than that I might be a philosopher; and that I have neither hoped for any pay from my studies, from my labors by lamplight, nor sought any other reward than the cultivation of my mind and the knowledge of the truth I have ever longed for above all things. I have always been so desirous, so enamored of this, that I have relinquished all interest in affairs private and public and given myself over entirely to leisure for contemplation, from which no disparagements of those who hate me, no curses of the enemies of wisdom, have been able in the past or will be able in the future to discourage me. Philosophy herself has taught me to rely on my own conscience rather than on the opinions of others, and always to take thought not so much that people may speak no evil of me, as, rather, that I myself may neither say nor do aught that is evil.

23. For my part, reverend Fathers, I was not unaware that this very disputation of mine would be as grateful and pleasing to you who favor all good sciences, and have been willing to honor it with your most august presence, as it would be offensive and annoying to many others. And I know there is no lack of those who have heretofore condemned my project, and who condemn it at present on a number of grounds. Enterprises that are well and conscientiously directed toward virtue have been wont to find no fewer—not to say more—detractors than those that are wickedly and falsely directed toward vice. There are, indeed, those who do not approve of this whole method of disputation and of this institution of publicly debating on learning, maintaining that it tends rather to the parade of talent and the display of erudition than to the increase of learning. There are those who do not indeed disapprove this kind of practice, but who in no wise approve it in me because I, born I admit but twenty-four years ago, should have dared at my age to offer a disputation concerning the lofty mysteries of Christian theology, the highest topics of philosophy and unfamiliar branches of knowledge, in so famous a city, before so great an assembly of very learned men, in the presence of the apostolic senate. Others, who give me leave to offer this disputation, are unwilling to allow me to debate nine hundred theses, and misrepresent it as being a work as unnecessary and as ostentatious as it is beyond my powers. I would have yielded to their objections and given in immediately if the philosophy I profess had so instructed me; and I should not now be answering them, even with philosophy as my preceptress, if I believed that this debate between us had been undertaken for the purpose of quarreling and scolding. Therefore, let the whole intention to disparage and to exasperate depart from our minds, and malice also, which Plato writes is ever absent from the heavenly choir.[29] Let us in friendly wise try both questions: whether I am to debate and whether I am to debate about this great number of theses.

29. [*Phaedrus* 247a.]

24. First, as to those who revile this custom of debating in public I shall certainly not say a great deal, since this crime, if it is held a crime, is shared with me not only by all of you, excellent doctors, who have rather frequently engaged in this office not without the highest praise and glory, but also by Plato, also by Aristotle, and also by the most worthy philosophers of every age. For them it was certain that, for the attainment of the knowledge of truth they were always seeking for themselves, nothing is better than to attend as often as possible the exercise of debate. For just as bodily energy is strengthened by gymnastic exercise, so beyond doubt in this wrestling-place of letters, as it were, energy of mind becomes far stronger and more vigorous. And I could not believe, either that the poets, by the arms of Pallas which they sang, or that the Hebrews, when they called the sword the symbol of wise men, were indicating to us anything else than that such honorable contests are surely a necessary way of attaining wisdom. For this reason it is, perchance, that the Chaldaeans desired in the horoscope of one who was to be a philosopher that Mars should be to Mercury in the trinal aspect, as much as to say, "If these assemblies, these disputations, should be given up, all philosophy would become sluggish and drowsy."

25. But truly with those who say I am unequal to this commission, my method of defense is more difficult. For if I say that I am equal to it, it seems that I shall take on myself the reproach of being immodest and of thinking too well of myself, and, if I admit that I am not equal to it, the reproach of being imprudent and thoughtless. See into what straits I have fallen, in what a position I am placed, since I cannot without blame promise about myself what I cannot then fail to fulfil without blame. Perhaps I could refer to that saying of Job: "The spirit is in all men,"[30] and be told with Timothy, "Let no man despise thy youth."[31] But out of my own conscience I shall with more truth say this: that there is nothing either great or extraordinary about me. I do

30. [Job 32:8.]   31. [I Tim. 4:12.]

not deny that I am, if you will, studious and eager for the good sciences, but nevertheless I neither assume nor arrogate to myself the title of learned. However great the burden I may have taken on my shoulders, therefore, it was not because I was not perfectly aware of my own want of strength but because I knew that it is a distinction of contests of this kind, that is, literary ones, that there is a profit in being defeated. Whence it is that even the most feeble are by right able and bound not only not to decline but even more to court them, seeing that he who yields receives no injury but a benefit from the victor, in that through him he returns home even richer, that is, wiser and better equipped for future contests. Inspired by this hope, I, who am but a feeble soldier, have feared not at all to wage so burdensome a war with the strongest and most vigorous men of all. Whether this action be ill considered or not may be judged from the outcome of the battle and not from my age.

26. It remains in the third place to answer those who take offense at the great number of my propositions, as if the weight of these lay on their shoulders, and as if the burden, such as it is, were not rather to be borne by me alone. It is surely unbecoming and beyond measure captious to wish to set bounds to another's effort and, as Cicero says, to desire moderation in a matter which is the better as it is on a larger scale.[32] In so great a venture it was necessary for me either to give complete satisfaction or to fail utterly. Should I succeed, I do not see why what is laudable to do in an affair of ten theses should be deemed culpable to have done also in an affair of nine hundred. Should I fail, they will have the wherewithal to accuse me if they hate me and to forgive me if they love me. For the failure of a young man with but slender talent and little learning in so grave and so great a matter will be more deserving of pardon than of blame. Nay, according to the poet: "If strength fails, there shall surely be praise for daring; and to have wished for great things is enough."[33] And if many in our time, in imitation

32. [*De finibus* i. 1.]   33. [Propertius ii. 10. 5–6.]

of Gorgias of Leontini, have been wont, not without praise, to propose debates not concerning nine hundred questions only, but also concerning all questions in all branches of knowledge, why should I not be allowed, and that without criticism, to discuss questions admittedly numerous but at least fixed and limited? Yet they say it is unnecessary and ostentatious. I contend that this enterprise of mine is in no way superfluous but necessary indeed; and if they will ponder with me the purpose of studying philosophy, they must, even against their wills, admit that it is plainly needful. Those who have devoted themselves to any one of the schools of philosophy, favoring, for instance, Thomas or Scotus, who are now most in fashion, are, to be sure, quite capable of making trial of their particular doctrines in the discussion of but a few questions. I, on the other hand, have so prepared myself that, pledged to the doctrines of no man,[34] I have ranged through all the masters of philosophy, investigated all books, and come to know all schools. Therefore, since I had to speak of them all in order that, as champion of the beliefs of one, I might not seem fettered to it and appear to place less value on the rest, even while proposing a few theses concerning individual schools I could not help proposing a great number concerning all the schools together. And let no man condemn me for coming as a friend whithersoever the tempest bear me. For it was a custom observed by all the ancients in studying every kind of writer to pass over none of the learned works they were able to read, and especially by Aristotle, who for this reason was called by Plato ἀναγνώστης, that is, "reader." And surely it is the part of a narrow mind to have confined itself within a single Porch or Academy. Nor can one rightly choose what suits one's self from all of them who has not first come to be familiar with them all. Consider, in addition, that there is in each school something distinctive that is not common to the others.

27. And now, to begin with the men of our faith, to whom

34. [Cf. Horace *Epistles* i. 1. 14.]

philosophy came last: There is in John Scotus something lively and subtle; in Thomas, sound and consistent; in Aegidius, terse and exact; in Francis, acute and penetrating; in Albert, venerable, copious, and grand; in Henry, as it always seems to me, something sublime and to be revered. Among the Arabs, there is in Averroes something stable and unshaken; in Avempace....; in Alfarabi, serious and thoughtful; in Avicenna, divine and Platonic. Among the Greeks philosophy as a whole is certainly brilliant and above all chaste. With Simplicius it is rich and abundant; with Themistius, graceful and compendious; with Alexander, harmonious and learned; with Theophrastus, weightily worked out; with Ammonius, smooth and agreeable. And if you turn your attention to the Platonists, to examine a few: in Porphyry you will rejoice in the abundance of his material and in the complexity of his religion; in Jamblichus you will revere an occult philosophy and the mysteries of the East. In Plotinus there is no isolated aspect you will admire; he shows himself admirable on every side. The toiling Platonists themselves scarcely understand him when he speaks divinely of things divine and, with learned obliquity of speech, far more than humanly of human things. I prefer to pass over the later Platonists: Proclus abounding in Asiatic richness, and those stemming from him, Hermias, Damascius, Olympiodorus, and several others, in all of whom there ever gleams that $\tau\grave{o}$ $\theta\epsilon\hat{\iota}ov$. that is, "the Divine," which is the distinctive mark of the Platonists.[35]

28. Add to this that any sect which assails the truer doctrines, and makes game of good causes by clever slander, strengthens rather than weakens the truth and, like flames stirred by agita-

35. [This catalogue is a brief survey of the philosophers utilized in Pico's nine hundred theses. John Scotus is Duns Scotus (d. 1308), Thomas is Thomas Aquinas (d. 1274), Aegidius is Giles of Rome (d. 1316), Francis is Franciscus de Mayronis (d. 1325), Albert is Albertus Magnus (d. 1280), and Henry is Henry of Ghent (d. 1293), Averroes (d. 1198), Avempace (d. 1138), Alfarabi (d. 950), Simplicius (*fl. ca.* 530), Themistius (*fl. ca.* 350), and Alexander of Aphrodisias (*fl. ca.* A.D. 200). Most of the remaining thinkers are Neo-Platonists.]

tion, fans rather than extinguishes it. This has been my reason for wishing to bring before the public the opinions not of a single school alone (which satisfied some I could name) but rather of every school, to the end that that light of truth Plato mentions in his *Epistles*[36] through this comparison of several sects and this discussion of manifold philosophies might dawn more brightly on our minds, like the sun rising from the deep. What were the gain if only the philosophy of the Latins were investigated, that is, that of Albert, Thomas, Scotus, Aegidius, Francis, and Henry, if the Greek and Arabian philosophers were left out—since all wisdom has flowed from the East to the Greeks and from the Greeks to us? In their way of philosophizing, our Latins have always found it sufficient to stand on the discoveries of foreigners and to perfect the work of others. Of what use were it to treat with the Peripatetics on natural philosophy, unless the Platonic Academy were also invited? Their teaching in regard to divinity besides has always (as Augustine witnesses) been thought most hallowed of all philosophies;[37] and now for the first time, so far as I know (may no one grudge me the word), it has after many centuries been brought by me to the test of public disputation. What were it to have dealt with the opinions of others, no matter how many, if we are come to a gathering of wise men with no contribution of our own and are supplying nothing from our own store, brought forth and worked out by our own genius? It is surely an ignoble part to be wise only from a notebook (as Seneca says)[38] and, as if the discoveries of our predecessors had closed the way to our own industry and the power of nature were exhausted in us, to produce from ourselves nothing which, if it does not actually demonstrate the truth, at least intimates it from afar. For if a tiller of the soil hates sterility in his field, and a husband in his wife, surely the Divine mind joined to and associated with an

36. [Cf. *Epistle* vii. 341c–d.]

37. [Cf. *City of God* ix. 1 and many other passages.]

38. [*Epistles* xxxiii. 7.]

infertile soul will hate it the more in that a far nobler offspring is desired.

29. For this reason I have not been content to add to the tenets held in common many teachings taken from the ancient theology of Hermes Trismegistus, many from the doctrines of the Chaldaeans and of Pythagoras, and many from the occult mysteries of the Hebrews. I have proposed also as subjects for discussion several theses in natural philosophy and in divinity, discovered and studied by me. I have proposed, first of all, a harmony between Plato and Aristotle, believed to exist by many ere this but adequately proved by no one. Boethius among the Latins promised that he would do it, but there is no trace of his having done what he always wished to do. Among the Greeks, Simplicius made the same declaration, and would that he had been as good as his word! Augustine also writes, in the *Contra Academicos*, that there were not lacking several who tried with their keenest arguments to prove the same thing, that the philosophies of Plato and Aristotle are identical.[39] John the Grammarian[40] likewise, although he did say that Plato differs from Aristotle only in the minds of those who do not understand Plato's words, nevertheless left it to posterity to prove. I have, moreover, brought to bear several passages in which I maintain that the opinions of Scotus and Thomas, and several in which I hold that those of Averroes and Avicenna, which are considered to be contradictory, are in agreement.

30. In the second place, I have next arranged the fruit of my thinking on both the Platonic and the Aristotelian philosophy, and then seventy-two new physical and metaphysical theses by means of which whoever holds them will be able (unless I am mistaken—which will soon be made manifest to me) to answer any question whatever proposed in natural philosophy or divinity, by a system far other than we are taught in that philosophy which is studied in the schools and practised by the doctors of this age. Nor ought anyone, Fathers, to be so amazed that I, in

39. [*Contra academicos* iii. 42.]   40. [Joannes Philoponus.]

my first years, at my tender age, at which it was hardly legitimate for me (as some have taunted) to read the books of others, should wish to introduce a new philosophy; but rather one should praise it if it is sustained or condemn it if it does not find favor, and finally, when these my discoveries and my scholarship come to be judged, number not their author's years so much as their own merits or faults.

31. There is, furthermore, still another method of philosophizing through numbers, which I have introduced as new, but which is in fact old, and was observed by the earliest theologians, principally by Pythagoras, by Aglaophamos, Philolaus, and Plato, and by the first Platonists, but which in this present era, like many other illustrious things, has perished through the carelessness of posterity, so that hardly any traces of it can be found. Plato writes in the *Epinomis* that, of all the liberal arts and theoretical sciences, the science of computation is the chief and the most divine.[41] Likewise, inquiring, "Why is man the wisest of animals?" he concludes, "Because he knows how to count," an opinion which Aristotle also mentions in his *Problems*.[42] Abumasar writes that it was a saying of Avenzoar of Babylon that he knows all things who knows how to count. These statements cannot possibly be true if by the science of computation they mean that science in which, at present, merchants in particular are most skilled. To this also Plato bears witness, warning us with raised voice not to think that this divine arithmetic is the arithmetic of traders.[43] I therefore promised, when I seemed after much nocturnal labor to have discovered that arithmetic which is so highly extolled, that I myself would (in order to make trial of this matter) reply in public through the art of number to seventy-four questions considered of chief importance in physics and metaphysics.

32. I have also proposed theorems dealing with magic, in which I have indicated that magic has two forms, one of which depends entirely on the work and authority of demons, a thing to

41. [*976c* ff.]   42. [xxxi. 6. 956 *a* 11 ff.]   43. [*Republic* 525*b* ff.]

be abhorred, so help me the God of truth, and a monstrous thing. The other, when it is rightly pursued, is nothing else than the utter perfection of natural philosophy. While the Greeks make mention of both of them, they call the former γοητεία, in no wise honoring it with the name of magic; the latter they call by the characteristic and fitting name of μαγεία, as if it were a perfect and most high wisdom. For, as Porphyry says, in the Persian tongue *magus* expresses the same idea as "interpreter" and "worshiper of the divine" with us. Moreover, Fathers, the disparity and unlikeness between these arts is great, nay, rather, the greatest possible. The former not only the Christian religion but all religions and every well-constituted state condemn and abhor. The latter all wise men, all peoples devoted to the study of heavenly and divine things, approve and embrace. The former is the most deceitful of arts; the latter a higher and more holy philosophy. The former is vain and empty; the latter, sure, trustworthy, and sound. Whoso has cherished the former has ever dissembled, because it is a shame and a reproach to an author; but from the latter the highest renown and glory of letters was derived in ancient days, and almost always has been. No man who was a philosopher and eager to study the good arts has ever been a student of the former; but Pythagoras, Empedocles, Democritus, and Plato all traveled to study the latter, taught it when they returned, and esteemed it before all others in their mysteries. As the former is approved by no reasonable arguments, so is it not by established authors; the latter, honored by the most celebrated fathers, as it were, has in particular two authors: Zamolxis, whom Abaris the Hyperborean copied, and Zoroaster, not him of whom perhaps you are thinking but him who is the son of Oromasius.

33. If we ask Plato what the magic of both these men was, he will reply, in his *Alcibiades*,[44] that the magic of Zoroaster was none other than the science of the Divine in which the kings of the Persians instructed their sons, to the end that they might be

44. [122a.]

taught to rule their own commonwealth by the example of the commonwealth of the world. He will answer, in the *Charmides*,[45] that the magic of Zamolxis was that medicine of the soul through which temperance is brought to the soul as through temperance health is brought to the body. In their footsteps Charondas, Damigeron, Apollonius, Osthanes, and Dardanus thereafter persevered. Homer persevered, whom I shall sometime prove, in my *Poetic Theology*, to have concealed this philosophy beneath the wanderings of his Ulysses, just as he has concealed all others. Eudoxus and Hermippus persevered. Almost all who have searched through the Pythagorean and Platonic mysteries have persevered. Furthermore, from among the later philosophers I find three who have scented it out—the Arabian al-Kindi, Roger Bacon, and William of Paris.[46] Plotinus also mentions it when he demonstrates that a *magus* is the servant of nature and not a contriver. This very wise man approves and maintains this magic, so hating the other that, when he was summoned to the rites of evil spirits, he said that they should come to him rather than that he should go to them; and surely he was right.[47] For even as the former makes man the bound slave of wicked powers, so does the latter make him their ruler and their lord. In conclusion, the former can claim for itself the name of neither art nor science, while the latter, abounding in the loftiest mysteries, embraces the deepest contemplation of the most secret things, and at last the knowledge of all nature. The latter, in calling forth into the light as if from their hiding-places the powers scattered and sown in the world by the loving-kindness of God, does not so much work wonders as diligently serve a wonder-working nature. The latter, having more searchingly examined into the harmony of the universe, which the Greeks with greater significance call συμπάθεια, and having clearly perceived the

45. [156e–157a.]

46. [Alkindi (d. *ca.* 870); Roger Bacon (d. 1294); William of Paris, better known as William of Auvergne (d. 1249).]

47. [Cf. Porphyry's *Life of Plotinus* 10.]

reciprocal affinity of natures, and applying to each single thing the suitable and peculiar inducements (which are called the ἴυγγες of the magicians) brings forth into the open the miracles concealed in the recesses of the world, in the depths of nature, and in the storehouses and mysteries of God, just as if she herself were their maker; and, as the farmer weds his elms to vines, even so does the *magus* wed earth to heaven, that is, he weds lower things to the endowments and powers of higher things. Whence it comes about that the latter is as divine and as salutary as the former is unnatural and harmful; for this reason especially, that in subjecting man to the enemies of God, the former calls him away from God, but the latter rouses him to the admiration of God's works which is the most certain condition of a willing faith, hope, and love. For nothing moves one to religion and to the worship of God more than the diligent contemplation of the wonders of God; if we have thoroughly examined them by this natural magic we are considering, we shall be compelled to sing, more ardently inspired to the worship and love of the Creator: "The heavens and all the earth are full of the majesty of thy glory."[48] And this is enough about magic. I have said these things about it, for I know there are many who, just as dogs always bark at strangers, in the same way often condemn and hate what they do not understand.

34. I come now to the things I have elicited from the ancient mysteries of the Hebrews and have cited for the confirmation of the inviolable Catholic faith. Lest perchance they should be deemed fabrications, trifles, or the tales of jugglers by those to whom they are unfamiliar, I wish all to understand what they are and of what sort, whence they come, by what and by how illustrious authors supported, and how mysterious, how divine, and how necessary they are to the men of our faith for defending our religion against the grievous misrepresentations of the Hebrews. Not only the famous doctors of the Hebrews, but also from among men of our opinion Esdras, Hilary, and Origen write that

48. [From the "Sanctus" of the Mass.]

Moses on the mount received from God not only the Law, which he left to posterity written down in five books, but also a true and more occult explanation of the Law. It was, moreover, commanded him of God by all means to proclaim the Law to the people but not to commit the interpretation of the Law to writing or to make it a matter of common knowledge. He himself should reveal it only to Iesu Nave,[49] who in his turn should unveil it to the other high priests to come after him, under a strict obligation of silence. It was enough through guileless story to recognize now the power of God, now his wrath against the wicked, his mercy to the righteous, his justice to all; and through divine and beneficial precepts to be brought to a good and happy way of life and the worship of true religion. But to make public the occult mysteries, the secrets of the supreme Godhead hidden beneath the shell of the Law and under a clumsy show of words —what else were this than to give a holy thing to dogs and to cast pearls before swine?[50] Therefore to keep hidden from the people the things to be shared by the initiate, among whom alone, Paul says, he spoke wisdom, was not the part of human deliberation but of divine command.[51] This custom the ancient philosophers most reverently observed, for Pythagoras wrote nothing except a few trifles, which he intrusted on his deathbed to his daughter Dama. The Sphinxes carved on the temples of the Egyptians reminded them that mystic doctrines should be kept inviolable from the common herd by means of the knots of riddles. Plato, writing certain things to Dion concerning the highest substances, said: "It must be stated in riddles, lest the letter should fall by chance into the hands of others and what I am writing to you should be apprehended by others."[52] Aristotle used to say that his books of *Metaphysics*, in which he treated of things divine, were both published and not published. What further? Origen asserts that Jesus Christ, the Teacher of life, made many revelations to his disciples, which they were unwilling to write down

49. [Cf. Ecclus. 46 : 1.]   51. [Cf. Rom. 1 : 17 and I Cor. 2 : 13.]
50. [Cf. Matt. 7 : 6.]   52. [*Epistle* ii. 321*d*.]

lest they should become commonplaces to the rabble. This is in the highest degree confirmed by Dionysius the Areopagite, who says that the occult mysteries were conveyed by the founders of our religion ἐκ νοῦ εἰς νοῦν διὰ μέσον λόγου, from mind to mind, without writing, through the medium of speech.

35. In exactly the same way, when the true interpretation of the Law according to the command of God, divinely handed down to Moses, was revealed, it was called the Cabala, a word which is the same among the Hebrews as "reception" among ourselves; for this reason, of course, that one man from another, by a sort of hereditary right, received that doctrine not through written records but through a regular succession of revelations. But after the Hebrews were restored by Cyrus from the Babylonian captivity, and after the temple had been established anew under Zorobabel, they brought their attention to the restoration of the Law. Esdras, then the head of the church, after the book of Moses had been amended, when he plainly recognized that, because of the exiles, the massacres, the flights, and the captivity of the children of Israel, the custom instituted by their forefathers of transmitting the doctrine from mouth to mouth could not be preserved, and that it would come to pass that the mysteries of the heavenly teachings divinely bestowed on them would be lost, since the memory of them could not long endure without the aid of written records, decided that those of the elders then surviving should be called together and that each one should impart to the gathering whatever he possessed by personal recollection concerning the mysteries of the Law and that scribes should be employed to collect them into seventy volumes (about the number of elders in the Sanhedrin). That you may not have to rely on me alone in this matter, Fathers, hear Esdras himself speak thus: "And it came to pass, when the forty days were fulfilled, that the Most High spake unto me, saying, The first that thou hast written publish openly, and let the worthy and the unworthy read it: but keep the seventy last books, that thou mayst deliver them to such as be wise among thy people: for in them is

the spring of understanding, the fountain of wisdom, and the stream of knowledge. And I did so." And these are the words of Esdras to the letter.[53] These are the books of cabalistic lore. In these books principally resides, as Esdras with a clear voice justly declared, the spring of understanding, that is, the ineffable theology of the supersubstantial deity; the fountain of wisdom, that is, the exact metaphysic of the intellectual and angelic forms; and the stream of knowledge, that is, the most steadfast philosophy of natural things. Pope Sixtus the Fourth who last preceded the pope under whom we are now fortunate to be living, Innocent the Eighth, took the greatest pains and interest in seeing that these books should be translated into the Latin tongue for a public service to our faith, and, when he died, three of them had been done into Latin. Among the Hebrews of the present day these books are cherished with such devotion that it is permitted no man to touch them unless he be forty years of age.

36. When I had purchased these books at no small cost to myself, when I had read them through with the greatest diligence and with unwearying toil, I saw in them (as God is my witness) not so much the Mosaic as the Christian religion. There is the mystery of the Trinity, there the Incarnation of the Word, there the divinity of the Messiah; there I have read about original sin, its expiation through Christ, the heavenly Jerusalem, the fall of the devils, the orders of the angels, purgatory, and the punishments of hell, the same things we read daily in Paul and Dionysius, in Jerome and Augustine. But in those parts which concern philosophy you really seem to hear Pythagoras and Plato, whose principles are so closely related to the Christian faith that our Augustine gives immeasurable thanks to God that the books of the Platonists have come into his hands.[54] Taken altogether, there is absolutely no controversy between ourselves and the Hebrews on any matter, with regard to which they cannot be refuted and

53. [II Esdras 14 : 5–6.]
54. [Cf. *Confessions* viii. 2.]

gainsaid out of the cabalistic books, so that there will not be even a corner left in which they may hide themselves. I have as a most weighty witness of this fact that very learned man Antonius Chronicus[55] who, when I was with him at a banquet, with his own ears heard Dactylus, a Hebrew trained in this lore, with all his heart agree entirely to the Christian idea of the Trinity.[56]

37. But let me return to surveying the chapters of my disputation. I have introduced also my own idea of the interpretation of the prophetic verses of Orpheus and Zoroaster.[57] Orpheus is read among the Greeks in a nearly complete text, Zoroaster only in part, though, among the Chaldaeans, in a more complete text, and both are believed to be the fathers and authors of ancient wisdom. Now, to pass over Zoroaster, the frequent mention of whom among the Platonists is never without the greatest respect, Jamblichus of Chalcis writes that Pythagoras followed the Orphic theology as the model on which he fashioned and built his own philosophy. Nay, furthermore, they say that the maxims of Pythagoras are alone called holy, because he proceeded from the principles of Orpheus; and that the secret doctrine of numbers and whatever Greek philosophy has of the great or the sublime has flowed from thence as its first font. But as was the practice of the ancient theologians, even so did Orpheus protect the mysteries of his dogmas with the coverings of fables, and conceal them with a poetic veil, so that whoever should read his hymns would suppose there was nothing beneath them beyond idle tales and perfectly unadulterated trifles. I have wished to say this so

55. [Antonio Vinciguerra, called Chronicus, a Venetian diplomat and writer (see Arnaldo della Torre, *Di Antonio Vinciguerra e delle sue Satire* [Rocca S. Casciano, 1902]).]

56. [For Dactylus, one of Pico's Jewish teachers, see U. Cassuto, *Gli Ebrei a Firenze nell'età del Rinascimento* (Florence, 1918), pp. 317–19.]

57. [For the influence of the Orphic texts in the Italian Renaissance see P. O. Kristeller, "The Scholastic Background of Marsilio Ficino," *Traditio*, II (1944), 271–72. For the influence of the Chaldaic Oracles then attributed to Zoroaster see B. Kieszkowski, *Studi sul Platonismo del Rinascimento in Italia* (Florence, 1936), pp. 34 ff. and 155 ff.]

that it might be known what a task it was for me, how difficult it was to draw out the hidden meaning of the secrets of philosophy from the intentional tangles of riddles and from the obscurity of fables, especially since I have been aided, in a matter so serious, so abstruse, and so little known, by no toil, no application on the part of other interpreters. And yet like dogs they have barked that I have made a kind of heap of inconsequential nothings for a vain display of mere quantity, as if these were not all questions in the highest degree disputed and controversial, in which the main schools are at swords' points, and as if I had not contributed many things utterly unknown and untried to these very men who are even now tearing at my reputation and who consider that they are the leaders in philosophy. Nay, I am so far from this fault that I have taken great pains to reduce my argument to as few chapters as I could. If I myself had (after the wont of others) wished to divide it into parts and to cut it to pieces, it would undoubtedly have grown to a countless number.

38. And, to hold my peace about the rest, who is there who does not know that a single proposition of the nine hundred, the one that treats of reconciling the philosophies of Plato and Aristotle, I could have developed, beyond all suspicion of my having wooed mere quantity, into six hundred, nay, more chapters, by enumerating one after the other all those points in which others consider those philosophers to differ and I, to agree? But I must certainly speak (for I shall speak, albeit neither modestly nor in conformity with my own character), since my enviers and detractors compel me to: I have wished to give assurance by this contest of mine, not so much that I know many things, as that I know things of which many are ignorant. And now, in order that this, reverend Fathers, may become manifest to you by the facts and that my oration may no longer stand in the way of your desire, excellent doctors, whom I perceive to be prepared and girded up in the expectation of the dispute, not without great delight: let us now—and may the outcome be fortunate and favorable—join battle as to the sound of a trumpet of war.

V

PIETRO POMPONAZZI

Translated by WILLIAM HENRY HAY II, *revised by*
JOHN HERMAN RANDALL, JR., *and annotated
by* PAUL OSKAR KRISTELLER

INTRODUCTION

By JOHN HERMAN RANDALL, JR.

PIETRO POMPONAZZI of Mantua (1462–1525) was the Italian Aristotelian who, heir to the great tradition of the Italian universities, opposed the reigning Averroism and introduced into the academic tradition the new humanistic emphasis on the dignity and worth of the individual soul. With Ficino and Pico he opposed the impersonal and collectivistic views of the older tradition, and with them he sought to defend a more personal conception of human nature. But where the Platonists vindicated the dignity of the individual soul by elevating it in freedom above nature, Pomponazzi made the soul rather a natural inhabitant of an orderly universe.

To understand Pomponazzi's accomplishment, and the rather technical arguments by which he defended his position, it is necessary to know something of the long tradition of Italian Aristotelianism within which he was effecting a revolution.[1] The

1. There is little accurate knowledge or writing, especially in English, about the history of Aristotelianism in Italy. Guido de Ruggiero, *Storia della filosofia*, Part III: *Rinascimento, riforma e controriforma* (2 vols.; 2nd ed.; Bari, 1937), Introduction, Sec. III, and chap. v, is probably the best recent account. Ernst Cassirer, *Das Erkenntnisproblem* (3d ed.; Berlin, 1922), Part I, "Die Reform der Aristotelischen Psychologie," pp. 98–120, is the best philosophical analysis. R. Hönigswald, *Denker der italienischen Renaissance* (Basel, 1938), chaps. vi–viii, is not seriously wrong. E. Garin, "Aristotelismo e Platonismo del Rinascimento," *La Rinascita*, II (1939), 641–71, emphasizes the influence of Renaissance ideas on the Aristotelian tradition. Of the older studies, Francesco Fiorentino, *Pietro Pomponazzi: Studi storici sulla scuola Bolognese e Padovana del secolo XVI* (Florence, 1868), is fundamental. The writings of Pietro Ragnisco loyally defend the importance of Padua against Fiorentino and are beyond question the most accurate studies of the School of Padua. They are cited in detail later. Ernest Renan's *Averroès et l'Averroïsme* (Paris, 1852) initiated the whole study, but his work is superficial and highly selective. E. Troilo, *Averroismo e Aristotelismo padovano* (Padua, 1939), is the most recent work; it emphasizes the "modern" tendencies in Padua Aristotelianism.

[257]

Florentine circle and most of the Humanists were not academic scholars but men whose Platonic enthusiasm crowned other interests, literary, artistic, or professional. During the Renaissance the organized intellectual life of the universities remained loyal to the Aristotelian tradition. In most countries the fifteenth-century schools saw the teaching and refinement of earlier philosophies—Scotism, Ockhamism, and Thomism—with little basically new. But in northern Italy, at Padua, Bologna, and Pavia, and to a lesser extent at Siena, Pisa, and the brilliant new university of Ferrarra, Aristotelianism was still a living and growing body of ideas. What Paris had been in the thirteenth century, and Oxford and Paris together in the fourteenth, Padua became in the fifteenth: the center in which ideas from all Europe were combined into an organized and cumulative body of knowledge. A succession of great teachers—Paul of Venice (d. 1429),[2] Cajetan of Thiene (d. 1465),[3] and Nicolettus Vernias (d. 1499)[4]—carried that knowledge to the point where in the next century it could find fruitful marriage with the new interest in the mathematical sciences.

Scientific Padua felt the effects of the same Humanistic impulse and the same revival of learning that were inspiring Florence in the second half of the *quattrocento*.[5] To the challenge of Ficino's Platonism it responded by proving that Aristotle as well as Plato spoke Greek. To Ficino's attack on their traditional Averroism, with its fatalism and its strange conception of human nature that minimized all that was personal and individual, the Paduans replied, not by accepting his Platonic religious modernism, but by reorganizing their own naturalistic and scientific

2. See Felice Momigliano, *Paolo Veneto e le correnti del pensiero religioso e filosofico nel suo tempo* (Udine, 1907).

3. A. D. Sartori, "Gaetano de' Thiene, filosofo averroista nello Studio di Padova." *Atti della Società italiana per il progresso delle scienze, Riunione 26* (Venice, 1937), III (1938), 340–70.

4. Pietro Ragnisco, *Nicoletto Vernia: Studi storici sulla filosofia Padovana nella seconda metà del secolo XV* (Venice, 1891).

5. *Ibid.*, chap. i: "L'Umanesimo e l'averroismo padovano"; Garin, *op. cit.*

thought around a more individualistic conception of man and his destiny. To the Florentine Platonic Humanism they opposed an Aristotelian Humanism close to the naturalism of Aristotle himself and fitting in well with their dominant scientific interests. Not until Spinoza and the eighteenth-century Newtonians does there appear another figure who manages to effect so "modern" a blend between Humanism and scientific naturalism as Pomponazzi and Zabarella.

In 1497 the Faculty of Arts at Padua petitioned the Senate of Venice for a new chair for the teaching of Aristotle in Greek. The Senate acceded, and Leonicus Thomaeus, who knew Greek from his native Epirus, was installed as the first to expound the Stagirite, as well as Plato, in their own tongue.[6] This event marks not only the end of several decades of effort to rediscover Aristotle himself; it marks also the end of the older literal-minded Averroism. Vernias and Nifo, its last defenders, had already, with better texts, and under pressure from the Humanist bishop of Padua, abandoned the crudities of Averroes' view of man's nature.[7] Thereafter not even Achillini was prepared to defend the literal unity of the intellect; and Averroism thenceforth meant primarily a vision of knowledge and a freedom from theological compromise.

Bruni had begun a fresh translation of Aristotle; Bessarion had done the *Metaphysics*. The Paduans used in part the new version of the Venetian Humanist and anti-Scholastic Ermolao Barbaro,[8] but chiefly that of Argyropolus, a Byzantine who taught at Padua before joining the Medici circle. The orthodox Averroists had emphasized the logical side of Aristotle, using the traditional Latin terms and distinctions from which the master's own functional meaning had evaporated. These abstract nouns reinforced

6. Ragnisco, *op. cit.*, p. 7.   7. *Ibid.*, p. 142.

8. See T. Stickney, *De Hermolai Barbari vita atque ingenio* (Paris, 1913); and the less satisfactory work of A. Ferriguto, *Almorò Barbaro* (Venice, 1922); Ermolao Barbaro, *Epistolae, orationes et carmina*, ed. V. Branca (2 vols.; Florence, 1943).

the Platonizing tendencies of the Averroistic commentaries to make independent existences out of the substantives of discourse. Verbs were turned into nouns, and operations into substances. The result can best be described as a very Neo-Platonic or dialectical naturalism.

The first effect of Humanism in Padua was to send men directly to the Greek text and the ancient commentators. The group of innovating "Alexandrists" who appear at the end of the century derive their name from Alexander of Aphrodisias, the best of the Greek commentators on Aristotle, whom they studied and cited; a selection from his writings dealing with human nature was published in Latin in 148–.[9] But the Averroists had likewise cited Alexander; his views they found discussed in the Commentator himself. The significant difference is not that another commentator is followed but that we find a group of Aristotelians thinking in terms of the Greek words and distinctions and considering not isolated texts but the whole course and spirit of the argument. We suddenly discover a functional Aristotle as the setting for the Aristotelian logical distinctions; we find the operations of things given more importance than the statement of their essences. And we find strong Humanistic interests. Whereas before the *Physica* had been the center of attention, now it is the *De anima* and the interpretation of human nature that awaken controversy. Like the Platonists, the Aristotelians began discussing God, freedom, and immortality in relation to the individual soul; but, unlike them, they arrived through Aristotle at naturalistic conclusions.

Though the older Averroists had been more concerned with the world than with man, they had maintained an essentially impersonal and collectivistic view of human nature. Man is a composite of animal body and "cogitative soul": he is an individual substance with a matter and form of his own. His body is a mixture of the four elements; his proper form, the "cogitative

9. Alexandri Aphrodisei, *De intellectu* (Venice: Bernardinus Venetus de Vitalibus, no year, but clearly printed during the 1480's).

soul," is a power of the senses or the imagination—that is, it is a bodily function, a "material form," which comes into being with the body and suffers corruption with it. But man could not know without an additional rational soul, which, by becoming the forms of all things, understands them. In order to be able to assimilate the forms of things without their matter, this passive or "possible" Intellect must be, as Aristotle said, "separable and impassive and unmixed."[10] It cannot therefore be the form or entelechy of any particular body, joined to and subject to that body's matter; that would make it a "material form." It is not united to the body save in conferring upon it the function of knowing. This possible Intellect is a perfect and eternal substance, the lowest in that hierarchy of "Intelligences" which inform and animate the heavenly spheres. United to men, not in its being but in its operation of intellection or knowing, this possible Intellect uses the human body as art uses an instrument, or a workman a knife. In this operation of intellection, it combines with man's power of receiving sense images, with his "cogitative soul," to form the "speculative" or theoretical intellect by which an individual man actually knows and thinks.

On this Averroistic view, explains Zabarella, "the rational soul is thus like a sailor coming into a ship already constituted, and giving to man his outstanding operation, which is to contemplate and understand, just as a sailor steering a ship gives it the operation of navigation."[11] Being immaterial and eternal and apart from all matter, the possible Intellect "is not multiplied in accordance with the number of men but is only one in number in the whole human species; it is the lowest of the Intelligences, to which is assigned the whole human species as its own proper 'sphere,' and that species is thus like one of the heavenly orbs. When any man dies, this Intellect does not perish but remains the same in number in those that are left."[12] This single Intellect

10. *De anima* iii. 4 and 5, 429*b*–430*a*.

11. Zabarella, *De rebus naturalibus libri 30* (Venice, 1590), Lib. 27, *De mente humana*, cap. 3.

12. *Ibid.*, cap. 10.

of mankind thus enjoys an impersonal immortality; but individuals and their proper cogitative souls suffer dissolution and death. Men perish; only in the function of knowing do they partake of the Eternal. Or, rather, knowing is not a personal function at all; it is Truth which knows itself, now in this man, now in another. For though this single human Intellect is independent in its existence, it cannot know truth save as it employs the sensitive powers of this or that human body.

The motives for this conception are in part dialectical, like the arguments advanced for it; they aim at achieving consistency in the Aristotelian concepts rather than at taking account of the facts of experience. Aristotle had said that intellect is "separable" from matter and independent of it, a deathless and eternal activity. He had also made clear that whatever is eternal, independent of matter and not individuated by it, can be only one in number in a single species. Moreover, if each body had its own intellect, then those intellects would depend on the bodies for their separate existence and die with them. They would be themselves parts of the body or bodily powers; as particular and material things they could never know universals or indivisibles or abstract things but could receive only particulars. They would thus be indistinguishable from sense. Nor could intellect be multiplied and individuated miraculously by a special act of creation, as the faithful (and the Thomists) held, thus escaping these natural consequences. As Vernias puts it, "The moderns receive such an impossibility because they have been accustomed to hear it from childhood. For custom is second nature."[13]

But though these arguments are technical and dialectical, the motives behind them are fundamentally Platonic. The mind that knows Truth must be itself a member of a Platonic realm of Truth, itself an Idea, eternal and nonexistent, unchanging and impersonal, and not bound by the limitations of any particular body. "The possible Intellect is a form capable of existing with-

13. Nicoleti Verniatis Theatini .... *Contra perversam Averrois opinionem de unitate intellectus* (Venice, 1505; dated 1492), fol. 7ʳ.

out matter. For it has an operation which does not depend on the body; neither therefore does its being. And if it does not in fact operate without sense phantasms, nevertheless it is capable of so doing."[14] "For there is no mean between the abstract and the material. Every form is thus either derived from the power of matter, and subject to generation and corruption, or else eternal in past and future, and separated from matter in its being."[15] There must indeed be one realm of Truth common to all men. How could pupil learn from teacher were there two truths in two intellects? And such an eternal Truth always actualized is just what we mean by "intellect." Truth must be ever kept alive in some mind and, to be humanly accessible, in a human mind. As the great teacher of the middle of the fifteenth century, Cajetan of Thiene, put it: "The speculative intellect is born and dies in this or that individual; in the human species as a whole it is eternal. There is always some thought being imagined in the imagination of someone, and consequently intelligible species and intellection being received in the possible Intellect. In this way are first principles eternal and the arts and sciences. And thus the possible Intellect never ceases, absolutely speaking, from knowing,"[16] as it would if it depended on any particular individual.

Under the criticism of the Florentines, this Platonic emphasis grew stronger. Plato, Aristotle, and Averroes agree in everything but words, says Vernias. Philosophy is always perfect somewhere, in some human mind. "The Intellect is always in act with respect to some individual of whatever species. And if not in this northern quarter in which we are, it will be so in the southern habitable region. The being of the world is never wholly without some such individual being. Hence universals

14. Alexandri Achillini Bononiensis .... *Opera omnia* (Venice, 1545; 1st ed., Venice, 1508), *De intelligentiis*, Quod. III, Dubium i.

15. Augustini Niphi Suessani. ... *De intellectu libri 6* (Venice, 1554; dated 1492), Lib. II, par. 15.

16. Caietanus Thienensis super libros *De anima* (Venice, 1514), Lib. III, Text. 5, Qu. 2.

are the same in all men; whence comes the knowledge of all that is known."[17] And the later Averroists, like Zimara, came more and more to identify this unity of the Intellect with the unity of the rational principles in all men.

There is discernible here also a strong social sense of the unity of all men in the knowledge of the Truth. Knowledge is not a fragmentary individual possession; it belongs to all mankind, which forms, as it were, taken as a whole, a single man. Men are essentially communistic in knowing—a psychological position that accords well with the theory of popular sovereignty advanced in the *Defensor pacis* of the two early Averroists, John of Jandun[18] and Marsilio of Padua.[19] In a word, for the Averroists mind or intellect is not so much a personal activity as a realm of being. As befitted their impersonal interest in nature, their sense of the intelligibility of the world was far stronger than their sense of the individual intelligence of the knower.

Alexander Achillini,[20] who taught a vigorous and independent Averroism first at Bologna, from 1506 to 1508 at Padua, and from 1508 to his death in 1512 at Bologna, tried to find a place for human individuality within this framework. Man is a true substance, made single and individual by his cogitative soul in conjunction with the possible Intellect. Differences in intellec-

---

17. Vernias, *De unitate intellectus*, Opinio Averrois.

18. On John of Jandun, see É. Gilson, "La Doctrine de la double verité, avec des textes de Jean de Jandun," in his *Études de philosophie médiévale* (Strasbourg, 1921), pp. 51-75. On his contribution to the *Defensor pacis* (1324) see G. H. Sabine, *History of Political Theory* (New York, 1937), pp. 290-91.

19. On Marsilio see Sabine, *op. cit.*, pp. 290-304. The *Defensor pacis* has been edited by C. W. Previté-Orton (Cambridge, 1928) and by Richard Scholz (Hannover, 1933). On the connection of Averroism with political theory see M. Grabmann, "Studien über den Einfluss der Aristotelischen Philosophie auf die mittelalterlichen Theorien über das Verhältnis von Kirche und Staat," *Sitzungsberichte der Bayerischen Akademie der Wissenschaften, Philosophisch-historische Kl.* (1934), Heft 2.

20. On Achillini see L. Münster, "Alessandro Achillini, anatomico e filosofo, professore dello Studio di Bologna (1463-1512)," *Rivista di storia delle scienze mediche e naturali*, XV, No. 24 (1933), 7-22, 54-77. Cf. Ragnisco, *op. cit.*, p. 95. For *Opera omnia* see n. 14 above.

tual power come from the body rather than from the intellect, from the senses and the bodily spirits, from the greater efforts of different cogitative souls. "And thinking is in our own power, not only because the Intellect is our form, but also because the operation of the senses which thinking follows is in our power."[21] But Padua had already found a better defense for Humanistic values in the thought of Achillini's lifelong antagonist, Pomponazzi.

This Averroistic view of man was vigorously maintained by Nicoletto Vernias, holder of the first chair in philosophy at Padua from 1468 to 1499, "so that almost all Italy was converted to the error."[22] Vernias became involved in a quarrel with the Scotist theologians, who had little intellectual standing at Padua; and the bishop finally got him and his pupil Nifo to cover their views with a transparent veil of submission. But, writing of the last decade of the century, Contarini could say, "When I was in Padua, in that most celebrated university of all Italy the name and authority of Averroes the Commentator were most esteemed; and all agreed to the positions of this author, and took them as a kind of oracle. Most famous with all was his position on the unity of the Intellect, so that he who thought otherwise was considered worthy of the name neither of peripatetic nor philosopher."[23]

Contarini goes on to say that he, too, was convinced that Aristotle believed in a single immortal Intellect. Unable to accept such a view, and like all the Paduans holding that Thomas' theory of special creation violated the principles of natural reason, he judged "the opinion of Alexander of Aphrodisias preferable to all others."[24] Confronted by a choice between an impersonal immortality of the soul and a personal mortality,

21. *De intelligentiis*, Quod. III, Dubium ii.

22. Antonii Riccoboni, *De gymnasio patavino* (Padua, 1598), VI, cap. x, fol. 134. The whole of cap. x deals with Vernias' influence and controversies.

23. Gasparis Contarini Cardinalis, *Opera* (Paris, 1571), p. 179.

24. *Ibid.*, p. 180; cf. *Apology*, Lib. III, cap. 3, concl. 2.

like many Paduans of that day he sided with human individuality and joined the *sectatores Alexandri*.[25] For Alexander had figured in all the Averroistic discussions from Siger de Brabant[26] and John of Jandun on as the foil to Averroes. He was the Aristotelian with a naturalistic and biological interpretation of the human mind; against him Averroes had insisted on the immaterial and abstract and therefore immortal nature of the operation of knowing, and hence of "intellect" as such. In the Commentator men found that Alexander believed that "intellect is multiplied with the multiplication of individuals of the human species; and that it is subject to generation and corruption like other natural forms, through the most noble mixture of primary qualities and the dissolution of that mixture."[27] Generated naturally from the elements, it is inseparable from matter and, though the highest power of the soul, has a bodily instrument like sense.

What kept the Paduans from accepting this view was not its naturalism and its denial of personal immortality: that they had long welcomed, and the Thomists they regarded as mere compromising theologians. What they missed in it was rather that Platonic vision of Truth they deeply felt and thought they found in Aristotle himself. For, in the act of knowing, man seemed to them to lift himself above the limitations of a particular animal body and to see what is with a transparency and a clarity no merely biological creature has a right to possess. The Paduans were not merely anticlericals; they believed in a rational science. And, until some way could be found to reconcile the rational vision of Truth with its biological conditions, they persisted in their Platonism. Intellect could not be mere matter. It is significant that the atomism of Lucretius was always held at Padua to

25. Contarini, *op cit.*, p. 211. Cf. "sectatores Alexandri" in Zabarella, *De mente*, c. 9, 14; *Com. de Anima* iii. T. 5 (731); "Alexandristae," *ibid*. T. 3 (691).

26. On Siger de Brabant see Pierre Mandonnet, *Siger de Brabant* (Louvain, 1911).

27. Pauli Veneti, *Summa naturalium* (Venice, 1476; ed. Venice, 1503, as *Summa philosophiae naturalis*), Lib. V: *De anima*, Sec. II, cap. 37.

be crudely unscientific. So long as there seemed to be no mean between the purely material and the abstract intellect, they insisted that human nature participates in the latter.

When the actual text of Alexander was made known and read,[28] it was found that he did provide such a mean. He was no mere materialist, as Averroes had charged; he made a place for reason and intellect. "Alexander maintained," explains Zabarella, "that the intellective soul is a form constituting matter and derived from the power of matter; yet it is not 'organic,' for it is not localized in any organ of the human body."[29] And Pomponazzi writes in his *Commentary to the De anima*: "Alexander held intellect to belong to the things that are generated; but with some part of itself it agrees with things eternal, namely, in understanding and willing, which comes from its being a mean between the eternal and the noneternal, and the first of material forms."[30]

The man who solved this dilemma of the Paduan theory of human nature was Pietro Pomponazzi of Mantua.[31] Called "the

28. See n. 9 above.

29. Zabarella, *Commentarii in 3 Aristotelis libros de anima* (Frankfurt, 1606), Lib. III, Text 6, col. 743.

30. Luigi Ferri, *La Psicologia di P. Pomponazzi secondo un manoscritto della Biblioteca Angelica di Roma* (Rome, 1877), containing selections from an unpublished commentary on the *De anima*: Lib. III, Text 8 (p. 156).

31. There are two collected editions of Pomponazzi's writings, each incomplete: (a) Petri Pomponatii Mantuani, *Tractatus acutissimi, utillimi, et mere Peripatetici* (Venice, 1525), containing *De intensione et remissione formarum ac de parvitate et magnitudine*, *De reactione*, *De modo agendi primarum qualitatum* (or *Questio an actio realis immediate fieri potest per species spirituales*), *De immortalitate animae*, *Apologiae libri tres*, *Contradictoris tractatus doctissimus*, *Defensorium Autoris*, *De nutritione et augmentatione;* and (b) Petri Pomponatii philosophi et theologi doctrina et ingenio praestantissimi, *Opera* (Basel, 1567), containing *De naturalium effectuum admirandorum causis, seu De incantationibus*, *De fato*, *libero arbitrio, praedestinatione, providentia Dei libri V*. In addition, Pomponazzi published *Dubitationes in quartum meteorologicorum Aristotelis librum* (Venice, 1563). Luigi Ferri published selections from a set of lecture notes on the *De anima* (see n. 30 above). Francesco Fiorentino, *Studi e Ritratti della Rinascenza* (Bari, 1911), pp. 63–79, gives an account of manuscripts in the library of the Fraternità de' Laici in Arezzo of com-

last Scholastic and the first man of the Enlightenment," he did indeed partake of the natures of both: of the latter in his fiery zeal against the theologians, his scorn for all comfortable and compromising modernism in religion, and his sober vision of the natural destiny of man; of the former in his refusal to leave the bounds of the Aristotelian tradition, in his meticulous use of the medieval method of refutation, and in his painstaking attention to the reasons by which a position was defended. But as the Renaissance mean between the two, he shared the spirit of his age: its concentration on man and his destiny, its view of human nature as the link between heaven and earth, its reverence for the authority of the ancients—for him, Aristotle—and, despite all theory, its Stoic temper of mind. Like his great Platonic rival Ficino, he sought to examine man's destiny in independence of all dogma. Within his close-knit argument there burns a vision of man more akin to the insight of that other Florentine, Machiavelli, than to the rather sentimental piety of the Academy—and to that of the lens-grinder of Amsterdam. Nor is Pomponazzi merely the realist as against aspiration, the man who came closer to the biological Aristotle than any save his own follower Zabarella. To our way of thinking today, though he stripped

mentaries on the *Physica*, I, II, III, VII, VIII, on the *Metaphysica*, XII, and on the *Parva naturalia*, Pomponazzi's last work before his death in 1525.

On Pomponazzi see: Francesco Fiorentino, *Pietro Pomponazzi: Studi storici su la scuola Bolognese e Padovana del secolo XVI* (Florence, 1868); Pietro Ragnisco, *Nicoletto Vernia: Studi storici sulla filosofia Padovana nella seconda metà del secolo decimoquinto* (Venice, 1891), the most accurate of all the studies, especially valuable for Pomponazzi's intellectual development; Ragnisco, *Giacomo Zabarella il filosofo: Pietro Pomponazzi e Giacomo Zabarella nella questione dell' anima* ("Estratto degli Atti del R. Istituto Veneto di scienze, lettere, ed arti," Tomo V, Serie vi [Venice, 1887]); Erminio Troilo, *Averroismo e Aristotelismo padovano* (Padua, 1939); Ernst Cassirer, *Individuum und Kosmos in der Philosophie der Renaissance* (Leipzig, 1927), pp. 143–49, and *Das Erkenntnisproblem*, I, 105–17; E. Weil, "Die Philosophie des Pietro Pomponazzi," *Archiv für Geschichte der Philosophie*, XLI (1932), 127–76 (dissertation by a student of Cassirer); John Owen, *The Skeptics of the Italian Renaissance* (London, 1893), pp. 184–241; A. H. Douglas, *The Philosophy and Psychology of Pietro Pomponazzi* (Cambridge, 1910).

both Thomism and Averroism of their accretions of Platonism, he had a better understanding of Plato than Ficino or Pico; for he knew that Plato's insight is vision and not metaphysics, and that vision he respected and fought for.

Pomponazzi did not start as an Averroist. With his fellow-students Contarini and De Vio, he was brought up by his teachers, especially Francesco di Nardò or de Neritone, the Thomist professor of metaphysics at Padua, as a thoroughgoing Thomist; and he early distinguished himself against the Averroistic pupils of Vernias, winning the post of lector or professor extraordinarius in 1488.[32] Indeed, he seems to have remained a good Thomist, within the free spirit of Padua, lecturing mainly on the *Physica,* until, having as yet published nothing, he left for Ferrara in 1509 when the wars closed the university. The Padua system provided every professor with an antagonist or *concurrens* of different views who lectured at the same hours. Pomponazzi taught, from 1496 to the latter's departure in 1499, against Nifo.[33] He was appointed professor ordinarius, in the second place next to Vernias, in 1495; after Cardinal Bembo secured him Vernias' first chair on the latter's death in 1499, his *concurrens* was Antonio Fracanciano. In 1506 Achillini returned to Padua, succeeding Fracanciano as Pomponazzi's *concurrens,* and a bitter rival; both were later at Bologna together. During 1510 Pomponazzi was lecturing at Ferrara on the *De anima;* in the *Apology* he says he taught the opinions of the *De immortalitate* at that university. In 1511 he was elected to the first place in philosophy at Bologna for a term of four years, but because of the wars he did not go until 1512. In 1515 the Riformatori confirmed his chair, at a greater salary, we are told, than any other professor of philosophy had ever received in Italy.[34]

All these opponents of Pomponazzi—Achillini, Nifo, and Fracanciano—were Averroists and pupils of Vernias. In partic-

32. Ragnisco, *Vernia,* chap. 5; *Zabarella,* p. 22.

33. Ragnisco, *Vernia,* chaps. v, vi.

34. Fiorentino, *P. Pomponazzi,* 26; Ragnisco, *Vernia,* p. 89.

ular, the disputes with his young rival Fracanciano, in which he defended the Thomistic views of his teacher Neritone against those of Vernias, seem to have shaken his own Thomism.[35] They were over the relation of the Intelligences to the heavenly spheres, a question fundamental to the conception of human nature, since for the Averroists the Intellect was also an "Intelligence" and mankind its proper "sphere." They convinced him that a *forma informans et dans esse*, that is, a true substantial form, cannot be separable from its matter. Too proud to admit defeat, and still too much of a Thomist to become a narrow Averroistic partisan, he left for Ferrara to reconstruct his thought. His new views had probably already taken form at Padua, but he did not make them known until he arrived in Ferrara; and they were not set forth in print until there appeared in Bologna, in 1516, his short but epoch-making essay, *De immortalitate animae*.

Pomponazzi was thus a Thomist half-converted to Averroism. He consistently uses Thomas against the unity of Averroes' position, and Averroes against the separability and immortality of Thomas'. The naturalism and, he would have said, the Aristotelianism of each he employs against the Platonism of the other. It is significant of the co-operative character of the Padua school that he advances hardly a new argument but merely collects and marshals with great skill the arguments elaborated for generations. He may have found the inspiration for his intermediary position in Alexander, and he certainly puts it in Alexander's mouth; and his conception of man as "of twofold nature, and a mean between the mortal and the immortal" may well have been influenced by Ficino.[36] But in neither his commentaries nor in his less formal treatises does he follow Alexander in detail or any of the Greeks; Averroes, Thomas, Jandun,

35. Ragnisco, *Vernia*, chap. v.

36. *De immortalitate animae*, chap. i; P. O. Kristeller, "Ficino and Pomponazzi on the Place of Man in the Universe," *Journal of the History of Ideas*, V (1944), 224.

and the Latins in general are his chief supports. And though he argues against Ficino in the *Apologia*,[37] and quotes Pico in the *De immortalitate*,[38] he follows the older custom of not mentioning recent writers by name. And yet out of this largely traditional material comes a position of striking originality and power: that a natural bodily function, a *forma materialis*, can behold rational truth. Pomponazzi may have derived his interpretation of Aristotle, as he certainly drew support, from his fellow-student under Neritone, the celebrated Thomist, Thomas de Vio, later Cardinal Gaetano,[39] a Dominican teaching at Padua with him after 1494, who in 1509 published a commentary on the *De anima* maintaining that Aristotle taught the mortality of the soul. But his problem and its solution are his own.

For it is the problem of man's nature, his operations and their conditions, and their unity in a single being. Man's nature is not simple but multiple, not certain but ambiguous, a mean between mortal and immortal.[40] How are these two natures combined in man? Pomponazzi contemptuously brushes aside the Averroistic answer: Aristotle never even thought of such nonsense, let alone believed it.[41] Thomas' despised refutation is conclusive. If the

37. *Apologia*, Lib. I, cap. 9.

38. *De immortalitate animae*, chap. xiv (see below, p. 376).

39. See Ragnisco, *Vernia*, p. 97. Gaetano was professor of Thomist metaphysics, the *concurrens* of Trombetta, professor of Scotist metaphysics. In his *Commentaria de anima* (Florence, 1509) he says: "Know that it is not my intention to wish to say or maintain that the possible intellect is subject to generation and corruption according to the principles of philosophy.... This is shown to be false from faith; hence it cannot follow from the principles of philosophy. Whence I have not written these words as true or as consistent or as probable in philosophy, but merely as setting forth the opinion of this Greek, which I shall endeavor to show to be false according to the principles of philosophy" (ed. Palermo, 1598, p. 205).

Gaetano was the first Dominican to find Aristotle maintaining the mortality of the soul. A fellow-Dominican, Bart. de Spina, wrote three polemics: against Gaetano, Pomponazzi's *De immortalitate*, and his *Apologia*. De Spina attacked Gaetano, in *Propugnaculum Aristotelis de immortalitate animae contra Thomam Gaetanum* (Venice, 1519), as the source of Pomponazzi's interpretation.

40. *De immortalitate animae*, chap. i (see below, p. 282).

41. *Ibid.*, chap. iv (see below, pp. 286 ff.).

intellect of Socrates were the same as that of Plato, both would have the same being and operations. What could be more foolish?[42] Nor does the Platonic view, that man is a soul using a body, a combination of mover and moved, serve better to account for the individual unity experience reveals; this position also Thomas has abundantly refuted. For it soul and body have no more unity than oxen and a cart, and there would be two men joined together in me.[43]

But the view of Thomas himself, though true in faith, seems contrary to Aristotle and to natural reason. Thomas is right in taking the intellect as the true form and entelechy of the human body, as its natural functioning. He is wrong in making it separable from matter and capable of continued existence after death. Pomponazzi goes on to give a thoroughly naturalistic and functional interpretation of Aristotle. In all its operations the intellect needs the body and the corporeal sense images it furnishes. Aristotle is clear on this point, and he is confirmed by our own experience.[44]

The answer to his problem which Pomponazzi thinks agrees with Aristotle and natural reason is that the soul is essentially and truly mortal, relatively and improperly speaking immortal. He bases this position on an analysis of the operations of the soul, particularly those connected with the function of knowing, and on their necessary conditions. All knowing, both sensitive and intellectual, is a function of the same soul; and it is true that in some sense all knowing abstracts from matter. But there are three modes of separation from matter, corresponding to the three ways of knowing found in the universe. There is the total separation from matter by which the Intelligences know; there is the lowest separation from matter by which the sensitive powers know, needing a body both as their subject and as their object and limited to particulars. But there is a third and intermediary

42. *Ibid.*, chap. v (see below, p. 297).
43. *Ibid.*, chap. vi (see below, pp. 298–99).
44. *Ibid.*, chap. viii (see below, p. 305).

kind of separation—here Pomponazzi diverges from Averroes—in which the body is needed as object but not as subject. And this "mean" is the human intellect.[45]

Hence, on the one hand, the soul is a material form, a bodily function generated by the parents and not by special creation, the supreme and most perfect of material forms, but not capable of operating in any way or existing without the body.[46] On the other hand, the soul's essential operation of knowing shows that in a certain manner it participates in immortality: it can grasp the universal and the immaterial.[47] In a word, while knowing requires material conditions, and is thus the activity of a human body, it does not function materially but rises above the limitations of those conditions to grasp universals and truth. Knowing needs a body, but it does not take place in any localized part of the body; it would then be "organic" and limited by the conditions of its organ. Knowing takes place in the body as a whole, as Alexander held, since intellect includes all the powers of the body.[48]

Although Pomponazzi follows the whole Greek tradition in deriving the nature of the soul from an analysis of the function of knowing, he examines also and refutes all the extraneous moral and pragmatic arguments for immortality. To know the soul is mortal is in fact a great gain, for it makes possible at last a secular and human morality, a way of life that can aim at those values the Humanists held dear. And since the Averroists had also denied personal immortality, Pomponazzi seems in his restrained tones to be delivering to that age, so eager to find a way of living based on the nature of man himself, the wisdom of the long Padua tradition: the community of mankind in intellect and truth. The whole human race is like a single man with differing members. All men should communicate in three intellects—the

45. *Ibid.*, chap. ix (see below, p. 315).
46. *Ibid.* (see below, pp. 321–22).
47. *Ibid.* (see below, pp. 317 ff.).
48. *Ibid.*, chap. x (see below, p. 334).

theoretical, the practical, and the productive—for no man fails to possess something of each. The general end of mankind is to participate relatively in the theoretical and productive intellects but perfectly in the practical. If man is mortal, every man can have the end which suits man universally, though not what suits the most perfect part. And this power can make almost everyone blessed.[49]

For the rewards and punishments of the hereafter Pomponazzi has only scorn. The essential reward of virtue is virtue itself, and the real punishment of vice is vice itself. Nay, if one acts virtuously with hope of reward, his act is not considered so virtuous as that of one who expects no external reward; and he who is punished externally thereby diminishes that guilt which is the greatest and worst punishment of vice. "Whence those who claim that the soul is mortal seem better to save the grounds of virtue than those who claim it to be immortal. For the hope of reward and the fear of punishment seem to import a certain servility which is contrary to the grounds of virtue."[50]

This striking statement and defense of a thoroughly naturalistic ethics owes more to the Stoics than to Aristotle; Pomponazzi makes happiness consist in the perfection not of the theoretical intellect but of the practical, though it must include a relative participation in production and in knowing, which is among mortal things most excellent, and the function of the most perfect part of mankind.

Although Pomponazzi concluded his essay with the formal contention that the immortality of the soul is a "neutral problem,"[51] like that of the eternity of the world, and that neither its affirmation nor its denial can be demonstrated by natural reason, an uproar broke out among the clergy in Venice.[52] They persuaded the Patriarch and the Doge to burn the book and pro-

49. *Ibid.*, chap. xiv (see below, pp. 350 ff.).
50. *Ibid.* (see below, pp. 359 ff. and 373 ff.).
51. *Ibid.*, chap. xv (see below, pp. 377 ff.).
52. Fiorentino, *Pomponazzi*, pp. 35, 36.

claim him a heretic. A copy was sent to his patron, Cardinal Bembo, the Platonist, to be condemned in Rome. But Bembo found no heresy in it, and Leo X, who loved a good fight, encouraged both sides in the controversy. They urged him to write an *Apologia*,[53] in which he answered his various detractors in 1517; and in 1519 he wrote a *Defensorium*[54] against the voluminous and labored defense of Thomas by Nifo, who had the reputation of being a time-server. In 1518 the Riformatori of Bologna reappointed Pomponazzi to his chair for a term of eight years at a doubled salary.[55]

The *Apologia* is a more detailed and a better book than the first. Stung by the attacks, Pomponazzi replies with passion to the monks and priests and with searching analysis to the criticisms of his old fellow-student and Thomist, Contarini. Immortality is no longer a neutral problem; it is wholly contrary to natural principles. He is prepared to die for its truth as an article of faith; but he will not teach that it can be demonstrated by reason. "A philosopher cannot do this; especially if he be a teacher, for in so teaching he would be teaching falsehood, he would be an unfaithful master, his deception could be easily detected, and he would be acting contrary to the profession of philosophy."[56] Natural theology is indeed so weak and ridiculous that it brings Christianity itself into disrepute. Like so many rationalists since, Pomponazzi defends the letter of orthodoxy against the liberals and Platonists. Only with the resurrection of the body, with supernatural grace and redemption, is immortality consistently conceivable. Indeed, were the soul by nature immortal, how would grace be a merit? With great clarity he works out the logic of personal immortality—all founded, of course, on the

---

53. *Apologia Petri Pomponatii Mantuani* (Bologna, 1518); Lib. III, cap. 2.

54. *Defensorium Petri Pomponatii Mantuani: Petri Pomponatii Mantuani Defensorium sive Responsiones ad ea quae Augustinus Niphus Suessanus adversus ipsum scripsit De immortalitate animae* (Bologna, 1519).

55. Fiorentino, *Pomponazzi*, p. 38.

56. *Apologia*, Lib. III, cap. 3.

abrogation of natural knowledge and reason. The plea from ignorance receives short shrift.

Contarini, however, pushed him to a more exact analysis of the soul's functioning and to an interpretation of all the doubtful Aristotelian passages. At first he had maintained that intellect does not need the body as subject; Contarini forced more radical views.[57] In the *Apologia* intellect has become extended, like other forms, but is still indivisible;[58] finally, in *De nutritione* (1521), he admits divisibility also.[59] The intellect is in its nature no different from any other material form. It is indissolubly united to the body in its existence, both as subject and as object;[60] it is in its functioning that it rises above the body, acts independently, and receives universals. Thus a mortal soul can know immortal truths; it is in its function of knowing, not in any substantial character, that it is "separable and impassive and unmixed"—an interpretation thoroughly Aristotelian in spirit. Only for Contarini's question, "Why, then, has the intellect no localized or-

57. Ragnisco, *Zabarella*, pp. 15 ff. Cf. F. Fiorentino, "La psicologia di Pietro Pomponazzi," in *Studi e Ritratti della Rinascenza* (Bari, 1911), p. 8. This is a review of Luigi Ferri, *La psicologia di Pietro Pomponazzi* (Rome, 1877), in which Fiorentino attacks Ferri's contention, that there is no evolution or change in Pomponazzi's conception of the soul. In support, he quotes from G. Cardano, *Opera* (Leyden, 1663), II, 487: "But Pomponazzi is not at all consistent in his position that the question of the immortality of the soul is a neutral problem. Thus, forgetful of what he has said, he maintains that the immortality of the intellective soul, speaking of the human soul, contradicts natural principles. He says this, however, when he is angry because he has been accused of heresy."

58. *Apologia*, Lib. I, cap. 3: "It seems to me that it can be said with sufficient probability . . . . that the human intellect is extended in its knowing and willing; still it knows and reasons in terms of universals; nor does Aristotle contradict this view." Cf. F. Fiorentino, *Studi e Ritratti*, p. 10.

59. *De nutritione*, Lib. I, cap. 11: "But, with no prejudice to truth, I believe that according to Aristotle not only are the souls of plants and beasts to be accounted divisible, but that every soul conferring perfection on lower matter is divisible; although according to the truth, which Aristotle did not know, the human soul is to be pronounced absolutely indivisible. But I judge that this position is to be held merely on the grounds of faith, and not on account of any natural reason." Cf. Fiorentino, *Studi e Ritratti*, p. 12.

60. Fiorentino, *Studi e Ritratti*, p. 8.

gan?" did Pomponazzi have no answer; it remained for Zabarella to make the "imagination" the organ of intellect.[61]

Pomponazzi did not confine his naturalism to psychology. He saw in nature an orderly uniformity of law that admitted no miracles, no demons or angels, not even any direct divine intervention. In *De naturalium effectuum admirandorum causis* (1520)[62] he sought to explain all miraculous cures and events through purely natural causes, through natural powers not ordinarily experienced, and through the constant and regular influence of the heavens. Against Pico's denial of astrology as incompatible with human freedom, he tried to make an orderly and rational science of the stars, opposed to all superstition—the naturalist's answer to the Humanist. "All prophesy, whether vaticination, or divination, or excess, or speaking with tongues, or the invention of arts and sciences, in a word, all the effects observed in this lower world, whatever they be, have a natural cause."[63] The recorded miracles of religion are not events contrary to the natural order; they are merely unaccustomed and rare. The very conception of an immaterial spirit precludes any particular operation. "In vain do we assume demons, for it is ridiculous and foolish to forsake what is observable, and what can be proved by natural reason, to seek what is unobservable, and cannot be proved with any verisimilitude."[64] "No effect is produced upon us by God immediately but only through the means of his ministers. For God orders and disposes everything in an orderly and smooth manner and imposes an eternal law on things which it is impossible to transgress."[65]

Pomponazzi goes on to give a naturalistic account of the origin and development of religions themselves. "Those men who are

61. Ragnisco, *Zabarella*, p. 47; *Vernia*, p. 96; Cassirer, *Das Erkenntnisproblem*, I, 117-20, 136-44.

62. Petri Pomponatii Mantuani .... *De naturalium effectuum causis, sive de incantationibus* (Basel, 1556; finished 1520); cf. Cassirer, *Individuum und Kosmos*, pp. 108-15.

63. *Apologia*, Lib. II, cap. 7.

64. *De .... causis*, cap. 1.   65. *Ibid.*, cap. 10.

not philosophers, and who indeed are like beasts, cannot understand how God and the heavens and nature operate. Therefore,
angels and demons were introduced for the sake of the vulgar,
although those who introduced them knew they could not possibly exist. For in the Old Testament many things are alleged
which cannot be understood literally. They have a mystic sense
and were said because of the ignorant vulgar, which cannot understand anything not bodily. For the language of religions, as
Averroes said, is like the language of poets: poets make fables
which though literally impossible yet embrace the truth of the
intellect. For they make their stories that we may come into
truth and instruct the rude vulgar, to lead them to good and
withdraw them from evil, as children are led by the hope of reward and the fear of punishment. By these bodily things they are
led to the knowledge of what is not bodily, as we lead infants
from liquid food to food more solid."[66]

Religions are born and die like all things human; for their re-
newing, striking signs are needed among men, and therefore
powers are placed in nature whose exercise is rarely called for.
"Since a change of religion is the greatest of all changes, and it is
difficult to pass from the familiar to what is most unfamiliar, for
the new religion to succeed there is need that strange and surprising things be done. Whence on the advent of a new religion men
making 'miracles' are produced by the heavenly bodies and are
rightly believed to be sons of God..... It is with religions as
with other things subject to generation and corruption: we
observe that they and their miracles are weak at first, then they
increase, come to a climax, then decline, until they return to
nothing. Whence now too in our own faith all things are growing frigid, and miracles are ceasing, except those counterfeit and
simulated, for it seems to be near its end."[67]

In *De fato, libero arbitrio, et de praedestinatione* (1520)[68]

66. *Ibid.*   67. *Ibid.*, cap. 12.

68. *De fato, libero arbitrio, et de praedestinatione* (Basel, *Opera*, 1567;
finished 1520); cf. Cassirer, *Individuum und Kosmos*, pp. 85–87.

Pomponazzi, starting from a treatise of Alexander's, made his choice between human freedom and natural law. After a detailed survey of the attempts to reconcile freedom and providence, he concludes that none has succeeded: it is either fate and providence, or free will, but not both. No view is satisfactory; the Stoics had the most consistent answer.[69] And thus the Paduans ended by opposing a Stoic determinism to the freedom of the Florentines. Pomponazzi's whole view of natural law is in fact more Stoic than scientific in the seventeenth-century sense: it is the universe as a whole acting through "the heavens" that determines particular events rather than some determinate sequence. And his "Alexandrianism" can well be called a rather Stoic Aristotelianism.

There are two modern editions of the *De immortalitate animae*: that edited by Giovanni Gentile ("Opuscoli filosofici: testi e documenti inediti o rari," Vol. I [Messina and Rome: Casa Editrice Giuseppe Principato, 1925]); and that edited by William Henry Hay II (Haverford College, Haverford, Pa., 1938), containing a facsimile of the *editio princeps* and an English translation. Gentile's edition contains some useful emendations, together with a number of unfortunate errors and omissions. Mr. Hay has very kindly permitted his translation, based on the edition of 1516, to be published in this volume with certain editorial revisions; the responsibility for the final redaction rests on J. H. Randall, Jr.

69. *Ibid.*, Lib. II, cap. 1.

ON THE IMMORTALITY OF THE SOUL

Pietro Pomponazzi of Mantua sends his warmest greetings to the Magnificent Noble of Venice Marcantonio Flavo Contarini, dear godfather of his child

I WAS hoping, magnificent Contarini, that during these summer holidays from our studies here I would be free to visit Venice and there to greet after a long absence so many great and old friends, and my illustrious patrons, and to pay my respects to them in person, and to you especially, of whom I am ever duly mindful and observant. But I was greatly deceived in my hope, for, as I was just making ready for the journey, I suddenly contracted a severe and dangerous disease, which troubled me greatly for a long time. In the meantime, throughout the period of my illness, there came to see me every day to pay their respects, as is the custom, many students and friends of mine, soundly learned and courteous men. They tried to mitigate my affliction in many ways. For some time they aroused the sick man with various and diverse questions. At last, by some chance, discussion arose on the immortality of the soul. On which matter at the request of all who were there I gave a long and full discourse, which I afterward decided to publish and dedicate to you, after having gone over it and arranged it more carefully, so that, though we, being separated by space, are prevented from exchanging actual spoken words, we may at least be drawn together by the bond of my writings, such as they are, and that I may talk with you in the only way given me. You, in accordance with your kindness, will receive my little gift with joyful countenance, though it is hardly suitable for so great a man as you. Farewell.

The Calends of October, 1516.

PREFACE

CONTAINING THE PURPOSE OR MATTER OF THE BOOK AND
THE OCCASION OF THIS PURPOSE, ETC.

Brother Hieronymus Natalis of Ragusa of the Order of Preachers, since he is a very kind man, and very dear to me, used to come frequently to visit me when I was suffering from ill-health. And when one day he saw I was less troubled by the illness, with truly humble countenance he began thus: "Beloved teacher, in former days when you were expounding the first book of *De caelo* to us, and had come to that place[1] in which Aristotle tries to show by many arguments that the ungenerated and the incorruptible are convertible, you set forth the position of St. Thomas Aquinas on the immortality of the soul. Although you were in no doubt that it is true and most certain in itself, yet you judged that it is in complete disagreement with what Aristotle says. Therefore, unless it is too much trouble for you, I should very much like to know two things from you. First, leaving aside revelation and miracles, and remaining entirely within natural limits, what do you yourself think in this matter? And, second, what do you judge was Aristotle's opinion on the same question?"

Now I, when I saw the same great desire in all there present— and indeed there were many there—then answered him thus: "Dear son, and all you others, although you ask no small thing, for a business of this sort is very profound, since almost all the famous philosophers have worked upon it; yet since you ask only something which I can answer, namely, what I myself think, for it is easy to make this known to you; therefore I gladly comply. Yet whether things actually are as I think, you must consult more learned men. Therefore, with God's guidance, I shall begin the question.

1. i 12, 282 b 5 ff.

CHAPTER I

IN WHICH IT IS SHOWN THAT MAN IS OF A TWOFOLD
("ANCIPITIS") NATURE AND A MEAN BETWEEN
MORTAL AND IMMORTAL THINGS

Now, I hold that the beginning of our consideration should be made at this point. Man is clearly not of simple but of multiple, not of certain but of ambiguous (*ancipitis*) nature, and he is to be placed as a mean between mortal and immortal things. This is plain to see if we examine his essential operations, as it is from such operations that essences are made known. For in performing the functions of the vegetative and of the sensitive soul, which, as is said in *De anima*, Book ii,[2] and in *De generatione animalium*, Book ii, chapter 3,[3] cannot be performed without a bodily and perishable instrument, man assumes mortality. However, in knowing and willing, operations which throughout the whole *De anima* and in *De partibus animalium*, Book i, chapter 1,[4] and in *De generatione animalium*, Book ii, chapter 3,[5] are held to be performed without any bodily instrument, since they prove separability and immateriality, and these in turn prove immortality, man is to be numbered among the immortal things. From these facts the whole conclusion can be drawn, that man is clearly not of a simple nature, since he includes three souls, so to speak —the vegetative, the sensitive, and the intellective—and that he claims a twofold nature for himself, since he exists neither unqualifiedly (*simpliciter*) mortal nor unqualifiedly immortal but embraces both natures.

Therefore the ancients spoke well when they established man between eternal and temporal things for the reason that he is neither purely eternal nor purely temporal, since he partakes of both natures. And to man, who thus exists as a mean between the two, power is given to assume whichever nature he wishes.

2. Cf. ii 4–5. 4. Cf. 641 b 4 ff.
3. Cf. 736 b 22 ff. 5. Cf. 736 b 27 ff.

Hence there are three kinds of men to be found. Some are numbered with the gods, although such are but few. And these are the men who, having subjugated the vegetative and the sensitive, have become almost completely rational. Some from total neglect of the intellect and from occupying themselves with the vegetative and the sensitive alone, have changed, as it were, into beasts. And perhaps this is what the Pythagorean fable means when it says that men's souls pass into different beasts. Some are called normal men; and these are the ones who have lived tolerably according to the moral virtues. They have not, however, devoted themselves entirely to the intellect or held entirely aloof from the bodily powers. Each of these two latter sorts has a wide range, as is plain to see. With this agrees what is said in the Psalm: "Thou hast made him but a little lower than the angels,"[6] etc.

CHAPTER II

IN WHICH ARE SET FORTH THE WAYS IN WHICH THE AFORESAID MULTIPLICITY OF HUMAN NATURE CAN BE UNDERSTOOD

We have seen that human nature is multiple and ambiguous—not that nature which results from the union of matter and form but the nature which comes from the form or soul itself. It now remains to be seen, since the mortal and the immortal are opposites, which cannot be affirmed of the same thing, whether anyone may justly doubt how it can happen that the two may be affirmed of the human soul at the same time. For, indeed, this is not easy to see.

Now either one and the same nature must be assumed, which is at once mortal and immortal, or two different natures. And if the second is posited, this can be understood in three ways. Either, first, the number of mortal and immortal natures will be according to the number of men—that is, in Socrates there will be one immortal nature and one or two mortal ones, and similar-

6. Ps. 8:6.

ly of the rest, so that each man will have his own mortal and immortal natures. Or, second, in all men there will be assumed but one immortal nature, while the mortal ones will be distributed and multiplied in each man. Or, third, and conversely, we shall posit the immortal as multiplied, but the mortal as common to all.

If, however, the first position is taken, that is, that through one and the same nature man is both mortal and immortal, since it would not seem possible to affirm opposites of the same thing, it is impossible for the same nature to be unqualifiedly mortal and immortal. It will be either unqualifiedly (*simpliciter*) immortal and relatively (*secundum quid*) mortal; or, vice versa, unqualifiedly mortal but relatively immortal; or embrace each relatively, and be relatively mortal and relatively immortal. Now the contradiction can be satisfactorily avoided in these three ways. In summary, therefore, this question can be formulated in six ways, as appears to one examining it and summing it up.

CHAPTER III

IN WHICH IS SET FORTH THE WAY THAT AFFIRMS THAT THE IM-
MORTAL SOUL IS ONE IN NUMBER, WHILE THE MORTAL IS
MULTIPLIED; WHICH IS THE WAY THEMISTIUS AND AVER-
ROES FOLLOWED

Now of these six ways just enumerated, judicious men have accepted four, while two have disappeared. For no one has maintained that the immaterial soul is multiplied, while the material is one in number. And this for good reason, because it is unimaginable for one bodily thing to be in so many distinct places and subjects, and above all if it is corruptible. Likewise, no one has maintained that the same thing is equally mortal and immortal; inasmuch as nothing can be constituted equally of two contraries, but one must always predominate over the other, as is plainly shown in *De caelo*, Book i, text and comment 7;[7] in *De genera-*

7. Cf. i 2, 269 a 1–2, and the commentary of Averroes (*Opera Aristotelis* [Venice, 1560], Vol. V, fols. 10ᵛ and 11).

tione, Book ii, 47;[8] in *Metaphysica,* Book x, 23;[9] and in *Colliget,* Book ii.[10]

In turn, therefore, let us see about the remaining four ways. In the first place, Averroes[11] and, as I believe, Themistius[12] before him agreed in maintaining that the intellective soul is distinct in its existence (*realiter*) from the corruptible soul, but is one in number in all men, while the mortal soul is multiplied. Now the reason for the first statement is that, since they saw that Aristotle demonstrates that the possible intellect is unqualifiedly unmixed and immaterial, and in consequence eternal, and that all his words tend to this conclusion, as is plain to one examining the *De anima,* and since they believed the demonstration of Aristotle to be true in itself, they affirmed unqualifiedly that the intellect is immortal. Since, however, they saw further that the sensitive and the vegetative soul necessarily require bodily organs for their functioning, as appears from the passages cited above, while such organs are necessarily bodily and perishable, they concluded that such a soul is unqualifiedly mortal. But since the same thing cannot be unqualifiedly and absolutely mortal and immortal, they were forced to maintain that the immortal soul is distinct in its existence from the mortal soul. Themistius tries to bring Plato also into this opinion and cites the words of Plato in the *Timaeus,*[13] which clearly seem to assert it. Now, that there is a single intellect in all men, whether it be held active or possible, can be shown from the fact that there is among the Peripatetics a celebrated proposition, that the multiplication of individuals in the same species is not possible except by a certain quantity of mat-

8. Cf. ii 3, 330 a 31 ff.

9. Cf. x 7, 1057 b 26 ff.

10. *Opera Aristotelis* (Venice, 1560), Vol. IX, fol. 17ᵛ.

11. Cf. Averroes, Commentary on the *De anima,* Book iii (*Opera Aristotelis,* Vol. VII, fols. 101 ff.).

12. Cf. Themistius, *In libros Aristotelis de anima paraphrasis* (ed. R. Heinze, in *Commentaria in Aristotelem Graeca,* V, Part III [Berlin, 1899]), p. 106.

13. Themistius (*ibid.*), who cites *Timaeus* 69 c ff. and 72 d.

ter, as is stated in *Metaphysica*, Books vii[14] and xii,[15] and in *De anima*, Book ii.[16] Moreover, how the doubts against this way are resolved appears from reading their books and those of their followers. For here we intend to be brief, and to bring in only what is necessary.

CHAPTER IV

IN WHICH THE AFORESAID OPINION OF AVERROES IS REFUTED

Although this opinion is widely held in our time and by almost all is confidently taken to be that of Aristotle, it nevertheless seems to me that it is not only in itself most false; it is unintelligible and monstrous and quite foreign to Aristotle. Indeed, I think that Aristotle never even thought of such nonsense, let alone believed it.

As for the first point, I intend to introduce nothing new about its falsity but only to refer the reader to what the glory of the Latins, St. Thomas Aquinas, writes in his own book, *Against the Unity of the Intellect*,[17] in the first part of the *Summa*,[18] in *Contra Gentiles*, Book ii,[19] in the *Disputed Questions about the Soul*,[20] and in many other places. For he indeed inveighs against this opinion so lucidly and so subtly that in my judgment he leaves nothing untouched and lets go unrefuted no answer which anyone could bring forward in behalf of Averroes. For he refutes the whole position and dissipates and annihilates it; and no refuge is left the Averroists but railing and curses against the godly and very holy man.

14. Cf. vii 8, 1034 a 7–8.

15. Cf. xii 2, 1069 b 30, and 8, 1074 a 33 ff.

16. Cf. ii 2, 414 a 25 ff.

17. *Opusculum XV, De unitate intellectus contra Averroistas* (*Opera omnia*, ed. Fretté, XXVII [Paris, 1875], 311 ff.).

18. *Summa theologiae*, Part I, Question 76, Article 2 (*Opera omnia, Editio Leonina*, V [Rome, 1889], 216 ff.).

19. Chap. 73.   20. Articles 2–3 (ed. Fretté, XIV, 66 ff.).

But as for the second point, I have resolved to bring forward these few things which confirm my faith. This view is foreign to Aristotle and is indeed a fiction and a monstrosity contrived by this Averroes. First, because such an intellective soul either has some operation entirely independent of the body as subject and object, or it has none. The latter cannot be maintained, since he would be contradicting himself and reason. Himself, because in *De anima*, Book i, comment 12, toward the end, he says: "And he does not mean by that what appears superficially from this passage, that there is no knowing without imagination; for then the material intellect will be generated and corruptible, as Alexander understands it."[21] From this it is clear that, according to Averroes, the intellect has some operation entirely independent of the body. This is also confirmed by reason, because the intellect is not a form constituted in its being by the subject and therefore is not dependent on the subject for its being, or therefore for its operating, since operation follows being. But that this view does not agree with Aristotle and is contrary to his opinion is plain enough, since Aristotle says at the end of the cited text 12 of *De anima*, Book i: "Knowing is either imagination or not without imagination."[22] And, although he there speaks conditionally, in *De anima*, Book iii, text 39,[23] he nevertheless says most clearly that there is no knowing without some phantasm—which experience also proves. In no way, therefore, according to Aristotle, does the human intellect have any operation entirely independent of the body, which is the opposite of what was conceded.

To this I see no other answer except what Averroes' argument shows about human knowing and in what respect man is called intelligent because of this intellect. For thus it is verified that it always needs some phantasm. Now this is clear in a new intellection and before its completion (*adeptionem*); but in an eternal intellection or in the completion itself it also holds true, since, according to Averroes, the possible intellect is disposed for receiv-

21. *Opera Aristotelis*, Vol. VII, fol. 8ᵛ.

22. i 1, 403 a 8–9.   23. iii 7, 431 a 16–17.

ing the active intellect as form by its speculative habits, which depend for their preservation on the sensitive power, as he says in *De anima*, Book iii, comment 39: "But if the intellect is taken by itself it is no wise dependent on any phantasm."[24] But, although this is said rather cleverly, it nevertheless seems to profit nothing, because, according to the common definition of the soul, the soul is the act of a body physical and organic, etc. Therefore, the intellective soul is the act of a physical and organic body. Since, therefore, in its being the intellect is the act of a physical and organic body, it will thus also depend in all its functioning on some organ, either as subject or as object. Hence it will never be totally released from some organ.

To this it is perhaps said that the soul is like the other Intelligences. And indeed the Commentator himself maintains, in *De anima*, Book iii, comment 19,[25] that it is the lowest of the Intelligences. The other Intelligences, however, can be considered in two ways. In one way in themselves and not as they actuate a heavenly body; and in this way they are not souls and have operations in no wise dependent on a body, like knowing and desiring. But they can be considered in another way, as the acts of the heavenly bodies; and in this way it befits them to be souls, indeed, even the above definition of soul fits them. For in this sense they are the acts of a physical and organic body, although that definition applies rather equivocally, as the Commentator says, in *De anima*, Book iii, comment 5.[26] For the celestial bodies are animated, as Aristotle maintains in *Physica* viii,[27] *De caelo* ii,[28] and *Metaphysica* xii;[29] although rather equivocally, as the Commentator himself says in *De substantia orbis*.[30] Therefore the intellective soul also can be considered in two ways. In one way, as the lowest of the Intelligences, and not in relation to its own sphere, that is,

24. *Op. cit.*, Fol. 131.

25. *Ibid.*, fol. 112ᵛ.

26. *Ibid.*, fol. 102ᵛ.

27. Cf. viii 2, 252 b 24 ff.

28. ii 12, 292 a 20 ff.

29. Cf. xii 8.

30. Cf. chap. 2 (in *Joannis de Janduno in libros Aristotelis de coelo et mundo .... quaestiones* [Venice, 1564], fol. 50).

mankind. In this way it is no wise dependent on any body, neither in its being nor in its functioning, and hence as such it is not the act of a physical and organic body. However, it can be considered in another way, in relation to its own sphere, and as such it is the act of a physical and organic body. Hence it is not released from the body as such, neither in its being nor in its functioning. For this reason, as it is the form of man, it always requires some phantasm for its functioning, but not unqualifiedly, as above. And in this way the customary doubt can be resolved as to how the natural philosopher treats of the intellective soul, since he says in *De partibus*, Book i, chapter 1,[31] that it does not belong to the natural philosopher to treat of the intellective soul, since it is a mover and not something moved, and the rest there set forth. It is solved, I say, because, in so far as it is a soul, it is something natural. Indeed, from this point of view the Intelligences are considered by the natural philosopher. But in so far as the human soul is an intellect, it is the affair of the metaphysician, just like the rest of the higher Intellects.

But as a matter of fact this answer seems deficient in many ways. First, because if there were the same judgment about the human soul as about the rest of the Intelligences, when in *Metaphysica* xii[32] Aristotle treats of the Intelligences, he ought to have treated the human soul thoroughly also; and he does not do this. Moreover, if there is the same judgment about the human intellect as about the Intelligences, why then does Aristotle, in *Physica* ii, text of comment 26,[33] hold that the limit of the natural philosopher's field is the human soul? Because if Aristotle understands this as concerning the soul's existence (*quia est*), it is false. For the existence of God and the Intelligences is demonstrated by the natural philosopher, and according to the Commentator himself, in *De anima* i, comment 2,[34] and *Metaphysica* xii, comment 36,[35] the theologian receives these proofs from the natural

31. 641 b 33 ff.   33. Cf. ii 2, 194 b 9 ff.
32. Cf. chap. 8.   34. *Op. cit.*, Vol. VII. fol. 5ᵛ.
35. *Opera Aristotelis,* Vol. VIII, fols. 337–38.

philosopher. But if he is speaking of their essence (*quid est*) it is clear enough, according to the answer given, that it does not belong to the natural philosopher, since as such it is a mover, not something moved. Indeed, as the answer says, this is what Aristotle meant in *De partibus* i, chapter cited.[36]

Further, it seems ridiculous to say that the intellective soul, which is a power single in number, has two ways of understanding, one dependent on and one independent of the body. For thus it would seem to possess two kinds of being. For an Intelligence, even though it be intellect and soul, and in its understanding does not need the body, still might need the body in causing motion. But causing motion in place and understanding are very different functions. In the soul, moreover, are placed intellections, of which one depends on the body, while the other is unqualifiedly absolute. This does not seem in harmony with reason, since of a single function, with respect to one and the same thing, there does not seem to be but a single manner of functioning.

Moreover, it seems superfluous and incredible that something one in number should have almost infinite functions with respect to the same object at the same time. But this follows from the present opinion. For that intellect knows God by an eternal intellection, and by a new intellection has as many intellections with respect to God as there are men who know God. Now this seems to be a pure fiction, as can appear from many reasons. However, if an Intelligence knows without body, but does not cause motion in place without a body, no inconsistency follows; since knowing and causing motion in place are functions of very different kinds, and one is immanent and the other transitive, whereas the complete opposite occurs with regard to the intellective soul. For both are intellections and both are immanent functions.

Second, as to the principal question: if according to Aristotle the intellective soul is truly immaterial, as the said Commentator pretends, since this is not known immediately (per se) and on

36. Chap. 1, 641 b 33 ff.

the contrary is exceedingly doubtful, it ought to be made clear by some evidence. But it is enough to conclude its inseparability, according to Aristotle, that it is either an organic power, or, if not organic, that at least it cannot come into operation without some bodily object. For he says in *De anima* i, text 12,[37] that whether the intellect is imagination or is not without imagination, its separation does not take place. Since, however, separability is the opposite of inseparability, and a disjunctive affirmative contradicts a copulative affirmative formed of two opposites; if then it is enough for inseparability alternatively to be in an organ as in a subject or to depend upon it as upon an object, then for separability there is required jointly neither to depend upon an organ as upon a subject nor as upon an object, at least in some one of its operations. Since, however, this is just what is in question, how can Averroes ascertain that the soul is immortal, particularly since Aristotle says that it is necessary to have a phantasm before one in knowing, and every man experiences this in himself?

To this it is perhaps said that the argument of *De anima* iii[38] demonstrates unqualifiedly that the soul is immaterial because it receives all material forms; whence it follows strictly that it has an operation entirely independent, since operation follows being.

But this does not seem valid, because that argument of Aristotle assumes that the intellect is moved by the body, since he says that knowing is just like sensing, and the possible intellect is a passive power; and further on he says that its mover is a phantasm. But what needs a phantasm is inseparable from matter, for the reasons given. Therefore, that argument proves rather that it is material than immaterial.

But still perhaps it is said that, inasmuch as the intellect does not need an organ as subject, then it is unqualifiedly immaterial (this argument Aristotle puts directly after the above). But this does not seem to help, because either that condition alone suf-

<hr>

37. i 1, 403 a 8–9.   38. Chap. 4.

fices or another is required, that it be not moved by the body. If both, the earlier argument stands; if that alone, the judgment of Aristotle is destroyed, since he maintains that both are required.

But still perhaps it is said that indeed only one thing is required. For not to need the body as a subject implies absolutely that it is an immaterial power and conversely. Because, however, in addition to being immaterial, it may have some operation entirely independent (for indeed if it is immaterial it has some independent operation, and conversely)—since, however, it happens that besides an operation independent of any object it may have one that is dependent; lest perchance someone might think from the fact that it has some dependent operation that all its operations may be dependent, Aristotle then added: "that if knowing were not without imagination" so that it needed imagination in every operation, then the intellect would undoubtedly be inseparable.

But this does not seem able to stand. First, because Aristotle would have added that condition superfluously, since the other is enough to imply the conclusion, which is scandalous to ascribe to so great a philosopher. Secondly, because, if from the fact that the intellect needs some phantasm in all its functions, it is inferred that it is inseparable; this cannot be unless because it is assumed to be organic, I mean organic in its subject. For, according to what has been assumed, what is organic in its subject is convertible with a material cognitive power; whence something not organic in its subject is also convertible with something immaterial. Hence to say always to need the body as an object is to say to need the body as subject; and thus nothing new would be said when he adds, "if knowing is not without imagination." For to be imagination and never to be without imagination are simply convertible, and the one states the other. Hence it would be as if someone should say, if Socrates is not a man, or is not a rational animal, he is not teachable. How ridiculous and foreign to the majesty of Aristotle this statement is I leave to the judgment of others.

[292]

Further, when something has two causes of its truth, and one be taken away and the other remains, nonetheless the thing remains, as is self-evident, since for the truth of a disjunction it is enough that one part be true. But it is proved that the intellect is inseparable from matter, since it is imagination, or is not without imagination, as is clear in *De anima* i.[39] If we set aside, therefore, that it is imagination, it would be nonetheless proved that it is material, provided that it is not without imagination. But according to the assumption that is false, because, according to it, it is impossible for the intellect to be inseparable and not to be imagination, since by it the two are convertible. Therefore the proposition asserting that a thing organic in its subject and a material thing are convertible, and likewise their opposites, that a thing inorganic in its subject and an immaterial thing are convertible, is false.

Further, whenever two modes are attributed to anything disjunctively, that thing can be separated indifferently from either of them, or at least from one of them, and itself remain. For example, parsimony occurs in two ways, either through avarice or through prodigality. Hence a parsimonious miser is found without prodigality, and a parsimonious prodigal without avarice. For if they could not be separated, there would not be two modes of parsimony, but they would either coincide or both necessarily combine copulatively and not disjunctively into parsimony. For, indeed, if no one were parsimonious unless he were at the same time prodigal and avaricious, it would not properly be said that prodigality or avarice is required for parsimony but that prodigality and avarice together constitute parsimony. If then it suffices for the inseparability of the soul for it to be imagination or not without imagination, either then it is established that it is inseparable without either of these conditions indifferently, or at least determinately. If the first, then it will be established that the intellect is not without some phantasm, and yet is not imagination; and, consequently, that it always needs

39. i 1, 403 a 8–9.

the body as object and not as subject, which is contrary to what was conceded by our adversary. But if the second is affirmed, that is, determinately and not indifferently, since it cannot be that anything should need the body as subject, and not as object, it will then be established that it needs the body as object and not as subject. Hence the same as before.

Further, according to the assumption, the intellect has some operation entirely independent of the body. Since this is doubtful, it must be proved by some mark; and one can imagine nothing by which it can be proved except because it is immaterial. But since this too is no less doubtful than the first, it needs demonstration. Therefore, a question arises as to that middle, whether it is that it does not depend on the body at the same time as subject and object, or only that it does not depend on the body as subject. The first cannot be affirmed; for one thing, because then there would be a begging of the question, since, intending to prove that the intellect in some of its operations does not depend upon the body, we are assuming that it is immaterial, and, in proving that it is immaterial, we accept that in some operation it does not depend on the body. For another, because there is no such middle in which it is not assumed that the intellect depends upon the body as upon an object. And indeed the first demonstration of *De anima* iii[40] proves that the intellect is immaterial because it receives all material forms. Now since to receive such forms consists in being acted upon, as Aristotle there says, it will thus be moved by some bodily thing and will need it as object. The second demonstration is that the intelligible species is received not in the organ but in the intellect itself; hence the same as before, since to receive is to be acted upon. We must then state another proposition as the middle, that it does not need the body as subject, though it does as object. But if this is so, why then is it that Aristotle, calling the attention of his hearer, said in the Preface to *De anima:* "It is necessary to know beforehand concerning its operations,"[41] and adds, "If

40. iii 4, 429 a 18 ff.   41. i 1, 403 a 3 ff. and a 8–9.

knowing is like imagination, or not without imagination, it is impossible that it be separated"?

Hence to prove separability as the opposite of inseparability, we must prove at the same time both that it is not imagination and that in some operation it does not depend on the imagination; and, consequently, that it does not depend on the body as subject nor as object, at least in some operation, which is the opposite of what is conceded. This likewise is so affirmed by our adversary. To need the body as subject and to be a material power are convertible; their opposites also are convertible, not to need the body as subject and to be an immaterial power. For in *Analytica posteriora* i,[42] if an affirmation is the cause of an affirmation, a negation is the cause of a negation. Why then does Aristotle in proving materiality add, besides imagination, not to be without imagination? For he sins through the fallacy of the non-cause as cause, since the precise cause of materiality is to need the body as subject. This also is most evidently confirmed again. Because for immateriality, besides not needing the body as subject, it is either necessary in addition not to need the body as object in any determinate operation or it is not necessary. The second cannot be affirmed because of what has been conceded, since not to need the body as subject and not to need the body as object in any determinate operation are convertible. Hence, if one be posited, the other is posited. It thus remains that immateriality needs both copulatively. Hence, since materiality is the contrary of immateriality, it would be enough for materiality itself to need the body as subject, or the body as object. Either, then, these things are separable, and thus not convertible, which is contrary to what was conceded; or they will be inseparable, and thus will not be predicable by disjunction. But this is just what Aristotle does. Now a final corollary is plain, that what is stated disjunctively is proved alternatively and not copulatively. For *Metaphysica* x, text 17,[43] and the Commentator in

42. i 13, 78 b 20–21.
43. Cf. x 5, 1055 b 37 ff.

De caelo iii, comment 56,[44] and Boethius in *De syllogismo hypothetico*[45] say: "A disjunctive question in which both parts are proved is vain and ridiculous." And, further, a copulative affirmative would be contradicted by a copulative made of opposite and not disjunctive parts, which is plainly false. Therefore, unless I am mistaken, the Commentator, St. Thomas, and whoever thinks that Aristotle judged the human intellect to be truly immortal are far from the truth.

Moreover, it is strange that Aristotle should have maintained that at times the intellect knows without any phantasm and nevertheless say in every passage that there is no knowing without some phantasm. For he ought not to have stated it so absolutely.

Thirdly, as to the principal question: according to the Commentator we ought to place human happiness in the union of the active with the possible intellect, as he clearly shows in *De anima* iii, comment 36.[46] But how futile this is and how contrary to Aristotle is not difficult to see. Futile, because, so far as history tells, no such union has ever been found to this day. And thus the goal of man is vain, since no one has attained it, nay, no one can attain it, since the means appointed for that goal cannot be possessed. For it is impossible for any man to know all things, as Plato says in the *Republic*, Book x,[47] nor even all visible things. Indeed, no science has been perfectly known up to the present day, as is plain from experience. That it is also contrary to Aristotle is clear, since in the *Ethics*,[48] where he concludes about the final end of man as man, he places it in a state of wisdom. Nor can anyone say that that book was not finished, since in the end of that book[49] he plainly concludes and continues to the *Politics*. Hence I very much wonder when he ascribes to Aristotle this unity of the intellect, inasmuch as the latter nowhere maintains

44. Cf. *Opera Aristotelis*, Vol. V, fols. 223–24.

45. Cf. Book ii (in Migne, *Patrologia Latina*, Vol. LXIV, cols. 873 ff.).

46. *Op. cit.*, Vol. VII, fol. 129ᵛ.   48. x 7.

47. Cf. 598 c–d.   49. x 10.

it. But in the *Physica* ii, text 26,[50] where he mentions the human soul, he says that they are multiplied. For he speaks in this way, up to the point where it reads, "by cause of which each thing is, and in regard to these things which are separate species in matter, for man generates man from matter, and the sun." Whence it is clear that he maintains not one only but many. It is another matter in regard to that union, since no such man has been found, nor did Aristotle make any mention of it. Hence it seems to me that this is not only a fiction in itself but is also contrary to Aristotle.

CHAPTER V

IN WHICH IS SET FORTH THE SECOND WAY, ASSERTING THAT THE INTELLECTIVE SOUL IS DISTINCT IN EXISTENCE FROM THE SENSITIVE BUT CORRESPONDS TO THE SENSITIVE IN NUMBER

Since the foregoing opinion has been rejected as unintelligible, there is the second of the ways enumerated. It agrees with the first that the intellective soul is distinct in existence from the sensitive, seeing that contradictories cannot be truly predicated of the same thing; but it differs from the first in a second respect. For it holds that the number of intellective souls corresponds to the number of sensitive. For Socrates is distinguished from Plato as this man from that man; but he is this man only through his intellect, as Averroes himself admits in *De anima* iii, comment 1.[51] Hence the intellect of Socrates is different from the intellect of Plato. For if the intellect of both were one, both would have the same being and operations; but what greater folly can be thought of?

But those who agree in this view also differ among themselves. Some of them have maintained that the soul is related to a man as a mover to what is moved rather than as form to matter. And this seems to have been the view of Plato, who says in *I Alcibiades:*

50. ii 2, 194 b 11 ff.　　51. *Op. cit.*, Vol. VII, fols. 94ᵛ–95.

[297]

"Man is a soul using a body."[52] With this seem to agree the words of Aristotle in *Ethics* ix: "Man is an intellect."[53] However, others have asserted the opposite, saying that the soul is related to a man as form to matter, and not only as a mover to what is moved; and that it is more truly to be said that man is a composite of soul and body than that he is a soul using a body. But certain other things they adduce are not necessary for our purpose.

CHAPTER VI

IN WHICH THE AFORESAID OPINION IS REFUTED

Now this way is refuted in both its parts by St. Thomas in *Summa* i,[54] and in many other places, and in my opinion with abundant and clear argument. For if man were not composed of matter and form, but of mover and thing moved, then soul and body would have no greater unity than oxen and a plow. And many other inconvenient consequences follow, which he adduces. Moreover, to posit a plurality of substantial forms in the same composite, as the second part asserts, seems foreign to Aristotle and many Peripatetics. But I adduce two reasons, for which all the above ways seem to me far from the truth and from Aristotle.

First, this seems to contradict experience. For I who am writing these words am beset with many bodily pains, which are the function of the sensitive soul; and the same I who am tortured run over their medical causes in order to remove these pains, which cannot be done save by the intellect. But if the essence by which I feel were different from that by which I think, how could it possibly be that I who feel am the same as I who think? For then we could say that two men joined together have common cognitions, which is ridiculous. Moreover, how far a belief of this sort is from Aristotle is not difficult to see. For in *De anima*

52. 129 e.   53. Cf. ix 4, 1166 a 22–23.   54. Question 76, article 2.

ii[55] he places the vegetative soul in the sensitive, as the triangle in
the quadrilateral. But it is plain that the triangle is not in the quadrilateral as something distinct from it in existence: what is potentially a triangle is actually a quadrilateral. Hence, since for Aristotle the sensitive soul is related to the intellective in mortals in
the same way, the sensitive soul will not be a thing distinct from
the intellective. Wherefore it seems to me that both the first way
of Averroes and these two ways are contrary to truth and to
Aristotle.

CHAPTER VII

IN WHICH THERE IS SET FORTH A WAY AFFIRMING THAT THE MOR-
TAL AND THE IMMORTAL ARE THE SAME IN EXISTENCE IN MAN,
BUT THAT THAT ESSENCE IS UNQUALIFIEDLY IMMORTAL, WHILE
RELATIVELY MORTAL

Since therefore that way is completely rejected which thinks
that the intellective and the sensitive souls in man are distinct in
existence, it remains that the intellective and the sensitive are the
same in man; and, although this can be understood in three ways,
as has been said before, still only two are reasonable.

Now one was that the immortal is in man unqualifiedly, but
the mortal relatively. And, although according to the nature of
division this way can be divided into two, either one in number
in all men, or multiplied to the number of men; yet, since no one
has maintained the first way, we shall omit it and discuss only the
second. Although many very famous men have held it, yet, since
it seems to me that St. Thomas[56] has stated it more fully and more
clearly, I shall refer to his words alone. That it may be understood in orderly fashion, I shall collect his opinion into five
propositions:

55. ii 3, 414 b 31–32.

56. Cf. *Summa theologiae*, Part I, Question 75 and 76 (*op. cit.*, pp.
194 ff.).

First, that the intellective and the sensitive in man are the same in existence.

Secondly, that this soul is truly and unqualifiedly immortal, while relatively mortal.

Thirdly, that such a soul is truly the form of man and not only as it were the mover.

Fourthly, that this same soul corresponds in number to the number of individuals.

Fifthly, that a soul of this kind begins its existence with the body but that it comes from without and is produced by God alone, not indeed by generation, but by creation; however, it does not cease to be with the body, but is perpetual from that time on.

The first of these is plain enough from the above, not only because many substantial forms cannot exist in the same subject but also because it seems to be the same essence that knows and senses and also because in mortals the sensitive exists in the intellective, just as the triangle in the quadrilateral.

But the second, in which all the strength consists, that such a soul is truly immortal, but relatively mortal, is stated in many ways. And, first, primarily in the argument of Aristotle, in *De anima* iii,[57] because such a soul is receptive of all material forms; but what is of this kind cannot be material, as Aristotle there sets forth, since the receiver must be stripped of the nature of the thing received. This proposition is also conceded by Plato in the *Timaeus*,[58] and, as Averroes says in *De anima* ii,[59] it is universally verified in material and spiritual action. For the eye, receptive of the species of color, must be without color, and thus universally of the other senses. Secondly, because if the intellect were material, the form received in it would be known potentially; and thus it would either not know, or know only particulars. Thirdly, because thus it would be an organic power, whence it would be limited to a certain genus of beings, or at least to the singular mode; whence it would either not know everything, or not know

57. iii 4, 429 a 15 ff.   58. Cf. 36 e–37 a.   59. *Op. cit.,* fol. 96.

in the universal mode. This is also conclusively proved by its effects (*a signo*). For the mode of desiring naturally follows the mode of knowing; but the intellect apprehends the universal, which is eternal, whence the will also will desire the eternal. Now such desire is natural, since all wills strive for the eternal. But a natural appetite cannot be in vain, since, in *De caelo* i,[60] God and nature do nothing in vain. Whence it is proved that the intellect is unqualifiedly immortal. The words of Aristotle are also so clear on this point that they need no interpreter, since he maintains in *De anima* i, ii and iii[61] that the intellect is separate and not the act of any body. In the part also that treats of the active intellect, he says that the active intellect is truly immaterial, because the possible intellect is of this kind, and the active is superior to the passive. He affirms the same thing also in *De partibus* i, chapter 1,[62] and *De generatione animalium* ii, chapter 3.[63] But that a soul of this kind is relatively mortal can be made clear by two reasons. First, since this intellective soul is also sensitive and vegetative, as follows from what has been said; but the sensitive and vegetative, if they are separated from the intellective, are corruptible. Whence the intellective is not mortal in itself but because it contains a degree which taken by itself is mortal. Secondly, since the human soul does not exercise the functions of the sensitive and the vegetative except through a perishable instrument. Hence it is not mortal in itself but by reason of such functions and instruments.

The third proposition, that it is the form of man, is plain from the universal definition of the soul, since it is the act of a physical body, etc., and is the principle by which we know, as Aristotle there clearly demonstrates.

Now the fourth follows from the third. For if the intellective soul is the form by which man is man, if it were one in all men, the being and operations of all men would be the same, as has been demonstrated against the Commentator. Aristotle also, in *Physica*

---

60. i 4, 271 a 33.
61. i 4, 408 b 29–30; ii 2, 413 b 24 ff.; iii 4–5.
62. Cf. 641 b 4 ff.
63. Cf. 736 b 27 ff.

[301]

ii, text 26,[64] expressly holds that they are in the plural number, as has been said before.

The fifth, however, that it has been produced, is clear, not only from *Physica* ii, text 26:[65] "Since the sun and man generate man," but also since, according to the third proposition, it is "the form by which man is man," and in *Metaphysica* xii, text 17,[66] "the form begins to be at the same time as that of which it is the form." Also from *De generatione animalium* ii, chapter 3,[67] where he says that the intellect alone comes from without. But that it does not come into being through generation is clear, since what is produced through generation is material and perishable. But it has already been demonstrated in the second proposition that the soul is immaterial and incorruptible. That it is indeed made by God alone is clear, since as it is not through generation it must be through creation. But that God alone creates has been demonstrated elsewhere. This can also be shown through that passage in *De generatione animalium* ii, chapter 3,[68] where it is said: "Hence only the intellect exists divine and immortal." But that it remains after death, since it is immortal, is clear. It follows also from the words of Aristotle in *Metaphysica* xii, text 17,[69] since he says that nothing prevents the intellect from remaining after death. And thus the whole position is made clear.

CHAPTER VIII

IN WHICH DOUBTS ARE RAISED CONCERNING
THE AFORESAID WAY

Of the truth of this position there is for me no doubt at all, since the canonical Scripture, which must be preferred to any human reasoning and experience whatever, as it was given by God, sanctions this position. But what for me is subject to doubt

---

64. ii 2, 194 b 12–13.

65. ii 2, 194 b 13.

66. Cf. xii 3, 1070 a 23–24.

67. 736 b 27–28.

68. 736 b 28.

69. Cf. xii 3, 1070 a 24 ff.

is whether these propositions exceed the natural limits, so that they presuppose something from faith or revelation, and whether they are in conformity with the words of Aristotle, as St. Thomas himself declares. But as the authority of so learned a Doctor is very great with me, not only in divinity but also in the interpretation of Aristotle, I would not dare to affirm anything against him. I only advance what I say in the way of doubt and not of assertion; and perchance the truth will be disclosed to me by his most learned followers. Of his first proposition, then, I have no doubt, that in man the sensitive and the intellective are the same in existence. But the other four are very doubtful to me.

And, first, that such an essence is properly and truly immortal, but improperly and relatively mortal. First, then, because by the same reasons by which St. Thomas proves this, the opposite can be proved. For from the facts that such an essence receives all material forms, that what is received in it is known actually, that it does not use any bodily organ, that it strives for eternity and heavenly things, it was concluded that it is immortal. But equally, when it operates materially as the vegetative soul, it does not receive all forms; when, as the sensitive soul, it uses a bodily organ; and strives after temporal and perishable things; and these facts will prove it is truly and unqualifiedly mortal. But, in so far as it knows, it will be relatively immortal, not only because the intellect, when not joined to matter, is incorruptible, but when joined to matter is corruptible; but also because in such an operation it does not use any bodily instrument. Thus even St. Thomas says that in such a way it is accidentally or relatively material. For the argument for the one conclusion seems to be no stronger than for the other.

Secondly, because since in this essence there are some things that imply that it is mortal, and some that it is immortal, and since many more tend toward mortality than toward immortality, and in *Physica* i and vi,[70] "the denomination comes from what is greater," it must rather be pronounced mortal than immortal;

70. Cf. i 1, 184 b 10–11; vi 9, 240 a 23 ff.

and not only must it be pronounced but it will also be so in actual fact.

Now the assumption is proved as follows. For if we consider the number of powers in man, we find only two which attest to immortality, the intellect and the will; but innumerable powers of the sensitive and the vegetative soul, which all attest to mortality.

Further, if we examine the habitable regions, many more men resemble beasts than men, and in the habitable regions you will find that those who are rational are most rare. Among rational men also, if we will consider, even they can be called essentially irrational; they are called rational in comparison with others who are most beastlike, just as is said of women, that none is wise except in comparison with others who are most foolish.

Further, if you examine knowing itself, especially that which is concerning the gods—why concerning the gods?—nay, even concerning natural things, and what belongs to the senses, it is so obscure and so weak that it ought more truly to be called a twofold ignorance, of negation and of disposition, than cognition. In addition, how little time men spend on the intellect, and how much more on the other powers! Whence it is that truly such an essence is bodily and corruptible and is scarcely the shadow of intellect. This indeed seem to be the cause why from so many thousand men hardly one may be found who is devoted to study and intellectual things.

The cause is indeed natural, since the effect is natural; for it has always been so, though at times more or less. The cause, I say, is that by nature man's existence is more sensuous than intellective, more mortal than immortal. This is apparent also, since many in defining man put mortal as the differential. If, I say, you will consider these things, the opposite view will seem closer to the truth than that of St. Thomas.

Thirdly, it is argued against this position, that the soul is immortal is not known immediately; then the question arises, just as was said against Averroes, "By what evidence is it known?"

Either from the fact that in its operation it needs no organ, more precisely, as subject, or with something else added. The first cannot be affirmed, according to Aristotle himself, in *De anima* ii, text 12.[71] For to infer inseparability it is enough alternatively, either that its operation be in the subject or that in all its operations it need the body as object. Since he says, "If then knowing is either imagination, or is not without imagination, it is impossible for it to be separated." Hence for separability both conditions are required, because a copulative affirmative is opposed to a disjunctive made of opposite parts. Hence for knowing that the soul is separable it is necessary that it should neither need the body as subject, nor as object, at least in some operation. But how can this be known, since Aristotle also says,[72] "It is necessary for the knower to have some phantasm before him"? And by experience we know that we always need phantasms, as every one observes in himself, and as an injury to the organs demonstrates. And everything which was adduced against the Commentator in regard to the immortality of the soul is also opposed to this opinion, since they agree on this point, though they differ on others.

Fourthly, it is argued thus: if the human soul is dependent in all its operations on some organ, it is inseparable and material; but in all its operations it is dependent on some organ; hence it is material. The major follows from *De anima* i, where Aristotle says, "If knowing is imagination, or is not without imagination, it is impossible for it to be separated."[73] The minor follows from the universal definition of the soul, "It is the act of a physical and organic body."[74]

But to this it is perhaps replied that the human soul, as regards the intellect, is not the act of an organic body, since the intellect is not the act of any body, but only as regards the operations of the sensitive and the vegetative soul. But it does not seem that this can stand. First, because then the intellective soul would not be a soul, since as such it would not be the act of a physical and organ-

71. i 1, 403 a 8 ff.   73. i 1, 403 a 8 ff.
72. Cf. *De anima* iii 7, 431 a 17.   74. *De anima* ii 1, 412 a 19 ff.

ic body, which is contrary to Aristotle, who maintains that this is the definition common to every soul—which even by Thomas himself is said univocally of all souls. Secondly, because if the intellective soul needed some organ even for sensing, as long as it were a soul, it would sense, or could sense, which seems obviously false. The conclusion follows, since if the definition stands, everything in the definition stands also. Thirdly, because, according to Thomas himself, in Part I (of the *Summa*),[75] and Book ii *Contra Gentiles*,[76] the Intelligences are not the forms of the celestial bodies, because if they were, they would stand in great need of a body for knowing, just like the human soul. Hence if the human soul is the act of an organic body as regards sensation, this is for its knowing; hence in all its knowing it needs imagination. But, if this is so, it is material. Hence the intellective soul is material.

But to this it is perhaps replied that it is not necessary for the intellective soul always to depend actually on an organ, although an organ is included in its definition. It is enough that it do so in aptitude; just as upward motion is the definition of the light, although the light is not always moving upward, but it is enough that it so move or be able to move.

But this answer is deficient in many ways. First, because if aptitude alone were enough in definitions, then it could be said that something is a man, and yet is not actually a rational animal. For it would be enough, according to the answer, that it would be so in aptitude. Secondly, since it would be said that if the soul depends on imagination in aptitude, it will be nonetheless inseparable and material, even though it does not always actually so depend.

To these points it is perhaps said that that is not a true definition but, as it were, a description or characterization. To the second point it is said that for inseparability it is not enough to depend on the body in aptitude, because what exists as separate and immaterial can in fact depend on a body. But if it were always actu-

75. Cf. Question 51 (*op. cit.*, pp. 14 ff.).   76. Chap. 51.

ally dependent, so that it could never exist without a body, then it would indeed be material.

But none of these statements seems suitable. First, because all say that those two asserted definitions are asserted of the soul, the one by formal cause, and the other by material cause, and by the one the other is demonstrated. The second statement also seems deficient in many points. First, because if the human soul has two ways of knowing, the one through phantasms and the other without phantasms, it seems very irrational that an immaterial substance should be moved by a material thing. For however much the immaterial acts on the material, it does not seem that the action can go the other way. Whence also even among theologians doubt has arisen as to how souls can be tortured by bodily fire. Secondly, because if a soul after separation has an aptitude for its body, it will then either be reunited with it or not. If the first, then we must return to the opinion of Democritus, who held to resurrection, or to Pythagoras, who held to the transmigration of souls into different animals, which is refuted as erroneous in every quarter. But if the second be affirmed, then it is contrary to the order of nature. For in *Physica* viii, text 15,[77] Aristotle refutes Anaxagoras' position that the world has not existed for infinite time and began at a later period. For nature proceeds either in one way or in several. Even if in several, it still proceeds in orderly fashion. But there is no order or proportion of the finite to the infinite. Whence if the soul is joined to the body for a finite time, but separated for an infinite time, the order of nature will not remain. Thirdly, because such different ways of being as joined and separate, and such different ways of operating as through phantasms and without phantasms, seem to argue a diversity of essence.

For when this way is rejected, there remains no way of proving a specific diversity between anything. In *De historiis* vi, chapter 24,[78] Aristotle says that the she-mules which in Syria bear offspring, although they are so exceedingly like ours that they

77. Chap. 1 ff.   78. 577 b 23 ff.

can scarcely be distinguished, are yet not of the same genus, because of having so different a manner of generation. And he seems to assert throughout the whole *De animalibus* that what is generated from putrefaction and from seed are not of the same species, just as Averroes also affirms. And Averroes says the same thing at the end of *De somno et vigilia:* "If there were any men who did not know in the same way as we do, they would not be of the same genus as we."[79]

The second statement, also, that if the soul were always joined to phantasms, it would be material, does not seem well said, because, just as to be joined for a certain time does not destroy immateriality, so neither does being always joined; as the Philosopher says in *Ethics* i against Plato, "The length of time does not destroy the species."[80] This is confirmed, because an Intelligence in moving its orb always depends upon a body, and yet though it so depends is immaterial. Whence the intellect also; assuming that it were always joined to a body, it still does not follow that it is material. But perchance it is said that this is true of an Intelligence, because its body is eternal, but that the human intellect has a perishable body; whence either, when the body is destroyed it would not itself exist, which is contrary to the assumption, or, if it did exist, it would be without operation, since it would be without phantasms, and according to the assumption could not know, and would thus be functionless.

But this statement does not seem to be rationally asserted. First, because it does not seem to follow logically. For although the intellect after its separation would not be moved by an imagination already destroyed, what would prevent it from being moved by existing imaginations, since they are all of the same species, and it does not seem to be prevented by distance in place, as it is not in place? And this especially, since many very weighty theologians assert that both angels and separated souls are moved by what is below them. Next, the consequence deduced does not seem in-

79. Cf. *Opera Aristotelis,* Vol. VII, fol. 171.
80. i 4, 1096 b 3 ff.

appropriate that in separation it would be functionless; because, when two opposites naturally inhere in anything, it is not necessary that both should inhere all the time. Indeed, that is impossible, just as sleep and waking naturally inhere in an animal, and waking, for example, is fitting by day but sleep at night. Whence a soul joined will know, but one separated will be functionless. But if it is said to be unfitting to operate for a very short time and to be without function for an infinite time, this answer destroys itself. For if, separated for an infinite time, it knows, and then without phantasms, but for a very short time with phantasms, surely it will be more natural for it to know without phantasms than with phantasms. Whence it is inappropriately stated in the definition of the soul that it is the act of a physical and organic body, etc.

Fifthly, because such an essence is truly sensitive and vegetative. Either, therefore, after separation it has powers by which it can perform its functions, or not. If the second, it seems contrary to nature that for all eternity it should be crippled and wholly deprived, unless resort be had to the resurrection of Democritus or to the Pythagorean fables. If, however, it has such powers, since it lacks organs by which to perform its proper functions, it follows again that those powers are in vain, which Aristotle would scarcely concede.

Sixthly, that such a soul is more truly called relatively immaterial and immortal, in the manner already set forth, appears from the Philosopher himself, in *De anima* iii, in the chapter on the active intellect.[81] For there, when he had said that both intellects are separated and immortal, he said afterward, but "this one," namely, the active intellect, "truly exists, which is immortal and always knowing, but that one," namely, the possible intellect, "does not, since at times it knows and at times it does not know." For it is destroyed when something in it is destroyed, which is because it is joined to matter; whence it is destroyed at the destruction of the sensitive soul. Therefore, it will be essentially cor-

81. Cf. iii 5, 430 a 22 ff.

ruptible but relatively incorruptible, because intellect which is not joined to matter is incorruptible. These points thus raise doubts for me as to the second proposition.

The third proposition is that such a soul is truly the form of man and not merely as it were the mover. I, too, agree to this proposition if it is asserted as material. But if it is asserted as immaterial, as he himself says, it does not seem to be known. For it is necessary for such an essence to be individual (*hoc aliquid*) and self-subsisting. Then how will it be possible for it to be the act and perfection of matter, since such a thing as the act of matter is not a substance (*quod est*) but an essence (*quo aliquid est*), as appears from *Metaphysica* vii?[82] But if it is said, this is peculiar to the intellective soul, this is very suspicious and arbitrarily said. Thus the Averroists could also say that the intellective soul is a form giving being and not merely operations. According to them, Averroes himself believed the opposite. There would be also a difficulty about the being of the composite, which is asserted to be distinct from the being of the soul. What is that being and how is it destroyed? Although they say much about it, I confess that I know their words but not their sense. Whence Plato[83] seems to me to have said wisely, when asserting that the soul is immortal, that "man is more truly a soul using a body" than "a composite of soul and body," and "more truly its mover," that is, the body's, "than its form, since the soul is that which truly is, and truly exists, and can assume a body and be deprived of it." For I do not see but that St. Thomas has to say this.

The fourth proposition was about the multiplication of souls. This also is no less doubtful with me, since in *Metaphysica* xii, text 49,[84] Aristotle says that such multiplication occurs through matter. But what is said by some, that souls are distinguished by their aptitude for different matters, or, what Aristotle says, by principles of individuation which can be called matter, to me all these seem intricacies and new inventions for upholding the posi-

82. Cf. vii 6.
83. I Alcibiades 129 e.

84. Cf. xii 8, 1074 a 33–34.

tion, and by no means the views of Aristotle. For in this way we could multiply Intelligences in the same species, nay, God himself. How far this agrees with the Peripatetics, I leave to the consideration of others. And although some concede it in regard to the Intelligences and deny it of God, adducing new arguments why God cannot be multiplied, it is certain that Aristotle neither devised nor saw those arguments, and God knows how much they are worth in Aristotle's philosophy; but it is supported only by the above argument. Further, because, according to the principles of Aristotle, the world is eternal, and man is eternal, since "the sun and man generate man," *Physica* ii,[85] and viii,[86] "man has always been begotten by man." Whence, either there will be an actual infinite, which he everywhere plainly denies, or recourse must be had to the Pythagorean fables, refuted as errors, or to the resurrection of Democritus, which is accounted no less foolish.

The fifth proposition also seems no less deficient. For what it asserts, that the intellective soul is produced anew, that indeed we concede. But that it is produced not through generation but through creation, this does not seem to agree with the words of Aristotle, since he has never made mention of such a creation. Indeed, if he had asserted it, he would have clearly sinned through the fallacy of the consequent in *Physica* viii[87] when he endeavored to prove that the world has never begun, since he demonstrates it for true generation alone. But if besides generation he had maintained creation also, it was for him to prove that it was not through creation, and this he did not do at all. Whence he would obviously have sinned.

What is also added further, that it is created immediately by God, seems also not to agree with Aristotle, since he asserts that God does not act upon these things here below except through intermediary causes and that this is the essential order.

Moreover, what is added further, that the soul does not cease

85. ii 2, 194 b 13.   87. Chaps. 1 ff.
86. ii 1, 193 b 8; cf. viii 5, 257 b 10.

[311]

to be from that time on, this seems to contradict Aristotle's intention completely. First, for everything incorruptible is ungenerated, *De caelo* i, text 125,[88] where he proves their convertibility. But by what is conceded the intellective soul is incorruptible, hence ungenerated, hence it never began, which is the opposite of what is conceded. But to this it is replied by denying the last consequence, "hence it never began"; it follows only that it never began through true generation. But this obviously contradicts the text, as I have already noted when I was expounding that passage. For Aristotle says, "I call ungenerated what is, and of what it was never true to say that it was not." If then the intellective soul is ungenerated as the Philosopher says there, it never was true to say that it was not. For, as he expressly shows, he means that that is generated not only which has true causes of its generation but whatever begins to be, in whatever way it begins, which he means to be convertible with the corruptible taken proportionally; and thus he takes the ungenerated and the incorruptible. Moreover, it is remarkable that Aristotle should adduce so many and such strong arguments for proving their convertibility and should never have excepted the intellective soul. Certainly he would have given great cause for erring.

Moreover, what he says further, that souls remain after death, although Aristotle makes no mention of them, seems exceedingly improbable, since Aristotle, so diligent an examiner of nature in the *Poetics*, the *Rhetoric*, and other works, would have been so diligent yet negligent in so important a thing.

Further, because in *Ethics* i[89] he seems to assert no happiness after death; nay, what is more, St. Thomas, in *Ethics* iii, lecture 1,[90] on the text "That anyone ought to choose death rather than commit a great crime," as if doubtful as to how Aristotle affirms this, says that Aristotle said this because after death glory remains, or because he judged it better to persist in that virtuous activity for a short time than to live long in vicious activity. Now

88. i 12, 282 b 5 ff.

89. Cf. chap. 11.

90. Lectio 2 (ed. Fretté, XXV, 325).

if St. Thomas believes that Aristotle upheld immortality, none of these causes would be fitting. For it would at once be clear: because of a future state. Whence the Blessed Thomas rather wondered why, since Aristotle holds that after death there is nothing, he wants anyone to prefer to die rather than to live in evil ways. For he himself also in the *Exposition of the Apostles' Creed*[91] says of the resurrection of the flesh: "that unlesss we expect to rise again, a man ought to commit any crime rather than to die." Further, as has been said, it would be strange that Aristotle should have made no mention of such a state after death, nor have promised to explain it, which is contrary to his custom. Moreover, he ought either to have asserted resurrection, or to have contrived Pythagorean fables, or to have left such very noble beings without any function; all of which seem very far from the Philosopher. However, these things have been said not to contradict so great a philosopher (for what is a flea against an elephant?) but from desire of learning. Whence, etc.

CHAPTER IX

IN WHICH IS SET FORTH A FIFTH WAY, NAMELY, THAT THE SAME ESSENCE OF THE SOUL IS MORTAL AND IMMORTAL BUT UNQUALIFIEDLY MORTAL AND RELATIVELY IMMORTAL

Since therefore the first way, asserting that the intellective soul is distinct in existence from the sensitive in mortals, has been refuted in all its modes; and the second, asserting that intellective and sensitive are the same in existence, and that this soul is unqualifiedly immortal and relatively mortal, is exceedingly doubtful and does not seem to agree with Aristotle, it remains to assert the last way, which, holding that the sensitive in man is identified with the intellective, maintains that this soul is essentially and truly mortal but relatively immortal.

91. *Opusculum* vii, *In symbolum apostolorum expositio*, chap. 14 (ed. Fretté, XXVII, 226).

And that we may proceed in due order, we shall speak according to those five propositions in the previous chapter. And the first we concede unqualifiedly, that the intellective and the sensitive in man are identified in existence. But we are at variance on the second, because we assert that such a soul is truly and unqualifiedly mortal, but relatively and improperly speaking immortal. For evidence of this it must be known and thoroughly committed to memory in this matter, that all cognition in some fashion abstracts from matter. For, as the Commentator says, *De anima* iii, comment 5,[92] matter hinders cognition; and this is to be seen in the senses, which do not know according to real qualities but according to their intentions; whence in *De anima* ii[93] it is said that the property of each sense is to be receptive of species without matter. Therefore, three modes of cognition are found in the universe, corresponding to three modes of separation from matter. For there are some things which are totally separated from matter and hence in their knowing neither need a body as subject nor as object. For their knowing is not received in any body, since they are not in a body, nor are they moved by any body, since they are unmoved movers. And these are the separated substances which we call Intellects or Intelligences, in which is discovered neither discursive thought, nor composition, nor any motion. But there are some things which, although they know not through sensible qualities but through their species, which assume some manner of immateriality, for they are both said to be without matter and are spiritual; yet because they are the lowest in the genus of knowing things and are exceedingly material, they hence need the body for their operations both as subject and as object. For such cognitions are both received in an organ, whence also they represent only singulars, and are moved by some corporeal thing. And these are all the sensitive powers, although some of them are more spiritual and some less, as the Commentator says (*De anima* iii, comment 6,[94] and *De sensu et sensato*[95]).

92. *Op. cit.*, fol. 96ᵛ.   94. *Op. cit.*, fol. 106ᵛ–7.
93. ii 12, 424 a 17 ff.   95. Cf. *Opera Aristotelis*, Vol. VII, fols. 150ᵛ ff.

Now since nature proceeds in orderly fashion, as is said in *Physica* viii[96] between these two extremes, of not needing a body as subject or as object, and of needing a body as subject and object, there is a mean, which is neither totally abstracted nor totally immersed. Whence, since it is impossible for anything to need a body as subject and not as object, as is obvious, it remains that such an intermediary does not need the body as subject but as object. Now this is the human intellect, which by all the ancients and moderns or almost all is held to be halfway between things abstract and things not abstract, that is, between the Intelligences and the sensitive level, below the Intelligences and above the sensitive. Whence it is said also in the Psalm, "Thou hast made him a little less than the angels."[97] And a little further on, "Thou hast established him above the works of thy hands, the sheep and the oxen," etc. And this way of knowing is that of which Aristotle spoke, in *De anima* i, text 12: "If knowing is either imagination or not without imagination, it is impossible for it to exist without a body."[98] And when in *De anima* iii he declared that knowing is not imagination, since it is not through an organ, and it cannnot be without imagination;[99] and in the same book, texts 29 and 39: "The soul does not know at all without some phantasm."[100] Hence the human soul does not need an organ as subject but as object.

Now, according to Aristotle and Plato, it is fitting that there be souls corresponding to all these levels of cognition. Hence, at least according to Aristotle, any knowing thing is the act of a physical and organic body, though each kind in a different way. For Intelligences are not the acts of bodies as Intelligences, since in their knowing and desiring they in no wise need a body. But in so far as they actuate and move the heavenly bodies, they are souls and are the acts of a physical and organic body. For a star is an organ of the heavens, in *De caelo* ii;[101] and in *Metaphysica*

---

96. viii 1, 252 a 11–12.

97. Ps. 8 : 6 ff.

98. i 1, 403 a 8–9.

99. Cf. iii 3, 427 b 14 ff., and 4, 429 a 26–27.

100. iii 7, 431 a 16–17.

101. Cf. ii 12, 292 b 25 ff.

xii, text 48,[102] the whole sphere exists for the sake of the star. Hence the Intelligences actuate a physical and organic body; and, as such, they need the body as object. But, in thus actuating and moving, they receive nothing from the body but only give to it. The sensitive soul, moreover, is unqualifiedly the act of a physical and organic body, because it both needs the body as subject, since it performs its office only in an organ, and needs the body as object. But the mean, which is the human intellect, is in none of its operations wholly freed from the body or wholly immersed in it, whence it will not need the body as subject but will as object. And thus in a fashion halfway between abstract things and things not abstract it will be the act of an organic body. For Intelligences as Intelligences are not souls, because as such they are no wise dependent on a body but in so far as they move the heavenly bodies. But the human intellect in all its operations is the act of an organic body, since it always depends on the body as object.

There is also a difference in the way an Intelligence and a human intellect depend on an organ, because the human soul receives and is completed by a bodily object when it is moved by it, but an Intelligence receives nothing from a heavenly body but only gives. Moreover, the human intellect differs from the sensitive power in its way of depending on the body, because the sensitive depends subjectively and objectively, but the human intellect objectively only. And thus in a fashion halfway between the material and the immaterial the human intellect is the act of an organic body.

Wherefore heavenly things, men and beasts are not animated in the same way, since their souls are not in the same way the acts of a physical and organic body, as has been seen. Hence Alexander in his *Paraphrase of the De anima* said that an Intelligence is rather equivocally called the soul of a heaven, and the heaven an animated being.[103] With this, Averroes seems also to

102. Cf. xii 8, 1074 a 1 ff.

103. This passage is probably quoted from Averroes. It cannot be verified in Alexander's *De anima* (*Scripta Minora*, ed. I. Bruns, Part I [Berlin, 1887], in *Supplementum Aristotelicum*, Vol. II).

agree in *De substantia orbis*.[104] But beasts are properly called animals, as is the common usage. But men are called animals in an intermediate manner.

Nor is it to be pretended that, with Aristotle, this way of knowing of the human intellect is accidental to it, that is, being moved by an object and not needing a subject; not only because a single thing has but a single essential way of operating but also because just as the way of the sensitive is never transformed into the way of the Intelligence or of the human intellect, nor the way of the Intelligence into the way of the human intellect or of the sensitive; so equally the human way of understanding does not seem capable of transformation into the way of the Intelligence. This would be the case if it knew without needing the body as subject and object. This is also confirmed, because then a nature would be transformed into another nature, since its essential operations would also be transformed.

Further, by no natural mark can the human intellect be known to have any other way of knowing, as we understand from experience, because we always need some phantasm. Whence it is concluded that this way of knowing by phantasms is essential to man.

From these considerations we must now syllogize the principal conclusion we are seeking—that the human soul is unqualifiedly material and relatively immaterial. And, first, the prosyllogism is divided as follows: The human intellect is immaterial and material, as is shown by the above reasons. But it does not partake of these equally; nor is it more immaterial than material, as has been proved in the preceding chapter. Hence it is more material than immaterial and will thus be unqualifiedly material and relatively immaterial.

Secondly, it is essential to the intellect to know by means of phantasms, as has been demonstrated, and is clear from the definition of the soul, as the act of a physical and organic body; whence in all its operations it needs an organ. But what knows

104. Cf. chap. 2 (in *Joannis de Janduno in libros Aristotelis de coelo et mundo .... quaestiones* [Venice, 1564], fol. 50).

in this way is necessarily inseparable; hence the human intellect is mortal. The minor is evident not only from Aristotle's words: "If knowing is imagination or not without imagination, it is impossible for it to be separated"; but also, if it were separable, it would either not have any operation, and would thus be functionless, or it would have one and would operate without phantasms, which is contrary to the demonstrated major.

And again this is confirmed as follows: Since Aristotle did not posit any Intelligence without a body, as in *Metaphysica* xii,[105] he maintains that the number of Intelligences corresponds to the number of spheres; much less, therefore, can he posit the human intellect without a body, since it is far less abstracted than an Intelligence. Indeed, if the world is eternal, as Aristotle believed, infinitely infinite forms exist actually without a body. This seems ridiculous according to Aristotle. Whence the human soul, according to Aristotle, must be declared to be absolutely mortal. But since it is halfway between what is unqualifiedly abstracted and what is immersed in matter, it partakes in some fashion of immortality, which its essential operation also shows. For it does not depend on the body as subject, in which it agrees with the Intelligences and differs from the beasts; and it needs the body as object, in which it agrees with the beasts. Whence it is mortal.

For a complete understanding of what has been said it is necessary to know what it is to need an organ as subject and as object and what it is not to need them. To need an organ as subject, then, is to be received in the body in a manner both quantitative and corporeal so as to be received with extension. In this way we say all organic powers receive and perform their functions, as the eye in seeing and the ear in hearing, for vision is in the eye and in an extensive manner. Whence not to be in an organ, or not to need it subjectively, is either not to be in the body or not to be in it in a quantitative manner. Whence we say that the intellect does not need the body as subject in its know-

105. Cf. xii 8, 1073 a 30 ff.

ing, not because knowing is in no wise in the body, since if the intellect is in the body it cannot be that its immanent operation is not in it in some fashion. For where the subject is, there must be the accident of the subject. But knowing is said not to be in an organ and in the body only in so far as it is not in it in a quantitative and corporeal manner. Wherefore the intellect can reflect upon itself, think discursively, and comprehend universals, which organic and extended powers cannot do at all. But all this comes from the essence of the intellect, since as intellect it is not dependent on matter or on quantity. But if the human intellect depends on matter, this is as it is joined to sense; whence as intellect it is accidentally dependent on matter and on quantity. Wherefore its operation also is no more abstracted than its essence. For, unless the intellect possessed something that could exist by itself without matter, its knowing could not be exercised except in a quantitative and corporeal way.

But although the human intellect, as has been considered, does not use quantity in knowing, nevertheless, since it is joined to sense, it cannot be released entirely from matter and quantity, since it never knows without a phantasm, as Aristotle says in *De anima* iii: "The soul does not know at all without a phantasm."[106] Hence it thus needs the body as object. Nor can it know a universal unqualifiedly but always sees the universal in the singular, as everyone can observe in himself. For in all cognition, however far abstracted, we form some bodily image. On this account the human intellect does not know itself first and directly; and it composes and thinks discursively, whence its knowing is in succession and time. The complete opposite of this occurs in the Intelligences, which are utterly freed from matter. The intellect, then, existing thus halfway between the material and the immaterial, is neither completely here and now nor completely released from here and now. Wherefore its operation is neither completely universal nor completely par-

106. iii 7, 431 a 16–17.

ticular; it is neither completely subjected to time nor completely removed from time.

Yet nature proceeds duly and in orderly fashion, so that it arrives at its ends from first things by way of those in between. For Intelligences, since they are unqualifiedly abstracted, in knowing no wise need the body as subject or as object; wherefore they know nature absolutely, first knowing themselves by a simple intuition; wherefore they are released from time and from succession. But the sensitive powers, since they are immersed in matter, know only singulars, not reflecting on themselves or thinking discursively. But the human intellect, just as it is a mean in its existence, so also is it in its operations, as has already been said. Whence the things received in it are known neither wholly in potentiality nor wholly in actuality. Hence it is clear what it is to need the body as subject and as object and not to need them, what things need them and what do not, and in what manner.

Further, it must be known that those who assert that the human soul is immortal and multiplied say that from the fact that it is of an immaterial nature it is a self-subsistent individual (*hoc aliquid per se subsistens*). Whence it can also exist and function without a body, and, when it so exists separated, it possesses none of the powers of the soul save intellect and will, just like the Intelligences. Hence it possesses none of the sensitive or vegetative powers, except as in their very remote beginning. But since it is the lowest of abstracted substances, besides that way of being it possesses another: for it can also be that by virtue of which something exists (*quo aliquid*). Whence it can truly inform a body and because of its imperfection be numbered according to the number of bodies; and it assumes all the sensitive and vegetative powers, whence it exercises them through organs and in so doing becomes perishable. Yet although thus united to the body it may possess intellect and will, still it has not the power to exercise them freely, since without a bodily instrument, at least as object, it cannot perform their functions. The opposite of this occurs in separation, since it can go forth in act entirely apart from any bodily organ.

But there is another opinion that judges these things to be absurdities and contrary to the principles of philosophy: that the same thing should be a self-subsistent individual and also that by which an individual is distinguished, as having disparate ways of operating; that separated way of being proved by neither argument nor experience but held quite arbitrarily; the now having sensitive and vegetative powers and now relinquishing them, knowing in one way when joined, in another when separated; joined for an exceedingly short time, separated for infinity, unless we imagine the transmigration of souls into bodies; that it has begun and will never cease to be, now assuming a body and now getting rid of it, as the vulgar say of vampires; and, when it is separated from the body, it ceases to be actually the act of a body, whence it is either nowhere, or if somewhere, how did it get there? For either by alteration, or by motion in place. Not by alteration, as is obvious; neither by motion in place, since, in *Physica* vi,[107] what is indivisible cannot move in place. But if it is asserted to be nowhere, what then, according to Aristotle, prevents the positing of some Intelligences also which do not move spheres? And that infinitely infinite multitude will be posited nor can it be known whether it be without function or operate, unless something fictitious or arbitrary be posited. And whereas an actual infinity of material things cannot be, in which multiplication is clear and even necessary, in immaterial things, in which multiplication is not necessary, nor is distinction in the same species possible, an actually infinite multitude is here posited.

Wherefore, since all these things seem to be irrational and foreign to Aristotle, it seems more rational that the human soul, since it is the highest and most perfect of material forms, is truly that by virtue of which something is an individual, and in no wise is truly itself an individual. Whence it is truly a form be-

107. Cf. vi 10, 241 a 26.

ginning with and ceasing to be with the body, nor can it in any way operate or exist without the body; and it possesses only a single way of being or operating. Whence also it can be multiplied, since that is truly the principle of multiplying in the same species. Nor are souls actually infinite, but only potentially, like other material things. And the soul possesses powers that are organic and unqualifiedly material, those of the sensitive and the vegetative soul. But since it is the noblest of material things and lies at the boundary of immaterial things, it savors somewhat of immateriality, but not unqualifiedly. Whence it possesses intellect and will, in which it agrees with the gods; but rather imperfectly and equivocally, since the gods themselves are completely abstracted from matter, while it knows always with matter, since it knows with phantasms, with succession, with time, with discursiveness, with obscurity. Whence in us intellect and will are not truly immaterial things but relatively and to a slight extent. Whence it ought to be called more truly reason than intellect. For, so to speak, it is not intellect but the trace and shadow of intellect. What is said in *Metaphysica* ii[108] bears witness to this: "As the eye of the owl is to the light of the sun, so is our intellect to what is most clear in nature," though Averroes interpreted the passage wrongly. And as the moon is of the nature of earth, as Aristotle says in *De animalibus*,[109] so is the human soul of the nature of Intelligence. But in the moon earth is present only according to its properties, not according to its essence; whence knowing is also in the human soul according to the participation of property and not of essence.

Now all this agrees with nature, which proceeds by degrees. For vegetable things possess something of a soul, since they operate in themselves, though very materially, since they do not perform their functions except through first qualities, and their operations are limited to material being. Then come animals

108. ii 1, 993 b 9 ff.

109. Cf. Averroes, Commentary on the *De coelo* (*Opera Aristotelis*, Vol. V, fol. 137). Cf. also *De generatione animalium* iii 11, 76; b 22.

having only touch and taste and an indeterminate imagination. After them are animals which arrive at such perfection that they are thought to have intellect. For many operate like craftsmen, as by building houses; many like citizens, as bees; many have almost all the moral virtues, as is shown in the *De historiis animalium*, in which marvelous things are set down which would be too long to recount. Indeed, almost an infinite number of men seem to have less intellect than many beasts. There is also posited the cogitative power among the sensitive powers. What ought we to say about its excellence when, according to the Commentator, *De anima* ii, comment 60,[110] it knows individuals under ten categories, and particular reason is posited by all? Nay, Homer, Galen, and many excellent men thought it to be intellect itself. But if we ascend a little, we shall place the human intellect immediately above the cogitative and below immaterial things, partaking of both, so that it clearly does not need the body as subject in the way already set forth and needs it as object, which manner is essential to it and inseparable. Whence it must be placed absolutely among material forms. Witness the fact that it belongs only to mortals, unless we imagine, like the ancients, that men become gods and are carried up to heaven; all of which Aristotle thought fables, in *Metaphysica* iii and xii,[111] and devised by the laws for the advantage of men.

Nothing unfitting seems therefore to follow from this position; it all agrees with reason and experience, it maintains nothing mythical, nothing depending on Faith. But if anything seems to contradict this way, as that when the soul is in warm and cold matter, how is it that it does not itself assume those qualities, and in its operation not employ any organ and not receive universals? —these and similar rather slight things surely create no less difficulty against the earlier position, since that also admits that form is in matter. But if anyone says that neither opinion is true, but rather that of Averroes, certainly for me whoever imagines

110. *Op. cit.,* Vol. VII, fol. 58.
111. Cf. iii 4, 1000 a 18–19, and xii 8, 1074 b 3 ff.

that opinion has a very powerful imagination, and I believe painters have never contrived a finer monster than this monster; besides, it is contrary to Aristotle, as has been demonstrated above.

Wherefore this position just set forth seems to me the most probable of all and closest to Aristotle's view. From all of which it is obvious that many things said by Aristotle about the intellect seem mutually contradictory, when they really are not at all. For he says at times that it is material and mixed, or not separable, but at times that it is immaterial and separable. For in the definition of the soul it is said that it is the act of an organic body; but at times it is said that it is not the act of any body. These seem indeed contradictory. Whence different men have turned into different paths, and some think that Aristotle did not understand himself. But from what has been said everything is plain, nor is there any contradiction. For the intellect, absolutely and as intellect, is entirely unmixed and separate. But the human intellect retains both, for it is separated from the body as subject but is not separated as object. Moreover, intellect as intellect is in no wise the act of an organic body, since the Intelligences do not need any organ in knowing, though they do in moving. But the human intellect as human is the act of an organic body as object, and thus it is not separated. But not as subject, and thus it is separated. Whence there is no contradiction.

Moreover, in the third proposition, that the soul is truly the form of man, it seems that it is far better preserved by this way than by the former. For, as we said, it is extremely difficult to imagine that a single thing existing by itself is truly a form. Whence Gregory of Nyssa, as St. Thomas reports,[112] when he saw Aristotle say that the soul is the act of the body, said that Aristotle believed that the human soul is corruptible, since a form existing by itself cannot truly be the act of an organic body. Indeed, some say that Gregory of Nazianzus also thought this about Aristotle.

112. *Summa contra Gentiles*, Book ii, chap. 79.

The fourth proposition, however, that human souls are numbered, we affirm; but the questions that tortured the former way do not torture us, for, since souls are material, they are distinguished through matter. Nor does the infinity of souls disturb us.

Of the fifth proposition, we also say that the human soul is produced, though not by creation but by generation, since the sun and man generate man, in *Physica* ii,[113] and the soul is the highest being in natural philosophy. And what is said in *De partibus* i, chapter 1,[114] about the intellect not belonging to natural philosophy, is true of true intellect. For that is an unmoved mover, while the human intellect is a moved mover; whence the human intellect is a matter for the consideration of the natural philosopher, but intellect as such not at all, since, in *Physica* ii,[115] unmoved movers do not belong to the field of natural philosophy. The Philosopher also touches on this argument in the passage in *De partibus* i. And when further it was said that it comes from without, this must be understood as mind unqualifiedly, not as the human mind; or, if as the human mind, it must be understood not absolutely, but because in comparison with the sensitive and the vegetative it partakes more of divinity. For, in *De partibus* iv, chapter 9,[116] only man is of an erect nature, because only man partakes of much divinity.

We do not, however, assert that man remains after death so far as his soul is concerned, since its existence has a beginning. And in *De coelo* i,[117] whatever begins ceases to be; and Plato says, in *Laws* viii, "Whatever in any way at all begins to be, ceases also to be."[118] And as for what is said in *Metaphysica* xii, text 17,[119] I do not approve the answer of Alexander which the Commentator[120] there repeats from the account of Themistius, that the passage is to be understood as about the active intellect. For

113. ii 2, 194 b 13.
114. 641 a 33 ff.
115. Cf. chap. 2.
116. iv 10, 686 a 27–28.
117. i 10, 279 b 20–21.
118. Cf. x 893 e–894 a.
119. Cf. xii 3, 1070 a 24 ff.
120. *Opera Aristotelis*, Vol. VIII, fol. 324v–25.

the active intellect is not the form of man; but it is understood about the possible intellect, which at times knows and at times does not, for it is destroyed when something within it is destroyed, that is, the sensitive, with which it is identified. But Aristotle understands the passage as referring to intellect in itself and not accidentally, as if he were to say that nothing prevents it from remaining as intellect but not as human intellect; since it has already been demonstrated in *De coelo* i[121] that anything that comes into being passes out of being.

That this was the opinion of Aristotle about the human soul can also be shown from the passage in *Metaphysica* xii, text 39, where he says: "Pleasure, moreover, such as the best we enjoy for a very short time; for it is everlasting for them, though impossible for us."[122] From these words it is clear, first, that the gods are unqualifiedly immortal. For if they are always enjoying pleasure, it is since they always know, for it follows in the same text: "Waking, sensing and understanding are exceedingly pleasant." If therefore they eternally enjoy pleasure, they eternally exist; hence they are immortal beings. But men are mortal, since they take pleasure for a very short time, for operation follows being. But if man is at times called immortal, this is understood relatively, since it is said, in *De partibus* ii, chapter 10: "Man alone among mortals partakes in the highest degree of divinity."[123] Compared to other mortals, he can be called immortal, for, as has been said, man is halfway between the gods and the beasts. Whence, just as grey compared to black is called white, so man compared to the beasts can be called God and immortal, but not truly and unqualifiedly. "But if our ancestors report that men have at times been changed into gods," says Aristotle in text 50 of *Metaphysica* xii," they told these as fables to persuade the many and for the advantage of the many, and as an aid to the laws; but God alone is properly called immortal."[124] And in the end of text 39 he says: "We say, moreover, that God

121. i 10, 279 b 20–21.   123. ii 10, 656 a 7–8.
122. xii 7, 1072 b 14 ff.   124. Cf. xii 8, 1074 b 3 ff.

is a living being, eternal and good; wherefore life and continuous and eternal duration exist in God. For this is God."[125]

A second point also appears from these words, that the human intellect does not know without phantasms. For if eternal beings always take pleasure because they always know, in their knowing they need no phantasm. For if they did, they would not be eternal, since in *De anima* ii[126] imagination is a motion produced by actualized sense. Indeed, they are not moved by anything when they know, as the Philosopher says in text 50: "What is most divine and most honorable does not change."[127] For quite unworthy would be such change and motion for them; nay, in those who know, what is known and the knowing are the same, as is said in the same texts cited. But the human intellect, since it takes pleasure for a very short time, as it knows for a very short time, cannot be released from phantasms, since it does not know unless it is moved; for knowing consists in a kind of being acted upon. The mover of the intellect, however, is a phantasm, as appears from *De anima* iii.[128] Wherefore it does not know without phantasms; although it does not know like the imagination, since, existing as a mean between the eternal beings and the beasts, it knows the universal, according to which it agrees with eternal beings and differs from beasts. Yet it sees the universal in the singular, by which it differs from eternal beings and in some fashion agrees with beasts. But beasts themselves, established in the lowest rank of knowing things, understand neither the universal unqualifiedly nor the universal in the singular, but only the singular as singular.

There are therefore in the universe three kinds of animated beings, and, since every animated being knows, there are also three ways of knowing. For there are animated beings entirely eternal, there are also those entirely mortal, and there are the mean between these two. The first are the heavenly bodies, and, in knowing, these in no way depend upon a body. The second

125. xii 7, 1072 b 28 ff.   127. *Metaphysica* xii 9, 1074 b 26.
126. iii 3, 429 a 1–2.   128. Cf. iii 7, 431 a 16–17.

are the beasts, which depend on the body as subject and as object, whence they know only singulars. The intermediate beings are men, not dependent on the body as subject but only as object; whence they regard neither the universal unqualifiedly, like the eternal beings, nor the singular alone, like the beasts, but the universal in the singular.

These three ways of knowing, Aristotle implies in *De anima* i when he says: "If knowing is imagination, or is not without imagination."[129] For by imagination he understands sense, which needs the body in both ways, as subject and as object. By not being imagination and not being without it, he understands the human intellect; whence it needs the body as object and not as subject. But that which is not imagination and is completely without imagination is truly intellect and belongs to divine beings. No further ways of knowing are found by Aristotle in any place, nor would it conform to reason. For to say, as they do who assert that the human intellect is absolutely immortal, that the intellect possesses two ways of knowing, one without phantasms at all and the other with phantasms, is to change human nature into divine. And this is not very different from the fables of Ovid in his *Metamorphoses*. For the Philosopher grants that the ancients had maintained this as a myth for the advantage of the laws, as has been said.

But perhaps someone shall resort to false arguments, that the proposition that we enjoy pleasure for a very short time is to be understood of man and not of his soul; that man does not know without phantasms, for man is mortal, but his soul is immortal, whence it knows as in separation without phantasms. I beg one who falsely reasons in this manner, nay, who thus quibbles, to take care lest, while he strives to interpret Aristotle, he corrupt Aristotle. First, because Aristotle here makes no distinction between man and his soul, as he makes none between God and a heavenly body; for he says that God is an eternal animated being. Secondly, because if he understands it as applying only to man

129. i 1, 403 a 8–9.

and not to his soul, where then does he speak about the knowledge of the separated soul? For there was the place, since it is in the *Metaphysica*, which is about separated substances. Thirdly, because thus the human soul would become unqualifiedly divine, since it would take on the way of operating of the divine. And thus we should be asserting the fables of Ovid that a nature is changed into another nature. Fourthly, because if in so important a matter Aristotle should make no mention of it, he would be very much at fault. Whence those excusing Aristotle in this way are gravely accusing him.

But perhaps someone may say that Aristotle in *De anima* iii, text of comment 36,[130] promises to treat of the being of the separated soul, when he says that he will later examine thoroughly whether the human intellect can know separated substances. Whence either the *Metaphysica* was not finished by Aristotle, who was perhaps prevented by his death; or because the completion has not yet come down to us, whence it is not strange if we have nothing of Aristotle's about its separated being. This is confirmed by the Commentator, *De anima* iii, comment 36,[131] since he himself says that that question was not finished by Aristotle, so far as we yet have his books, whence it is very difficult. To this I answer that Aristotle's words argue the opposite more than the proposition. For he says thus: "But whether or not it may be possible to know some one of the separated things for something itself existing not separated from magnitude, is to be considered later."[132] From this it appears, first, that the human intellect is not separable from magnitude, whence it does not know without imagination, and, if so, is inseparable; because if it is imagination or not without imagination, it is inseparable. But as to the statement "to be examined later," St. Thomas in his exposition of *Metaphysica* ix, last text,[133] says

130. iii 7, 431 b 17 ff.
131. Cf. *Opera Aristotelis*, Vol. VII, fol. 121.
132. *De anima*, iii 7, 431 b 17 ff.
133. Lectio 5 (ed. Fretté, XXV, 92).

that in that text Aristotle is determining the question he left unresolved in *De anima* iii; although St. Thomas himself in *De anima* iii[134] said otherwise, but in the *Metaphysica* changed his
opinion for the better. But the kind of knowledge which in that
passage of the *Metaphysica* ix[135] we are asserted to have of Intelligences is not without phantasms, since in the beginning of
Metaphysica ii[136] also Aristotle says that our intellect is related
to separated beings as the owl to the light of the sun; whence St.
Thomas also said in *Contra Gentiles* iii, chapter 48,[137] that the
opinion of Aristotle about our knowledge of separated beings is
that we only understand them according to the course of speculative science. Hence not without phantasms, as we know. And
note carefully that he seems there to suggest this opinion of ours,
that Aristotle thought the human soul is not truly intellect but
possesses only a kind of participation in intellect, whence it is,
improperly speaking, immortal. Yet I think that the phrase "to
be examined later" can also be understood of the *Ethics*. For in
it he declares[138] that the ultimate happiness of man lies in the
contemplation of abstracted beings by metaphysics, whence the
same as before, etc.

CHAPTER X

IN WHICH THE OBJECTIONS OF OTHER OPINIONS ARE ANSWERED

So that our position may be still stronger, it is worth while to
answer the arguments offered in opposition by the other opinions. And since we hold that in man the vegetative, sensitive,
and intellective are the same in existence, it is answered that
contradictories cannot be asserted absolutely of the same thing;
yet it is not inconsistent for one to be asserted absolutely, and
the other relatively, as Aristotle says in the *De sophisticis elen-*

---

134. Lectio 12 (ed. Fretté, XXIV, 176).

135. Cf. ix 10, 1051 b 15 ff.

136. ii 1, 993 b 9 ff.

137. Cf. chaps. 41 ff.

138. Cf. x 7.

chis;[139] and thus it is in the proposition. For the human intellect is absolutely mortal and relatively immortal.

Now it is said to the first point against the second proposition that the human soul, thus able to receive all species of material forms, has two conditions. The first is that in itself it is immaterial and does not need an organ as subject, as far as it receives and knows those forms, which we admit. But it has another in that it does not receive those forms without being moved by phantasms, as Aristotle plainly teaches there; whence it needs an organ as object. But from what has been demonstrated, what is so ordered is unqualifiedly material, and relatively immaterial. And this is the conclusion we maintain. But if it is asked, whether it is itself a material form, we say that it is in part and in part not. As for the point that it partakes of immateriality, although it does not know itself through its proper species, but through species of others, as is said in *De anima* iii,[140] yet according to that being it can in some fashion reflect upon itself and know its acts, though not first and perfectly like the Intelligences. Nor is it strange, since the soul in knowing does not use a bodily organ or material appendages.

If it be pressed further, the soul itself has no being save in matter, and through first qualities together with quantity; but, since operations follow being, it cannot operate without them, and hence it cannot operate without appendages of matter, which is the opposite of what you say. Moreover, according to the Philosopher, in *De anima* ii and iii,[141] in order for the pupil to receive all colors, not only must its essence not be color, but it must also not be joined to color. Hence, if the intellective soul is to receive all material forms, not only must it be immaterial, but also not joined to any material form, and consequently neither with the warm nor the cold. But this is false. For one making this objection does not see that all these things are contrary to the other opin-

139. Chap. 5, 167 a 7 ff.
140. Cf. iii 4, 429 a 28–29, and 7, 431 a 16–17.
141. Cf. ii 7, 418 b 26–27, and iii 4, 429 a 13 ff.

ions also. For, according to them, too, the soul is not in matter except by quality and quantity, whence for them also it will not be able to operate without the latter. But if any defense is made of these opinions, it will also hold for mine.

However, it is replied to the first proposition that the human intellect cannot indeed know unless in matter there exist sensible qualities and quantities, since it cannot operate unless it exists, and it cannot exist without the required conditions. But it does not follow that it knows by means of these conditions. Indeed, as is clear enough, it does not follow in sense. For the visual power does not see unless the eye is warm, yet it does not see by means of warmth or any other material quality but by the visible species.

It is replied to the second that a material thing is not universally prevented from knowing by its coexistence with another material thing (for thus sight would not know colors, since to sight are joined first qualities) but is indeed prevented by its coexistence with any one of those of which it is itself perceptive. For it is prevented by redness from knowing other colors, of which together with redness it is perceptive. Wherefore, if the intellect were a pure material form, since it is perceptive of all material forms, it would be prevented from knowing them. But that it is immaterial is proved, though it is not unqualifiedly immaterial; hence it is not prevented by its coexistence with material forms. For the material and the immaterial are of different nature. For the active intellect does not prevent the possible from receiving species, however much it completes the possible, as the Commentator says, in *De anima* iii, comments 4 and 5.[142]

Moreover, to the second point advanced in opposition, it is said that the things which are in the Intelligences are known unqualifiedly in act and completely stripped of matter. But the things which are in sense are known merely potentially, while those which are in the human intellect are known in an intermediate manner, since the species represents the universal primarily, but

142. Cf. *Opera Aristotelis*, Vol. VII, fols. 95 v ff.

secondarily as in the substratum. For it cannot be wholly released from matter, since the intellect, for any of its cognitions at all, is always moved by an object and sees the universal in the singular, as has been said. But from what has been demonstrated, this argues a power relatively but not unqualifiedly immaterial. But if it is said, since the intellect itself is in this quantity, how, then, will the species received in it be able to represent universals? The answer is: Nothing hinders it. First, because it is an accident that as intellect it is in quantity. Secondly, because, although it is in quantity, yet quantity is not the principle of that operation, nor in that operation does it use quantity essentially. Thirdly, because, as is plain from what has been said, it is not completely released from quantity and its conditions, since it always sees the universal in the particular. For the human intellect is both intellect and human. For as intellect it knows the universal, but as human it cannot perceive the universal except in the singular. And to that about the organ it is said, in accordance with the above, that it needs one as object, not as subject. And what each of these is has been said in the previous chapter.

If it is pressed further, is it not joined to matter by first qualities, and will it not then certainly take on some quality? Whence being either the warm or the cold, it will thus not know all qualities. It is answered that the intellect is not joined to matter as intellect, but in so far as it is joined to sense; whence, although in the operation of sensing it takes on a quality, yet it does not in the operation of knowing; on account of which it is not as intellect of some quality or organic. But if it be asked further, since human knowing is an accident which cannot exist without some subject, in what subject then will knowing be located? The answer is: Truly and essentially knowing is in the intellect itself, in accordance with the passage in *De anima* iii: "The soul is the place of species, not the whole soul, but the intellect."[143] But since the human intellect is in matter as though by a kind of concomitance, knowing itself also is in some fashion in matter, but rather acci-

143. iii 4, 429 a 27–28.

dentally, since being in matter is an accident of the intellect as intellect. However, knowing is not located in any particular part of the body but in the whole body taken categorematically. For it is not located in any particular part, since then the intellect would be organic and would either not know all forms, or, if it did, it would, like the cogitative soul, know them only as singulars and not as universals. Wherefore, just as the intellect is in the whole body, so also is knowing.

Hence not unfittingly then did Alexander hold that the whole body is the instrument of the intellect, since the intellect includes all powers and not some determinate part; because then it would not know all forms, just as none of the sensitive powers does. But although the whole body is thus made the instrument of the intellect, as though it were its subject, yet it is not truly as its subject, since knowing is not received in it in a bodily way, as has been said before. And if it be asked further whether the human intellect receives indivisibly, it is answered that, in so far as it knows, it receives indivisibly, but, in so far as it senses or vegetates, divisibly. Nor is it inconsistent for so multiple a nature to have so many different ways of receiving and operating.

As for the argument from experience, first, I wonder how St. Thomas adduces it, since Aristotle, in *Ethics* iii, says: "The will is of impossible things, as in desiring immortality."[144] Then, if our will does not exist except in the intellective soul, and if desiring immortality is, according to Aristotle, desiring the impossible, the human soul can hence not be immortal. Whence it is said in refutation that mark is not conclusive, since, as the Philosopher says there, the will is naturally of possibles and impossibles, since in the impossible the order of good can be preserved. And what was said further, that a natural appetite is not in vain, is true, taking natural as distinguished from intellective. For the former is the function of an intelligence that does not err; whence that toward which the will is directed without knowledge cannot be in vain. But if by knowledge, it can be in vain unless it be right.

144. iii 4, 1111 b 22–23.

For when the highest good is presented, even that appropriate for the gods, the will is directed toward it if it is not shown that it is impossible. Whence lest it be in vain the will must be ruled by right reason. Granted also that we could say that just as the mule, halfway between the ass and the horse, participates in both yet does not truly possess the properties of the horse or the ass; so also the human soul, halfway between material and immaterial things, aspires to eternity, granted that it cannot perfectly attain it. For the mule also, though it has all the organs of generation, cannot attain it perfectly, although it desires it exceedingly. Indeed, it is not inconsistent for something to be in vain for a whole species, provided it be not in vain for the genus; just as has been said of mules, in which the organs of generation are in vain, but are useful for their genus. And the mole, though it has eyes, does not see; but for the animal genus they are not in vain, as is considered in *De historiis animalium*.[145] Wherefore also the human soul desires immortality, which it cannot achieve absolutely, but it is enough that separated substances achieve it unqualifiedly. Whence Aristotle in *Metaphysica* ii[146] compared the human intellect to the owl, and not to the mole; for the owl sees a little but the mole not at all. Whence also, in *Metaphysica* ix, last text, he said: "The human intellect in knowing abstract things is not blind," but dim of sight, wherefore it aspires to eternity but does not desire it with a perfect desire.[147]

Moreover, the answer to Aristotle is plain enough from what has been said. For universally the heavenly bodies, men, beasts, and plants possess souls, and their souls are included in the universal definition of soul but not in the same way. For the Intelligences, in so far as they actuate the heavenly bodies, are the acts of a physical and organic body, but not as Intelligences. Likewise they receive nothing as they actuate, but only give. But the human soul is unqualifiedly the act of a physical and organic body, since it has no operation in which it does not depend in some way

145. i 9, 491 b 28 ff.   147. ix 10, 1052 a 2 ff.
146. ii 1, 993 b 9 ff.

[335]

on the body; and if not as subject, at least as object; whence it receives something from the body. This does not happen to the Intelligence in moving its body. For it gives only and does not receive. But the sensitive soul and the vegetative soul are deeply immersed in matter, though the vegetative more than the sensitive; wherefore they are altogether the acts of an organic body, both as subject and as object.

Nature has instituted this in due and orderly fashion. For just as we descend from things altogether without motion, which are the Intelligences, to the heavenly bodies, which are moved only in place, and these not as a whole but in part; and after them to things subject to generation and corruption, which are changed as a whole and in accord with all the ways of moving; so also the Intelligences are among all souls the least acts of an organic body; then the human intellect, thirdly sense, and fourthly the vegetative soul. For needing a body in any way whatever is not free from imperfection. Whence this order is most fitting.

Now to what was said about the active intellect, that since it is truly immortal the passive is also, inasmuch as they are both essential parts or powers of the human soul. To this it is replied that that passage is rather for the opposite than for the proposition. For Aristotle says there that only the active intellect is truly immortal and is always actual, while the passive is not, since at times it knows and at times it does not. Wherefore, since it does not have a perpetual operation, neither does it have a perpetual essence. Whence it is replied to the argument that the possible intellect is relatively immortal, but the active intellect is truly immortal, since it is one of the Intelligences. Nor is it any part of the human soul, as Themistius and Averroes judged, but only a mover.

That Aristotle said it is part of soul is true, as soul is common to the Intelligence and the human intellect, from which it does not follow that it is part of the human soul. For that is the fallacy of the consequent and is similar to what is said about first matter. For the latter is receptive in their true being of all material forms;

but the intellect only in their intentional being, since the stone is not in the soul, but its species. But what draws first matter out from potentiality to act in the existence of its forms is not anything of first matter, or anything joined to it in existence, but the universal mover, which can be called "the active nature." Thus the human intellect, since it has the same proportion in the genus of intelligibles as first matter in the genus of sensibles, as even Themistius and Averroes admit, will be moved to the reception of all species by something which is not a part of itself or joined to it. And this is called the active intellect, just as what universally moves matter is called the natural mover. Nor is it true what Themistius adds, that we are the active intellect, or that it is part of us as truly form. But only as mover, for that union is a pure fiction. But the other arguments advanced further are either not against the proposition or are answered by what has been said in another chapter, such as in what manner the intellect comes from without and remains after death, etc.

CHAPTER XI

IN WHICH THREE DOUBTS ARE RAISED CONCERNING
WHAT HAS BEEN SAID

Concerning what has been said some doubts arise. First, it has been said that the human soul is truly mortal but relatively immortal. But that does not seem to be well said. Indeed, it seems that it ought rather to be said that it is unqualifiedly immortal and relatively mortal. For higher things contain lower and not lower higher. For, we say, the heavenly bodies contain what is generated and corrupted and not the converse. Whence, since the immortal is above the mortal, it ought rather to be said that the human soul is unqualifiedly immortal and relatively mortal, since immortal contains mortal, than that we should say that it is unqualifiedly mortal and relatively immortal, since mortal does not contain immortal.

There is a second doubt, since, if the soul is immortal only relatively, then it is either truly and properly speaking immortal or not truly, and improperly speaking. Not the first, as has been said; nor the second, because, if it is improperly called immortal, it could no less be called any other thing it is not; for it could also be improperly called a dog or a hare. Why, then, is it rather said that it is immortal than that it is a dog or a hare, since immortal is improperly said of it?

The third doubt is, because the whole root of this position is supported on this foundation, that the human intellect has but one way of knowing, as both sense and the Intelligences have one way of knowing. But this way is a mean between the way of knowing of unqualifiedly abstracted substances and that of the sensitive soul, since it participates in both. As it knows universals, it agrees with abstracted substances; but as it sees such universals only in the phantasm and the singular, it agrees with sense, since it does not know entirely without the appendages of matter; whence it was concluded to be a mean between the material and the immaterial.

But this raises a doubt, because if such dependence of the knowing of the intellect on phantasms is to see the universal in the singular, then the intellect would know singulars, which is denied by many. For some say that the material singular can be known only by sense; or, granted, as we admit, that the intellect knows the singular, it still seems to many that it cannot be known except reflexively, as Aristotle seems to say in *De anima* iii, text 10.[148] But this too admitted, since that reflection cannot be imagined except as a kind of discursive thought, as almost all interpret it; and this discursive thought does not take place except in time and after the cognition of simple things; hence before composition and division, and consequently before discursive thought, it will see the universal and not in the singular. Therefore the position is supported on a false foundation, etc.

148. Cf. iii 4, 430 a 6–7.

CHAPTER XII

IN WHICH AN ANSWER IS MADE TO THESE DOUBTS

To the first doubt, then, it is replied that containing is far different from participating. For containing takes place by way of form, and being contained by way of matter. Whence the container is perfect and superexcellent, but what is contained is imperfect and exceeded. But the contrary holds of the participant and what is participated in. For what is participated in exists rather by way of cause and exceeding; the participant by way of effect and exceeded. Wherefore we do not appropriately say that the human intellect contains the divine and immortality, but the contrary. But we rightly say that the human intellect participates in divinity and immortality, and not the contrary. Whence Aristotle, *De partibus* i, chapter 10,[149] did not say, "Only man contains divinity and immortality," but he said, "Only man participates in divinity and immortality, or especially man." This last phrase is added, because other mortal things also participate in divinity, for "in all natural things is divinity," as Aristotle says from the maxim of Heraclitus in *De partibus* i, last chapter.[150] But other mortal things not so much as man. He also repeats the same thing in *De partibus* iv, chapter 9.[151] Wherefore the argument required that the human intellect should not contain immortality, but not that it should not participate in immortality, which we affirm.

You may know also that just as something truly mortal partakes of immortality, nay, everything productive of something like itself thus participates in immortality, as is said in *De anima* ii, texts 34 and 35,[152] so anything immortal seems to participate in mortality and corruption. For the Commentator, *De coelo* ii, comment 49,[153] giving the cause of the spots on the moon, says

149. ii 10, 656 a 7–8.
150. i 5, 644 a 16 ff.
151. iv 10, 686 a 27 ff.
152. ii 4, 415 a 28 ff.
153. *Opera Aristotelis*, Vol. V, fol. 137.

that this is because the moon is of the nature of earth, and cites Aristotle's *De animalibus*. But he says this more clearly in *De proprietatibus elementorum*.[154] For he asserts that the rest of the elements participate in the erratic ones. It is hence not unfitting for mortal to participate in the immortal, and for immortal to participate in the mortal.

To the second doubt it is replied that, although between properly and improperly there is no mean, yet there is one by participation of properties; just as although between substance and accident there is no mean (for there is nothing which is not either substance or accident), still something is asserted to participate in the properties of both; just as moving by part is placed as a mean between moving of itself and moving by accident, as is said in *Physica* v.[155] Whence the human soul, although it is improperly called immortal, because it is truly mortal, still participates in the properties of immortality, since it knows the universal, although this sort of knowledge is very slight and obscure. But it is not so with the dog and the hare, as regards that operation. Whence the objection there advanced falls.

But if it is said that we greatly vilify the human intellect, when we assert that it is hardly the shadow of intellect, to this it is replied, that truly in comparison with the Intelligences it is a shadow. Aristotle teaches this also, both in scattered passages in the *De anima*[156] and in the *Metaphysica* ii.[157] For it is not truly called intellectual but rational. For intellect perceives all things by a simple intuition; but reasoning by composition, discourse, and time. All this bears witness to its imperfection and materiality. For these are the conditions of matter. But if you will compare the human intellect to the other things that are generated and corrupted, it will obtain the first rank of nobility, although the body is very weak and subject to an almost infinite number

---

154. Cf. Ps. Aristotle, *De causis proprietatum elementorum*, chap. 1 (in *Opera Aristotelis*, Vol. VI, fols. 283–84).

155. v 1, 224 a 21 ff.   157. Cf. ii 1, 993 b 10–11.

156. Cf. iii 4–5.

of infirmities, and is of a worse condition than almost all beasts, as Pliny the Elder shows very ably in his *Natural History* vii.[158] Add, besides, that man is either a subject or else rules others. If he is subject, let him consider his most miserable lot, since of a thousand thousand rulers hardly one is found of even moderate virtue; indeed, almost always those established in power are mad, ignorant, and filled with every sort of vice. How hard indeed is this kind of fate is plain enough, since no race of animals is thus oppressed by one of its own species. But if he rules others, how unjust a tyranny is both Plato in the *Republic*[159] and Aristotle in the *Politics*[160] make clear at sufficient length and maintain that the condition of a tyranny is far worse than that of a subject in any subjection whatever. Let him then who so greatly magnifies man not consider what he does not experience but those things which he knows and has before his eyes.

In answer to the third doubt it must be said that certain very weighty interpreters of St. Thomas, expounding the *Summa*, Part I, article 7, question 84,[161] in which St. Thomas treats of this conversion, say that the singular is known reflexively and that reflection of this sort is a kind of argument; and they say that the universal is not known in any singular, but in some particular; for example, that man is not known in Socrates or in Plato, but in some man. But "some man" is related to "man" within the limits of the first mode of speaking per se; and, although it is not primarily in that mode, it is still within its limits, just as the perfect and the imperfect are related to each thing. Nor is "man" prior to "some man," since the consequence of subsisting is convertible. For if "man" exists, "some man" exists; and if "some man" exists, "man" exists; which could not be if "man" were prior to "some man."

But to me these statements are exceedingly doubtful. And,

158. Cf. *Nat. Hist.* vii, prooemium and chaps. 6 ff.
159. ix 571 a ff.
160. Cf. v 10 ff.
161. Editio Leonina, V, 325–26. See also Question 86, article 1 (p. 347).

first, that man is known in some man but not in Socrates, nor in any singular, seems especially contrary to experience; because, however far we know the immaterial or the universal, we always form some image in the cogitative soul, in which we see it; as even St. Thomas says in that passage: "But the image is something singular and represents a singular, and reason draws toward it." For he is trying to prove that we know by turning to the phantasm, which cannot be formed except as a singular, since man is in Socrates and horse in this horse. For these are his words: "Whence from the fact that man is in this singular, he knows in this phantasm." For otherwise the proof would not be appropriate. For not from the fact that it is indifferently in some man does he know in this phantasm. And certainly the assertion of this interpreter contradicts the letter, for the letter runs thus: "He knows in some individual." This is manifest from the following words, for it follows: "Human nature is in this man, and equine nature in this horse."

Further, it is very hard for me to understand that line of argument, because in addition it seems to me deficient in many ways. For, from *Analytica priora* i,[162] every true argumentation has some universal proposition, since singulars are not inferred from singulars; but a universal proposition is obtained by induction, as appears in the *Posteriora* i and ii.[163] But induction is of singulars, as is well known. Whence in knowledge of the universal[164] there is presupposed knowledge of the singular. Further, if for knowing Socrates we need that most obscure course of argument, as he says, then a great time would be taken for knowing Socrates after knowing man. I also admit that I know Socrates is a man, and I know nothing of that course of argument; and children and idiots lacking discourse would be ignorant that this is a man and this a dog, since they do not possess this course of argument.

162. Cf. i 21, 40 a 1-2.

163. Cf. i 13, 81 b 2 ff., and ii 7, 92 a 37–38.

164. The edition of 1516 reads: *singularis*. We follow Gentile's correction, which reads: *universalis*.

Furthermore, "some man," according to him, is not singular, though it determines man. But it seems that there can be nothing in "some man" determinative of man except that adjective "some" (*aliquis*). This does not seem to be so, since it is of greater extension than "man," and yet the determiner ought to be of less extension than the determined. Moreover, he says, that "man" and "some man" are on the same logical level, since they mutually imply each other. But by the same argument, if all the singulars contained under "man" be taken, they imply each other disjunctively in the same way with the consequences of subsisting. Yet no one doubts that for the intellect man is prior to the singular, although not in existence. And the discussion is about the first. For Porphyry in his *Communitates* (*Isagoge*)[165] proves that genus is prior to differentia and species, since, if genus be removed, there is neither species nor differentia; but if the latter be removed, the genus is not. This, of course, cannot be understood of existence, but only for intellect. Whence it seems to me we must say that the intellect knows man in the singular but indeterminately; since although I now know man in Socrates, yet I can also in Plato and in any other, provided it be in some singular; just as every body is in one singular place, though indeterminately. And it is said that it knows the universal and the singular at the same time, although the universal is prior by nature; though there are not lacking some who affirm that the singular is known first and, as I think, not only by nature but also in time, since they assert that knowledge of the universal is obtained from a comparison of singulars. But for the present let us continue with the first opinion.

When it was said that the singular is not known except reflexively, according to the *De anima* iii,[166] it is true, although Themistius and Averroes do not so interpret the words. This now granted, we say that truly and properly such knowing is a

---

165. Porphyry, *Isagoge*, ed. A. Busse (in *Commentaria in Aristotelem Graeca*, Vol. IV [Berlin, 1887]), pp. 14-15.

166. Cf. iii 4, 430 a 6-7.

reflecting upon and a turning to the phantasm, to use the words of St. Thomas. This is plain to see. For in *Physica* viii[167] in that part in which Aristotle shows that reflexive motions are not continuous, he defines reflexive motion to be that which ends in the same point from which it began. But since the human mind understands through the cogitative soul the singular first, then through the intellect understands the universal, which however is seen in the same singular which is known by imagination; it makes truly a return (*reditus*) and consequently a turning-back; since from the singular, known by the imagination, the soul returns by the intellect to the same point. Nor do I see how a syllogism or a course of argument can be fittingly called reflection or conversion, since they proceed not from the same to the same but from the diverse to the diverse; and both are comprehended by the same species, though one is prior to the other. Nor is it unfitting for many things to be known at the same time, provided they are known through a single species. Yet the species comprehends this present singular rather than another, since the phantasm is of this one and not of that. For from the inspection of this lion I know lion and this lion, yet no more do I know lion from this one than from that which remains in the forest. For if I should inspect that one, I should no less know lion. But I know this one and not the one in the forest, because I have a phantasm of this one and not of that. Whence the foundation stands, etc.

CHAPTER XIII

IN WHICH MANY ARDUOUS DIFFICULTIES ARE RAISED AGAINST WHAT HAS BEEN SAID

But against this position greater difficulties arise, which, as far as I see, are not easy to satisfy.

167. viii 8, 262 a 17.

First, because if the human soul is mortal, as has been concluded, then there will be no final end of man as man, and thus he will not be capable of happiness. But the opposite is maintained by Aristotle in *Ethics* i,[168] as is clear enough. It is also contrary to the common saying, which runs that man is an animal capable of happiness since he is capable of reason. This is also plain from its opposite, since in *Physica* ii[169] misfortune or unhappiness does not fall to beasts but only to rational beings. Hence the soul is not mortal.

These propositions are all plain except the conditional, which is the major: that if he were mortal, there would be no final end of man as man. This is proved as follows: because, if there were any such final end, since it could be placed neither in the vegetative or the sensitive part, nor in the goods of the body or of fortune, as Aristotle quite briefly demonstrates in *Ethics* i,[170] and Boethius fully and clearly in *De consolatione* ii and iii,[171] and St. Thomas in *Contra Gentiles* iii,[172] hence his happiness would be placed in the goods of the soul or its virtues. But since the virtues of the soul are divided into the moral and the intellectual, and happiness cannot be placed in the moral virtues, as the men cited clearly show, it remains that it must be placed in the intellectual. Yet when the intellectual virtues are divided into their parts, as appears in *Ethics* vi,[173] in none does it seem rational to place happiness except in the state of wisdom, which is especially concerned with God, as the plain meaning of Aristotle seems in *Ethics* x.[174]

But this also is refuted by many arguments. First, because such knowledge demands a man of very superior ability, and moreover wholly withdrawn from worldly affairs, of a good constitution, that is, of a healthy one, and not lacking the necessities. But such men may be most rare; even in long centuries

168. Chaps. 5 ff.
169. ii 6, 197 b 8–9.
170. i 6, 1097 b 33 ff., and 8, 1098 b 12 ff.
171. ii 4 ff., and iii 2 ff.
172. Chaps. 27 ff.
173. vi 2 ff.
174. x 7.

hardly one is found. This our daily experience teaches and history declares. But this is contrary to the nature of happiness, because that is a good appropriate to any man who is not disabled, since every man naturally desires it.

Further, because such knowledge is exceedingly feeble and very uncertain, since it belongs to opinion rather than to science. This is shown by men's diverse opinions, since hardly two are found to agree in such matters. And our way of knowing demonstrates the same point, for it is by sense, and such things are far removed from sense; whence it is that it ought to be called ignorance rather than knowledge and suspicion rather than certainty. Moreover, who will assert this knowledge to be happiness, since in happiness we are at peace, but in this we are tossed about and not at peace? Besides, happiness has the nature of an end; but this is all on the road, since no man knows as much as he can know; nay, the more he knows, the more he desires to know. Moreover, in striving for this knowledge how many arts, how many sciences, how many labors, how many sleepless nights are needful? Wherefore, since life scarcely suffices for attaining a single art, how shall man be able to reach such an end? And when one sees that he is uncertain of his life, of his powers, of events able to hinder him and to remove him from the midst of things, how shall he set forth on so great and so difficult a journey? Further, since the time needed for producing such happiness is very great, and the way of arriving at it most difficult, for a man ought to renounce the body almost completely while he is in the body; and he is doubtful of the outcome, and even after he has succeeded he may lose it in a moment, by dying or by going mad or by some other chance: how then will that not be more truly called unhappiness than happiness? Wherefore many have not unreasonably said, if the human soul is mortal, the condition of man is far worse than that of any beast, considering the weakness of man in regard to his body, which is subject to so many infirmities, and the restlessness of his soul, which is ever turning this way and that.

Secondly, and principally, because, if the mortality of the human soul is established, man ought not to choose death in any case, no matter how urgent. And thus courage would be done away with, which teaches us to despise death, and that we ought to choose death for our country and for the public good. Nor ought we to risk our life for a friend; nay, we ought even to commit any crime or sin whatever rather than suffer death. This is contrary to Aristotle, in *Ethics* iii and ix,[175] and contrary to nature. A mark of this is that we naturally hate those who do these things, even to save their lives, and revile them; and naturally love and praise those who do the opposite. But that this should follow is plain enough; because choice considers the nature of its own good, but death destroys all good, and there is in it nothing to choose. This appears also from Plato in the *Phaedo*,[176] where he testifies that death is not to be borne with equal mind were there no hope of a better life. And he says also in the *Laws* v, "He who thinks this life the highest good disgraces it."[177] And St. Thomas too in *Ethics* iii[178] rather doubts how those who assert the soul to be mortal can choose death. In the *Exposition of the Apostles' Creed*[179] he says, in the part on the resurrection of the flesh, that beyond all doubt, were there no hope of resurrection, one ought to commit any crime whatever rather than die.

Thirdly, because it follows, either God is not the governor of the universe or he is unjust, of which each is an enormity. For if he did not govern everything, he would not be God; and if God, he is the highest good, since he possesses nothing of potentiality; and if he is the highest good, how can there be injustice in him? Now this is plain to see, since so many evils take place in this world which are unknown to men, and if known are left unpunished. Nay, very often men obtain the greatest goods for their evil. It is the opposite with regard to

175. Cf. iii 1, and ix 1 ff.
176. 63 b.
177. 727 c-d.

178. Lectio 2 (ed. Fretté, XXV, 325).
179. Chap. 14 (ed. Fretté, XXVII, 226).

good deeds, which either are not known, or if they are known remain without reward, and many times they incur death and injury. But these things God either does not know, or, if he knows, and leaves them thus unpunished or without reward, as Jerome says,[180] he is not God.

Fourthly, because all religions, not only those which have been but those which now exist, maintain that the soul remains after the body; and so this is of very great renown and celebrated throughout the whole world. Wherefore either we must say that the soul is immortal or that the whole world is deceived and that a widespread belief is completely false. But the Philosopher denies this in *De somno et vigilia*.[181]

Fifthly, because there are many experiences from which the soul's immortality can be conclusively grasped. For Plato in the *Phaedo*[182] relates that around tombs the shadowy phantasms of souls have been seen, and these are the souls of evil men. In the *Laws* ix[183] also he says that the souls of the slain often pursue their murderers with hostile intent, wherefore some have thought that blood flows from wounds in the presence of the murderer. In the *Republic* x[184] also he relates how there had risen from the dead a certain Pamphylian who told horrible things of the punishments and tortures of the wicked. And the younger Pliny says[185] that at Athens there had been a notorious house in which both the apparition of a frightful old man was seen and noises heard. Athenodorus, a philosopher from Tarsus, had seen that apparition after he had rented the house and, led by it, had discovered in the courtyard of the house under the ground bones bound by chains, and, as was customary, he had buried them; from that time on the house was free from noise.

---

180. Cf. Epistle 39 (ad Paulam) chap. 2 (*Sancti Eusebii Hieronymi Epistulae*, Part I, ed. I. Hilberg [Vienna, 1910], pp. 296–97).

181. *De divinatione per somnia*, chap. 1, 462 b 14 ff.

182. 81 c–d.   184. 614 b ff.

183. 865 d–e.   185. *Epistles* vii 27, 5 ff.

And Posidonius the Stoic tells[186] that two Arcadian friends, when they arrived at Megara, had parted to spend the night, one at an inn, the other at a friend's house. After they had dined and retired, it seemed to the one in the friend's house at night in his sleep that the other begged his companion to come to his aid, because the innkeeper was plotting his death. Frightened from sleep, he arose at first; then, when he had collected himself, and had decided that that vision meant nothing, lay down again. Then it seemed to the sleeping man that the other begged him, that since he had not come to his friend's aid while alive, he would at least not allow his death to pass unavenged; that he had been killed by the innkeeper, had been thrown into a cart, and dung thrown on top; he asked that in the morning his friend go to the gate before the cart went out of the town. Disturbed by this dream, he was at the gate in the morning to meet the plowman, and asked what was in the cart. The plowman fled in fright, the dead man was dug out, and the innkeeper, now that the affair had come to light, was punished. Simonides also,[187] when he had seen some unknown dead man lying stretched out, and had buried him, and was intending to board a ship, seemed to be warned not to do so by the man he had aided by burial; if he sailed he would perish in a shipwreck. Simonides returned, the others suffered shipwreck. And an infinite number of incidents of this sort could be adduced. I myself can also testify that I have had many things through dreams which are somewhat similar. Wherefore these facts clearly seem to show that the souls of the dead exist.

Sixthly, because we read many things and observe by experience that some are disturbed by demons who prophesy past and future, and say that they are the souls of certain dead men. And to deny experience is audacity and madness.

Seventhly, because Aristotle also seems to maintain that souls are immortal, not only because he says in *Ethics* i[188] that the mis-

---

186. Cicero *De divinatione* i 27, 57.
187. *Ibid.* 56.   188. i 11, 1100 a 18 ff.

fortune of a great-grandson affects the souls of the dead, but also because he holds that they are rewarded after death. For in *Oeconomica* ii, chapter 2, speaking of Alcestis and Penelope, he says that, "made faithful in evil, they had prepared for themselves immortal glory and are justly honored by men, nor are they unrewarded by the Gods."[189]

Eighthly, because all the followers of this position have been and are most impious and wicked men, like cowardly Epicurus, base Aristippus, mad Lucretius, Diagoras called the Atheist, the Epicurean and most bestial Sardanapalus, and all whose conscience is burdened with base crimes. But, on the contrary, holy and just men, whose conscience is spotless, vehemently declare the soul to be immortal. Wherefore Plato, in the *Epistle to Dionysius*,[190] which begins, "I have heard from Archedemus," there says the following: "For it chances by some natural principle that the most base men care not at all what may be the future opinion about them, yet the most upright men do everything so that in future ages they may hear men speaking well of them. Hence I conjecture that there is some feeling in those who are dead for our affairs, since the best souls so strongly divine it, the worst in no way. More powerful indeed are the prophesies of divine men than those of others, etc."

CHAPTER XIV

IN WHICH THE OBJECTIONS ARE ANSWERED

It seems to me arduous indeed and burdensome to satisfy these arguments, and especially since it is common repute that souls remain after death; and, as it is written in *Metaphysica* ii,[191] it is difficult to speak against common custom. But so far as we are

---

189. Ps. Aristotle, *Oeconomica*, Book ii, chap. 1 (*Opera Aristotelis* [Venice, 1560], Vol. III, fol. 475v). This second book which was translated from the Arabic is not found in the Greek text of the *Oeconomica*.

190. *Epistle* ii, 311 b–c.   191. Cf. ii 3, 995 a 1 ff.

given power we shall endeavor to speak in this matter with probability at least.

For answer then to the first objection, it must be known that each thing, at least each complete thing, has some end. And although the end has the nature of good, as is said in *Metaphysica* ii,[192] nevertheless there must be assigned to each thing as its end not what is good to a greater degree, but only according to what suits its nature, and has a due proportion to it. For although it is better to sense than not to sense, it does not suit a stone to sense, nor would it be the good of the stone; for then it would no longer be a stone. Whence also in assigning an end to man, if it were such as we should assign to God and the Intelligences, that would not be fitting, since he would thus not be man.

Secondly, it must be accepted and particularly committed to memory that the whole human race can be compared to one single man. But in one human individual there are multiple and divers members, ordered to divers offices or to divers proximate ends; yet all are also directed to a single end, whence they must all share in some things. Now if that order were violated either he would not be a man or would be so with great difficulty. But all the members are ordered to the common advantage of that man, and the one is either necessary to the other and vice versa, or at least useful, though at times one more, and another less. Whence the heart is necessary to the brain, and the brain to the heart, and the heart is necessary to the hand while the hand is useful for the heart; and the right hand is useful to the left, and the left to the right, and all the members share in life and natural heat, and need spirits and blood, as is plain to see from the *De animalibus*.[193] And besides what they share in, each single member has a single function; for the heart has one, the brain another, the liver a third, and so of the rest, as Aristotle declares in the same *De animalibus*,[194] and Galen more fully in his *De utilitate*

192. Cf. ii 2, 994 b 9 ff.
193. Cf. *De historiis animalium*, iii 2, 511, b 1 ff., and 19, 520 b 10 ff.
194. Cf. *De historiis animalium* i 16–17.

particularum.[195] Moreover, these functions or operations are not equal, but one is prior and the other posterior, one is more perfect and the other less perfect. For, according to Aristotle, since the heart is the noblest and the first, so also is its function the noblest and the first. And so of the rest in order. And although the brain, for instance, is not so perfect as the heart, still in its kind it can be perfect. Wherefore, just as all the members have latitude and diversity among themselves, so also each genus of member, yet within fixed limits. For neither are all hearts equally great nor similarly warm; and so of the other members. This, too, is to be observed, that, although among these members there may exist so great a diversity, yet it is not such as to produce discord; but it must be a commensurate diversity. But if it becomes beyond measure, either the destruction of the individual or sickness will follow. If indeed there were not that commensurate diversity, the individual could in no way endure. For if all the members were either heart or eye, there would be no animal; just as in instrumental and vocal music, if all the voices were of a single order, no harmony and pleasure would be caused. And they are so disposed that neither the whole individual nor any part of it can be disposed in a better way than it is. Just as Plato says in the *Timaeus*[196] that God gave to each what is best for it and for the whole, in the same way we must think of the whole human race.

For the whole human race is like a single body composed of different members, also with different functions, yet ordered to the common advantage of the human race. And each gives to the other, and receives from him to whom he gives, and they have reciprocal functions. Nor can all be of equal perfection, but to some are given functions more perfect, to some less perfect. And were this inequality destroyed, either the human race would perish or it would persist with great difficulty. Yet there

195. *Claudii Galeni Opera omnia,* ed. C. G. Kuehn, III (Leipzig 1822), 1 ff.

196. Cf. 29 e–30 a.

are some things in which all or almost all share. For otherwise they would not be parts of one genus and with a tendency toward a single common good, just as was said of the members of a single individual man. Nor ought the inequality among men, provided it be commensurate, to produce discord. Indeed, just as in a musical group a commensurate diversity of voices makes a delightful harmony, so a commensurate diversity among men generates the perfect, the beautiful, the suitable, and the delightful; but an incommensurate diversity the contrary.

Therefore, having thus disposed of these things, let us say that all men in pursuing this sort of common end must share in three intellects: the theoretical, the practical or operative, and the productive. For no man who is sound and of due age fails to possess something of these three intellects, just as there is no member which does not participate in blood and natural heat. For each man has something of speculation, and perhaps in each theoretical science. Because he knows the principles at least, as is said in *Metaphysica* ii,[197] which are as the doors of the house, which no one does not know. For who is there who does not know first principles like "Of anything it is said to be or not to be," "It does not happen that the same thing at the same time both is and is not"? Who is altogether ignorant of God? Of being, of one, of true, of good? And so of the rest, which it would be too burdensome to run through. But these things belong to metaphysics. It is also clear of natural philosophy, since those things are subject to the senses which first meet the intellect. In mathematics also it is clear to see, since human life could not be carried on without numbers and figures; and all men know hours, days, months, and years and many other things which are the business of astronomy. And no less, unless he be blind, does he know something of sight, which is the task of optics; and unless he be deaf, of harmonies, which belong to music. What shall I say, moreover, of rhetoric and dialectic,

197. Cf. ii 1, 993 b 1 ff.

since Aristotle in the Preface to the *Rhetoric* says, "wherefore and in a certain fashion all participate in both"?[198]

Now in regard to the operative intellect, which is concerned with morals, public and private affairs, it is very clear, since to each it is given to know good and evil, to be part of the state and the family. For intellect of this sort is truly and properly called human, as Plato in the *Republic*[199] and Aristotle in the *Ethics*[200] testify. And as regards the productive intellect, it is plain, since no man can maintain life without it. For without things mechanical and necessary to life man could not endure.

But it must be known that, although no man is completely deprived of these three intellects, yet man is not equally related to them. For the theoretical intellect is not of man but of the gods, as Aristotle teaches in *Ethics* x.[201] And Plato in the *Timaeus:* "The greatest gift of the Gods is philosophy."[202] Wherefore man in no way shares it with other creatures. Hence even if all men possess something of it, yet very few have it and can have it exactly and perfectly. Wherefore it happens that that part of the human race which gives itself wholly to speculation holds that proportion in the race of men which the heart holds in the genus of members; although there is also latitude for some to be mathematicians, some to be physicists, and some metaphysicians. Among all these ways there is latitude, as is clear enough. But the productive intellect, which is lowest and mechanical, is common to all men; nay, even beasts participate in it, as Aristotle teaches in *De historiis*,[203] since many beasts build houses, and many other things which indicate the productive intellect. And this is most necessary, inasmuch as the greater part of men have been occupied with it. Whence the female sex apply themselves almost completely to it, as in weaving, spinning, sewing, etc. And the greatest part of men spend their time in agriculture, then in the different crafts. Nor can he who applies himself to

198. i 1, 1354 a 3–4.
199. Cf. iv 420 b ff.
200. Cf. vi 5.

201. Cf. x 7, 1177 b 26 ff.
202. Cf. 47 a–b.
203. viii 1, 588 a 29 ff.

one craft easily apply himself to another. Wherefore Plato in the *Republic*[204] and Aristotle in the *Politics*[205] ordered that, just as one member does not easily perform different functions, so one artisan ought not to spend his time at different crafts. For he will master neither. Yet the practical or operative intellect is truly fitting for man. And every man not incapacitated can pursue it perfectly. And according to it man is called unqualifiedly and absolutely good and evil, but according to the theoretical and the productive intellects only relatively and within limits. For according to his virtues and vices a man is called a good man or a bad; but a good metaphysician is not called a good man but a good metaphysician, and a good builder is not called good absolutely but a good builder. Wherefore a man submits without offense if he is not called a metaphysician, a philosopher, or a smith; but if he is called a thief, intemperate, unjust, imprudent, or something vicious of this sort, he is much offended and gets excited, since being righteous or vicious is human and is in our power, but being a philosopher or a builder is not our task, nor is it necessary to man. Whence it is that all men can and ought to be of good character, but not all philosophers, mathematicians, builders, and the rest. For mankind would not endure if there were not such diversity, as was said above about the members.

Returning then to the proposition, we say that the end of the human race in general is to participate in these three intellects, by which men communicate with each other and live together; and one is either useful or necessary to the other, just as all the members in a single man share in vital spirits and have mutual operations together. And from this end man cannot be absolved. But as to the practical intellect, which is proper to man, every man should possess it perfectly. For in order that the human race be rightly preserved, every man must be morally virtuous and as far as possible lack vice; and a vice is imputed to him as his, in whatever condition he be found, whether destitute or

204. Cf. iv 442 c. 205. Cf. iv 4.

poor or rich or moderately wealthy or quite wealthy. With the other intellects this is not necessary, nor is it possible. Nor does it suit the human race; for the world would not endure if everyone were theoretical, nor would he himself, for it is impossible for one kind of men, like philosophers, to be self-sufficient; nor for a race of builders alone, or anything of this sort. Nor can it be that one should perfectly perform the functions of another, still less of all, just as happens in the members.

Wherefore the universal end of the human race is to participate relatively in the speculative and the productive intellects but perfectly in the practical. For the whole would be most perfectly preserved if all men were righteous and good, but not if all were philosophers or smiths or builders. Nor is it thus in the moral virtues as in the arts and sciences, that one hinders another, and applying one's self to one prevents applying one's self to another. Indeed, as is said in the *Ethics*,[206] the moral virtues are bound up together, and he who possesses one perfectly possesses them all. Wherefore all ought to be righteous and good. But to be a philosopher, a mathematician, or an architect is a particular end: just as the brain has its own function, and the liver its. Nor ought that inequality in the human race to beget envy and quarrels among them, just as the diversity in the members does not; nay rather union and peace, especially since every man ought to be moral, by which such things are expelled. And as each element has its proper place in the whole categorematically, yet some part of it is better than another; for not every part of fire touches the sphere of the moon unless as it is joined to the whole, nor is every part of earth the center of the world, except by reason of the whole; so not every man has the final end which suits the part, except as part of the human race. It is enough that he have the common human end.

Wherefore it is said to the argument, that if man is mortal, every man can have the end which suits man universally; the end that belongs to the most perfect part he cannot, nor is it fit-

206. Cf. vi 13, 1144 b 32 ff.

ting. Just as not every member can have the perfection of the heart or the eye, indeed, the animal would not persist; so, if every man were theoretical, the human community would not persist. Whence many climates and different regions are necessary. Happiness then does not consist in the theoretical power of demonstration, as suitable for the whole human race, but as suiting its first principal part. And though the other parts cannot arrive at such happiness, they are still not wholly deprived of all happiness, since they can possess something of the theoretical and something of the productive, and the practical perfectly. This power can make almost everyone blessed. For farmer or smith, destitute or rich, if his life be moral, can be called happy, and truly so called, and can depart contented with his lot. In addition, besides moral happiness he can be called a happy farmer or a happy builder, if he operates successfully in agriculture or in house-building, although he is not on this account so properly called happy. For these things are not in human power, like the virtues and vices. Hence the human race is not frustrated in its end, unless it make itself so.

And what was added further, that such speculation does not seem to be able to make man happy, since it is very weak and obscure; to this I say that, although it is of this sort in relation to eternal things and to that of the Intelligences, yet among mortal things nothing can be found more excellent, as Plato says in the *Timaeus*.[207] Nor ought a mortal to desire immortal happiness, since the immortal is not fitting for the mortal: just as immortal wrath is not fitting for mortal man, as Aristotle says in *Rhetoric* ii.[208] Whence we first suppose that to each thing a proportionate end is assigned. For if man will be moderate, he will not desire the impossible, nor does it suit him. For to have such happiness is proper to the gods, who are in no wise dependent on matter and change. The opposite of this occurs in the human race, which is a mean between the mortal and the immortal.

And when it was further said, that the end ought to bring

207. Cf. 47 a-b.   208. ii 21, 1394 b 21-22.

peace but this does not set man's intellect and will at rest; to this I say that Aristotle at the end of *Ethica* i[209] does not assert human happiness as perfect peace; nay, he holds that no matter how happy a man be, yet he is not so steadfast that many things do not disturb him (for he would not be man), but they do not remove him from happiness; just as every wind does not strip a tree, though it moves the leaves. Whence in human happiness a steadfastness that cannot be destroyed is enough, although it may be disturbed somewhat; nay, what is more, also at any age: for in youth, if he does not have exact knowledge, which belongs to manhood, provided he have what belongs to youth he is content for that age; nor does he desire more than suits him. Wherefore he will not be perturbed, as was said.

And when it proceeded further, that man never knows as much as he can know, nor so clearly but that it might be more clear; I say that this does not destroy his happiness, so long as he have as much as suits his condition, and that he is not deficient on his part. For it is characteristic of a temperate appetite to desire as much as it can digest; so it is characteristic of the temperate man to be content with what suits him and what he can have.

And when it was further added, since man knows he will soon lose this happiness, and that it can be destroyed in many ways, he will have more misery than happiness; to this I say that it belongs to an illiberal man not to wish to give back what he has received freely, when man is assumed to be mortal; for the ancients also called life a purgatory, since man receives it with the provision that he knows he must give it back to nature. He will give thanks to God and nature, and will always be ready to die, nor will he fear death, since fear of the inevitable is vain; and he will see nothing evil in death.

And when further it was inferred that the condition of man would be far worse than that of any brute, surely in my opinion this is not said philosophically, since the works of beasts, though

209. i 11.

they bring content to their kind, are here preferred to the restless works of the intellect. Who would prefer to be a stone or a stag of long life, rather than a man of however low degree? Inasmuch as a prudent man can maintain a contented mind in any condition or time, though he be troubled by bodily distresses. Indeed the wise man would much prefer to be in extreme necessity and the greatest troubles rather than to be stupid, cowardly, and vicious under the opposite conditions.

Nor is it true that one who sees immense labors, withdrawal from bodily pleasures, obscure knowledge of things, the easy loss of what has been acquired, would turn aside to vice and bodily things rather than be moved to acquire knowledge, if that man acts according to reason. For the slightest modicum of knowledge and virtue is to be preferred to all bodily delights, nay, to kingdoms themselves, in which abound tyrannies and vices. Wherefore the first argument seems in no way to prove that the soul is immortal.

But in answer to the second objection, which asserted that if the mortality of the soul is established, then we ought never to choose death, I say that it on no account follows but rather the opposite. For in *Topica* iii it is said: "Of two evils the lesser is to be chosen."[210] And in *Ethica* iii: "Choice is of goods, rejection of evils."[211] Since then in choosing death for the sake of country, of friends, and of avoiding sin the greatest virtue is acquired, and it is greatly to the advantage of others, since men naturally praise an act of this sort, and nothing is more precious and more happy than virtue itself, it is above all things to be chosen. But, in committing a crime, a man very greatly harms the community, and hence also himself, since he is part of the community. And he falls into vice, than which there is nothing more unhappy, since he ceases to be a man, as Plato says in so many places in the *Republic*;[212] and therefore this has the nature of a thing to be avoided. And happiness follows the attainment of that

210. Cf. iii 2, 117 a 8–9.   212. Cf. i 354 a.
211. Cf. iii 4, 1111 b 33 ff.

virtue, or a great part of happiness, even though it be of short duration. But misery follows sin, for, as Plato witnesses, sin is misery and in the end death, since immortality may not follow on account of the crime committed, except perhaps through infamy and vituperation. But it is plain that the former rather than the latter is the lesser evil. Nor is living long with infamy to to be put above living a brief time with praise, just as the life of man however brief is to be set above the life of beasts however long. For Aristotle, in *Ethica* i, says: "A long life is not to be preferred to a short life, unless other things are equal."[213]

Nor is death chosen in such a case for itself, since it is nothing; but rather a righteous act, though death follow it; just as in not committing a sin life is not refused, since life is good in itself, but the sin is refused whose consequence is life. But as to the objection based on the statement in the *Phaedo*,[214] Plato holds in the *Republic*[215] and the *Crito*,[216] that just as life with an incurable infirmity ought to be rejected, nay, even taken from the living, so the soul with sin ought to be eradicated; and the soul, were it to live forever in sin, is the highest misery, since there is nothing worse for the soul than sin itself. But Plato said this in regard to what would actually happen. For if men hoped for no better life after death, they would doubtless endure this one uneasily, because they do not know the excellence of virtue and the ignobility of vice. For only the philosophers and the righteous, as Plato says in the *Republic*[217] and Aristotle in *Ethica* ix,[218] know how much delight the virtues produce and how much misery ignorance and vice. Nay, Socrates, in Plato's *Apology*, says: "Whether the soul be mortal or immortal, death is nonetheless to be despised."[219] Nor ought we in any way to turn aside from virtue, whatever may happen after death. I think in the same way also the words of St. Thomas in *On the Apostles'*

213. Cf. i 4, 1096 b 3 ff.
214. 63 b.
215. Cf. x 608 d ff.
216. 47 d ff.

217. Cf. ix 582 e ff.
218. Cf. ix 8.
219. Cf. 40 c ff.

Creed[220] are to be interpreted, not that crimes ought to be committed rather than to suffer death, if the soul were mortal—for that I judge to be said neither wisely nor in accordance with theology—but that men who did not know the excellence of virtue and the foulness of vice would commit every crime rather than die. Wherefore to restrain the abominable desires of men there is given the hope of reward and the fear of punishment.

That also, if the mortality of the soul be assumed, death is in some cases to be suffered, is clear from many actions of beasts, in which there is no doubt that the souls are mortal and guided by natural instinct. For Aristotle tells, in *De historiis* ix, chapter 30,[221] which our Vergil recalls in *Georgics* iv,[222] that bees risk death to protect their ruler and their community. And he writes in the same place that the male cuttlefish suffers death to save his mate. And he tells in *De historiis* ix, chapter 37,[223] that a camel killed a camel-driver with a piercing bite, because he compelled it by a trick to couple with its mother; and a horse, deceived in the same way, committed the same crime; but when it recognized what it had done, suddenly killed itself. Now since these things were done by nature, they were done according to reason, inasmuch as in the opinion of Themistius and Averroes nature is directed by an unerring intelligence. Hence in man also this is not contrary to reason.

But to the third principal objection, which asserted that either God is not the governor of the universe or he is unjust; to this I say that neither follows. And, I say, no evil remains in essence unpunished, nor any good in essence unrewarded. In proof it must be known that reward and punishment have two meanings: one is essential and inseparable, the other accidental and separable. The essential reward of virtue is virtue itself, which makes man happy. For human nature can possess nothing greater than virtue itself, since it alone makes man secure and removed from every perturbation. For all things work together

220. Chap. 14 (ed. Fretté, XXVII, 226).   222. Cf. iv 67 ff.
221. Cf. ix 40, 626 a 13 ff.   223. ix 47, 630 b 31 ff.

for him who loves the good: fearing nothing, hoping for nothing, but in prosperity and adversity ever the same, as is said in the end of *Ethica* i.[224] And Plato says in the *Crito:* "To the good man neither alive nor dead can any evil happen."[225] But it is the opposite with vice. For the punishment of the vicious is vice itself, than which nothing can be more miserable, nothing more unhappy. But how perverted is the life of the vicious man, and how greatly it is to be shunned, Aristotle makes clear in *Ethica* vii,[226] where he shows that for the vicious man all things are discordant. Faithful to no one, not even to himself, neither awake nor asleep is he at peace; he is beset by horrible tortures of body and soul: a most unhappy life. So that no wise man, however destitute, infirm in body, deprived of the goods of fortune, would choose the life of a tyrant or of some vicious ruler, and the wise man would prefer to remain in his own condition. And so every virtuous man is rewarded by his virtue and happiness. Wherefore Aristotle, in *Problemata* 30, problem 10,[227] when he asks why rewards are set for contests, but not for virtues and knowledge, says that this is because virtue is its own reward. For since the reward ought to be more excellent than the contest, and since nothing is more excellent than prudence, it is thus its own reward. But the contrary takes place with vice. Hence no vicious man is left unpunished, since vice itself is the punishment of the vicious man.

Moreover, accidental reward or punishment is what can be separated, like gold, or penalties of any sort. And not every good is rewarded thus nor is all evil punished. Nor is this unfitting, since they are accidents. These two things should be known: first, that accidental reward is far more imperfect than essential reward, for gold is more imperfect than virtue. And accidental punishment is far less than essential punishment; for accidental punishment is the punishment of a penalty, but essential, that of guilt. But the punishment of guilt is far worse than

224. Cf. i 11, 1100 b 20–21. 226. Cf. vii 6 ff.
225. *Apology*, 41 d. 227. Cf. xxx 11, 956 b 16–17 and 30 ff.

the punishment of a penalty. Whence it does not matter if sometimes the accidental is lacking, provided the essential remains. Secondly, in addition it should be known, that when good is accidentally rewarded, essential good seems to be diminished, nor does it remain in its perfection. For example, if one man acts virtuously without hope of reward, and another with hope of reward, the act of the second is not considered as virtuous as that of the first. Whence he is rewarded more essentially who is not rewarded accidentally than he who is rewarded accidentally. Likewise, he who acts viciously and is punished accidentally, seems to be punished less than he who is not punished accidentally; for the punishment of guilt is greater and worse than the punishment of a penalty; and when the punishment of a penalty is added to guilt, it diminishes the guilt. Whence he who is not punished accidentally is punished more essentially than he who is punished accidentally. Witness also on this what Laertius[228] wrote of Aristotle: for when Aristotle was asked what he had acquired from philosophy, he answered, "What you do from the hope of reward and shun from fear of punishment, I do from love and nobility of virtue, and shun from hatred of vice." But why some are rewarded or punished accidentally, and others not, does not concern the present proposition.

But in answer to the fourth objection, that almost the whole world would be deceived, since all religions hold the soul to be immortal, I say that if the whole is nothing but its parts, as many think, since there is no man who is not deceived, as Plato says in the *Republic*,[229] it is not wrong, nay, it is necessary to admit that either the whole world is deceived or at least the greater part. For assuming that there are only three religions, those of Christ, of Moses, and of Mohammed; then either they are all false, and thus the whole world is deceived; or at least two of them, and thus the greater part is deceived.

But it must be known that, as Plato and Aristotle say, the

228. Diogenes Laertius v 1, 20.   229. Cf. i 334 c.

statesman is the physician of souls, and the purpose of the statesman is to make man righteous rather than learned. Now, according to the diversity of men, one must proceed by different
devices to attain this end. For some are men of ability and of a
nature well formed by God, who are led to the virtues by the
nobility of the virtues alone, and are restrained from vices by
their foulness alone. And these are of the best nature, though
they are very few. Some, however, have a nature less well
ordered, and these, besides the nobility of virtue and the foulness of vice, perform righteous acts and shun vice from rewards,
praise, and honors, from punishments like censure and infamy.
And these are on the second level. Some, however, are made
righteous on account of the hope of some good and the fear of
bodily punishment. Wherefore, so that they may attain such
virtue, statesmen establish either gold or dignity or some other
such thing; and that they may shun vice, they establish that they
shall be punished in money, or in honor, or in body, either by
mutilating a member or by killing. But some from the fierceness
and perversity of their nature are moved by none of these, as
daily experience teaches. Therefore they have set up for the
virtuous eternal rewards in another life, and for the vicious,
eternal punishments, which frighten greatly. And the greater
part of men, if they do good, do it more from fear of eternal
punishment than from hope of eternal good, since punishments
are better known to us than that eternal good. And since this
last device can benefit all men, of whatever degree, the lawgiver
regarding the proneness of men to evil, intending the common
good, has decreed that the soul is immortal, not caring for truth
but only for righteousness, that he may lead men to virtue.

Nor is the statesman to be blamed. For just as the physician
feigns many things to restore a sick man to health, so the statesman composes fables to keep the citizens in the right path. But
in these fables, as says Averroes in the prologue to *Physica* iii,[230]
there is, properly speaking, neither truth nor falsity. So also

230. This prologue is not given in the edition of 1560.

nurses bring their charges to what they know to benefit children. But if a man were healthy or of sound mind, neither physician nor nurse would need such fictions. Wherefore if all men were on the first level mentioned, even granting the mortality of the soul, they would be righteous. But almost none are of that nature. Whence it has been necessary to proceed by other devices. Nor is this unfitting, since human nature is almost entirely immersed in matter, and participates very little in intellect; whence man is farther from the Intelligences than a sick man from a healthy one, a boy from a man, and a fool from a wise man. Wherefore it is not strange that the statesman uses such devices, etc.

In the fifth principal objection two points were touched upon: one concerning the things that have been seen in tombs, and the other concerning dreams. To the first of these I say, first, that many things are counted among histories which nevertheless are mere fables. Secondly, it is said that in the neighborhood of tombs, as in many places, the air is rather heavy, partly from the evaporation of the corpses, partly from the coldness of the stones, and from many other reasons which cause density of the air. But as is said in *Meteora* iii,[231] in the chapter on the rainbow, "Such air easily receives the image of the things near by, just as a mirror receives figures." Whence things seen in air so disposed are thought by simple men to be the things which seem to be there, just as children looking in a mirror or in water believe that the things seen in them are really there. For Aristotle tells of a certain man of weak sight who, seeing his shadow at night, thought it was a man following him. Whence it is that simple men on account of such incidents think that those things are the souls of the dead. Imagination and universal repute also help. Wherefore, as Aristotle tells in *De somno et vigilia*, chapter 2,[232] many things are thought to be seen by those living in fear or other passions, even though they be awake, which yet do not exist; just as happens to those ill.

231. Cf. iii 4, 373 b 8–9.   232. *De somniis*, chap. 2, 460 b 3 ff.

Thirdly, it is said that this happens often because of the illusions and tricks of wicked priests, as is said in the last chapter of Daniel[233] of the idol Bel. For many priests and guardians of temples have changed the four cardinal virtues into ambition, avarice, gluttony, and riotous living. And upon these sins all others follow. Wherefore that they may fulfil their desires they employ these frauds and fictions; just as in our time we know to have happened occasionally. Fourthly, it is said because many histories of the Greeks and the Romans recount marvels. For on the birth and death of men worthy of record it is most certain that portents appeared. For Suetonius Tranquillus in his *On the Twelve Caesars* tells of great signs both by birds and by answer of the gods, and many others. No less does Plutarch in his *Lives of Illustrious Men*. And our Vergil at the end of the first *Georgic* sang these verses:

> But at the time the earth and sea besides,
> Unseasonable birds and hell-sent dogs,
> Gave portents. Often Etna 'neath our gaze
> Burst her great furnaces and shed her heart
> O'er Cyclopean fields, a boiling flood
> Of liquid rocks and solid balls of flame!
> The Germans heard the din of heavenly wars;
> Unwonted tremors shook the Alps; a voice
> Of awful power rang through the silent groves;
> Pale phantoms of strange aspect were espied
> Through the night shadows; beasts were heard to speak,
> O horror! rivers stood, earth oped her mouth,
> Bronze statues sweated, ivory shed tears.[234]

No less does Lucan relate many things. In Maccabees ii, chapter 5, also, it is written thus: "At the same time Antiochus prepared a second journey into Egypt. And it came to pass that through the whole city of Jerusalem for the space of forty days there were seen horsemen running in the air, in gilded raiment, and armed with spears, like bands of soldiers, and horses set in order by ranks, running one against another, with the shakings of shields, and a multitude of men in helmets with drawn

233. Dan. 14: 2 ff.   234. i 469–80 (translated by T. F. Royds).

swords, and casting of darts, and glittering of golden armor, and of harnesses of all sorts. Wherefore all men prayed that these prodigies might turn to good."[235]

Wherefore the oracular responses of old do not seem to be wholly without meaning. To deny such things, moreover, seems great obstinacy and impudence. Wherefore we must speak otherwise. Granted that they are not fictions or illusions or our imaginings, we must say that Christians, and almost universally all religions, and Plato and Avicenna and many others hold that these things are done either by God or by his servants, whom we call angels if they are good, and demons if they are bad. It is true that there is some difference between the two, with which we are not now concerned.

And these men grant that the human soul is unqualifiedly immortal and multiple, as is well known. But this clearly contradicts the words of Aristotle, since there is no immaterial substance which does not move a sphere; for in *Metaphysica* xii he holds that the number of Intelligences corresponds to the number of spheres.[236] Nor is there any effect here below which is not reducible, in his opinion, to first motion, as appears in *Physica* viii[237] and *Meteora* i.[238] Further, because it seems to me this cannot be demonstrated by conclusive natural reason. Whence we shall not remain within natural limits, which we nevertheless promised in the beginning. Hence Alexander of Aphrodisias, as St. Thomas relates in the disputed question *About Miracles*, Articles III and X,[239] in the body of the question, says that these things are produced by separated substances, by means of heavenly bodies, according to the powers of the stars, according to their conjunctions and oppositions. And truly if these effects are granted, according to the Peripatetics, it cannot be said otherwise; since the whole world here below borders on that above, so that every power is governed from there, as is said in

235. II Macc. 5: 1–4.   237. viii 6 ff.
236. xii 8.   238. i 2, 339 a 30 ff.
239. *Quaestiones disputatae, De potentia,* Questio: VI: *De miraculis,* articles 3 and 10 (ed. Fretté, XIII, 188 and 212).

the beginning of the *Meteora*.[240] And this also does not seem to be unreasonably said. For Alexander holds that God and the Intelligences exercise providence over things below, as St. Thomas notes as his opinion in the exposition of *De caelo* ii, text 56.[241] And Alexander expressly admits it in *De fato*.[242] Wherefore according to the conditions of time and place he rules things below, both kings and prophets, and other events. Therefore that at times such things have appeared as is said in *Maccabees*, marked future wars as the event made plain; although perhaps these too could have been avoided, according to Alexander, since he holds in *De fato* to free will.[243] Nor is it strange if such things can be shadowed forth by the heavenly bodies, since they are animated by a most noble soul and generate and govern all things below.

The same may be said of those things which Titus Livy, Suetonius, Vergil, Plutarch, and Lucan relate. For if signs precede spring, summer, and the other seasons, as is obvious, how much more ought those Intelligences to be solicitous for human nature! This is indeed very clear to see. For I do not remember having read the life of any man excelling in anything whatever, whose birth and death were not heralded by many signs, nay, many of his acts. And what the Platonists call the genius or familiar demon, is with the Peripatetics his natal star; because such a man is born under such a constellation, but another under another. If we can do without that multiplication of demons and genii, it seems superfluous to assume them; besides the fact that it is also contrary to reason.

Therefore the heavenly bodies according to their powers produce these marvels for the advantage of mortals, and especially of men, since human nature partakes of divinity.

240. i 2, 339 a 21 ff.

241. Lectio 14, par. 11 (Editio Leonina, III, 177).

242. *Alexandri Aphrodisiensis Praeter commentaria scripta minora*, ed. I. Bruns (in *Supplementum Aristotelicum*, Vol. II), Part II (Berlin, 1892), p. 188, 1 ff.

243. *Ibid.*, p. 180, 3 ff.

For Aristotle relates in *De historiis* iii, chapter 20,[244] that on the island of Lemnos so much milk had been drawn from the dugs of a he-goat—it had twin ones close to the genitals—that they made cheese from it; and when the master of the animal consulted an oracle, he received the answer that there would be a further increase of his cattle; which was discovered to be so. If therefore they give portents about cattle, how much more about men!

But St. Thomas attacks this opinion with many subtle arguments. First, because such events take place in irregular fashion; but what takes place by nature takes place regularly, in *Physica* ii and viii.[245] Secondly, because there are some effects in apparitions of this sort which cannot be traced back to the heavenly bodies, like sayings and especially predictions about the future, since such things cannot be done except by one who possesses intellect. But such things are very often inanimate, or lacking in intellect, as when beasts speak, or when in the air human voices are heard, or something else like that. Thirdly, because some things take place that cannot be done by the power of the heavenly bodies, as that branches are turned into serpents. Whence there seems to be no answer.

But these things do not seem to me to prove the conclusion. For the first is answered, that on the contrary such things occur in a regular manner, both as to time and to place, and by determinate causes, etc. The proof is that many astrologers know how to predict them, and future prodigies, changes in states, and in determinate places, as has often been seen. But that to us they seem indeterminate is due to our ignorance. And in regard to the second point, so emphasized by St. Thomas, I do not wish to say that I marvel, but that I do not rightly understand. For according to him effects and sayings of this sort are accomplished by Intelligences, sometimes good and sometimes evil, and by divine permission, sometimes by human souls now separated from the body. But all such things are then not forms of those bodies,

244. 522 a 13 ff.   245. ii 8, 198 b 35–36 and viii 1, 252 a 11–12.

whether animate or inanimate, which are heard to speak thus. Hence they are only movers. Why then cannot the Intelligences moving the heavenly bodies do this by means of their instruments, which accomplish so many and such great things, make parrots, magpies, crows, blackbirds, and so on speak? I do not see why he denies these so flatly, especially since he holds, in the *Summa*, Part I, question 51,[246] that an angel speaks or makes some other sound by means of an aerial body condensed and shaped. Now the heavenly bodies accomplish these and much greater things by means of their powers and the conjunctions of the stars, because they make animals and other amazing things, as appears from stones and plants; whence they can accomplish these things also.

And this is confirmed by the Conciliator, in expounding the twenty-sixth problem of the eleventh part, "The problem is, why some speak as soon as they are born."[247] He says, "Haly ben Ragel writes *De nativitatibus*: 'Our king called us because one of his wives bore a son, and the ascendent was 8 degrees of Libra, the terminus of Mercury, and in it were Jupiter, Venus, Mars and Mercury. And a group of astrologers gathered there, each one of whom gave his opinion. And I kept silent. Then the king said to me, What is the matter? Why do you not speak? I answered, Give me a limit of three days; because if your son survives the third day a great miracle will occur. And when the child completed twenty-four hours he began to speak and to make signs with his hands. And the king grew much frightened; wherefore I said, It is possible that he may say some prophecy and some miracle. And then we were with the king at the child's side. And the child said, I am born unfortunate, and I am born to foretell the loss of the kingdom of Agedeir and the destruction of the house of Almann. He at once fell back and was dead.'" And it was discovered to be as he said. Now this child either spoke by a

246. Article 2 (Editio Leonina, V, 16–17).

247. *Expositio....Petri de Ebano....in librum Problematum Aristotelis* (Venice: John Herbort, 1482, Hain 17), Part XI, Problem 27, fol. u 4.

spirit or of himself. Not the first, because Haly would not have known by astrology how to predict what he said; hence of himself, that is, from within, and not from any knowledge he had from any man; hence from the power of the Intelligences and the heavenly bodies. Wherefore it can happen thus in other things as well.

But if it be said that all teaching and instruction comes from pre-existing knowledge, I answer that this is not teaching or instruction, nor knowledge properly speaking. The mark of this can be that those soothsayers, when they have recovered from the madness, recall nothing, nay, deny that they have said those things. But they are moved by a heavenly impulse. Whence Plato says in the *Meno*[248] and in many other places, "Soothsayers announce very many true things, yet understand nothing of what they say." And in *Problemata* xxx, problem 1, "Sybils and seers and all who are believed to be stirred up by a divine inspiration, are directed by impulse."[249] And the Conciliator in that passage says, "I heard from a faithful physician that a certain illiterate woman spoke coherent Latin while she was delirious; when she was recovered it disappeared."[250] This does not seem to take place except from the disposition of the body with the motion of the stars.

Now to St. Thomas' third objection it is answered that the Peripatetics would say that such things are illusions, such as many produce by alteration of the medium or of the eyes. Or, if it was true, we are not within natural limits, because we exclude miracles. What was further added about dreams, those and greater things we grant. For Averroes, who did not hold that souls are multiplied, in the chapter *On the Divination of Dreams*[251] fully concedes it; and Galen, who thought the soul mortal. Nay, many things are accomplished in medicine by dreams. But this does not prove that the soul is unqualifiedly immortal, but that the gods concern themselves with things below.

248. 99 c.
249. Cf. 954 a 36–37.
250. Part XXX, Problem 1 (*op. cit.*, fol. N 3).
251. Cf. *Opera Aristotelis*, Vol. VII, fol. 169v ff.

Wherefore by signs in waking and by dreams they teach many things and exercise providence over human affairs; as Averroes fully says there. And what is said of those Arcadians is not strange since Plato says in the *Republic* v, "God is the avenger of those who do wrong to strangers."[252] What is adduced about the Pamphylian is a fable for restraining the citizens.

But why some are left unpunished or even others on the contrary rewarded does not belong to the present consideration. And the Commentator there touches upon many beautiful and difficult things, which are not in accordance with our intention.

Now to the fifth point concerning those possessed by demons, the answer can be clear through what has been said. For all such men are suffering either from black bile or insanity, or from a trance or are near to death and far from human thoughts; whence it is that they become almost lifeless and irrational. Hence they can receive the heavenly motions and are driven and led by the lymphatic impulse rather than act or lead themselves. The conclusive mark of which is that, as Plato says and Aristotle agrees, they do not understand what they are saying but are moved like beasts by another. Whence the proverb has it that children and fools prophesy, while wise and sane men are strange to this sort of thing. Nor should anyone wonder at this, inasmuch as Aristotle writes in *De historiis* ix, chapter 31, "At the time when the Median enemies were attacking at Pharsalus, there were no crows in the places of Athens and the Peloponnesus, as if they had some sense by which they made known to each other, and were moved by, the outcome of things."[253] For if crows sensed such future events from the heavens, why not those men too, who stand hardly above crows, since they have very little intellect. Let him who thus objects then consider the beasts from which augurs also derive their predictions. Now that the art of augury is not entirely without value, the histories of the Greeks and Romans make clear; and Plato establishes in the *Laws*[254] that in a well-

252. Cf. *Laws* v 729 e.
253. 618 b 13 ff.
254. Cf. viii 828 b.

ordered city the art of augury must not be overlooked. Aristotle also, in *De historiis* i, chapter 10, and also vi, chapter 2, and ix, chapter 1,[255] recalls some things about the art of augury. But if birds and many creatures lacking reason can foretell by the impression of the heavens, why not also men who are like them? This is also confirmed, since otherwise astrologers could not make such certain predictions, as has been seen, unless the heavenly powers act on things below. But if they sometimes seem to lie, it is because they are either unskilled or have not correctly taken the horoscope, or else it happens because free will is overcoming heavenly powers.

Now to the seventh objection it is answered that Aristotle in no wise believes that the soul remains after death but believes the opposite. And as to that passage in *Ethica* i[256] it is plain enough, since he says that it neither profits nor harms them, since they are nothing, but only the opinion held of them. For the kind of existence that Homer has in the mind the dead also have. As for the second passage in *Oeconomica* ii,[257] it is replied that either these women were rewarded by the gods in their lifetime, for it is not said there that it was after death, or if after death, this is understood as referring to the opinion held of them, or that it may induce other women to like performances.

Now to the eighth and last objection, in which it was said that men impure and sinful and conscious of their crimes assert that the soul is mortal, while those who are holy and just hold it immortal; to this it is answered that neither do impure men universally maintain mortality nor do the temperate universally maintain immortality. For obviously we see that many wicked men believe in religion but are seduced by the passions. And we also know that many holy and just men have maintained the mortality of the soul. For Plato in the *Republic* i[258] says that Simonides the poet was a divine and very good man, who nevertheless asserted it to be mortal. And Homer also, as Aristotle relates in

255. vi 2, 559 b 20.
256. Cf. i 11, 1100 a 16 ff.
257. See above, n. 189.
258. 331 e.

[373]

De anima ii,[259] thought that sense does not differ from intellect. But who does not know Homer's worth? Hippocrates also and Galen, most learned and good men, are reputed to have been of this opinion. Alexander of Aphrodisias, the great Alfarabi, Abubacher, Avempace, and of our countrymen also Pliny the Elder, Seneca and numberless others thought so. For Seneca, in the *Epistles to Lucilius* vii, epistle 54,[260] which begins, "Ill health had given me long companionship," and more clearly in *On Consolation to Martia*,[261] asserts that the soul is mortal, and he numbers many other upright and most learned men as being of the same opinion. And for this reason, that they thought that virtue alone is happiness, and vice misery, and neglected the other remaining goods except as they serve virtue, and cast from themselves those which hinder virtue.

And it must be considered that many men have thought the soul mortal, who nevertheless have written that it is immortal. But they did so on account of the proneness to evil of men who have little or no intellect, and neither knowing nor loving the goods of the soul devote themselves to bodily things alone. Whence it is necessary to cure them by devices of this sort, just as the physician acts toward the sick man and the nurse toward the child lacking reason.

By these reasons, I think, other points also can be resolved. For although it is commonly said that, if the soul is mortal, man ought to give himself over completely to bodily pleasures, commit all evils for his own advantage, and that it would be vain to worship God, to honor the divine, to pour forth prayers to God, to make sacrifices, and do other things of this sort, the answer is clear enough from what has been said. For since happiness is naturally desired and misery shunned, and by what has been said happiness consists in virtuous action, but misery in vicious action, since to worship God with the whole mind, to honor the divine, to raise prayers to God, to sacrifice are actions in the highest degree vir-

259. iii 3, 427 a 25–26.   261. Cf. chap. 19, 4 ff. and 23, 1 ff.
260. *Epistles* vi 54.

tuous, we ought hence to strive with all our powers to acquire them. But on the contrary, thefts, robberies, murders, a life of pleasures are vices, which make man turn into a beast and cease to be a man; hence we ought to abstain from them. And note that one who acts conscientiously, expecting no other reward than virtue, seems to act far more virtuously and purely than he who expects some reward beyond virtue. And he who shuns vice on account of the foulness of vice, not because of the fear of due punishment for vice, seems more to be praised than he who avoids vice on account of the fear of punishment, as in the verses:

> The good hate sin from love of virtue,
> The evil hate sin from fear of punishment.[262]

Wherefore those who claim that the soul is mortal seem better to save the grounds of virtue than those who claim it to be immortal. For the hope of reward and the fear of punishment seem to suggest a certain servility, which is contrary to the grounds of virtue, etc.

To complete this opinion it must be known that, as Aristotle teaches in *De generatione animalium*,[263] nature proceeds by degrees and in orderly fashion, so that it does not join an extreme immediately with an extreme, but an extreme with a mean. For we see that shrubs serve as a mean between grasses and trees; between vegetables and animals are unmoving animal things, like oysters and the rest of this sort; and so on ascending further. The Blessed Dionysius also suggests this in *De divinis nominibus*, chapter 7,[264] when he says that the divine wisdom joins the ends of higher things to the beginnings of lower things. But man, as has been said, is the most perfect of the animals. Wherefore since among material things the human soul holds first place, it will hence be joined to the immaterial, and is a mean between the material and the immaterial. But a mean compared to the extremes is called the other of the extremes; whence compared to

262. This seems to be a medieval verse proverb.

263. Cf. iii 10, 760 a 31.   264. *Dionysiaca*, I (Paris, 1937), 407.

the immaterial the soul can be called material, and with respect to the material, immaterial. Nor is it only those names that it deserves; indeed, it participates in the properties of the extremes. For green compared to white is not only called black; it truly gathers sight like black, though not so intensely.

Wherefore also the human soul has some of the properties of the Intelligences and some of the properties of all material things; whence it is that when it performs functions through which it agrees with the Intelligences, it is said to be divine and to be changed into a God; but when it performs the functions of beasts, it is said to be changed into a beast; for because of malice it is said to be a serpent or a fox, because of cruelty a tiger, and so on. For there is nothing in the world which because of some property cannot agree with man himself; wherefore man is not undeservedly called a microcosm, or little world. Therefore some have said that man is a great marvel, since he is the whole world and can change into every nature, since to him is given the power to follow whatever property of things he may prefer. Therefore the ancients were telling the right fable when they said that some men had been made into gods, some into lions, some into wolves, some into eagles, some into fish, some into plants, some into stones, and so on; since some men have attained intellect, some sense, some the powers of the vegetative soul, and so on.

Therefore those who place bodily pleasures above moral or intellectual virtues rather produce a beast than a god; those who put riches first, rather gold; whence the former are to be called beasts, the latter insensate. Therefore, though the soul is mortal, the virtues are not to be despised, and pleasures sought, unless one prefers to be a beast rather than a man, and insensate rather than sensate or knowing. For we must know that however much man thus participates in the material and in the immaterial, yet he is properly said to participate in the immaterial, because he lacks much of immateriality; but he is not properly said to participate in the brute and the vegetable, but rather to contain them, for he is below the immaterial and above the material. Wherefore he cannot arrive at the perfection of the immaterial, whence men are not to be called gods, but godlike or divine. But man cannot only make himself equal to the beast, nay exceed the beast; for there are some men far crueler than any beast, as Aristotle says in *Ethica* vii: "An evil man is ten thousand times worse than a beast."[265] And just as it was said of cruelty, so of the other vices. Since, therefore, vice is so foul, and so unjust the life of a vicious man, but the contrary of virtue, who then, even if the soul be mortal, would prefer vice rather than virtue, unless he preferred to be a beast or worse than a beast, rather than to be a man? Wherefore, etc.

CHAPTER XV AND LAST

IN WHICH IS AFFIRMED THE FINAL CONCLUSION IN THIS MATTER, WHICH IN MY OPINION MUST BE MAINTAINED AS BEYOND DOUBT

Now since these things are so, it seems to me that in this matter, keeping the saner view, we must say that the question of the immortality of the soul is a neutral problem, like that of the eternity of the world. For it seems to me that no natural reasons can be brought forth proving that the soul is immortal, and still less any proving that the soul is mortal, as very many scholars who hold it immortal declare. Wherefore I do not want to make answer to the other side, since others do so, St. Thomas in particular, clearly, fully, and weightily. Wherefore we shall say, as Plato said in the *Laws* i,[266] that to be certain of anything, when many are in doubt, is for God alone. Since therefore such famous men disagree with each other, I think that this can be made certain only through God.

But it does not seem to be fitting or expedient for man to lack such certainty. For if he were in doubt on this matter, he would have actions uncertain and without any end; since if the end be

265. vii 7, 1150 a 7–8. 266. 641 d.

unknown, the means thereto would also be necessarily unknown. Whence if the soul is immortal, earthly things are to be despised, and eternal things to be pursued; but if its existence is mortal, a contrary way is to be pursued. But if other things besides man have their own determinate ends, how much more man himself, since man is the most perfect of mortals, and the only one, as Plato says in the *Republic*,[267] who worships God and justice! Wherefore I say, that before the gift or advent of grace "in many places and in many ways by the prophets" and by supernatural signs God himself settled this question, as is plain to see in the Old Testament. But "most recently by the Son whom he made the heir of all, through whom he also made the ages," he has made clear this question, as the Apostle says in the *Epistle to the Hebrews*.[268] That he is truly the Son of God, true God and true man, most fittingly and without doubt, the light of the Christian name, St. Thomas Aquinas, declares in *Contra Gentiles* i, chapter 6.[269] Which points John Scotus, in my opinion most subtle of all and a man above all most religious, reducing them to the number of eight enumerates in the prologue to the *Sentences*.[270] And indeed so clearly do these eight points set it forth that unless demented or stubborn no one could deny it. Since therefore he is the true God, he alone is truly that light by which all things are seen, as in *John* i,[271] and he alone also is the truth by which other things are true, as in *John* xiv: "I am the way, the truth and the life."[272] But since he himself has made manifest in word and deed that the soul is immortal, in word when he threatens the evil with eternal fire, but to the good promises eternal life; for he says,

267. *Menexenus* 237 d.

268. Heb. 1:2.

269. Cf. also iv 3 ff.

270. *Joannis Duns Scoti Commentaria Oxoniensia ad IV libros magistri Sententiarum*, Prologue, Question 2 (ed. P. Marianus Fernandez Garcia O.F.M., I [Quaracchi, 1912], 32 ff.).

271. Cf. John 1:9.

272. John 14:6.

"Come, blessed of my Father, etc.,"[273] and it follows, "Go, accursed ones, into eternal fires, etc.";[274] in deed, when he rose on the third day from the dead. But as far as the light differs from the lucid and truth from the true, and as much as the infinite cause is more powerful than the finite effect, the more efficaciously does this demonstrate the immortality of the soul.

Wherefore, if any arguments seem to prove the mortality of the soul, they are false and merely seeming, since the first light and the first truth show the opposite. But if any seem to prove its immortality, they are true and clear, but not light and truth. Wherefore this way alone is most firm, unshaken, and lasting; the rest are untrustworthy.

Moreover, every art ought to proceed by things proper and fitting to that art; for otherwise it errs and does not proceed according to the rule of art, as Aristotle says in *Posteriora*[275] and *Ethica* i.[276] But that the soul is immortal is an article of faith, as appears from the Apostles' Creed and the Athanasian Creed; hence it ought to be proved by what is proper to faith. But the means on which faith relies is revelation and canonical Scripture. Hence it is proved truly and properly only by them; but other reasons are foreign, and rely on a means that does not prove what is intended. Hence it is not surprising if philosophers disagree among themselves about the immortality of the soul, when they rely on arguments foreign to the conclusion and fallacious; but all followers of Christ agree, since they proceed by what is proper and infallible, since matters cannot be except in one way.

Further, he who is ill is concerned for health. Yet let no one be physician to himself, since it is said in *Politics* iii: "In his own affairs no one judges rightly, since he is in a state of passion."[277] Let him therefore ask another. But the good physician ought to be skilled in his art, and of good character, since neither the first without the second nor the second without the first suffices. But

273. Matt. 25 : 34.
274. Matt 25 : 41.
275. Cf. *Analytica priora*, i 30, 46 a 21 ff.

276. Cf. i 1, 1094 b 11–12.
277. iii 16, 1287 b 2–3.

as Plato says, just as distemper in the humors is sickness of the body, so ignorance is sickness of the soul. Therefore not knowing whether the soul is immortal or not, let him seek a man well informed and good. Yet two classes of men profess to know this: infidels and Christians. Now there have been many very learned men among the infidels, but almost all of spotted life. Not to speak of other things, at least of empty glory, they have understood only natural things, which produce an obscure and infirm knowledge. But many Christians, unless I am mistaken, have known no less than they in natural philosophy: like Paul, Dionysius, Basil, Athanasius, Origen, the two Gregories, of Nazianzus and of Nyssa, Augustine, Jerome, Ambrose, Gregory and countless others; and besides a knowledge of natural things they have also had a knowledge of divinity. Which things, as Jerome says, "learned Plato did not know, and eloquent Demosthenes was ignorant of,"[278] and they led most spotless lives. But who except a madman would rather believe infidels thus ignorant than Christians so well endowed? And to me it makes faith firm that Augustine, in my opinion second to none in learning (for I do not judge him less than Plato or Aristotle), first hostile to the Christian name, having become so virtuous of life, writes in the end of the *City of God*[279] that he had seen made visible by faith so many miracles, which shows a faith unlimited, inviolable, and most firm. And Pope Gregory also, comparable in learning and holiness with any man, adduces so many and such great things in his *Dialogues*,[280] that all doubt is completely removed.

Wherefore we must assert that beyond doubt the soul is immortal. But we must not go the way the wise men of this age have gone, who, when they call themselves wise, have become fools. For whoever goes this way, I think, will waver always uncertain and wandering. Wherefore I believe that even though

278. *Epistle* 53 (ad Paulinum) chap. 4 (*Sancti Eusebii Hieronymi Epistolae*, Part I, ed. I. Hilberg [Vienna, 1910], p. 449).

279. Cf. *De civitate Dei* xxii 29.

280. Cf. esp. ii 32 ff. and iv 1 ff. (*Gregorii Magni Dialogi*, ed. U. Moricca [Rome, 1924], pp. 124 ff and 229 ff.).

Plato wrote so many and such great things about the immortality of the soul, yet I think that he did not possess certainty. This I conjecture from the end of the *Apology*,[281] for there it seems to be left in doubt. In the *Timaeus*[282] also, when he was about to discuss the matter, he said that for him it would be enough if in so difficult a matter he should speak in probabilities. Wherefore, comparing everything he says, he seems to me to speak more as in opinion than in assertion. And it is his endeavor to make good citizens but not learned ones. Indeed, as says St. Thomas, in *Summa* ii a ii ae, question 1, article 3,[283] the act remains moral even with a false opinion. But those that go the way of the faithful remain firm and unshaken. This their contempt of riches, honors, pleasures, and all things worldly makes clear, and finally the martyr's crown, which they ardently strove after, and when striven for attained with the highest joy.

And therefore these are the things that seem to me must be said in this matter, yet always submitting myself in this and in other matters to the Apostolic See. Wherefore, etc.

The end has been put to this treatise by me, Peter, son of John Nicholas Pomponazzi of Mantua, the twenty-fourth day of the month of September, 1516.

At Bologna, in the fourth year of the Pontificate of Leo X. To the praise of the indivisible Trinity, etc.

281. Cf. 40 c ff.
282. 29 c-d.

283. Editio Leonina, VIII (1895), 12.

V I

JUAN LUIS VIVES

Translated by NANCY LENKEITH

INTRODUCTION

By NANCY LENKEITH

THE *Fabula de homine* was written by the Spanish Humanist Ludovicus Vives (1492–1540) shortly after he first met Erasmus in Louvain in 1518, while traveling in Flanders as tutor to the young cardinal, William of Croy. It is dedicated to his disciple, Antoine de Berges, a young Belgian nobleman of considerable erudition.[1] This essay on man reveals the author's devotion to the study of Cicero, his knowledge of contemporary philosophical thought, and his taste for literary refinement. Vives' praise of man's work on earth inevitably recalls similar utterances in Cicero's *De legibus* (i. 8–9) and *De natura deorum* (ii. 56. 60–61), adding overtones of classical eloquence to his own account of the mystery of human greatness. The story is directly based on Pico's conception of the dignity of man as sharing with God alone the power to be all things. As in Pico's *Oration*, body and soul are treated as equal parts of the human essence, which is universal because it is undetermined. Vives' version, in its mythological setting, is less precise than Pico's: man is the son of Jupiter, born to play upon a stage at his will. The idea of the theater as a symbol and simile of the human life had been developed by the Stoics (Marcus Aurelius, Epictetus) and by the Neo-Platonists (Plotinus *Ennead* iii. 2). This allegorical framework, however, does not fully account for the personal character of Vives' conception. There is also a biblical influence. The creation in time of the stage suggests Genesis, while the co-essentiality of Jupiter and his son reminds one of the dogma of the Incarnation.

1. For biographical information consult A. Bonilla y San Martin, *Luis Vives y la filosofia del Rinacimiento* (Madrid, 1903).

Jupiter specifically determines the creation of the world as a stage, but he does not prescribe any particular form for man the actor. To him alone he gratuitously gives an unlimited power of self-transformation, exempting his nature from the rule of the immutability of essences. Man's activity determines his being. As his substance comprises the substances of other natures, he has power over the material world and the animals, moral power over himself, political power over those with whom he chooses to become associated, as a member of a family, of a state, and of humanity. This *regnum hominis* is not, as in Bacon, conquered by man through his scientific knowledge but received from Jupiter as a free gift. The ability to become another is the highest sign of divinity which could be bestowed upon man, given the previous existence of an outer world and sky. His Protean activity reaches its climax as he transforms himself into the person of the god Jupiter, thereby earning as a reward the immortality of his body and soul.

This fable written by a friend of Erasmus to expound a conception of the dignity of man borrowed from the Italian Humanists may well illustrate the interdependence of the cultural movements of the Renaissance.

A FABLE ABOUT MAN[1]

I SHOULD like to begin this essay of mine on man by some
fables and plays, since man is himself a fable and a play. Once
upon a time, after a certain lavish and sumptuous feast given by
Juno on her birthday for all the gods, they, feeling carefree and
elated by the nectar, asked whether she had prepared some
plays which they might watch after the banquet. Thus nothing
would be lacking to complete their happiness on this august occasion.

To gratify this wish of the immortal gods, Juno earnestly asked
her brother and husband Jupiter, since he was all-powerful, to
improvise an amphitheater and to bring forth new characters,
after the manner of regular plays, lest in this respect a day which
she wanted most distinguished seem deficient to the gods. Thereupon, all of a sudden, at a command of almighty Jupiter, by
whom alone all things are done, this whole world appeared, so
large, so elaborate, so diversified, and beautiful in places, just as
you see it. This was the amphitheater: uppermost, to wit in the
skies, were the stalls and seats of the divine spectators; nether-
most—some say in the middle—the earth was placed as a stage for
the appearance of the actors, along with all the animals and
everything else.

When everything was ready and the banquet tables carried
away, Mercurius Braubeta announced that the players were already on the stage. Joyfully the spectators went forth and were
seated, each according to his rank. The great Jupiter was director
of the plays, and when he saw that all were there, he gave the
signal. Since he was the maker,[2] he ordered everything and ex-

1. [Joannis Ludovici Vivis Valentini, *Opera omnia* (Valentiae, 1783),
IV, 3–8.]

2. [Read *qui* (Jupiter) *omnia cum faceret* for *quod* (*signum*) *omnia
cum faceret*. When translated *quod cum omnia faceret* (concessive),
omnia is a pleonasm.]

plained it to all that they might understand. Lest something be done differently from what he himself liked, he prescribed to the company of actors the entire arrangement and sequence of the plays, from which not even by the breadth of a finger, as they say, should they depart.

Indeed, as soon as the voice and signal of the great Jupiter reached the actors, each in their turn they came onto the stage, and there with such skill and poise, and so much in the manner of Roscius, did they perform tragedies, comedies, satires, mimes, farces, and other things of the sort that the gods swore that a more beautiful spectacle they had never beheld. Overjoyed at the delight and satisfaction of the gods, and quite elated herself, Juno kept asking them, one by one, how they liked the games. All agreed wholeheartedly that there had never been a more admirable spectacle, nothing worthier of Juno herself and of the birthday which they were celebrating.

This greatest spouse of the greatest god could not contain her excitement; briskly she would skip among the stalls of the immortal gods and, besides other things, repeatedly asked everyone which of the actors they considered the greatest. The wisest of the gods answered that none was more praiseworthy than man, and the father of the gods himself nodded his assent. Indeed, the more intently they watched the gestures, the words, and all the actions of this character, the greater was the astonishment that struck them. It pleased Jupiter to see so much admiration and praise given to man, his own offspring, by all the gods.

Those who sat at Jupiter's side, seeing how much pleasure he took in this human archmime, easily understood that he himself had made this personage; nay, looking more carefully, they recognized in man himself a great resemblance to Jupiter, so that even the dullest of gods might have known that man was born of Jupiter. Verily, man, peering oft through the mask which hides him, almost ready to burst forth and revealing himself distinctly in many things, is divine and Jupiter-like, participating in the immortality of Jupiter himself, in his wisdom, prudence, memory, sharing so many of his talents that it was easy to know that these great gifts had been bestowed upon him by Jupiter from out of his treasury and even from his own person.

Then, as he of gods the greatest, embracing all things in his might, is all things, they saw man, Jupiter's mime, be all things[3] also. He would change himself so as to appear under the mask of a plant, acting a simple life without any power of sensation. Soon after, he withdrew and returned on the stage as a moral satirist,[4] brought into the shapes of a thousand wild beasts: namely, the angry and raging lion, the rapacious and devouring wolf, the fierce and wild boar, the cunning little fox, the lustful and filthy sow, the timid hare, the envious dog, the stupid donkey. After doing this, he was out of sight for a short time; then the curtain was drawn back and he returned a man, prudent, just, faithful, human, kindly, and friendly, who went about the cities with the others, held the authority and obeyed in turn, cared for the public interest and welfare, and was finally in every way a political and social being.

The gods were not expecting to see him in more shapes when, behold, he was remade into one of their own race, surpassing the nature of man and relying entirely upon a very wise mind. O great Jupiter, what a spectacle for them! At first they were astonished that they, too, should be brought to the stage and impersonated by such a convincing mime, whom they said to be that multiform Proteus, the son of the Ocean. Thereupon there was an unbelievable outburst of applause, and they prevented that great player from acting any longer. They begged Juno to let him into the stalls of the gods, unmasked, and to make of him a spectator rather than an actor. She was already eagerly going about obtaining this of her husband, when, at that very moment, man came out upholding the great Jupiter, the worthiest of gods,

3. [*Omnia* is omitted in printed text.]

4. [The *Ethologi* and *Ethopaei* were mimes impersonating moral traits. In the classical tradition the passions of men were symbolically represented by certain animals (cf. Cicero *De oratore* ii. 59–60.)]

and with marvelous and indescribable gestures impersonating his father. He had transcended the characters of the lower gods and was piercing into that inaccessible light surrounded by darkness where Jupiter dwells, of kings and gods the king.

When the gods first saw him, they were roused and upset at the thought that their master and father had stooped to the stage. Soon, however, with composed minds, they glanced repeatedly at Jupiter's stall wondering whether he himself was sitting there or whether he had appeared masked to play a part. Seeing him there, they gazed back again at man and then at Jupiter. With such skill and propriety did he play Jupiter's part that, up and down, from Jupiter's stall to the stage, they kept glancing, lest they be misled by a likeness or the accurate mimic of an actor. Among the other players there were some who swore that this was not man but Jupiter himself, and they underwent severe punishment for their error.

Yet the gods, out of respect for this image of the father of all gods, and by their own suffrage, unanimously decreed that divine honors be granted to man. They prevailed upon Jupiter, through Juno's intercession, that man, who had so rightly played the parts of Jupiter and the gods, put off his mask and be seated among the gods. Jupiter complied with the gods, granting them what he himself, long before, had decided to bestow gratuitously upon man. Thus man was recalled from the stage, seated by Mercury among the gods, and proclaimed victor. There were no cheers to greet him but a silence of wonder. The whole man lay bare, showing the immortal gods his nature akin to theirs, this nature which, covered with mask and body, had made of him an animal so diverse, so desultory, so changing like a polypus and a chameleon, as they had seen him on the stage. Jupiter was then declared and proclaimed the father not only of the gods but also of men. With a gentle and mild countenance, he took delight in both, and was hailed and adored as a parent by both. With pleasure he received this august double name; and now, using also this favored title, we proclaim him of gods and men the father.

Now, when Mercury first came into the stalls of the gods, carrying in his arms the stage costumes, the gods looked at them with great interest; having examined them attentively, a long while, they praised Jupiter's wisdom and skill and adored him, for the costumes which he had made were no less appropriate than useful for all the acts. There was the lofty head, stronghold and court of the divine mind; in it the five senses arranged and placed ornately and usefully. The ears, accordingly, did not droop with soft skin, nor were they firmly fixed with a hard bone, but both were rounded by a sinuous cartilage. Thus they could receive sounds from all directions, and the dust, straw, fluff, gnats which might be flying around would not penetrate into the head but be caught in the folds. The eyes in equal number, two indeed, were high up so that they could observe all things and protected by a fine wall of lashes and eyelids against the same bits of straw and fluff, dust and tiny insects. They were the gauge of the soul and the noblest part of the human face. Then came the very attire of the mask or the mask itself, so handsomely shaped, divided into arms and legs which were long and ending with fingers, so good-looking and useful for all purposes. As there is no time to go through all that which others have related at great length, I shall add this conclusion. All is so well fitted and interrelated that if one were to withdraw or change or add something, all that harmony and beauty and the whole efficacy would be immediately lost. By no ingenuity could a more appropriate mask be conceived for a man, unless someone perhaps wish for the impossible.

When the gods saw man and embraced their brother, they deemed it unworthy of him to appear on a stage and practice the disreputable art of the theater, and they could not find enough praise for their own likeness and that of their father. They investigated one by one and examined the many hidden secrets of man and derived more pleasure from this than from the spectacle of all the plays, "Nor having seen him once are they content;

they wish to linger on."[5] There indeed was a mind full of wisdom, prudence, knowledge, reason, so fertile that by itself it brought forth extraordinary things. Its inventions are: towns and houses, the use of herbs, stones and metals, the designations and names of all things, which foremost among his other inventions have especially caused wise men to wonder. Next and no less important, with a few letters he was able to comprise the immense variety of the sounds of the human voice. With these letters so many doctrines were fixed in writing and transmitted, including religion itself and the knowledge and cult of Jupiter the father and of the other brother-gods. This one thing, which is found in no other animal but man, shows his relationship to the gods. Of little good would all these inventions have been if there had not been added, as the treasury of all things and for the safe-keeping of these divine riches, a memory, the storehouse of all that we have enumerated. From religion and memory, fore-knowledge is almost obtained, with the prophecy of the future, evidently a spark of that divine and immense science which perceives all future events as if they were present.

The gods were gazing at these and other things, as yet sateless; just as those who contemplate their beautiful reflection in a mirror take delight in these things and willingly tarry on, so the gods, seeing themselves and Jupiter their father so well portrayed in man, wished to look more and more at what they had already beheld, inquiring about one thing after another. How did he act plants, herbs, even wild animals, man, gods, the god king Jupiter, by what craft and gesture?

While man explained all this calmly and clearly, Jupiter ordered that ambrosia and nectar from the remains of the feast be placed before him. Cheerfully neglecting the plays, many of the gods had their afternoon refreshment with him. They were charmed by their brotherly guest or fellow-citizen, who, refreshed by heavenly victuals after the toil of the plays, wrapped like the other gods in the purple *praetexta* and bearing the crown,

5. [Virgil *Aeneid* vi. 487.]

went forth to watch the spectacle. Many of the gods stood up for him, many gave up their seats. In different directions they pulled his cloak and retarded his progress that he might stay next to them, until the great Jupiter nodded to Mercury, who led him, that he was to be received in the orchestra among the gods of the first rank, who considered this a great honor. Far was it from those gods of the highest order to despise man, who had been an actor a short time before. He was received by them with respect and invited to the front seats. He sat in their company and watched the games which proceeded without interruption, until Apollo himself reduced the light at Juno's request (for the masters of the feast and other servants, warned by the cooks, announced that supper was more than ready), and night fell upon them. Chandeliers, torches, wax tapers, candlesticks, and oil lamps brought by the stars were lighted, and they were entertained at supper with the same pomp as they had been at dinner. Juno also invited man, and Jupiter the father "assented and with a nod made all Olympus tremble."[6]

Man, just as he had watched the plays with the highest gods, now reclined with them at the banquet. He put on his mask, which he had meanwhile laid aside, for this stage costume was so greatly honored. Since it had so well met the needs of man, it was deemed worthy of the most sumptuous feast and of the table of the gods. Thus it was given the power of perception and enjoyed the eternal bliss of the banquet.

6. [*Ibid.* ix. 106.]

SELECTIVE BIBLIOGRAPHY

SELECTIVE BIBLIOGRAPHY

GENERAL

BURCKHARDT, J. *The Civilization of the Renaissance in Italy.* New York, [1944].

CARBONARA, C. *Il Secolo XV.* Milan, 1943.

CASSIRER, E. *Das Erkenntnisproblem*, Vol. I. Berlin, 1906 (and other eds.).

————. *Individuum und Kosmos in der Philosophie der Renaissance.* Berlin and Leipzig, 1927.

CHARBONNEL, J. R. *La Pensée italienne au XVIᵉ siècle et le courant libertin.* Paris, 1919.

DURAND, DANA B.; BARON, HANS; et al. "Discussion on the Renaissance," *Journal of the History of Ideas*, IV (1943), 1–74.

FALCKENBERG, R. *History of Modern Philosophy from Nicolas of Cusa to the Present Time.* New York, 1893.

FIORENTINO, F. *Il Risorgimento filosofico nel Quattrocento.* Naples, 1885.

GARIN, E. *Der italienische Humanismus.* Berne, [1947].

————. *Filosofi italiani del Quattrocento.* Florence, 1942.

————. *La Filosofia.* 2 vols. Milan, [1947].

GENTILE, G. *La Filosofia.* Milan, n.d.

————. *Il Pensiero italiano del rinascimento.* Florence, 1940.

————. *Studi sul rinascimento.* Rev. ed. Florence, 1936.

HOENIGSWALD, R. *Denker der italienischen Renaissance.* Basel, 1938.

HØFFDING, H. *A History of Modern Philosophy.* London, 1900.

KRISTELLER, P. O. "Humanism and Scholasticism in the Italian Renaissance," *Byzantion*, XVII (1944–45), 346–74.

————. "The Philosophy of Man in the Italian Renaissance," *Italica*, XXIV (1947), 93–112.

KRISTELLER, P. O., and RANDALL, JOHN H., JR. "The Study of the Philosophies of the Renaissance," *Journal of the History of Ideas*, II (1941), 449–96. Reprinted in *Surveys of Recent Scholarship in the Period of Renaissance.* Vol. I. [Providence], 1945.

MONNIER, PH. *Le Quattrocento.* Paris, 1901.

RIEDL, J. O. *A Catalogue of Renaissance Philosophers.* Milwaukee, 1940.

RIEKEL, A. *Die Philosophie der Renaissance.* Munich, 1925.

RÜEGG, W. *Cicero und der Humanismus.* Zurich, 1946.

RUGGIERO, G. DE. *Storia della filosofia*, Part III. Bari, 1930 (and other eds.).

SAITTA, G. *Il Pensiero italiano nell'umanesimo e nel rinascimento*, Vol. I: *L'Umanesimo.* Bologna, 1949.

SYMONDS, J. A. *Renaissance in Italy.*

TOFFANIN, G. *Storia dell'umanesimo*. Naples, 1933.
TRINKAUS, CH. E. *Adversity's Noblemen: The Italian Humanists on Happiness*. New York, 1940.
UEBERWEG, F. *Grundriss der Geschichte der Philosophie*, Vol. III. 12th ed. Berlin, 1924.
VOIGT, G. *Die Wiederbelebung des classischen Alterthums*. 3d ed. Berlin, 1893.
WHITFIELD, J. H. *Petrarch and the Renascence*. Oxford, 1943.

FRANCESCO PETRARCA

Opera. Venice, 1501 and 1503; Basel, 1554 and 1581.
Epistolae de rebus familiaribus et variae, ed. J. FRACASSETTI. 3 vols. Florence, 1859–63.
Le Familiari, ed. V. ROSSI. 4 vols. Florence, 1933–42.
Rerum memorandarum libri, ed. G. BILLANOVICH. Florence, [1943].
CAPELLI, L. M. (ed.). *Le Traité De sui ipsius et multorum ignorantia*. Paris, 1906.
BILLANOVICH, G. *Petrarca letterato*, Vol. I: *Lo Scrittoio del Petrarca*. Rome, 1947.
CARLINI, A. *Il Pensiero filosofico religioso di Francesco Petrarca*. Jesi, 1904.
COSENZA, MARIO E. (trans.). *Petrarch's Letters to Classical Authors*. Chicago, 1910.
GENTILE, G. "Il carattere della filosofia del Petrarca," *Nuova Antologia*, CCCLXXIV (July–August, 1934), 488–99.
GEROSA, P. P. "L'Umanesimo agostiniano del Petrarca," *Didaskaleion*, New Series, Vols. III–VII (1925–29).
KRISTELLER, P. O. "Augustine and the Early Renaissance," *Review of Religion*, VIII (1944), 339–58.
NOLHAC, P. DE. *Pétrarque et l'humanisme*. 2d ed. Paris, 1907.
RAJNA, P. "Il Codice Hamiltoniano 493 della Reale Biblioteca di Berlino," *Rendiconti della Reale Accademia dei Lincei, Classe di Scienze Morali, Storiche e Filologiche*, Ser. V, Vol. XVIII (1909), pp. 479–508.
RAZZOLI, ELENA. *Agostinismo e religiosità del Petrarca*. Milan, 1937.
ROBINSON, J. H., and ROLFE, H. W. *Petrarch, the First Modern Scholar and Man of Letters*. 2d ed. New York, 1914.
SAPEGNO, N. *Il Trecento*. Milan, 1934.
TATHAM, EDWARD H. R. *Francesco Petrarca*. 2 vols. London, 1925–26.

LORENZO VALLA

Opera omnia. Basel, 1540 and 1543.
De libero arbitrio, ed. MARIA ANFOSSI. Florence, 1934.
BAROZZI, L. and SABBADINI, R. *Studi sul Panormita e sul Valla*. Florence, 1891.

FREUDENTHAL, J. "L. Valla als Philosoph," *Neue Jahrbücher für das klassische Altertum*, XXIII (1909), 724–36.

MAIER, E. *Die Willensfreiheit bei L. Valla*. Bonn, 1911.

MANCINI, G. *Vita di L. Valla*. Florence, 1891.

MARSILIO FICINO

Opera omnia. Basel, 1561 and 1576; Paris, 1641.

Supplementum Ficinianum, ed. P. O. KRISTELLER. 2 vols. Florence, 1937.

Marsilio Ficino's Commentary on Plato's "Symposium," ed. and trans. SEARS R. JAYNE. Columbia, Mo., 1944.

BURROUGHS, JOSEPHINE L. (trans.), "Marsilio Ficino, Platonic Theology, iii. 2; xiii. 3; xiv. 3–4," *Journal of the History of Ideas*, V (1944), 227–39.

FESTUGIÈRE, J. *La Philosophie de l'amour de Marsile Ficin et son influence sur la littérature française au XVIᵉ siècle*. Paris, 1941.

KRISTELLER, P. O. *The Philosophy of Marsilio Ficino*. New York, 1943.

———. "The Scholastic Background of Marsilio Ficino," *Traditio*, II (1944), 257–318.

ROBB, NESCA A. *Neoplatonism of the Italian Renaissance*. London, 1935.

SAITTA, G. *Marsilio Ficino e la filosofia dell'umanesimo*. 2d ed. Florence, 1943.

TORRE, A. DELLA. *Storia dell'Accademia Platonica di Firenze*. Florence, 1902.

GIOVANNI PICO DELLA MIRANDOLA

Opera. Bologna, 1495–96 (and other eds.).

De hominis dignitate, Heptaplus, De ente et uno e scritti vari, ed. E. GARIN. Florence, 1942.

Of Being and Unity, trans. VICTOR M. HAMM. Milwaukee, 1943.

FORBES, ELIZABETH L. (trans.). "Pico della Mirandola, Of the Dignity of Man," *Journal of the History of Ideas*, III (1942), 347–54.

WALLIS, CHARLES G. (trans.). "Pico della Mirandola's Very Elegant Speech on the Dignity of Man," *View*, Fall and December, 1944. Also published by St. John's College, Annapolis, 1940.

ANAGNINE, E. *G. Pico della Mirandola*. Bari, 1937.

CASSIRER, E. "Giovanni Pico Della Mirandola," *Journal of the History of Ideas*, III (1942), 123–44, 319–46.

DULLES, A. *Princeps concordiae: Pico della Mirandola and the Scholastic Tradition*. Cambridge, Mass., 1941.

FESTUGIÈRE, J. "Studia Mirandulana," *Archives d'histoire doctrinale et littéraire du moyen âge*, VIII (1933), 92–258.

GARIN, E. *Giovanni Pico della Mirandola.* Florence, 1937.
GAUTIER-VIGNAL, L. *Pic de la Mirandole.* Paris, 1937.
KIBRE, PEARL. *The Library of Pico della Mirandola.* New York, 1936.
SEMPRINI, G. *La Filosofia di Pico della Mirandola.* Milan, 1936.

PIETRO POMPONAZZI

Tractatus. Bologna, 1525.
Opera ... *De naturalium effectuum admirandorum causis seu de incantationibus; de fato, libero arbitrio, praedestinatione, providentia Dei.* Basel, 1567.
De immortalitate animae, ed. G. GENTILE. Messina, 1925.
Les Causes des merveilles de la nature, trans. H. BUSSON. Paris, 1930.
De immortalitate animae, ed. and trans. W. H. HAY II. Haverford, 1938. (Some passages are reprinted in the *Journal of the History of Ideas,* V [1944], 240–42.)
DOUGLAS, A. H. *The Philosophy and Psychology of Pietro Pomponazzi.* Cambridge, 1910.
FERRI, L. "Intorno alle dottrine psicologiche di Pietro Pomponazzi contenute nel manoscritto della Biblioteca Angelica di Roma, T,3,8 intitolato: Pomponatius in libros de anima," *Atti della Reale Accademia dei Lincei,* Anno CCLXXIII (1875–76), Ser. II, Vol. III, Part III: *Memorie della Classe di Scienze Morali, Storiche e Filologiche,* pp. 333–548.
FIORENTINO, F. *Pietro Pomponazzi.* . . . Florence, 1868.
GARIN, E. "Aristotelismo e Platonismo del Rinascimento," *Rinascita,* II (1939), 641–71.
KRISTELLER, P. O. "Ficino and Pomponazzi on the Place of Man in the Universe," *Journal of the History of Ideas,* V (1944), 220–26.
RANDALL, JOHN H., JR. "The Development of Scientific Method in the School of Padua," *Journal of the History of Ideas,* I (1940), 177–206.
RENAN, E. *Averroès et l'averroïsme.* 3d ed. Paris, 1866.
WEIL, E. "Die Philosophie des Pietro Pomponazzi," *Archiv für Geschichte der Philosophie,* XLI (1932), 127–76.

JUAN LUIS VIVES

Opera omnia. 8 vols. Valencia, 1782–90.
On Education, trans. F. WATSON. Cambridge, 1913.
BONILLA Y SAN MARTIN, A. *Luis Vives y la filosofia del renacimiento.* Madrid, 1903 and 1929.
DALY, WALTER A. *The Educational Psychology of Juan Luis Vives.* Washington, 1924.
WATSON, FOSTER. *Luis Vives, el gran Valenciano.* Oxford, 1922.

INDEX

INDEX

Abano, Pietro d' ("The Conciliator"), 8, 370
Abubacher, 374
Abumasar, 246
Academics, the, 89, 159
Achillini, Alessandro, 253, 262–65
Aegidius Romanus, 243–44
Albanzani, Donato degli, 30, 47, 49, 65
Albertus Magnus, 243–44
Alexander of Aphrodisias, 243, 260, 267, 270, 279, 325, 334, 367–68, 374
Alfarabi, 243, 374
Allegory, 28–29; characteristic example of, 38 ff., 387 ff.
Ambrose, 54, 108, 380
Ammonius, 243
Anjou, Robert of, king of Sicily-Naples, 60, 68
Appetitus naturalis, 12, 15, 188–89
Arabian philosophy, 8, 10, 23, 31–32, 142–43, 216, 223, 243, 246
Archimedes, 81
Argyropoulos, Johannes, 259
Aristotelianism, 2, 5, 8–9, 16, 245, 257 ff. (*passim*); Arabian, 23, 31–32; Christianized, 6, 149, 151, 221; English, 135; Humanistic, 8–14
Aristotle, 1, 5–7, 9–16, 23, 26, 31, 53, 63 ff., 75–78, 83, 94, 96, 101–4, 106 ff., 110 ff., 116, 124, 128, 136, 149, 151, 181, 188, 200, 221, 246, 251, 257 ff., 261 ff., 265–66, 271–72, 276, 280–381 (*passim*)
Ars bene beateque vivendi, 24
Asnarez de Añon, Garcia, bishop of Lerida, 155
Augustine, 6–7, 24, 26–28, 41–42, 44–45, 54, 75, 108, 111, 114–17, 140–41, 151–57, 186, 237, 245, 252, 380
Augustinianism, 6, 19, 27, 33
Avempace, 243, 374
Avenzoar, 246
Averroes ("The Commentator"), 9, 10, 31 ff., 108–9, 141, 143, 243, 245, 255–60, 263, 278, 284–90, 295–

301, 303, 308, 314, 323, 329, 332, 336–37, 339, 361, 364, 371
Averroism, 4, 7–9, 11, 13, 14, 16, 17, 99, 141, 220, 257–58, 260–61, 263–64, 269–70, 273, 310
Avicenna, 201, 243, 245, 367

Bacon, Roger, 248
Bagnolo, Guido da, 30, 52–62
Barbaro, Ermolao, 259
Barlaam, 113
Bembo, Pietro, 269, 274–75
Berges, Antoine de, 385
Berkeley, George, 8
Bessarion, 7, 259
Boethius, 156, 160 ff., 172, 176–80, 245, 296
Borgo San Sepolcro, Dionigi da, 28, 36
Bruni, Francesco, 23, 34
Bruni, Leonardo, 259

Cabala, 216, 237, 251–52
Caloria, Tommaso, 31–32, 134
Calvin, Jean, 153
Cato Maior, 61
Chain of being; *see* Hierarchy of being
Chaldaeans, 226–27, 236, 240, 245, 253
Cicero, 14, 24, 26, 53, 55–56, 64, 72, 74, 77–91, 95–100, 102–5, 114–15, 123, 125, 132, 136, 182, 241, 385
Classical learning, 18–19, 25 ff.
Coleridge, Samuel Taylor, 8
Commentator; *see* Averroes
Conciliator; *see* Abano
Contarini, Gasparo, 265, 275–76
Contarini, Marcantonio Flavo, 280
Contarini, Zaccaria, 29, 52–62
Creation: eternity of, 10, 98 ff.; and time, 307
Cusanus, Nicholas of Cusa, 6–7

Dandolo, Leonardo, 29, 59–62
Dialectic, value of, 134–39